Admin911™:

Windows® 2000 Group Policy

About the Author

Roger Jennings is an author and consultant specializing in Windows networking and client-server database systems. He's written more than 20 books on Windows 95, Windows NT, Windows 2000, Microsoft Access, and Visual Basic database applications. U.S. publishers have sold more than one million copies of his books, and his books have been translated into 22 languages. He's a contributing editor for Fawcette Technical Publication's *Visual Basic Programmer's Journal* and has co-authored articles for the *Microsoft Developer Network News* and the MSDN CD-ROM.

Prior to his writing career, Roger was an FM transmitter engineer and classical music disk jockey and semi-employed as a commercial pilot. He then went on to found a specialty chemical company that, among other endeavors, raised sunken ships with polyurethane foam. His next venture was manufacturing automated process control and medical instrumentation systems, which initially were programmed by the Wang 700 calculator/computer. The Wang 1100 gave Roger his first taste of BASIC, and he was hooked on computers from then on.

Admin911™:
Windows® 2000 Group Policy

ROGER **JENNINGS**

Osborne/**McGraw-Hill**

Berkeley   New York   St. Louis   San Francisco
Auckland   Bogotá   Hamburg   London   Madrid
Mexico City   Milan   Montreal   New Delhi   Panama City
Paris   São Paulo   Singapore   Sydney
Tokyo   Toronto

Osborne/**McGraw-Hill**
2600 Tenth Street
Berkeley, California 94710
U.S.A.

For information on translations or book distributors outside the U.S.A., or to arrange bulk purchase discounts for sales promotions, premiums, or fund-raisers, please contact Osborne/**McGraw-Hill** at the above address.

Admin911™: Windows® 2000 Group Policy

1234567890 DOC DOC 01987654321

ISBN 0-07-212948-4

Publisher
Brandon A. Nordin

Vice President & Associate Publisher
Scott Rogers

Editorial Director
Wendy Rinaldi

Series Editor
Kathy Ivens

Project Editor
Janet Walden

Acquisitions Coordinator
Timothy Madrid

Technical Editors
Dustin Sauter
Scott Hall

Copy Editor
Judy Ziajka

Indexer
David Heiret

Computer Designers
Gary Corrigan
Melinda Moore Lytle

Illustrator
Michael Mueller

Series Design
Gary Corrigan

Cover Design
Greg Scott

Cover Illustration
Joe and Kathy Heiner

This book was designed and composed with Corel VENTURA™ Publisher.

To my wife, Alexandra

Contents
at a Glance

Contents

Acknowledgments

Publishing books is a team effort, and Kathy Ivens, prolific author and Windows 2000 Registry guru, is the leader of the *Admin911* team. Kathy's constant encouragement and consistent good humor made the writing of this book a truly enjoyable experience.

Osborne/McGraw-Hill's Editorial Director and Acquisitions Editor, Wendy Rinaldi, had the foresight to recognize the need of system administrators for the specialized coverage of Windows 2000 topics offered by the *Admin911* series. Janet Walden, Senior Project Editor, managed the book's editorial process with the assistance of Acquisitions Coordinator Timothy Madrid, who handled the electronic logistics. Judy Ziajka, Copy Editor, corrected my grammatical lapses and repaired convoluted syntax.

Special thanks go to technical editors Dustin Sauter (MCSE, Master ASE, Cisco CCNA) and Scott Hall (MCSE, Compaq ASE, Novell CNA), whose experience with Active Directory in very large, complex networks is reflected in their skilled contribution to every chapter of this book. Dustin is Chief Architect and Scott is Technical Manager for the Active Directory implementation of Wells Fargo & Company's multisite Windows 2000 network, which supports more than 100,000 client workstations. Dustin and Scott are co-authors of *Admin911: DNS & WINS* (Osborne/McGraw-Hill, 2001; ISBN 0-07-213154-3). The responsibility for any errors or omissions that Dustin and Scott didn't catch is mine.

And, finally, thanks to Microsoft for replacing Windows NT's system policy with Windows 2000's Group Policy.

Chapter 1

Managing Windows 2000 with Group Policy

Group Policy is the primary component of Windows 2000's implementation of Change and Configuration Management (CCM) and is the primary mechanism for establishing uniform, effective security policies within Windows 2000 domains. Group Policy replaces Windows NT's system policy for client administration and desktop lockdown of workstations running Windows 2000 Professional.

CCM includes IntelliMirror features (user settings and data management, and software installation and management) and remote operating system installation. Group Policy Objects (GPOs), stored in Active Directory (AD), and the File Replication Service (FRS), which replicates Group Policy Templates (GPTs), provide the infrastructure for CCM. Group Policy Extensions to GPOs apply security settings, specify logon and other scripts and configure automatic installation of Windows 2000-compatible application software.

If you hope to achieve any long-term economic benefit by upgrading to Windows 2000 from Windows NT, NetWare, or both, you *must* implement Group Policy. The consensus of industry analysts, such as GartnerGroup and Giga Information Group, is that a return on an upgrade investment depends entirely on your implementation of effective policy management.

Windows 2000 Server and its upscale derivatives, such as Advanced Server and Datacenter Server, have wizards to aid administrators in setting up new features, such as AD, Dynamic DNS, and Virtual Private Networks that run L2TP over IPSec. You won't find a "Group Policy Wizard" in Windows 2000 Server. Group Policy is one of the most complex and, in many respects, counterintuitive features of Windows 2000; if any component of Windows 2000 deserves a wizard, it's Group Policy. The absence of built-in assistance for establishing a logical and consistent set of CCM policies is one of the primary reasons for the existence of this book.

You can't escape Group Policy in a Windows 2000 domain. When you use Dcpromo.exe to create your first Windows 2000 Domain Controller (DC) during a clean installation or an upgrade of a Windows NT PDC, the AD promotion process establishes a Default Domain Policy that applies to all Windows 2000 computers and users in the domain. DCs in AD's Domain Controllers organizational unit (OU) receive Default Domain Controllers Policy. The default policies represent only the starting point of the Group Policy journey. In particular, the basic domain and DC security policies are grossly inadequate for a production network. Default local security settings for workstations and member servers contribute to weak security. The first Group Policy management example in this chapter describes how to increase your domain security level.

Comparing Group Policy with Windows NT System Policy

The immediate ancestors of Group Policy are Windows NT and 9x system policy files, Ntconfig.pol and Config.pol, respectively, that you author with the Policy Editor (Poledit.exe). These files, which load from the PDC's or BDC's Netlogon share during the client logon process, alter settings in the client's HKEY_LOCAL_MACHINE (HKLM) and HKEY_CURRENT_USER (HKCU) Registry hives. If you've implemented (or tried to implement) system policy in a Windows NT 4.0 network, you'll appreciate Group Policy's substantial improvements to system policy's rudimentary CCM features.

System policies are an element of the oxymoronic Zero Administration for Windows (ZAW) initiative that Microsoft announced in October 1996. The original ZAW press release (http://www.microsoft.com/presspass/press/1996/Oct96/ZAWinpr.asp) promised the following features:

◆ **Automatic system update and application installation**   The operating system will update itself when the computer is booted, without user intervention, seeking the latest necessary code and drivers from a server, intranet, or the Internet, if available. The Automatic Desktop feature will provide users with all available applications, installing them automatically when invoked.

◆ **All state kept on server**   Users' data can be automatically "reflected" to servers, ensuring high availability and allowing mobile users to have access to information whether connected to the network or not. Additionally, users will be able to roam between PCs while maintaining full access to their data, applications, and customized environments.

◆ **Central administration and system lockdown**   All aspects of client systems will be controllable by a central administrator across the network. In a few simple steps, the system can be "locked down" to maintain controlled, consistent, and secure configurations across sets of users. The degree of flexibility can be altered on a per-user basis by the central administrator, without having to change hardware and software.

◆ **Application flexibility to design the best solutions** A full implementation of the Active Platform—key client and server Internet technologies—on Windows offers the flexibility to deploy both Web-style "thin client" applications and the full wealth of personal productivity and client-server applications. When combined with the lockdown feature, administrators will be able to tune the client environment to the exact needs of each user and be able to change these as business needs dictate.

Three and a half years after the ZAW announcement, Microsoft delivered all the promised ZAW features in Windows 2000. In the interim, a subset of the ZAW features became available to Windows NT, 95, and ultimately, Windows 98 clients.

Central Administration and Lockdown

System policy delivers ZAW's "central administration and system lockdown" feature by permanently altering HKLM and HKCU Registry values for Windows NT and 9x users. If you decide to remove system policy restrictions on clients by simply deleting Ntconfig.pol and Config.pol from the Netlogon share, users still have lockdown restrictions applied by persistent Registry entries. Microsoft calls this defect "tattooing the Registry." You must explicitly disable in Poledit.exe every system policy you previously enabled to reverse clients' Registry entries. This process isn't fun, especially if you've implemented a very restrictive set of system policies.

NOTE: Group Policy and system policy use template (.adm) files to define each policy and specify the Registry key and value modified by setting the policy. Group Policy .adm templates are similar but not identical to system policy templates. System policy stores its settings in a single .pol file; Group Policy stores its settings in AD and two Registry.pol files: one for Computer Configuration and the other for User Configuration.

Group Policy overcomes the tattooing problem by placing its Registry changes under the following two sets of protected keys:

◆ HKLM\Software\Microsoft\Windows\CurrentVersion\Policies and HKLM\Software\Policies\Microsoft for computers, which load when the computer boots

◆ HKCU\Software\Microsoft\Windows\CurrentVersion\Policies and HKCU\Software\Policies\Microsoft for users, which load when the user logs on

NOTE: Appendix A contains descriptions of all Windows 2000 policies and, where applicable, their Registry keys and value names.

Unlike changes to system policies, which load only when the user logs on, changes to Group Policy propagate to computers on a regular schedule, every 90 minutes (plus or minus a random interval between 0 and 30 minutes) by default.

To minimize network traffic, policies are sent from domain controllers to member servers and clients only when changes occur. If you disable or delete a policy or set of policies, the change updates all protected keys and takes effect within the approximately 90-minute replication window. Users don't need to reboot their computers or log off and on for the changes to take effect. Application installation and updating is an exception; these operations occur only on user logon. Updating a user's copy of Microsoft Word with a document open, for example, has very undesirable consequences.

NOTE: Overwriting the values of *all* protected keys when a Group Policy changes is the method Windows 2000 uses to avoid tattooing the Registry. This process is unlike the replication of AD changes between DCs, which processes only the changes to individual AD objects. A simple change to one policy value causes all affected computers to download all policy-based Registry settings, which is one of the reasons the Group Policy refresh interval has a random time offset. If you have a large number of policy settings, the network traffic for Group Policy changes on many clients occupies a significant percentage of network bandwidth.

You can apply system policies to specific global groups of Windows NT and Windows 2000 users in a Windows NT domain, but doing so increases the size of the Ntconfig.pol file and slows user logon. Group Policy uses membership in sites, domains, and organizational units (OUs) as the primary basis for selectively applying policies. The policies load in local, site, domain, and OU (LSDOU) order, and settings of policies applied last prevail. Group Policy, by default, implements inheritance in the opposite order, so OUs inherit domain-level settings, which in turn inherit site-level policies. You can block Group Policy inheritance, but doing so usually isn't a recommended practice. Group Policy uses group membership only to *filter* group policies. Filtering lets you specify that a particular group of settings contained in a GPO doesn't apply to members of particular groups, such as Domain Admins and local Administrators.

Group Policy with 650 or so individual policies is much more granular than system policy, which has a total of 72 policies for Windows NT and a few more for Windows 9x clients. You can enable or disable virtually every user-accessible feature of Windows 2000 Professional with Group Policy. The added granularity, however, has drawbacks: many policies interact by preempting or disabling other policies. For instance, some policies are duplicated in the Computer Configuration and User Configuration classes; in many cases, Computer Configuration policies you apply overwrite User Configuration policies. Fortunately, each individual policy created by an .adm template has a *PolicyName* Properties dialog with an Explain page. Explanations often reveal more than you want to know about a policy, but (for the most part) they're quite useful. Policy descriptions in Appendix A are briefer.

In addition to computer- and user-based Registry modifications stored in .adm templates, Group Policy also lets you specify the following user and computer settings with Group Policy extensions:

⬧ **Security policies** for sites, domains, and OUs, including the Domain Controllers OU. Security policies are applied to the client's local security database, \Winnt\System32\ Security\Database\Secedit.sdb, not directly to the Registry. When you install Windows 2000 Server and promote the server to a DC, the Administrative Tools menu gives you access to Domain Security Policy and Domain Controller Security Policy snap-ins (see Figure 1-1). Default values are provided for a few security policies.

⬧ **Startup/Shutdown and Logon/Logoff scripts** for computers and users, respectively. Startup and shutdown scripts are new Windows 2000 features that run when the computer boots and shuts down.

⬧ **Software installation** for assigned and published applications. You can specify assigned applications, which install automatically, to computers or users. Published applications, which users install from Control Panel's Add/Remove Software tool, apply to users only. Published applications can be specified to install automatically

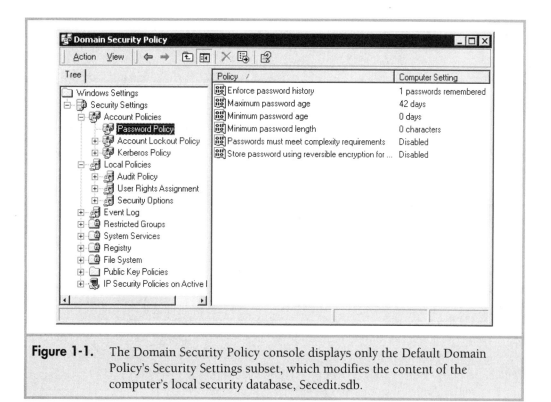

Figure 1-1.   The Domain Security Policy console displays only the Default Domain Policy's Security Settings subset, which modifies the content of the computer's local security database, Secedit.sdb.

when the user opens a file with an extension type that matches the application, such as .mdb for Microsoft Access. You also can assign or publish updates to or replacements for applications.

Windows Installer implements ZAW's "[a]utomatic system update and application installation" feature for Installer's .msi and downlevel .zap files.

✦ **Operating system installation.** A policy lets you specify the menu options for automatic RIS installation of Windows 2000 Professional and RIPrep installation of the OS and a set of applications you define.

✦ **Folder Redirection settings** to specify the location and processing of server-stored Application Data, Desktop, My Documents, and Start Menu folders.

Unless you're building a new Windows 2000 network from the ground up, you're faced with running Windows 2000 DCs and Windows NT BDCs in a mixed-mode environment and supporting a mix of downlevel (Windows 9x and NT) clients.

Unfortunately, Group Policy doesn't work with downlevel clients. Windows 2000 clients in Windows NT–only domains receive system policy, if implemented, not Group Policy. Windows NT clients upgraded to Windows 2000 receive computer- and user-based Group Policy only if the client's computer and user accounts are managed by a Windows 2000 DC.

It's a common practice in large Windows NT networks to maintain computer accounts in resource domains. Until you upgrade or migrate the resource domains to Windows 2000 or move client computer accounts to a Windows 2000 domain, upgraded clients receive computer system policy from the Windows NT resource domain.

The Zero Administration Kit and Group Policy Scenarios

The Zero Administration Kit (ZAK) for Windows NT 4.0, which Microsoft released in late June 1997, provided system admins with the capability to create a set of system policies and logon scripts and perform automatic installation of Windows NT 4.0 Workstation, service packs, and local applications or shortcuts to network-stored applications. ZAK also has versions for Windows 95 and 98 clients. ZAK dates from Microsoft's NetPC period, during the Network Computer Paranoia epidemic in Redmond, and was intended to deliver the remaining ZAW features that system policies alone couldn't implement.

ZAK defined the following two classes of workstations:

+ **TaskStation** for users who run only a single locally stored application, such as a database front-end for online transaction processing or, as Microsoft suggests, Internet Explorer (IE). When the user logs on, TaskStation starts the assigned application and locks down the desktop completely. The user doesn't have a Start button or taskbar, can't launch Control Panel or Task Manager, and can't see local files or network shares. The user is relegated to the equivalent of a cell in a maximum-security prison.

+ **AppStation** is a slightly relaxed version of TaskStation that permits users to choose from a set of administrator-specified applications (presumably members of Microsoft Office) that run from a network share. AppStation users can't get to the Control Panel or the file system, and store all documents on the server. AppStation users equate to inmates of an ordinary penitentiary.

ZAK generates an unattended setup file (Unattend.txt) and server shares for automated installation of the OS. You needed to do a substantial amount of manual tweaking to modify either of the two ZAK templates to match your sentencing guidelines for users. ZAK is a precursor to RIPrep and many new Windows 2000 policies that weren't included in system policy.

> **TIP:** For an independent review of ZAK and descriptions of some of its pitfalls, read Darren Mar-Elia's "Zero Administration Kit: The Answer to Your TCO Woes?" in the January 1998 issue of *Windows NT Magazine* (http://www.win2000mag.com/Articles/Index.cfm?ArticleID=3427). If you want to experiment with ZAK on a Windows NT test network, you can download it from http://www.microsoft.com/NTWorkstation/downloads/Recommended/Featured/NTZAK.asp.

Microsoft released on its Web site in February 2000 a set of Group Policy Scenarios that expands on ZAK to provide templates for the following six workstation classes, listed here in descending order of restriction:

◆ **Kiosk** runs a single application for access by the public, such as in an airport, train or bus station, or fast-food outlet. The configuration assumes a keyboard and mouse, but a touchscreen is much better suited for user input to a kisok.

◆ **TaskStation** is a clone of ZAK's TaskStation configuration.

◆ **AppStation** duplicates ZAK's AppStation configuration and is limited to a maximum of five user-accessible applications.

◆ **Public Computing Environment (PCE)** is intended for school computer laboratories where users can change and save a limited number of preferences, but can't alter computer-related settings, such as LAN or dial-up connections or hardware configuration. PCE users correspond to reform school candidates.

◆ **Low TCO Desktop** has minimal computer- and user-based management. Microsoft describes this configuration as suitable for power users and developers. Whether developers are inclined to accept *any* management of their workstation(s) is open to serious question.

◆ **Laptop** is intended for mobile users who primarily connect by low-speed dial-up, but occasionally or frequently connect directly to the LAN.

Installing, deploying, and customizing the Scenarios isn't a simple task. The Using Group Policy Scenarios (GroupPolicyScenarios.doc) documentation file runs 78 pages. Unlike ZAK, the Group Policy Scenarios don't generate Windows 2000 Professional installation files. You must create your own automated installation images with RIPrep or use SysPrep.

You can download the GroupPolicyScenarios.msi installer file from http://www.microsoft.com/windows2000/library/howitworks/management/grouppolicy.asp.

You might be able to use one or two of the Scenarios as starting points when designing policies for your network. The most useful components of the Scenarios for most system admins are the Excel workbooks for each Scenario. Figure 1-2 shows 22 of the 662 rows of LowTCO.xls, which lists every policy and has setting values for active (enabled or disabled) policies. Use one of the workbooks as the foundation for documenting your Group Policy implementation. Add columns for Domain Controllers and other OUs to which you apply Group Policy.

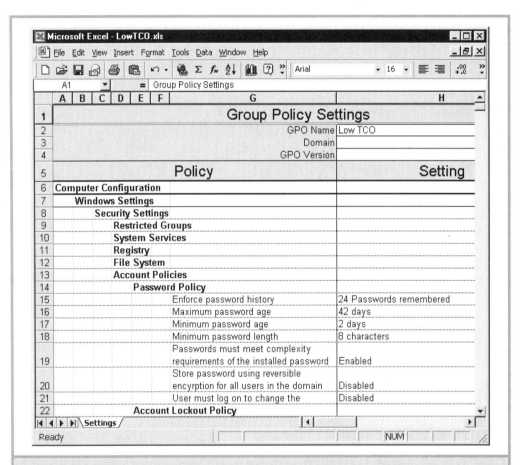

Figure 1-2. Use the Group Policy Settings worksheet for the Low TCO configuration as the template for documenting your Group Policy implementation.

NOTE: Microsoft didn't follow the GartnerGroup's classification of user roles when establishing definitions of the Scenarios. GartnerGroup's classifications (High Performance, Knowledge Worker, Mobile Worker, Process Worker, and Data Entry) have become a de facto standard for TCO analysis. The GroupPolicyScenarios.doc file has a table that equates Scenario names with GartnerGroup classifications. For example, High Performance corresponds to Low TCO Desktop with the user being a member of the Power Users group.

Getting Acquainted with Group Policy Management

Group Policy management falls into the two following categories:

✦ **Security management**, which you apply to all Windows 2000 servers and clients on the network. Setting security parameters with policies ensures consistency of password strength, account lockout, and Kerberos implementation on all machines. The most common practice is to specify security settings with the Domain Security Policy and Domain Controller Security Policy administrative tools or the Group Policy Editor (GPE) snap-in.

✦ **Computer and user management**, which you usually apply only to clients. There are a few Computer Configuration policies, such as verbose startup and shutdown messages, that you might want to apply to DCs and member servers. This book excludes security management from the computer and user management category.

You can apply Group Policy at the site level, but it's more common to establish a basic set of policies on a domain-wide basis and then establish policies that apply to individual OUs. The primary use of site-level Group Policies is to specify different servers to store redirected folders, roaming user profiles, or both, depending on clients' site membership.

Another reason to start at the domain level is that domains have a Default Domain Policy, and sites don't have a Default Site Policy. You display and alter policies in the GPE (GPEdit.msc) snap-in, which you load with the appropriate GPO in Active Directory Users and Computers (ADUC). You must be logged on with an account that's a member of the Domain Admins or Enterprise Admins group to configure Group Policy. In a production environment, you can delegate management of Group Policy to members of other Security Groups.

NOTE: The majority of the examples of this book are based on the oakmont.edu sample domain created with the GroupPol.exe application created to accompany this book. Appendix B tells you how to download, install, and use GroupPol.exe. The structure of the oakmont.edu domain is optimized for creating and testing Group Policy, but you can use your own test domain structure in all procedures described in the book.

To open the Default Domain Policy in the GPE, do this:

1. Launch ADUC on the PDC emulator DC of your domain, right-click the *DomainName* node, choose Properties to open the *DomainName* Properties dialog, and click the Group Policy tab (see Figure 1-3).

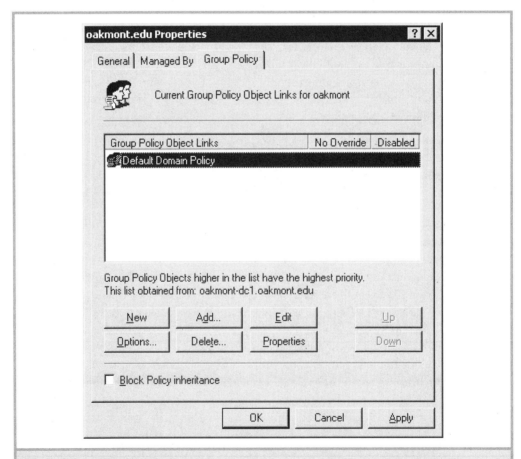

Figure 1-3. The *DomainName* Properties dialog's Group Policies page displays the Default Domain Policy GPO in the Group Policy Object Links list.

NOTE: You can run ADUC on any DC in your domain, but using the PDC emulator minimizes replication-induced delays in application to other DCs and clients.

2. Double-click the Default Domain Policy item to open the GPE, which automatically expands the two highest-level nodes: Computer Configuration and User Configuration.

3. Expand the nodes to display the third level of the hierarchy, and select one of the Administrative Templates subnodes. Computer Configuration's System node, for example, has subnodes and policies (see Figure 1-4).

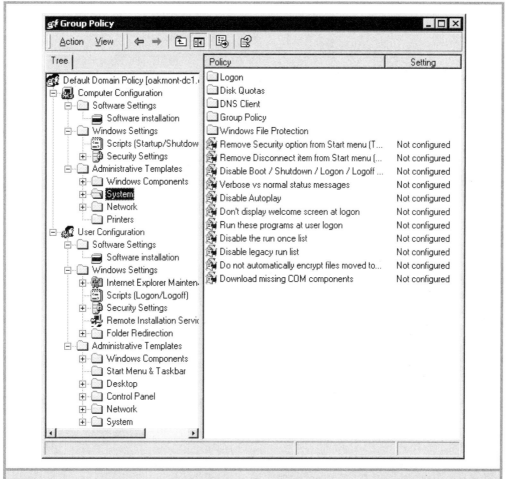

Figure 1-4. Many Administrative Templates subnodes include individual policies and nested nodes.

4. Double-click one of the items in the Policy list to open the Policy page of the *PolicyName* Properties dialog. Most policies have only Not Configured, Enabled, and Disabled option buttons, but some include controls, such as drop-down lists, text boxes, check boxes, and spin boxes (see Figure 1-5). You must select the Enabled option to activate the dialog's controls.

NOTE: Most policies disable Windows 2000 features that are enabled by default. Enabling a policy that disables or otherwise prevents normal behavior of a feature overrides the default (Not Configured) setting. Disabling such a policy explicitly enforces it. The use of negative logic (disabling a Disabled policy enables the feature) is one of the least intuitive elements of Group Policy management. When a policy name starts with "Enable" or "Allow," the feature usually is disabled by default.

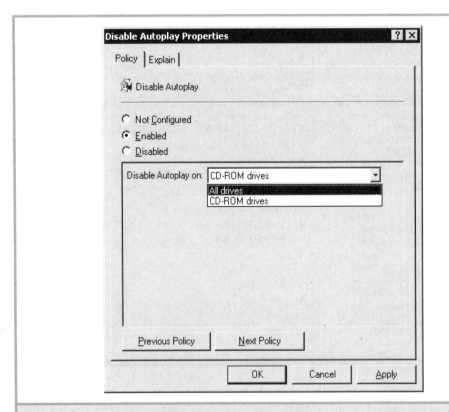

Figure 1-5. The Policy page of the Disable Autoplay Properties dialog uses a drop-down list to set the Registry value.

5. Click the Explain tab to read a discourse on the effects of enabling or disabling the policy (see Figure 1-6). If you set identically named policies in the Computer Configuration and User Configuration classes, the Computer Configuration policy prevails. The Previous Policy and Next Policy buttons provide convenient navigation between policies under the same node.

Setting values for all 650 or so policies obviously would be an overwhelming task. In a production environment, you seldom set more than 100 policy values in a single GPO. The most restrictive Group Policy Scenario, Kiosk, has 250 policy settings, but many of the settings aren't required to achieve total lockdown of the client. The Low TCO Desktop Scenario has 153 settings, but more than 50 of these settings aren't appropriate for the targeted Power Users and Developers categories.

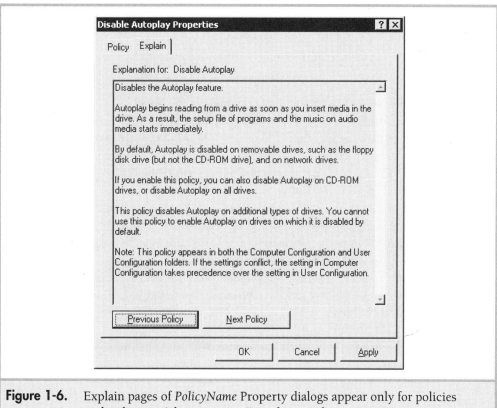

Figure 1-6.   Explain pages of *PolicyName* Property dialogs appear only for policies under the two Administrative Templates nodes.

> **TIP:** You can restrict the GPE's display of nodes under Administrative Templates to list only those policies that are enabled or disabled, and display nodes that contain configured policies. To impose the restriction, right-click either of the Administrative Templates nodes and choose View | Show Configured Policies Only. Setting the Show Configured Policies Only toggle makes it easier to explore currently enforced policies. The only Administrative Templates domainwide policy set by default is User Configuration\Administrative Templates\System\ Century interpretation for Year 2000. The "System Policy Templates" section later in this chapter describes use of the View | Show Policies Only choice.

Security Configuration Templates

Windows 2000 Server installs a set of incremental security configuration templates (.inf files) in \Winnt\Security\Templates. Security configuration templates apply only to clean or upgraded Windows 2000 installations on NTFS volumes, because Windows 2000 on FAT volumes can't be secured.

Applying the templates doesn't affect User Rights or Groups. These templates offer the following four levels of security for workstations and servers:

✦ **Basic** security establishes the default security settings for workstations, member servers, and DCs with Basicwk.inf, Basicsv.inf, and Basicdc.inf, respectively. Performing a clean installation of Windows 2000 automatically applies the Basic security settings to Local Computer Policy; upgraded computers require application of a Basic??.inf file to establish local security. When you establish a new domain, Default Domain Policy implements the settings shown in Table 1-1 under the Computer Configuration\ Windows Settings\Security Settings node. Basicsv.inf applies all but Account Policies\Kerberos Policy as local security settings when you install Windows 2000 Server. The Default Domain Policy inherits from Basicsv.inf settings all but the Local Policies when you promote the member server to a DC. Kerberos Policy is a system default policy for all Windows 2000 computers and isn't configured by a security template. Basicdc.inf makes only one change to the Basicsv.inf settings shown in Table 1-1; it enables the \Local Policies\Security Options\ Digitally Sign Server Communication (When Possible) policy.

\Account Policies\Password Policy\	Basic Security Setting
Enforce password history	1 password remembered
Maximum password age	42 days
Minimum password age	0 days
Minimum password length	0 characters
Passwords must meet complexity requirements	Disabled
Store passwords using reversible encryption for all users in the domain	Disabled
\Account Policies\Account Lockout Policy	
Account lockout threshold	0 invalid logon attempts
\Account Policies\Kerberos Policy	
Enforce user logon restrictions	Enabled
Maximum lifetime for service ticket	600 minutes
Maximum lifetime for user ticket	10 hours
Maximum lifetime for user ticket renewal	7 days
Maximum tolerance for computer clock synchronization	5 minutes
\Local Policies\Audit Policy	
Audit account logon events	No auditing
Audit logon events	No auditing
Audit object access	No auditing
Audit policy change	No auditing
Audit privilege use	No auditing
Audit process tracking	No auditing
Audit system events	No auditing

Table 1-1.   Default Policies Windows 2000 System and Basicsv.inf and Basicws.inf Templates Implement (Event Logs, System Services, Registry, and Settings Not Included)

\Local Policies\Security Options

Additional restrictions for anonymous connections	None. Rely on default permissions
Allow system to be shut down without having to log on	Disabled
Allowed to eject removable NTFS media	Administrators
Amount of idle time before disconnecting session	15 minutes
Audit the access of global system objects	Disabled
Audit use of Backup and Restore privilege	Disabled
Automatically log off users when logon time expires (local)	Enabled
Clear virtual memory page file when system shuts down	Disabled
Digitally sign client communication (always)	Disabled
Digitally sign client communication (when possible)	Enabled
Digitally sign server communication (always)	Disabled
Digitally sign server communication (when possible)	Disabled
Disable CTRL+ALT+DEL requirement for logon	Disabled
Do not display last user name on logon screen	Disabled
LAN Manager Authentication Level	Send LM and NTLM responses
Number of previous logons to cache (in case domain controller is not available)	10 logons
Prevent system maintenance of computer account password	Disabled
Prevent users from installing printer drivers	Enabled
Prompt user to change password before expiration	14 days
Recovery Console: Allow automatic administrative logon	Disabled
Recovery Console: All floppy copy and access to all drives and all folders	Disabled
Restrict CD-ROM access to locally logged-on user only	Disabled
Restrict floppy access to locally logged-on user only	Disabled
Secure channel: Digitally encrypt or sign secure channel data (always)	Disabled
Secure channel: Digitally encrypt secure channel data (when able)	Enabled

Table 1-1.   Default Policies Windows 2000 System and Basicsv.inf and Basicws.inf Templates Implement (Event Logs, System Services, Registry, and Settings Not Included) *(continued)*

\Local Policies\Security Options	
Secure channel: Digitally sign secure channel data (when able)	Enabled
Secure channel: Require strong (Windows 2000 or later) session key	Disabled
Secure system partition (for RISC platforms only)	Not defined
Send unencrypted password to connect to third-party SMB servers	Disabled
Shut down system immediately if unable to log security audits	Disabled
Smart card removal behavior	No Action
Strengthen default permissions of global system objects (e.g., symbolic links)	Enabled

Table 1-1.   Default Policies Windows 2000 System and Basicsv.inf and Basicws.inf Templates Implement (Event Logs, System Services, Registry, and Settings Not Included) (*continued*)

CODE BLUE

Never apply the Basicdc.inf template to any GPO, including the Default Domain Policy and Default Controllers Policy. Doing so causes errors to occur each time the policy is applied. Microsoft Knowledge Base article Q256000, "Error Messages after Importing Basicdc.inf into Group Policy," explains the reason for the errors and a complex procedure for stopping the error messages.

✦ **Compatible** security eliminates the need to promote ordinary members of the Users group to Power Users so they can run legacy applications that require extended permissions. Office 97 and 2000 run with Compatible security applied by the Compatws.inf template. Compatws.inf prevents anyone from being added to the Power Users group and relaxes security on six folders that many legacy applications modify. Compatible security applies only to workstations, and its use is uncommon.

✦ **Secure** configuration increases the security by applying from Securews.inf or Securedc.inf additional settings for policies under the Account Policy, Auditing, and Security Options nodes. Applying Securews.inf to a workstation removes all members from the local Power Users group. DCs don't have a Power Users group. You should consider the Secure configuration to be the minimum level of security for the domain. Secure configuration applied to the Default Domain Policy by Securedc.inf adds to the Basic configuration the settings described in Table 1-2, under the Computer Configuration\Windows Settings\Security Settings node. The Securews.inf settings differ only slightly from Securedc.inf. Securews.inf prevents anyone from being a member of the Power Users group, changes the Unsigned Driver Installation Behavior setting to Do Not Install, and changes the Unsigned Nondriver Installation Behavior setting to Warn, but Allow Installation.

\Account Policies\Password Policies\	Securedc.inf Changes to Basic Security
Enforce password history	24 passwords remembered
Maximum password age	42 days
Minimum password age	2 days
Minimum password length	8 characters
Passwords must meet complexity requirements	Enabled
Store passwords using reversible encryption for all users in the domain	Disabled
\Account Policies\Account Lockout Policies	
Account lockout duration	30 minutes
Account lockout threshold	5 invalid logon attempts
Reset account lockout counter after	30 minutes
\Local Policies\Audit Policy	
Audit account logon events	Success, Failure
Audit account management	Success, Failure
Audit logon events	Failure
Audit object access	No auditing
Audit policy change	Success, Failure
Audit privilege use	Failure
Audit process tracking	No auditing
Audit system events	No auditing

Table 1-2.   Settings for Secure Configuration

\Local Policies\Security Options	
Additional restrictions for anonymous connections	Do not allow enumeration of SAM accounts and shares
Allow server operators to schedule tasks (domain controllers only)	Disabled
Allow system to be shut down without having to log on	Disabled
Automatically log off users when logon time expires	Enabled
Digitally sign server communication (when possible)	Enabled
LAN Manager Authentication Level	Send NTLM response only
Smart card removal behavior	Lock workstation
Unsigned driver installation behavior	Do not allow installation
Unsigned nondriver installation behavior	Warn, but allow installation
\Public Key Policies	
Encrypted Data Recovery Agents	Administrator (untrusted)

Table 1-2. Settings for Secure Configuration (*continued*)

CODE BLUE

Do not apply the Securews.inf policy to Default Domain Policy or Default Domain Controllers Policy. Doing so results in a stream of errors, because the Power Users group isn't present of DCs. Applying Securedc.inf introduces potential problems with use of pre-Windows 2000 device drivers on domain computer. The "Resolving Security Configuration Template Issues" section of Chapter 6 provides additional information on these problems.

✦ **High Secure** configuration (Hisecws.inf and Hisecdc.inf) requires that all network communication use IP Security (IPSec), which requires digital signatures and encryption. This configuration removes the Terminal Server User from the system and requires Terminal Server Users to open a session with secure credentials. High Security requires configuration of an Enterprise Root Certificate Authority and

automatic certificate distribution to all network clients and servers. High Secure
changes only the Secure settings shown in Table 1-3, under the Computer
Configuration\Windows Settings\Security Settings\Local Policies\Security
Options node.

CODE BLUE

Don't apply the High Secure configuration unless all computers on the network are
running Windows 2000 and you have IPSec for network communication running
successfully. Applying this configuration prevents communication with computers on
which IPSec isn't or can't be implemented. If you apply this policy, then disable the
two Digitally Sign policies, but continue to require NTLMv2 authentication. Windows
9x and NT machines still can't authenticate with the domain. Windows 9x requires
installation of Dsclient.exe, Windows NT machines require SP4+, and both Windows
9x and NT machines require Registry hacks to authenticate with NTLMv2. Windows
NT 3.51 machines can't be patched to authenticate with NTLMv2. If you accidentally
apply this template to the Default Donain Policy, be sure to disable all three policies
listed in Table 1-3.

Steps to Apply a Security Template

You automate application of the security template settings to all computers in a Windows
2000 domain by importing the Securedc.inf file to the Default Domain Security GPO. If you
decide to reduce the security level of the domain's workstations by modifying the values
applied by the template to Default Domain Policy, the higher security settings of the Default

Security Options Policy	High Secure Setting
Digitally sign client communication (always)	Enabled
Digitally sign server communication (always)	Enabled
LAN Manager Authentication Level	Send NTLMv2 response only; refuse LM and NTLM

Table 1-3. Settings Changed for High Secure Configuration

Domain Controllers Policy of the Domain Controllers OU, except Account Policies, override those applied at the domain level. A domain can have only one set of Account Policies, which includes Password Policy, Account Lockout Policy, and Kerberos Policy. Group Policy ignores changes you make to any of the Account Policies at the site or OU level.

> **TIP:** If you want to apply different security settings (other than Account Policies) to member servers, create a Member Servers OU, move the computer accounts for member servers to the new OU, and add a new Default Member Server Policy to the OU. Creating OUs for application of specific policies is one of the subjects of Chapter 2.

You also can import the appropriate security configuration template to the Local Security Policy of an individual server or workstation. By doing so, you obtain the desired level of security prior to implementing Group Policy. It's a standard practice to apply the appropriate Basic??.inf template to the Local Security Policy of computers upgraded from Windows NT or 9x, because upgrading doesn't alter existing security settings. This is especially important for upgraded computers in a Windows NT domain that can't take advantage of Group Policy. The "Local Security Policy" section later in the chapter provides a brief introduction to Local Security Policy on workstations and servers. Chapter 5 explains local security policy in detail.

To increase the security level for all Windows 2000 computers in a test domain with the Securedc.inf template, do the following:

1. Open the Default Domain Policy in the GPE.

2. Right-click the Computer Configuration\Windows Settings\Security Settings node and choose Import Policy to open the Import Policy From dialog.

3. Select Securedc.inf (see Figure 1-7), and click Open to close the dialog and apply the settings for increased domainwide security.

4. Compare the changes made to policy settings with those in the list under the preceding Secure configuration item.

5. If you use or plan to use the GroupPol application to add user accounts to AD, navigate to the Computer Configuration\Windows Settings\Security Settings\Account Policies\Password Policy node, double-click the Minimum Password Length policy to open the Policy Settings dialog, and type 0 in the Characters spin box. Double-click the Passwords Must Meet Complexity Requirements policy and select the Disabled option in the dialog.

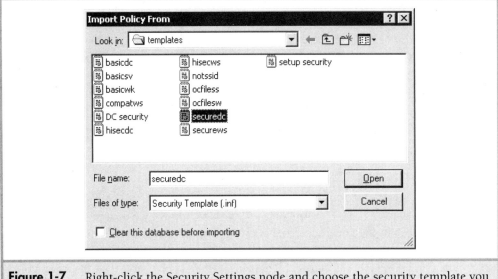

Figure 1-7. Right-click the Security Settings node and choose the security template you want to apply in the Import Policy From dialog.

 TIP: Right-click Security Settings and choose Reload to refresh the security policies after each change you make. This operation has an effect similar to running the command-line security editor, Secedit.exe, with the following arguments:

```
secedit /refreshpolicy machine_policy /enforce
```

Applying the Securedc.inf template enables Success/Failure auditing of policy changes. Each change you make to a policy adds a record to the Event Viewer's Security log. For example, changing the password policy adds an Event ID 643 record. Account management also is audited, so every modification you make to a user account adds an Event ID 624 record.

Undocumented Security Configuration Templates

The \Winnt\Security\Templates folder contains the following undocumented .inf files:

✦ **Setup Security.inf** establishes the default security settings by Access Control Entries (ACEs) on 74 Registry keys, 2,547 files and folders, and 32 services during the Windows 2000 setup process (see Figure 1-8). All files in the list are subject to Windows File Protection.

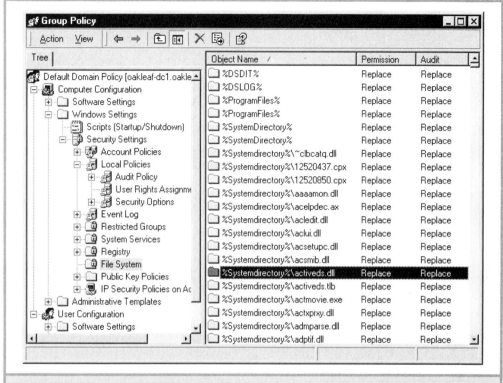

Figure 1-8. Setup Security.inf adds 2,547 protected system file and folder entries to the File System node. Activeds.dll is the COM component that implements the Active Directory Service Interfaces (ADSI).

CODE BLUE

Don't import Setup Security.inf into any GPO. Importing Setup Security.inf has a marked effect on the performance of the GPE, especially when importing other .inf files, and creates very large (approximately 500 kB) GptTempl.inf files in \Sysvol that must be replicated between DCs. The size of a GptTempl.inf file without the Security.inf entries is less than 10 kB.

♦ **DC Security.inf** adds DC-specific ACEs for 77 Registry keys and 33 files. The preceding warning also applies to this template, but the performance effects aren't as dramatic as those for Security.inf.

♦ **Ocfiless.inf** is a template for the Security Configuration Editor on servers. Ocfiless.inf adds entries to the File System node for the Program Files, Common Files, and System32 folders that aren't included in Setup Security.inf.

♦ **Ocfilesw.inf** is a version of Ocfiless.inf for workstations.

♦ **Notssid.inf** is a template for removing the Terminal Server User Security ID (SID) from Windows 2000 Server to accommodate the High Security configuration.

The \Winnt\Security\Templates\Policies folder holds several undocumented Unicode template files: Gpt00000.dom (and higher), Gpt00001.inf (and higher), and Tmpgptfl.inf. None of these templates includes a description of their purpose. Opening the files in Notepad and noting changes to file names and contents after rebooting the DC indicates the following:

♦ **Gpt00000.dom** contains the default settings for the Default Domain Policy's \Computer Configuration\Windows Settings\Security Settings\Account Policies Password Policy, Account Lockout Policy, and Kerberos Policy nodes. Promoting a server to a DC creates the file if it's not already present. Joining a domain creates this file on workstations and member servers.

♦ **Gpt000001.dom** and higher store the domain-level security settings when you add GPOs at the domain level. The settings in these files represent the settings immediately prior to the current settings. Rebooting the DC generates these files. Removing GPOs added at the domain level erases Gpt00001.dom and higher-numbered files.

♦ **Gpt00001.inf** stores copies of changes to Security Settings nodes made by the Default Domain Controllers policy. Promoting a member server to a DC creates this file during the required reboot.

♦ **Gpt00002.inf** and higher store the changes made by GPOs you add to the Domain Controllers OU. As you add GPOs and make policy changes, the file numbers increment; Gpt00001.inf becomes Gpt00002.inf, and so on when you reboot the DC. Removing links to the GPOs you added removes the higher-numbered files and regenerates Gpt00001.inf.

♦ **Tmpgptfl.inf** holds a list of modified policy values for the computer. All computers have this file after joining a domain. Combining Gpt00000.dom and Tmpgptfl.inf values re-creates the last-known good policy configuration for the computer.

Rebooting updates the Modified timestamps of each of the preceding files except Tmpgptfl.inf, which is the only file that doesn't include the GUID of a template. The apparent purpose of these files is for recovery in the event of security database corruption.

Custom Incremental Security Templates

The Security Templates snap-in lets you edit and save existing security templates or create your own from scratch. Customizing a template and saving it under a different .inf file name lets you quickly apply a common set of policies to multiple domains and their DCs. Applying common custom policies by creating an individual GPO for each domain is a better approach than linking custom GPOs from other domains, because cross-domain links to GPOs cause a significant performance hit. The Security Templates console isn't installed by default, so you must create a new console before you can edit the templates.

To edit an existing template and save it as a new custom template, run this drill:

1. Choose Start | Run, type **MMC /s** in the Open text box, and click OK to create a new Console 1.

2. Choose Console | Add/Remove Snap-in to open the dialog of the same name, and click Add to open the Add Standalone Snap-in dialog.

3. Scroll to the Security Templates item (see Figure 1-9), click Add, and click Close.

4. Click OK to add the snap-in to the console.

5. Choose Console | Save As and save the console as a .msc file—SecTempls.msc for this example.

6. Expand the Winnt\Security\Templates node to display a list of the template files the folder contains.

7. Expand one of the template nodes, such as Securedc, which displays the same set of Security Settings subnodes as the GPE. Make your changes to security policy settings, such as disabling the Passwords Must Meet Complexity Requirements policy.

TIP: It's a good practice to set Kerberos policies in your custom template, because these policy values sometimes revert to Not Configured after you make multiple changes to the Default Domain Policy GPO. Use the Kerberos Policy settings described in the earlier "Security Configuration Templates" section as a starting point.

8. Right-click the template name node (Securedc) and choose Set Description to open the Security Template Description dialog.

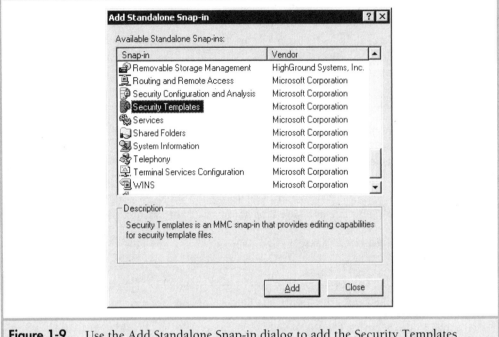

Figure 1-9. Use the Add Standalone Snap-in dialog to add the Security Templates snap-in to the new Security Templates console.

9. Replace the current description ("Assumes clean-install NTFS file\reg ACLs. Secures remaining areas." for Securedc.inf) with a brief description of the custom template (see Figure 1-10).

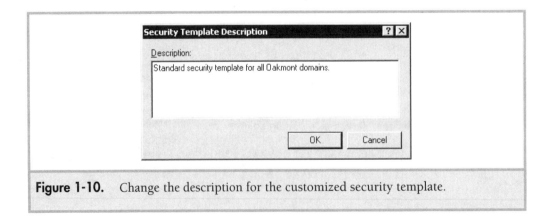

Figure 1-10. Change the description for the customized security template.

10. Right-click the template name node again and choose Save As; type a short, descriptive name for the template, and click OK to save the new .inf file (OMSecDom.inf for this example). The new template is added to the snap-in's list (see Figure 1-11).

Chapters 3, 6, and 7 show you how to take maximum advantage of incremental security templates in single- and multiple-domain topologies. These chapters also cover additional features of GPOs that aren't included in this introductory chapter, such as multiple GPOs applied to a single site, domain, or OU; GPO inheritance; and selective application of GPOs to groups and users.

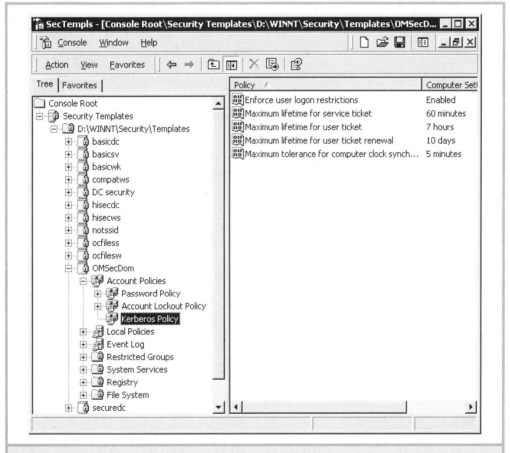

Figure 1-11.   The newly saved customized security template is added to the console's list.

Group Policy Documentation

The GPE has only rudimentary capability to export policy names and settings as tab- or comma-separated text files in conventional or Unicode format. To export a text list of policy names and their settings, right-click the node that contains the settings and choose Export List to open the Save As dialog. The feeble Export List feature writes only the items at the current node level, so exporting the Default Domain Controllers node results in a three-line file: Name, Computer Configuration, and User Configuration. The upshot of this impediment is that you must select every node containing the policies in which you're interested and save them to individual files. Figure 1-12 illustrates part of the text file exported from the Default Domain Controllers GPO's \Computer Configuration\Windows Settings\Security Settings\Local Policies\User Rights node.

NOTE: FullArmor Corporation (http://www.fullarmor.com) has come to the rescue of system admins faced with documenting production Group Policy objects. FullArmor's FAZAM 2000 consists of two snap-ins, Administrator and Policy Analysis, which aid in designing and managing Group Policy. FAZAM 2000 generates detailed GPO reports in HTML and Jet 3.51 (Access 97) .mdb formats. Using FAZAM 2000 is one of the subjects of Chapter 9.

Administrative Templates

Windows 2000 Server's Administrative Templates, as noted earlier in the chapter, are similar in format and structure to Windows NT .adm files. Each .adm file contains definitions and default setting values for the Computer Configuration and User Configuration policy classes. You can edit the standard .adm files or add new ones, so these files are replicated between all DCs in the domain. Replication permits editing Group Policy on any DC.

TIP: The Winnt\Inf folder stores working copies of all .adm files. This folder is hidden. If you haven't done so already, select the Show Hidden Files and Folders option on the View page of Explorer's Folder Options dialog. While you're there, also clear the Hide Protected Operating Files check box.

Following are Windows 2000's three standard .adm files:

✦ **Conf.adm** is the template for configuring NetShow. If you don't run NetShow on your network, you can disregard these policies. The size of Conf.adm is 33 kB.

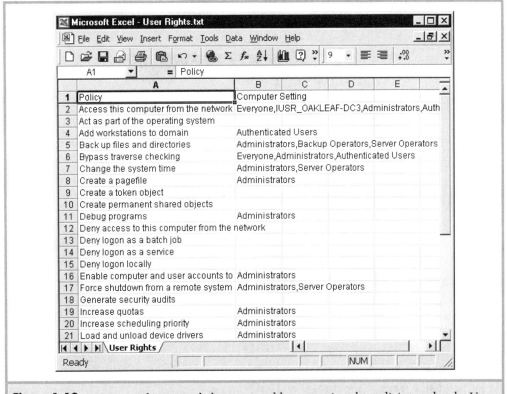

Figure 1-12. A two-column worksheet created by exporting the policies under the User Rights node of the Default Domain Controllers GPO.

✦ **Inetres.adm** configures Internet Explorer 5+. Not surprisingly, Microsoft provides a surfeit of detailed policy settings for IE, but none for alternative browsers. Inetres.adm is 110 kB.

✦ **System.adm** configures all other Registry-based policies and is 717 kB.

You can add and remove templates from the GPE by right-clicking the Administrative Templates node and choosing Add/Remove Templates to open the dialog of the same name.

If you don't use NetShow, you can remove Conf.adm in this dialog. Removing unneeded templates delivers a slight improvement in overall network performance.

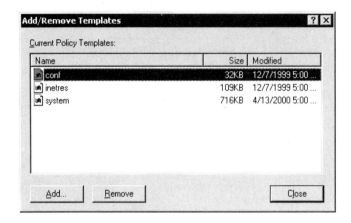

Administrative Template File Structure and Syntax

Policies defined by Administrative Templates primarily determine desktop, NetShow, and IE lockdown, and the behavior of IntelliMirror features, if implemented. Windows 2000 .adm files are in Unicode text format and, with a bit of experience, are easily readable. The files are divided into policy classes, CLASS USER and CLASS MACHINE, and have a [strings] section near the end to supply text for the Policy and Explain pages of the *PolicyName* Properties dialog (refer to Figures 1-5 and 1-6).

Figure 1-13 shows the Properties dialog for the \Computer Configuration\Administrative Templates\Group Policy\Group Policy refresh interval for computers. Figure 1-14 illustrates the template source code for this policy.

Following are the elements of the policy defined between the POLICY and END POLICY line of Figure 1-14:

✦ **KEYNAME** specifies the name of the Registry key that stores the value name and the saved value. If a KEYNAME entry is missing from the policy definition, search above the policy for a KEYNAME entry under a CATEGORY entry, which applies to policies within the category unless KEYNAME is specified within a policy.

✦ **EXPLAIN** holds a pointer to a string variable defined in the [Strings] section at the end of the template file. Two bangs (!!) indicate that the following identifier is a pointer to a string variable. The character string populates the Explain page.

✦ **PART...END PART** statements enclose code that creates an individual element of the Policy page, such as a block of text (TEXT).

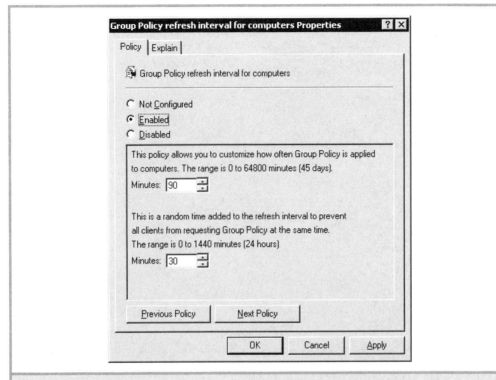

Figure 1-13.   The Policy page of the Group Policy Refresh Interval for Computers Properties dialog has two spin boxes for setting the refresh interval and random time offset.

✦ **PART** *ControlName* **NUMERIC** designates a spin box. REQUIRED specifies that the value can't be empty.

✦ **MIN 0 MAX 1440 DEFAULT 30** sets default and allowable range of the spin box. Other control types, such as drop-down lists, also have default values.

✦ **VALUENAME** is the name of the Registry entry under the key specified by KEYNAME.

You and third parties can modify System.adm (at your peril) or can extend the GPE's view of Administrative Templates to include other custom templates. As Windows 2000 matures, third-party server tool developers are likely to want to take advantage of templates for distributed management of their add-on software.

Figure 1-14. Code for the GroupPolicyRefreshRate policy generates the text and spin box controls for the policy Properties dialog shown in Figure 1-13.

NOTE: Administrative Templates are prime candidates for future conversion to XML. Moving Windows 2000 internals to open standards, however, isn't likely to be high on Microsoft's priority list.

Registry Entries for Policies

If you're interested in spelunking the Registry to track policies, copy the VALUENAME variable (GroupPolicyRefreshTime for this example) to the Clipboard and then launch Regedit.exe, choose Edit | Find, paste the value name into the text box, and click OK to start the search. After a few seconds, a highlighted key displays the VALUENAME entry. However, the first key Find encounters (HKEY_CURRENT_USER\Software\Microsoft\ Windows\CurrentVersion\Group Policy Objects\{31B2F340-016D-11D2-945F- 00C04FB984F9}Machine\Software\Policies\Microsoft\Windows\System for this example) isn't the key specified by KEYNAME (see Figure 1-15.) This entry is associated with the current user (usually Administrator when editing GPOs).

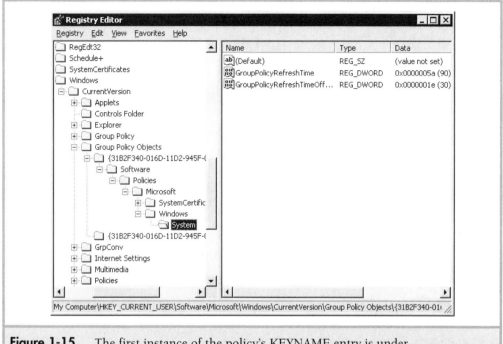

Figure 1-15.   The first instance of the policy's KEYNAME entry is under HKEY_CURRENT_USER, not HKEY_LOCAL_MACHINE.

TIP: You might have to wait up to five minutes (the default Group Policy refresh interval for DCs) after enabling the policy to find the value entry in the Registry.

Pressing F3 finds the value under its proper key in the protected region of the Registry, HKEY_LOCAL_MACHINE\SOFTWARE\Policies\Microsoft\Windows\System (see Figure 1-16). It's this key that applies the setting to the local computer.

Continuing the search finds another copy of the value in HKEY_USERS\S-1-5-21-3116961492-1656814436-3654400445-500\Software\Microsoft\Windows\CurrentVersion\Group Policy Objects\{31B2F340-016D-11D2-945F-00C04FB984F9}Machine\Software\Policies\Microsoft\Windows\System. S-1-5-21-*DomainGUID*-500 is the well-known Security ID (SID) for the Administrator of the domain specified by *DomainGUID*, the GUID of oakmont.edu for this example. Well-known SIDs identify Windows 2000's standard (generic) set of built-in or default users and Security Groups. This entry provides the values under the first-found key for the logged-on Administrator.

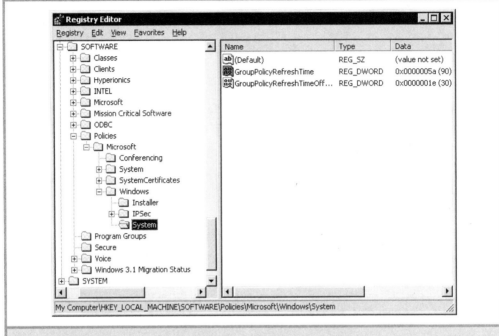

Figure 1-16.   The second KEYNAME instance is under HKEY_LOCAL_MACHINE. It's this key that applies the policy to the local computer.

 TIP: Appendix A lists the Registry entries for each policy in both classes of Administrative Templates. If you're seriously interested in (or just curious about) Windows 2000's Registry, purchase a copy of Kathy Iven's *Admin911™: Windows® 2000 Registry* (Osborne/McGraw-Hill, 2000; ISBN 0-07-212946-8).

System Policy Templates

System policy applies only at the domain level, but policies can be restricted to members of specific global groups. Windows NT 4.0's System Policy Editor, Poledit.exe, uses a combination of Winnt.adm and Common.adm to provide the definitions of system policies for creating Ntconfig.pol. Creating system policies for Windows 9x clients requires that you run Poledit.exe under Windows 9x, in which case the template files are Windows.adm and Common.adm, and the resulting system policy file is Config.pol. Common.adm contains definitions of polices that are shared by the downlevel operating systems. If you upgrade a Windows NT 4.0 PDC to a Windows 2000 DC, the system policy .adm files remain in their usual location, Winnt\Inf.

NOTE: This chapter provides only a brief overview of System Policy Templates. Chapter 8 delivers the details of how to establish system policies for Windows NT and 9x clients.

Running Adminpak.msi on a Windows 2000 server or client adds Poledit.exe to the \Winnt folder. When you launch Poledit.exe from the Run dialog on a DC that hasn't been upgraded from a Windows 2000 PDC with system policies in place, PolEdit's window has icons for Default Computer and Default User policies. These two icons correspond to the Computer Configuration and User Configuration nodes in the GPE. Computer system policies apply to Registry settings in the HKEY_LOCAL_MACHINE hive, and user system policies apply to HKEY_CURRENT_USER.

It's a common practice to add User objects whose policy settings apply by group membership. The Computer Configuration class of Windows 2000 GPOs apply when the computer boots. System policy computer and user settings don't apply until the user logs on and downloads his or her roaming user profile, if present. Computer and user policy settings can be applied by group membership. If users are members of more than one group, you can prioritize application of group-based system policy.

Each set of Computer and User objects has its own *IconCaption* Computer Properties and *IconCaption* User Properties dialogs. These dialogs combine tree-view elements of the GPE's UI with the settings pane of the Policies page of the GPE's *PolicyName* Properties dialog (see Figure 1-17). Tri-state check boxes, which are in the not-configured (gray) state by default, change to enabled (marked), disabled (cleared), and back to not configured with multiple mouse clicks.

After you define or edit system policy, you save the resulting policy (Ntconfig.pol or Config.pol) file in the folder shared as Netlogon. Windows NT 4.0 PDCs (and BDCs if LMREPL replication is working) store Ntconfig.pol and Config.pol in \Winnt\System32\Repl\Import\Scripts, the traditional Netlogon share. When you upgrade a Windows NT PDC or BDC to Windows 2000, the installation process moves all Netlogon files to \Winnt\Sysvol\Sysvol*DomainName*\Scripts, which Windows 2000 shares as Netlogon.

Microsoft discourages the use of system policies in Windows 2000 networks, because the company's objective is to sell Windows 2000 Professional upgrades for every client. The "To add or remove an Administrative Template" and ".adm files included with Windows 2000" topics of the GPE's online help file state that you can add system policy .adm files to the GPE, and that doing so causes icons for "true" Group Policy settings to turn blue and those for system polices to turn red. The information in online help is incorrect. Adding the

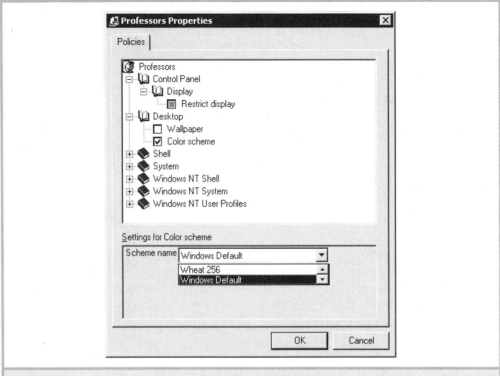

Figure 1-17. In this example of a user policy for a Professors group, the Wallpaper policy is disabled, Color Scheme is enabled and restricted to Windows Default, and the remaining nonvisible policies aren't configured.

Winnt.adm and Common.adm templates to one of the Administrative Templates nodes installs Unsupported Administrative Templates subnodes, each of which contains Not Configured entries for the two .adm files. Attempts to enable these two "policies" fail silently.

Local Security Policy

The Default Domain Policy GPO's Security Policy overrides local security settings on all computers for all users, and Default Domain Controllers Policy overrides Default Domain Policy to change local security settings of DCs. To open the GPE with only the Local Security Policy settings, choose Programs | Administrative Tools | Local Security Policy. On a workstation, open the Control Panel's Administrative Tools folder and double-click the

Local Security Policy tool. The columns in the list pane of the Local Security Setting window differ from those for Domain Security Policy and Domain Controller Security Policy. Local Security Setting has Local Setting and Effective Setting columns. Effective settings on a workstation are those applied by Default Domain Policy and, for DCs, Default Domain Policy and Default Domain Controllers Policy (see Figure 1-18).

Double-click a policy to open the Local Security Policy dialog, which has a list of the accounts and groups with Local Policy Setting and Effective Policy Setting check boxes that indicate the applicability of the policy. You can alter Local Policy Settings, but Effective Policy Settings check boxes are disabled. Effective Policy Settings can be changed only by

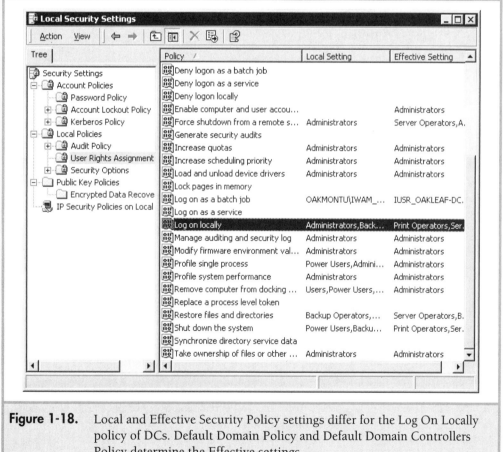

Figure 1-18.   Local and Effective Security Policy settings differ for the Log On Locally policy of DCs. Default Domain Policy and Default Domain Controllers Policy determine the Effective settings.

applying a GPO. Clicking Add opens the Select Users or Groups dialog, which lets you add Security Groups or user accounts to the list.

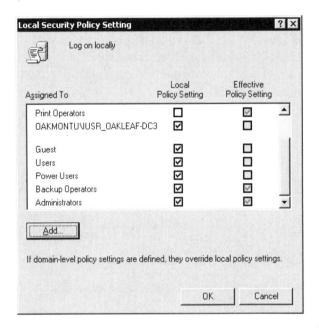

 TIP: Right-click Security Settings in the Local Security Policy Settings GPE and choose Reload to view changes made by altering a domain GPO. Otherwise, the changes may take up to five minutes to take effect locally.

Right-clicking the Security Settings node of Local Security Policy offers Import Policy and Export Policy choices. If you establish a custom local policy for workstations or servers, you can export it to a security template (.inf) file as either a local or effective policy. You can use the exported security template to import custom Local Security Policy to Windows 2000 workstations in Windows NT domains. You also can use the Security Configuration and Analysis snap-in to verify the conformance of local security policies of Windows 2000 workstations with a standard set of security policies you specify.

 NOTE: Chapter 5 provides much more detailed information about Local Security Policy and use of the Security Configuration and Analysis snap-in.

Filtering the Application of Group Policy Objects

Windows 2000's Group Policy provides much more flexible application criteria than Windows NT's system policies. System policies apply at the domain level only, and their effects can be restricted only to groups or individual users and their computers. Thus, system policies offer very coarse application granularity.

As mentioned early in the chapter, you can apply Group Policy at the site, domain, and OU levels. Creating GPOs at the OU level lets you apply policies by business functional groups, such as marketing or finance, rather than by the user's role within the group, which commonly is determined by GartnerGroup or similar classifications. You prevent application of GPOs to members of specific Windows 2000 Security Groups by a process called *filtering*. The first groups you'd obviously want to filter from restrictive domainwide User Configuration policies are Enterprise Admins and Domain Admins. By default, these two Admins groups and the System account are exempt from application of the Default Domain Policy's User Configuration policies. These policies *do* apply to Admins, however, because members of the Admins groups become members of the Authenticated Users group after logon, and all Authenticated Users receive User Configuration policies unless you filter this Security Group. The Admins' computers aren't exempt from Computer Configuration policies, because computer policies apply at bootup, and the DC doesn't know the user's group membership until logon. Computer objects are a subclass of AD's User object, so all computers in the domain also join the Authenticated Users group during the Winlogon process.

The Builtin, Computers, Foreign Security Principals, Lost and Found, System, and Users containers aren't OUs, so you can't apply Group Policy to these containers. You can apply special policies to Admins' computers by placing their accounts in an OU and adding a GPO for Admins.

TIP: You can verify that Computer Configuration policies apply to Enterprise Domain Admins by attempting to change the password for an account in these groups to less than the number of characters specified by the \Computer Configuration\Windows Settings\Security Settings\ Account Policies\Password Policies\Minimum password length policy. Right-click the account name in the Users container and type and confirm a short password. When you click OK, you receive a message that the password doesn't meet the password policy requirements.

To view and alter the application of GPOs by group and account, do this:

1. In the GPE, right-click the Default Domain Policy item and choose Properties to open the General page of the Default Domain Properties dialog. The two check boxes in the Disable frame let you disable either or both property classes.

2. Click the Security tab to display the list of groups to which the GPO applies. The initially selected Authenticated Users group has Allow Read and Apply Group Policy permissions. These two permissions are required to apply a GPO to a group. The Authenticated Users group includes all users who can log on to the network, so all users receive Group Policy, unless exempted by membership in another group.

3. Click each of the remaining groups to view its privileges. CREATOR OWNER (Microsoft, in this case, creator of the GPO) has special privileges for child objects only. The remaining groups have Apply Read, Write, Create All Child Objects, and Delete All Child Objects permissions. The Apply Group Policy check box is cleared for these groups.

4. To prevent Default Domain Policy from applying to Enterprise and Domain Admins because of their membership in Authenticated Users, mark the Deny Apply Group Policy check box for each of these groups (see Figure 1-19). When you click Apply, a message informs you that "Deny takes priority over Allow entries." Click Yes to acknowledge the message only if you have a specific reason to use Deny permissions, which can complicate Group Policy management. Microsoft recommends clearing the Allow Permissions check box rather than applying Deny permissions.

Combining application of GPOs at the domain and OU levels with group policy filtering can generate unforeseen conflicts in the effective group policy applied to particular users, especially when a user is a member of multiple security groups. You can prioritize application of multiple GPOs at the site, domain, and OU levels, but unlike with security groups, you can't explicitly set GPO application priorities by Security Group. One of the benefits of FAZAM 2000 is its ability to generate a Resultant Set of Policies (RSoP), which aids in predicting the actual policy settings applied to a computer/user combination. FAZAM 2000 also has a diagnostics utility that lets you log on as a user and create a local diagnostics file to determine the policy settings actually applied to the computer/user.

Storing, Replicating, and Processing Group Policy Objects

GPOs other than those for setting local security policy on workstations and servers store their data in the following two locations:

✦ **Group Policy Containers** (GPCs) are AD objects that contain version, status, component (Group Policy extensions), and policy setting information. GPCs also store Group Policy links, security settings, and other AD-related Group Policy data.

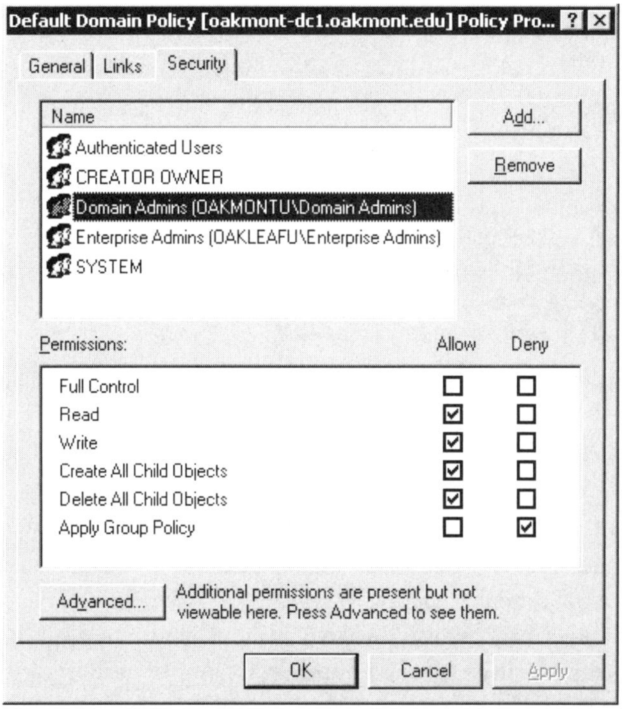

Figure 1-19. Marking the Deny Apply Group Policy check box prohibits application of a GPO to specific groups, regardless of inheritance of Allow Group Policy permission from other GPOs. Deny permissions should be used sparingly.

✦ **Group Policy Templates** (GPTs) are files that store policy information that's replicated between DCs by Windows 2000's FRS and delivered to computers in the site, domain, or both. GPTs are stored in the \Winnt\Sysvol\Sysvol*DomainName*\Policies*GUID* folder and its \Adm, \Machine, and \User subfolders.

The Default Domain Controllers GPT for the examples in this chapter is located in the \Winnt\Sysvol\Sysvol\oakmont.edu\Policies\{31B2F340-016D-11D2-945F-00C04FB984F9} folder. The GPT folder contains a single Gpt.ini file with a [General] section that has a single entry: Version = 131090. The version number displayed is the decimal equivalent of a 32-bit DWORD (double-word) value with the hexadecimal value of 0x00020012. The first word (0x0002, decimal 2) is the Computer Configuration (Machine) version, and the second word

(0x0012, decimal 18) is the User Configuration (User) version. During bootup and logon, and every 90 minutes (the default Group Policy refresh interval) thereafter, the system tests the DWORD version number stored in a DC's Gpt.ini with the DWORD version number stored by each computer. If the version numbers differ, a full update of protected Registry key values occurs.

> **TIP:** Use Calculator's Scientific view to convert decimal to hexadecimal values, and vice versa. To determine the DWORD value of the Version value, select Dec(imal), type the number, and select Hex(adecimal). If less than eight hex characters result, pad the resulting value to a DWORD by adding zeros to the left of the result.

Following are brief descriptions of the default contents of the subfolders of the \Winnt\Sysvol\Sysvol*DomainName*\Policies*GUID* folder:

✦ **Adm** contains copies of the current Conf.adm, Inetres.adm, and System.adm templates, unless you removed Conf.adm from the Administrative Templates node.

✦ **Machine** contains a Registry.pol file and Applications, Microsoft, and Scripts subfolders. Applications is empty. Microsoft has a Windows NT subfolder with a Secedit subfolder that contains the GptTempl.inf file mentioned in the earlier "Undocumented Security Configuration Templates" section. Scripts contains two subfolders, Shutdown and Startup, which are empty if you haven't defined startup and shutdown scripts.

✦ **User** contains a Registry.pol file, an empty Applications subfolder, a Documents & Settings subfolder with a Fdeploy.ini file (which has an empty [Folder Status] entry), a Microsoft subfolder with a Remote Install subfolder containing an Oscfilter.ini file for OSChoice values, and a Scripts subfolder with Logon and Logoff subfolders.

Defining production-grade group policy settings populates many of the Machine and User subfolders with files and, in some cases, additional subfolders.

The GptTempl.inf File

GptTempl.inf contains Security Settings values established by settings made in the Domain Security Policy and Domain Controller Security Policy GPE views or under the Computer Configuration\Windows Settings\Security Settings node of the GPE's Default Domain Policy and Default Domain Controllers Policy views. The values in this Unicode file update the computer's local security database, \Winnt\System32\Security\Database\ Secedit.sdb. Figure 1-20 shows the first 31 lines of a typical GptTempl.inf file containing Default Domain Policy values.

The last 36 entries of GptTempl.inf in the [Registry Values] section update values under the following 11 keys:

- ◆ MACHINE\Software\Microsoft\Windows NT\CurrentVersion\Winlogon

- ◆ MACHINE\Software\Microsoft\Windows NT\CurrentVersion\Setup\RecoveryConsole

- ◆ MACHINE\Software\Microsoft\Windows\CurrentVersion\Policies\System

- ◆ MACHINE\Software\Microsoft\Non-Driver Signing

- ◆ MACHINE\Software\Microsoft\Driver Signing

- ◆ MACHINE\System\CurrentControlSet\Services\Netlogon\Parameters

- ◆ MACHINE\System\CurrentControlSet\Services\LanmanWorkstation\Parameters

- ◆ MACHINE\System\CurrentControlSet\Services\LanManServer\Parameters

- ◆ MACHINE\System\CurrentControlSet\Control\Session Manager

- ◆ MACHINE\System\CurrentControlSet\Control\Print\Providers\LanMan Print Services

- ◆ MACHINE\System\CurrentControlSet\Control\Lsa

Registry.pol Files

The two Registry.pol files combine to form the Windows 2000 equivalent of Windows NT's Ntconfig.pol. The settings within the Registry.pol file in the Machine subfolder apply values set under Computer Configuration\Administrative Templates to the protected keys of the HKLM hive, and those from User Configuration\Administrative Templates in the User subfolder update the corresponding HKCU keys.

Unlike GptTempl.inf files, which consist of Unicode text only, Registry.pol files consist of a mixture of Unicode text and binary data. Thus, Registry.pol files aren't readable in Notepad or WordPad. Registry.pol files are relatively small (typically 2,440 bytes for Machine and 170 bytes for User), until you add many Administrative Template policy settings.

 CAUTION: Don't attempt to open Registry.pol in Regedit.exe or Regedt32.exe. You risk making changes to the file that might cause unexpected results, including problems booting the machine whose Registry is altered.

Figure 1-20. The GptTempl.inf file in the ...\Machine\Microsoft\Windows NT\Secedit folder updates the Secedit.sdb database and 36 Registry values.

Client-Side Extensions for Processing GPOs

Windows 2000 uses a set of protected system DLLs, called client-side extensions, to process GptTempl.inf, Registry.pol, and GPO-related ...\Machine and ...\User files on Windows 2000 computers. Table 1-4 lists the node names in the order of their appearance in the GPE and the name of the client-side extension that handles processing of the policy settings under the node.

Computer Configuration

Software Installation	Appmgmts.dll
Scripts (Startup/Shutdown)	Gptext.dll
Security Settings	Scecli.dll
Encrypted Data Recovery Agents	Scecli.dll
IP Security Policy	Gptext.dll
Administrative Templates	Userenv.dll

User Configuration

Internet Explorer Maintenance	Iedkcs32.dll
Scripts (Logon/Logoff)	Gptext.dll
Folder Redirection	Fdeploy.dll
Administrative Templates	Userenv.dll

Table 1-4.   Client Side Extensions for Computer and User Configuration Policies

CODE BLUE

Userenv.dll and Scecli.dll are two primary sources of inscrutable error events in the Application log, such as "The Groups Policy client-side extension Security was passed flags (17) and returned a failure status code of (13)." Events that repeat every five minutes usually are related to FRS problems between DCs or the Distributed File System (DFS) client, but some are due to loss of environmental variables for the Sysvol share or missing accounts for well-known security principals. To find fixes for Userenv.dll and Scecli.dll errors, search the Microsoft Knowledge Base with Windows 2000 in the My Search Is About list and Scecli in the My Question Is text box. New articles concerning these and related problems appear regularly.

Resource Kit Group Policy Tools

In addition to the Gpolmig.exe tool mentioned earlier in the chapter, the Windows 2000 Server Resource Kit's CD-ROM includes the following command-line tools specifically intended for Group Policy testing and troubleshooting the application of GPOs to computers and users:

✦ **Gpresult.exe** (the Group Policy Results tool) displays the policies in effect for the computer on which you run Gpresult.exe, along with those for the currently logged-on user. Command-line /c and /u switches display basic computer or user results, respectively. Basic results include domain and site information, group membership, the time of last application of Group Policy, and a list GPOs that applied the policies. The /v and /s switches expand the level of detail of the basic results.

✦ **Gpotool.exe** (the Group Policy Verification tool) runs on DCs to test the status of GPOs. Running the tool without command-line switches displays a list of the GPOs by GUID and the health of each policy. Adding the /verbose argument displays the friendly name of the policy, such as Default Domain Policy and its created and modified dates, version IDs, and machine and user Group Policy Extension GUIDs. Gpotool.exe is especially useful for verifying proper replication of GPOs between DCs, because it runs a recursive comparison of the content of GPOs on all DCs in the domain.

You use the preceding two tools, together with other Windows 2000 Support Tools such as Dcdiag.exe, Dsastat.exe, and Netdiag.exe, to troubleshoot DC and network connectivity problems that interfere with proper application of GPOs throughout the domain. Troubleshooting sections in later chapters of this book show you how to use Gpresult.exe and Gpotool.exe to track down failure of GPO updates to propagate to computer and user accounts.

TIP: If you haven't yet installed the Windows 2000 Support Tools on your server(s) and administrative workstation(s), run 2000Rkst.msi from the \Support\Tools folder of the Windows 2000 Server CD-ROM.

Chapter 2

Optimizing Active Directory Topology for Group Policy

The design of your organization's AD domain structure is your most important task as a Windows 2000 system admin. A substantial part of Microsoft's Windows 2000 Server documentation on Microsoft's Web site, the online help, and the Windows 2000 Server Resource Kit is devoted to optimizing your AD topology. Microsoft's design methodology takes into account geographical, organizational, political, networking, and Internet namespace constraints but devotes relatively little attention to the influence of AD topology on the effectiveness of Group Policy implementation.

Adapting Group Policy Implementation to Migration Strategy

Your Group Policy implementation strategy and, to a lesser degree, your final AD topology depends on your Windows 2000 migration strategy. The majority—probably 90 percent or more—of current Windows 2000 Server installations are upgrades to existing Windows NT networks. Microsoft's success in marketing Windows NT as application, file, and print servers means that upgrades probably will predominate over new Windows 2000 network installations through 2002 or later. A few courageous organizations began deploying Windows 2000 Server on an enterprisewide basis with release candidates. Most firms aren't willing to play the pilgrim role, so they delay migration to dramatically altered networking operating systems for a year or two after the initial release. The relatively slow initial acceptance of Windows NT Server 3.x followed by a very rapid increase of version 4.0 sales (and a corresponding decline in NetWare's market share) is indicative of the conservatism of IT departments of large organizations.

 NOTE: Microsoft's release in July 2000 of Service Pack 1 for Windows 2000 is indicative of the power of the "wait for the first service pack" dictum of respected industry analysts, such as GartnerGroup. It remains to be seen if fast-tracking SPs overcome IT departments' "if it ain't broke, don't fix it" policy for their existing Windows NT networks.

In the unlikely event that you're creating a Windows 2000 domain structure from scratch, for instance, for a new firm with no existing network (other than workgroup file and printer sharing), skip to the "Designing the Internal Domain Structure" section. If you've moved or intend to move NetWare users, groups, OUs, and other containers from a NetWare domain, start at the "Domain Restructure or Consolidation" section. For more information on migration strategies for NetWare, download Microsoft's NetWare to Windows 2000 Server Migration Planning Guide from http://www.microsoft.com/windows2000/library/ planning/incremental/netmigrate.asp.

Planning Client Migration to CCM

In contrast to the slow initial uptake of Windows 2000 Server licenses for production networks, Windows 2000 Professional is gaining corporate converts at a fairly rapid rate. Early adopters of Windows 2000 Professional fall into the following three migration categories:

- **Installation on newly purchased PCs only**   The average three-year useful life span for existing desktop and laptop workstations results in a relatively long transition to a fully managed Windows 2000 environment. Up to two-thirds of the new clients might connect to Windows NT networks when adoption of Windows 2000 Server is delayed.

- **Clean installs on new and some existing PCs**   Most business PCs purchased since early 1999 have the hardware horsepower to run Professional. This approach provides considerably faster migration to CCM-enabled clients, but doesn't solve the interim Windows NT networking problem. Microsoft recommends *de novo* installation where feasible and so does this book. If you've convinced your users to maintain all their local files under My Documents and, better yet, have desktop users storing My Documents in their home folder on a file server, clean installs on existing PCs are straightforward. Otherwise, backing up and wiping users' local disks, followed by a partial restore of user files, is a costly and chancy process.

- **Clean installs on new PCs and upgrades to existing PCs**   This process usually results in a heterogeneous mix of CCM-enabled clients and unmanageable PCs beset with application and local file system anarchy. If you can avoid upgrading Windows NT and 9x clients, do so. The move to Windows 2000 Professional is the ideal time to convince users accustomed to desktop and laptop autonomy (or anarchy) that centrally administered CCM will make their lives easier and more productive. It's virtually impossible to fully CCM-enable upgraded PCs that haven't been subject to a tightly controlled application configuration by system policies, such as Run Only Allowed Windows Applications.

TIP: Use of the term *personal computer* within a corporate environment leads users to the mistaken belief that the computers they use and the files they store are their personal property. It's not uncommon to find local disk drives or file servers filled with MP3 files downloaded from the Internet. Placing new restrictions on client PCs leads to user bickering and, in some cases, revolts reminiscent of those that occur when replacing Macintoshes with Wintel machines. Before you begin your Windows 2000 migration, make sure that executive management understands that CCM is necessary to achieve *any* return on the upgrade investment. You also need top-management backing to alter users' understanding of who owns and is responsible for the configuration of and content stored on the firm's computers. Implementing CCM offers a once-in-a-decade opportunity to minimize potential legal liability for unauthorized or improper use of client computers.

A typical Windows NT network has between 25 and 100 clients per server, so the decisions you make for migrating clients to Windows 2000 have a more profound effect on total network management costs than decisions about server upgrades. Synchronizing the timing of client and server upgrades, however, also is an important factor in gaining the maximum return from your investment in deploying Group Policy.

NOTE: The term *users* in this chapter applies to ordinary and power users, not admins, help desk technicians, and software developers.

Choosing the Server Migration Approach

There are two approaches to migrating from a Windows NT to 2000 network: *in-place upgrade* and *domain restructure*, which also is called *domain consolidation*. The choice you make between these two approaches, or how you combine them, has a major influence on the effectiveness of Group Policy deployment.

The first rule of AD topology is "simpler is better." A single domain for internal network users and computers in one tree of a forest is the optimal design, if your DNS namespace requirements permit. If not, consider changing your internal DNS namespace. Windows 2000's hierarchical OUs, and the ability to delegate administrative responsibility for OUs, takes the place of separate Windows NT domains created to distribute managerial tasks.

If your Web servers run under one or more ICANN-assigned (public) domain names, put them into separate domain trees that don't include the domain used for internal user and computer accounts. The "simpler is better" rule applies primarily to internal, not external, networks, where DNS namespaces and IP addresses are under your control, not that of ICANN or your ISP.

NOTE: An exception to the single-domain rule might be justified if you have a geographically disperse organization with several thousand clients and a large number of Security Groups whose membership changes frequently. In this case, intersite AD replication traffic over slow (128 kbps or less) WAN links can consume a significant part of available bandwidth.

In-Place Windows NT Server Upgrade

Microsoft calls in-place upgrade the "easiest, least-risky route" to Windows 2000 networking, because you retain the existing domain structure, its user and computer accounts, and all security groups. Home folders, logon scripts, and other files (hopefully) aren't affected by the upgrade. Least-risk endeavors, however, traditionally return low dividends, and in-place upgrades are no exception. Your Windows 2000 domain structure mirrors that of the upgraded Windows NT domains, including any resource domains you've established. If your clients have fixed IP addresses, which was common in early Windows NT networks, your new Windows 2000 network inherits them. You're also stuck, at least temporarily, with the Windows NT DNS namespaces you've implemented, if any.

It's a common practice to conduct incremental in-place upgrades in the following stages:

1. Upgrade the account domain PDC to a DC. The first PDC you upgrade becomes the initial root domain DC, a Global Catalog (GC) server, and the PDC emulator for downlevel clients. As with a PDC, all additions and changes to user accounts (and computer accounts not in a resource domain) occur on the PDC emulator and replicate to Windows NT BDCs. Trusts with other Windows NT domains remain nontransitive.

2. Designate subnets connected by WAN links to the PDC emulator's subnet as Windows 2000 sites in preparation for upgrading remote account BDCs and resource domains.

3. Upgrade account domain BDCs to Windows 2000 DCs and place them in the appropriate site. Each site needs at least one DC for each domain the site contains; two DCs per domain per site are necessary for redundancy. Each site must have at least one DC designated as a GC server.

TIP: It's a good practice to designate all DCs as GCs, except the DC that handles the Infrastructure Flexible Single Master Operations (FSMO) role. Doing this improves logon redundancy for Windows 2000 clients at each site where you install multiple DCs, and it doesn't have a significant effect on intersite replication traffic.

4. Upgrade each resource domain PDC to a DC and assign the DC to its site; then upgrade resource domain BDCs.

5. When all PDCs and BDCs are upgraded to Windows 2000, convert the mixed-mode domains to native mode, which lets you nest Global groups and take advantage of Universal groups, plus a few other native-mode-only features.

TIP: In each of the preceding steps, a full, known-good current backup is critical, and two backups are better than one. In-place upgrades are a one-way process. Although upgrade failures are rare, they usually are fatal, especially if the failure occurs during promotion of the server to a DC. Protect against extended domain downtime by adding a temporary BDC, synchronizing it with the PDC just before the upgrade, and removing it from the network. If the PDC upgrade fails, you can promote the BDC to a PDC and reconnect it to the network.

In-place upgrades of account and resource domains dump all user accounts and security groups in the Users container and computer accounts in the Computers container. Security IDs (SIDs) of groups and users don't change during the upgrade. Neither User nor Computers are OUs, so it's up to you to move the individual user and computer accounts into the OU hierarchy you create for classification and delegation of management. If computer accounts are in an upgraded resource domain, users and their computers remain in different domains. This isn't a problem for system policy, which depends only on the user account, but it does complicate application of Group Policy, because Computer Configuration comes from the upgraded resource domain and User Configuration from the account domain. You can create in the resource domain a cross-domain link to the Default Domain Policy GPO in the user domain, but doing so causes a significant slowdown of user logons.

NOTE: What does cause a problem with system policy is changing the group membership of a user subject to group-based system policy, which includes Windows 2000 clients whose user accounts are in Windows NT domains. If the user moves to a group with a different system policy (or no policy), the Registry of the user's computer is tattooed with the previous group's settings. Removing the spurious settings requires manual editing of the client's Registry.

Once you've converted the domains to native mode, you can consolidate the resource domains with the account domain by using Microsoft's Active Directory Migration Tool (ADMT) or a third-party Windows 2000 migration utility. Moving the computer accounts from resource domains into account domain OUs eliminates the need for individual domain GPOs or cross-domain GPO links. After the move, you decommission the upgraded resource domain by demoting the DCs to member servers and placing them in the account domain.

> **NOTE:** Microsoft describes the Computers container as the "Default container for upgraded computer accounts." In fact, it's the default container for all computer accounts, upgraded or not, unless you use RIS, RIPrep, or SysPrep to install Windows 2000 Professional on client PCs. Only automated installation lets you create Windows 2000 computer accounts in specified OUs. For reasons unknown, Microsoft didn't include a text box for a computer account OU in the installation dialogs. Unless you pre-create user accounts in OU(s), either individually or by scripts, manually added users fall into the Users container.

Domain Restructure or Consolidation

The alternative to in-place upgrade is to design your own domain and OU structure and use ADMT to import user and computer accounts into the structure. Domain restructure by cloning Windows NT directory objects in AD, called interforest migration, has the following advantages over in-place upgrade:

✦ You don't inherit the convoluted domain structure forced upon you by Windows NT's flat domain namespace.

✦ You can create and test your Group Policy and IntelliMirror implementations *before* you migrate users and computers to the new domain. This is an especially important feature of domain restructure. Altering desktop configuration and lockdown policies and adding or changing other features after new Windows 2000 users have joined the domain results in user dissatisfaction and a dramatic increase in help desk support cost.

✦ You can import user accounts directly into OUs by their group membership. This ability is contingent on your having a set of Windows NT security groups that correspond to your OUs for user accounts.

✦ You also can import computer accounts into OUs to selectively apply Computer Configuration policy, including security policies. Windows NT doesn't support security groups for computer accounts, but AD does. The Computer object is a subclass of the User object in Windows 2000, so you can treat Computer objects similarly to User objects.

NOTE: "Underclass of the User object" is a more apt description of the Computer object. Although you can assign individually named computer accounts to a Security Group from the Member Of page of the *ComputerName* Properties dialog, you can't select sorted or filtered computer accounts in Active Directory Users and Computers' pane for the Computers container and use the Adds the Selected Objects to the Group You Specify button to establish group membership. The button is disabled, and there's no Add Members to a Group context menu choice when you select the Computers container. If you try to add all computer accounts to a group by selecting the Computers container in the tree-view pane, the operation fails. Chapter 3 deals with this issue.

✦ You can import user, computer, and service accounts, plus security groups from multiple Windows NT domains, to perform domain consolidation, which also is called domain coalescence or collapse. For instance, you can move computer accounts from resource domains into OUs of the account domain.

✦ The final selling point of domain restructure is that cloning user and computer accounts and security groups creates duplicates in the Windows 2000 domain that retain their Windows NT identities. If users have difficulty logging on or have other problems with the Windows 2000 domain, they can simply log on to their old Windows NT domain. Moving the computer account back to the original domain requires opening the computer's System Properties dialog and clicking Properties to change domain membership in the Identification Changes dialog. In this case, however, the user gets a new local profile that doesn't contain settings for Internet Explorer, Outlook, or other messaging clients. Loss of long-established configuration settings is a serious inconvenience for most users.

TIP: The ability to move users and computers to and from the new domain is especially important when pilot-testing Group Policy with a small group of typical users of a particular category, such as Knowledge Worker or Mobile Worker. If your policies are too restrictive or cause users problems, you can return the user, computer, or both accounts to the original Windows NT domain until you fix the problems.

When you create a new User or Group object in AD (or in the Windows NT directory), it gets a new SID. The cloned user accounts, however, retain access to all resources in the Windows NT domain, and you can assign users and groups additional permissions for resources in new Windows 2000 domains. The attribute responsible for this magic is SIDHistory, which holds a copy of the SID of the user and groups from the Windows NT (source) domain. When users log on to a native-mode domain, the access token contains both the Windows 2000 SIDs and those in the SIDHistory attribute of the user's account. The Windows 2000 domain must run in native mode to support SIDHistory.

CODE BLUE

> To clone accounts from a trusted Windows NT domain to a native-mode Windows 2000 domain that was upgraded from a Windows NT PDC, you must re-create the DCs' trusts with other Windows NT source domains before using ADMT to migrate user accounts. Windows 2000 upgraded DCs have downlevel trusts with other Windows NT domains; downlevel trusts don't support SIDHistory. Use the DC's Active Directory Domains and Trusts tool to delete and re-create the trusts with other Windows NT domains before running ADMT. For more information on this issue, refer to Microsoft Knowledge Base article Q256250, "ClonePrincipal and ADMT Require Uplevel Trust to Migrate Objects Between Windows 2000 Domains."

NOTE: Appendix C describes how to use ADMT for interforest domain migration. Microsoft offers an 11-chapter "Domain Migration Cookbook" that you can download from http://www.microsoft.com/windows2000/library/planning/activedirectory/cookbook.asp. The "Cookbook" uses ADMT for domain migration and restructuring.

Interforest domain migration isn't limited to cloning Windows NT directory objects. You also can move AD objects between trees in two AD forests, but the move is subject to incomplete object migration if the schemas of the forests differ. Intraforest migration permits you to move objects between domains in the same forest of domain trees. It's the latter capability that lets you restructure multiple Windows NT domains you upgrade in place, assuming you adopted the standard practice of upgrading all domains into a single forest.

Domain Restructure Issues

Following are the primary problems you're likely to encounter when consolidating multiple domains with a large number of clients:

✦ **Duplicate user logon IDs** It's possible to duplicate account names in different domains, because the *DOMAINNAME\LogonID* combination identifies the specific account. User logon IDs within a domain, however, must be unique. ADMT offers an option to rename duplicate accounts by adding a prefix or suffix (see Figure C-15 of

Appendix C). You can apply an LDAP filter in Active Directory Users and Computers to search for the prefix or suffix to find which logon IDs are duplicates.

✦ **Identification of user accounts for classification by OU**   If security groups don't mirror OU membership, you need a method of identifying which users belong in a particular OU. Few admins take advantage of Windows NT's Description property of user accounts, and those who do aren't likely to have had OU membership in mind when adding the Description value. Consider adding a Description value with the OU name at the beginning or end of the field. LDAP filters have Begins With (*string) and Ends With (string*) conditions, but not an "Includes" (*string*) condition. This omission is the subject of many complaints that have gone unanswered by Microsoft.

✦ **Identification of computer accounts for OU classification**   The situation here is worse than for user accounts. Windows NT has a Description property for Computer objects, but AD doesn't. Even if you've added a description that can be used to classify computers, it doesn't propagate to the AD Computer object's Description attribute. This is another unsolved mystery of object migration from Windows NT to 2000. Create a worksheet with columns for NetBIOS names and the names of their target OUs.

NOTE: Duplicate computer account names should never occur, because computer NetBIOS names must be unique within the entire network.

The Windows 2000 Resource Kit includes a Deployment Scenarios foldout map that illustrates implementation of a child or grandchild domain at each site and use of a *site-domain-function-number* code (SEA-RK-DC-01, for example) for naming servers. This naming convention is quite satisfactory for servers, but isn't suitable for clients. A better approach for naming new clients is to use a prefix to uniquely identify the OU to which the computer belongs, followed by a serial number and, optionally, a suffix to identify the site, type of computer (such as desktop or laptop), or both. The examples in this book use three prefixes, FAC, NFS, and STU, to identify faculty member, nonfaculty staff, and student computers, respectively. A nine-digit ID number (the Employee ID of the user to which the computer is assigned) follows the prefix. When you run the Admin911: GroupPol application under Windows 2000, the program associates computer accounts with user accounts. The only location in which the association appears as *ComputerName* (*UserPrincipalName*) is in Active Directory Users and Computers' Select Users, Contacts, or Computers dialog (see Figure 2-1).

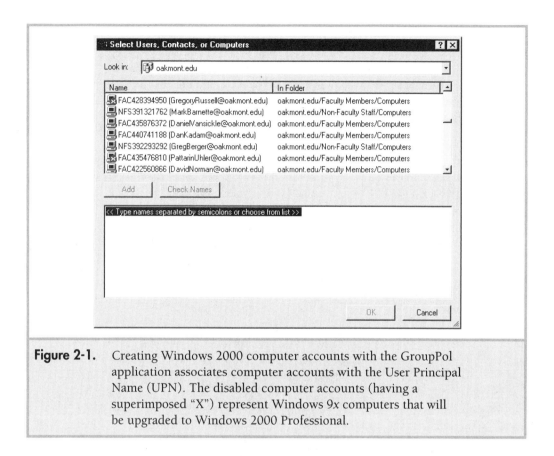

Figure 2-1.   Creating Windows 2000 computer accounts with the GroupPol application associates computer accounts with the User Principal Name (UPN). The disabled computer accounts (having a superimposed "X") represent Windows 9x computers that will be upgraded to Windows 2000 Professional.

Application of Group or System Policy to Windows 2000 Clients

If you install Windows 2000 Professional on clients in a Windows NT domain that implements system policies, the system policies are applied to Registry keys other than the protected keys that hold values set by Group Policy. The Registry tattooing occurs the first time the user logs on. Registry settings applied to Windows NT and 9x clients that you upgrade to Windows 2000 Professional remain in place. In either case, you're likely to find it difficult or impossible to reset the system policies by explicitly disabling them with the System Policy Editor. If you can't perform a full system policy reset from Poledit.exe, you must manually correct the errant Registry settings.

TIP: You can avoid tattooing the Registry of new Windows 2000 clients by installing the computers and their user accounts in a new Windows 2000 domain, rather than the production Windows NT domain. To accomplish this, you use ADMT to clone Windows NT groups in the new domain, but don't add existing Windows NT and 9x user or Windows NT computer accounts. Users gain access to resources in the Windows NT domain through the SIDHistory of the migrated security groups to which you add the user accounts. Be sure to establish Group Policy settings that emulate the existing system policy before you add production user accounts.

If you can't avoid having Windows 2000 user, computer, or both accounts managed by a Windows NT domain that implements system policy, or the clients already have their Registries tattooed, here's what you can expect:

◆ If both computer and user accounts are managed by a Windows NT domain, Local Security Policy is followed by computer and user system policy when the user logs on.

◆ If only the computer account is managed by the Windows NT domain, Local Security Policy is followed by computer system policy and the User Configuration class of Group Policy when the user logs on.

◆ If only the user account is managed by the Windows NT domain, Local Security Policy is followed by the Computer Configuration class of Group Policy and User System Policy when the user logs on.

The upshot of the preceding list is that Group Policy prevails over system policy when the Registry.pol file for computers or users is accessible to a Windows 2000 client.

Implementing the Internal Domain Structure

Using a single domain to hold all internal user and computer accounts, as mentioned earlier in the chapter, simplifies life for system and network admins. It's far easier to alter users' and computers' OU membership with the Move menu choice than to move these objects between domains with ADMT or another migration tool. The ability to apply specific policies to OUs is critical to client management in a single domain. The option to delegate management of client computer and user accounts to individuals who aren't members of the all-powerful Domain Admins group relieves the workload of network admins.

TIP: In several documents, Microsoft suggests using multiple domains if domains require different security policies. A domain can have only one set of Account Policies, but other security policies can differ. Placing computer accounts in OUs lets you easily apply more stringent security settings or other Computer Management policies to particular sets of computers. The default Domain Controllers OU, into which Dcpromo.exe automatically places the computer accounts, is an example of applying security policies (in the Default Domain Controllers Policy) to computer accounts in an OU. You also can apply less stringent policies by blocking inheritance from the Default Domain Policy and applying a new set of security-related policies. Blocking Group Policy inheritance, however, isn't a recommended practice.

The pragmatic approach to AD domain design is to start with a single domain for internal users and computers and then determine—preferably in production—whether it meets the functional requirements and performance standards of your organization. If you're worried about DC replication traffic between sites, you can determine the extent of potential WAN bandwidth problems only after you've achieved a steady-state production environment. The compression of intersite traffic is very efficient and, after you've added the bulk of your users and computers to the domain, quickly tapers off. You can use Network Monitor or a network sniffer to determine the percentage of intersite bandwidth consumed by AD and Group Policy change replication.

Don't let the number of physical sites interconnected by WANs influence your domain design. Windows 2000's Knowledge Consistency Checker (KCC) uses a very sophisticated least-cost algorithm to optimize the routing of intersite traffic between sites, but the KCC bogs down with a large number of sites and DCs. If you're considering a multiple-domain model, bear in mind that each site requires a minimum of one DC—preferably two or more—per domain to enable local logon to each domain. Increasing the number of domains can lead to a dramatic increase in the total number of servers in the network. If you have a very complex configuration with many DCs, you might find it necessary to configure your replication topology manually.

An Example of Single-Domain Topology

The ability to classify users and computers within a hierarchy of OUs is the primary feature that distinguishes Windows 2000 domains from those of Windows NT. OUs make single-domain structures feasible, even for very large organizations. In most cases, you base the upper levels of the OU hierarchy on the organizational chart for the enterprise, rather than geographic location. Classification of user accounts by region is better accommodated at the lowest OU level, but grouping computer accounts by physical location lets you delegate computer management and help desk assignments on a per-site basis. The complexity and size of your organization is the primary determinant of the depth of the OU hierarchy. One of your OU design goals should be to limit OU membership to a manageable set of user or computer accounts; a few hundred accounts per OU is a good target.

TIP: Active Directory Users and Computers sets a default 2,000-object limit for the right pane's list. To increase the number of viewable objects, you can choose View | Filter Options to open the Filter Options dialog. Type the maximum number of objects in the OU with the largest membership in the Maximum Number of Items Displayed per Folder text box. Browsing a large number of AD objects, however, consumes a substantial amount of server resources and, when conducted from a client, generates a large amount of network traffic. Use filters to generate LDAP queries that reduce the number of objects returned to a manageable value, such as 50 or fewer, to avoid swamping DCs with browse operations.

Most of the examples in this book use domains populated with AD objects by running the GroupPol application under Windows 2000. By default, GroupPol generates a single-domain (oakmont.edu) structure for Oakmont University, a fictional four-year institution in the Southwest. Oakmont U has 2,275 employees, of whom 1,448 are faculty members, and 25,344 full- and part-time students. If you don't have an existing test domain with numbers of user and computer accounts sufficient to emulate your anticipated production environment, you can use GroupPol to quickly create more than 27,500 user accounts and, optionally, the same number of computer accounts. Working with a large number of AD objects demonstrates the capabilities and pitfalls of Windows 2000's initial coterie of AD management tools.

Oakmont U classifies employees first as faculty members and nonfaculty staff and then by department, such as Anthropology and Information Technology. Students have their own top-level OU and are further classified by academic year—freshmen, sophomores, juniors, and seniors. Thus, employees and students both require a two-level OU structure. GroupPol adds optional computer accounts for employees and students in a Computers OU under each first-level OU. The program also installs 50 Computer Science laboratory computer accounts under the Lab Computers OU. Lab computers fall in the Public Computing Environment (PCE) category of the Microsoft Group Policy Scenarios discussed in Chapter 1. Figure 2-2 illustrates the structure of oakleaf.edu's three first-level OUs and their second-level OU members. Figure 2-3 shows Active Directory Users and Computers displaying the Non-Faculty Staff OUs and 10 of the 13 Security Groups in the top-level OU. Putting Security Groups in related OUs simplifies group management.

NOTE: Leicester University (http://www.leicester.ac.uk/) is an example of a very large organization (8,500 full-time students) that has implemented Windows 2000 with a single domain having multiple-level, nested OUs for organizing accounts. You can read an interview with Alistair Loew-Norris that describes Leicester University's Windows 2000 deployment at http://www.microsoft.com/TechNet/win2000/norris.asp. The resemblance between the oakleaf.edu and le.ac.uk domain architecture is purely coincidental. Loew-Norris spearheaded Leicester's early Windows 2000 migration, which began during the beta-testing stage. Microsoft's public relations spin on Leicester's implementation is at http://www.microsoft.com/windows2000/guide/platform/profiles/univofleicester.asp.

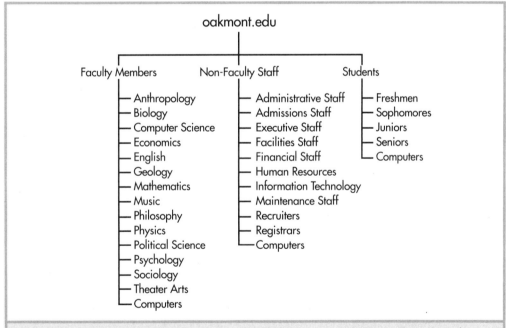

Figure 2-2. The oakleaf.edu domain example has a two-level OU hierarchy for classifying employees by department and students by academic year.

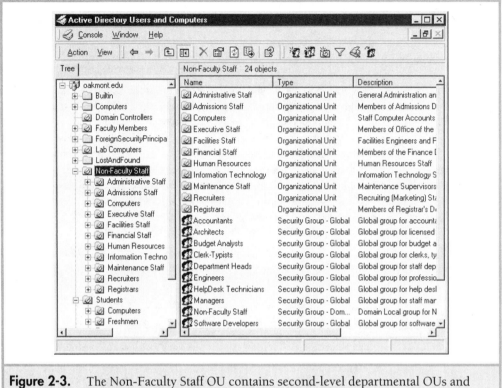

Figure 2-3. The Non-Faculty Staff OU contains second-level departmental OUs and Security Groups for staff members.

You use Security Group, not OU, membership to filter application of specific GPOs, as well as to control access to domain resources, including file shares, printers, scanners, CD burners, and the like. For example, faculty membership in five Security Groups (Deans, Chairpersons, Professors, Lecturers, and Teaching Assistants) is based on academic pecking order. Figure 2-4 illustrates group membership of a teaching assistant in the Anthropology department. If you were to use third-level OUs to classify faculty members by title, you'd end up with four sub-OUs for each of 14 academic departments, or a total of 71 OUs to manage. Of these OUs, 56 would require links to GPOs having policies suited to academic rank. Simplifying OU and GPO structures by applying Security Group filtering is the primary subject of Chapter 3.

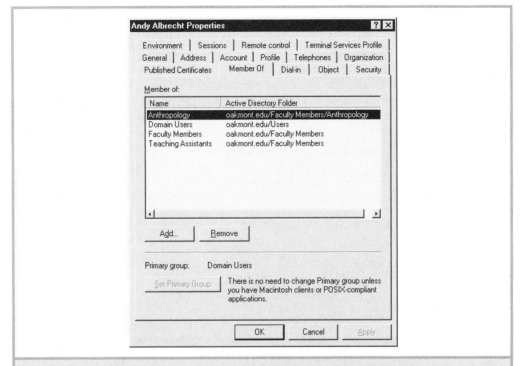

Figure 2-4. Oakmont U's faculty users are members of four Global groups, two of which reflect OU membership. The rank-based group (Teaching Assistants in this example) enables precise filtering of OUs by the users' authority levels.

Delegating Management of OUs

By default only Enterprise and Domain Admins and the System account have Full Control privileges for OUs. Local Administrators of DCs have Read, Write, and Create Child Objects permissions, but can't delete sub-OUs. Authenticated Users have only Read permission. After you've added user accounts, you can delegate management of the OU to an individual user or group with the Delegation of Control Wizard. To give the Wizard a test run, using oakleaf.edu's Anthropology OU as an example, do this:

1. Right-click the OU in the tree-view pane and choose Delegate Control to open the Wizard. Click Next to bypass the Welcome dialog.

2. In the Users or Groups dialog, click Add to open the Select Users, Computers, or Groups dialog.

NOTE: One incentive for the creation of multiple domains is the inane behavior of the Select Users, Computers, or Groups dialog. The dialog's Name list includes all security groups, and every member of the Domain Users *and* Domain Computers groups. Including computer accounts in the list more than doubles the number of objects loaded. In a domain with a very large number of users, populating the list takes *forever*. What's worse is that the list has no easily discernable order. Why one would even consider delegating control of an OU to a computer account is another Windows 2000 unsolved mystery. One explanation is an attempt by Microsoft to discourage browsing and encourage admins to type names in the text box and then click Check Names to run an LDAP query to find the desired object. Browsing a long list of AD object names is a very resource-intensive process for DCs and generates heavy network traffic.

3. Scroll to select or type the name of the user or group to whom you want to delegate control. You can add more than one user or group if you want. If you type the user names, separate multiple names with semicolons and click Check Names to verify your entries. Click OK to close the dialog and add the names to the Wizard's Users and Groups dialog (see Figure 2-5).

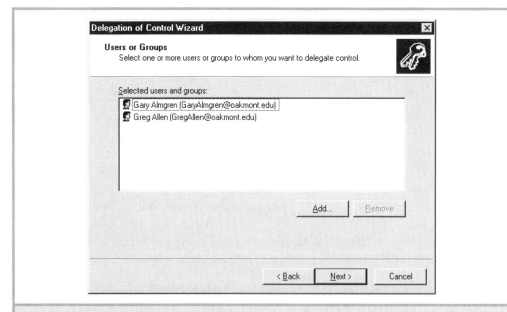

Figure 2-5. Add the user or group accounts to assume management of the OU in the Delegation of Control Wizard's second dialog. In this example, Gary Almgren is the chairperson and Greg Allen is the dean of the Anthropology department.

TIP: You can type a first name in the Select Users, Computers, or Groups dialog and then click Check Names to display the Select Matching Items dialog, which lists accounts containing the name. Typing last names doesn't work, because the search is left to right against the users' display names. Select the user from the list and click OK.

4. In the Tasks to Delegate dialog, mark the check boxes of the permitted tasks for the delegates. Ordinarily, the Create, Delete, and Manage Groups and Manage Group Policy Links tasks should be reserved for Domain Admins (see Figure 2-6).

5. Click Next to display a summary of your selections in the Completing the Delegation of Control Wizard dialog; click Finish to dismiss the wizard.

6. To confirm the preceding wizardry, right-click the selected OU, choose Properties to open the *OUName* Properties dialog, and click the Security tab. Surprisingly, selecting a delegated OU administrator, listed here by the full display name (including the prefix), doesn't display the task permissions you set in step 4 (see Figure 2-7). Permissions don't appear on this page, because they apply to objects contained in the OU, not to the OU itself.

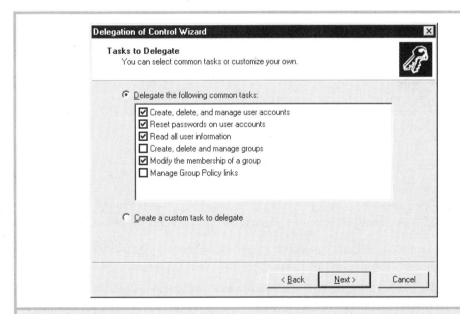

Figure 2-6.   The Delegate the Following Common Tasks option lets you choose the tasks to delegate. Selecting Create a Custom Task to Delegate and clicking Next leads to a dialog with a laundry list of more than one hundred AD objects that you can delegate.

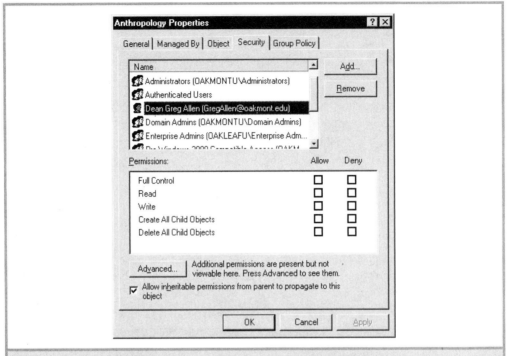

Figure 2-7. The Security page of the *OUName* Properties dialog adds the delegate names to the list, but doesn't display expected permissions for specific tasks.

NOTE: OUs inherit permissions from upper members of the hierarchy. The Allow Inheritable Permissions from Parent to Propagate to This Object check box, which is enabled by default, in this example inherits permissions from the Faculty Members OU and the oakleaf.edu domain.

7. Click the Advanced Button to open the Access Control Settings for *OUName* dialog, which displays the task permissions assigned to each delegate you selected in step 4 (see Figure 2-8).

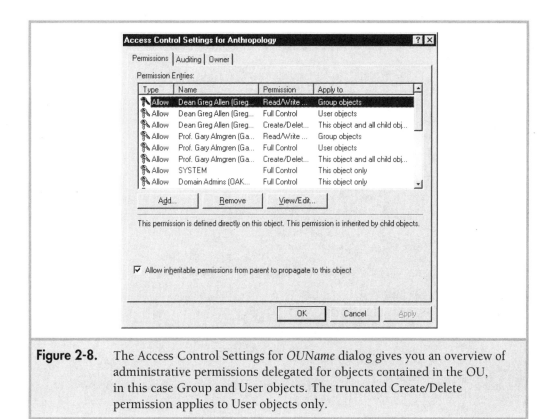

Figure 2-8. The Access Control Settings for *OUName* dialog gives you an overview of administrative permissions delegated for objects contained in the OU, in this case Group and User objects. The truncated Create/Delete permission applies to User objects only.

8. Double-click the permission entry or click View/Edit to open the Permission Entry for *OUName* dialog, which displays a list of additional tasks that you can delegate to the selected user or group (see Figure 2-9). Entries you make in this dialog apply directly to the Discretionary Access Control List (DACL) for the object(s), in this case group membership. The msExch... objects appear in the list only if you've installed Exchange 2000 or installed the Active Directory Connector (ADC) for Exchange 5.5+.

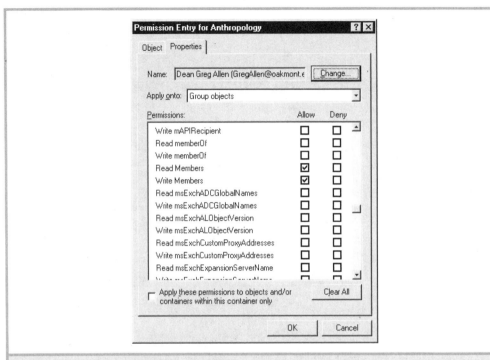

Figure 2-9. You can apply or deny permissions for additional tasks in the Permission Entry for *OUName* dialog. Opening the Apply Onto list displays a long list of AD objects to which you can assign permissions.

TIP: Even if the Apply These Permissions to Objects and/or Containers within This Container Only check box is marked, delegated OU administrators can't alter users' Security Group membership if the group isn't contained in the OU. The check box affects only sub-OUs. In this example, attempting to add a new user account to the Faculty Members or any rank-based group fails because these groups are in the Faculty Members container, not the Anthropology container. You must explicitly delegate prerequisite task permissions in other OUs. For this example, select the Faculty Members OU and use the Wizard to assign Greg Allen and Gary Almgren Modify the Membership of a Group permission only. You can save considerable time and effort by assigning the permission to the Deans and Department Chairpersons groups, which also prevents cluttering the Security page's list with a large number of individual users.

9. Click OK or Cancel three times to return to Active Directory Users and Computers.

You can verify the task permissions you delegated by logging on as the delegate and attempting each task. If you verify task permissions at a DC, you must give the Authenticated Users group Log On Locally permission under the \Windows Settings\Security Settings\Local Policies\User Rights Assignment node of the Domain Controller Security snap-in. Confirm that task permissions are limited to the selected OU by attempting the same operations in a different OU. Remove the Log On Locally permission for Authenticated Users after completing the tests on a DC.

Setting the Managed By Attribute and Finding OUs by Attribute Value

Delegating management of an OU doesn't set the Managed By attribute of the OU, because you can delegate management to groups or multiple users, and Managed By is a single-valued attribute. If you delegate management of a significant number of OUs, set the Managed By property to the user account of the person directly in charge of the OU. Doing so enables you to use Active Directory's Find feature to list, for instance, all OUs that have been assigned (or not assigned) managers.

To set the Managed By attribute, try the following:

1. Open the *OUName* Properties dialog and click the Managed By tab.

2. Click Change to open the Select User or Contact dialog.

3. Scroll the list, which has a totally random sort order, select the manager entry, and click OK to add the attribute values.

To find all managed OUs in the domain, do this:

1. Select the *DomainName* node to specify the starting point for the search.

2. Click the Find Objects in Active Directory toolbar button to open the Find Users, Contacts, and Groups dialog; click the Advanced tab.

3. Select Organizational Units in the Find list, which changes the dialog name to Find Organizational Units.

4. Click the Field button and select Managed By from the list.

5. Open the Condition list, select Present, and click Add to add the condition to the list box. If you want to find undelegated OUs, select Not Present as the condition.

6. Click Find Now to display the OUs that meet your search criteria (see Figure 2-10).

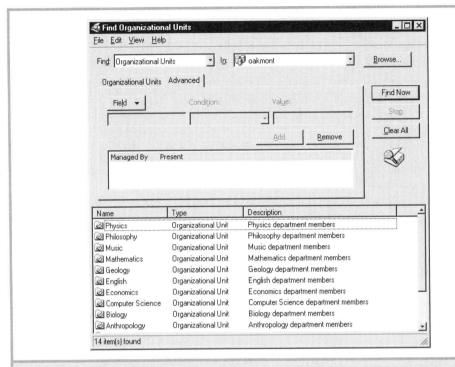

Figure 2-10. Active Directory Users and Computers' Find feature lets you use an LDAP query to search for OUs or other objects that have (as shown here) or are missing attribute values.

NOTE: The GroupPol application has an option to add the Managed By, Manager, and Direct Reports values to objects contained in the Faculty Members OU, plus those in the Computers OU of the Non-Faculty Staff OU. The option adds the dean of the department as the OU manager; members of the Information Technology OU's Helpdesk Technicians group become managers of individual computers. You must add all 2,275 employees before the message box for this option appears in GroupPol's main window.

Relocating an Object to an OU with the Move Command

As mentioned earlier, relocating objects from one OU to another is much easier than moving them between domains. For instance, you might want to move the Lab Computers OU from the domain root to the Computer Science OU, because members of the Computer Science department are responsible for managing these computers.

To move a single object between OUs, run this drill in Active Directory Users and Computers:

1. Right-click the object—Lab Computers for this example—and choose Move to open the Move dialog.

2. Expand the tree to display the destination OU: \Faculty Members\Computer Science in this case.

3. Click OK to move the object to its new location.

Filtering Objects to Move Objects by LDAP Attribute Value Strings

You can use custom LDAP filters to specify a subset of objects in a container to move to an existing or newly created OU. For example, the Faculty Members, Computers OU contains 1,635 computer accounts, which exceeds the recommended "few hundred" objects. The GroupPol application adds a Description attribute value to Computer objects, which conveniently includes a (*DepartmentName*) suffix that you can use as a filter criterion.

NOTE: Online help for Active Directory Users and Computers has only a single topic ("To select view filter options") on filtering objects, but the topic doesn't explain how to apply custom filters.

If you had the foresight to prefix or append a filterable criterion value to the objects you want to filter for movement to a new OU, you can do the following in Active Directory Users and Computers:

1. Create the new OU to contain the objects: in this case Anthro Computers under the Anthropology OU.

2. Select the source container—Faculty Members\Computers for this example—and click the toolbar's Set Filtering Options button (with the funnel icon) to open the Filter Options dialog.

3. Select the Create Custom Filter option and click Customize to open the strangely named Find Custom Search dialog. Select any existing criteria in the list and click Remove to delete them.

4. Click Field and choose Computer | Description to specify Description as the filtering attribute for computers.

5. For this example, select the Ends With condition, type (**Anthropology**) in the Value text box, and click Add (see Figure 2-11).

6. Click OK twice to close the two boxes and apply the filter to all objects except containers displayed in Active Directory Users and Computers.

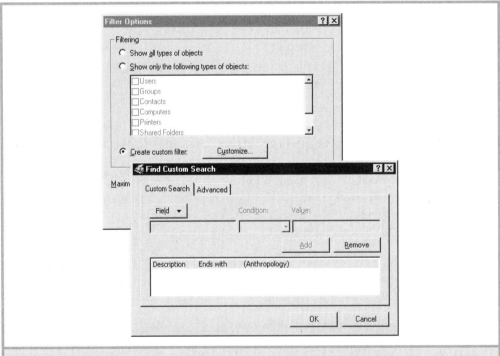

Figure 2-11. Custom filters let you select objects to move by attribute text values, but the Value string must be located at the beginning or end of the attribute value string.

7. Select the source container, which now displays only the objects meeting the filter criterion you specified in step 5 (see Figure 2-12).

8. Multiselect all objects in the list (click the first entry and then SHIFT-click the last entry), right-click the selection, and choose Move to open the Move dialog.

9. Expand the OU node to which you added the new OU in step 1, select the new OU, and click OK to move the selected objects. The Moving message box displays a progress bar during the move operation.

10. Click the Set Filtering Options button, select the Show All Types of Objects option, and click OK to remove the filter.

11. Verify the move by selecting the destination OU and checking its membership.

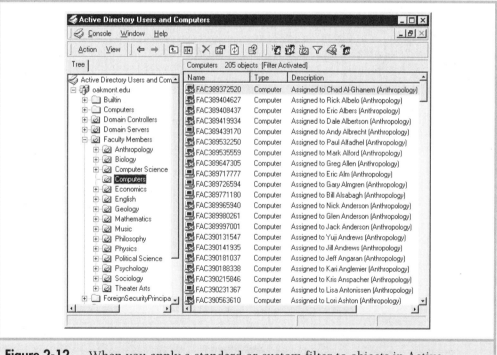

Figure 2-12. When you apply a standard or custom filter to objects in Active Directory Users and Computers, the header of the right pane includes a [Filter Activated] message. Microsoft's developers should have made [Filter Activated]'s color red and applied the flashing attribute.

TIP: Always remove the filter immediately after you move the selected objects. One of the primary sources of administrative confusion after filtering operations is accidentally leaving the filter in place when its job is done.

Filtering Objects to Move by Security Group Membership

Security Group membership is the most common criterion for selecting user accounts to move into a new OU. Group membership is ADMT's *only* criterion for assigning users to OUs during domain restructuring. It's reasonable to assume that the process of filtering by group membership be essentially the same as that for filtering by attribute value strings—so you select User, Group Membership, use Is Exactly as the condition, and type the group name in the Value text box. Unfortunately, this approach fails. It's ironic that Microsoft provides no online help topic or, when this book was written, no Knowledge Base article on this issue.

NOTE: Help topics for Advanced (LDAP) searches also are missing from online help and the Knowledge Base. Advanced searches use an obscure LDAP query dialect that's defined by RFC2254, "The String Representation of LDAP Search Filters," which you can read at http://www.cis.ohio-state.edu/htbin/rfc/rfc2254.html. If you're interested in learning more about LDAP queries, which the GroupPol application uses to set the Managed By attribute of OUs and Computer objects, download the Active Directory Service Interfaces (ADSI) 2.5 help file from http://www.microsoft.com/windows2000/library/howitworks/activedirectory/adsilinks.asp.

Filtering by group membership, which searches Member Of attribute values, requires you to supply the Distinguished Name (DN) of the group as the filter value. The DN specifies the LDAP path to an object in AD. You can use the ADSI Edit support tool to display the DN of each AD object in the default domain (see Figure 2-13) or any other accessible Windows 2000 domain. Choose Programs | Windows 2000 Support Tools | Tools | ADSI Edit to open the application, and expand the container that holds the Security Group by which to filter. CN is the LDAP abbreviation for Common Name, in this case the name of the group, followed by the OU in which the group is located and the two Domain Components (DCs) of the oakmont.edu domain.

NOTE: The GroupPol application displays the DNs of objects in the domain you specify in the startup dialog (see Figure B-6 in Appendix B). The LDAP:// prefix is a part of the full LDAP path to an AD object but is not a component of the DN.

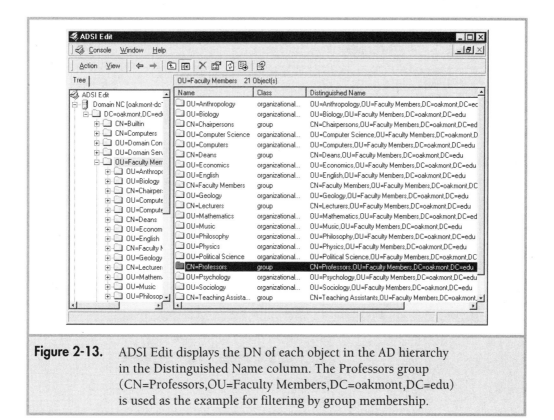

Figure 2-13.   ADSI Edit displays the DN of each object in the AD hierarchy in the Distinguished Name column. The Professors group (CN=Professors,OU=Faculty Members,DC=oakmont,DC=edu) is used as the example for filtering by group membership.

Do the following to move accounts filtered by group membership:

1. Create the new OU to contain the objects: in this case Anthro Profs under the Anthropology OU.

2. Click the toolbar's Set Filtering Options button to open the Filter Options dialog, select the Create Custom Filter option, and click Customize to open the Find Custom Search dialog. Delete existing criteria from the list.

3. Click Field and choose User, Group Membership from the context menus.

4. For this example, select the Is Exactly condition, type the DN in the Value text box, and click Add. For this example, the DN is CN=Professors,OU=Faculty Members, DC=oakmont,DC=edu, because the Faculty Members OU contains all faculty-specific groups.

5. Click OK twice to close the two boxes and apply the filter.

6. Select the source container, which now displays only the objects meeting the filter criterion you specified in step 4 (see Figure 2-14). If you've provided values for an attribute that corresponds to the group, horizontally scroll to the attribute's column to verify that the selection met your objectives. For this example, "Professor" in the Job Title column confirms membership in the Professors group.

TIP: If the attribute you need to use to confirm the filtered list isn't present in the Name pane, choose View | Choose Columns to open the Modify Columns dialog. Double-click the column name in the Hidden Columns list to add it to the Displayed Columns list and then click OK. You can change the new column's location by selecting its title bar and dragging it to the left or right.

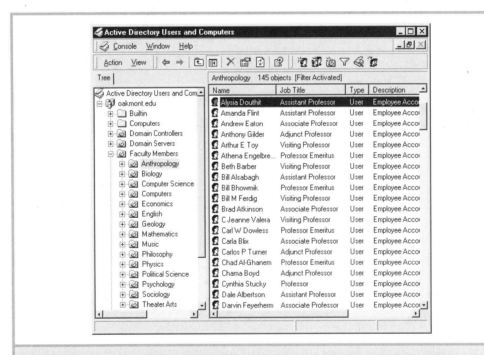

Figure 2-14. In the oakleaf.edu sample domain, successful filtering by Group Membership displays only users with membership in the Professors Security Group.

7. Multiselect all filtered objects in the list (excluding groups or OUs), right-click the selection, choose Move to open the Move dialog, select the new OU, and click OK to move the selected objects.

8. Click the Set Filtering Options button, select the Show All Types of Objects option, and click OK to remove the filter.

TIP: You can narrow membership in a filtered set by adding multiple filter criteria. For example, you can limit the filtered set to users who are members of two or more specified Security Groups (that is, members of Group1 *and* Group2). Unfortunately, Microsoft developers didn't implement a logical *or* feature (members of Group1 *or* Group2).

Multidomain Topology

Circumstances might dictate a multiple-domain design, either at the start of the design process or during development and testing. For instance, you might not want to mix special external and internal user accounts in a single domain because of security issues. You might have become frustrated with the Users, Computers, and Groups dialog's slowly generating a list of 2,000 AD objects each time you open it. You can add new domains as children of the first (parent) domain you created or as the first member of a new tree in the initial forest. Administrative costs are the primary factor in the decision between adding child domains or new trees in the forest.

If you decide to split a domain after adding user and computer accounts, you usually perform an intraforest migration of selected user and computer accounts into the added domain. For example, Oakleaf U's system admin might decide that students should have their own domain, students.oakleaf.edu, for security purposes or to apply a significantly different set of policies to students. Following are the basic steps for adding a new child domain and then using ADMT to move or copy selected user groups and accounts to the new domain:

1. Add the new domain by running Dcpromo.exe on a Windows 2000 member server.

2. Create a set of Global groups containing the members of each user account OU you intend to migrate, if such groups don't exist.

3. Create a corresponding set of OUs in the new domain to hold the user accounts.

4. Use ADMT to migrate (copy) Global groups to which users belong, but don't determine user membership in OUs. This step is required for users to maintain their group memberships during migration.

5. Migrate the Global groups created in step 2 and their user accounts to the OUs you added in step 3.

6. Migrate computer accounts.

NOTE: You can use the Movetree.exe command-line program, a member of the Windows 2000 Support Tools, to move objects between domains in a forest, but using ADMT is much easier.

Adding a New Child Domain

The process of creating a child domain is quite similar to that which you used when promoting your first Windows 2000 member server to the initial root domain for your network. To add a child domain, do this:

1. If you have an OU in the parent domain with the same name as the child domain you intend to create, change the OU's name.

NOTE: You receive a misleading "Directory service is busy" error message during the server promotion process if a parent domain OU has the same name as the child domain. A similar error message appears if you attempt to create a new OU in the parent domain with the same name as that of a child domain. The problem is a duplication of Relative Distinguished Names (RDNs), which Knowledge Base article Q240147, "Cannot Create an Organizational Unit in the Parent Domain with the Same Name as a Child Domain in Windows 2000," explains. For this example, you can rename the Students OU in the oakmont.edu domain to Student. Changing the Students OU name prevents adding more student accounts with GroupPol. Alternatively, specify Student as the child domain name in step 7.

2. Verify in the DNS page of the Internet Protocol (TCP/IP) Properties dialog of your network connection that the Preferred DNS Server text box contains the IP address of the parent domain's DNS server.

3. Run Dcpromo.exe to start the Active Directory Installation Wizard and click Next to bypass the Welcome dialog.

4. In the Domain Controller Type dialog, select the Domain Controller for a New Domain option and click Next.

5. In the Create Tree or Child Domain dialog, select the Create a New Child Domain in an Existing Domain Tree option and click Next.

6. In the Network Credentials dialog, type your user name and password for your Domain Admins account in the parent domain and change the Domain entry, if necessary. Click Next.

7. In the Child Domain Installation Dialog, accept or change the Parent Domain value and type the Child Domain name. As you type, the Complete DNS Name of New Domain text box displays the full *childdomain.parentdomain.ext* value: students.oakmont.edu for this example. Click Next.

8. In the NetBIOS Domain Name dialog, accept the default or change the NetBIOS name (STUDENTS) used by downlevel clients; then click Next.

9. In the Database and Log Locations dialog, accept the default folders, unless you have a reason to change them, and click Next.

10. In the Shared System Volume dialog, again accept the default unless you want to put Sysvol on another drive. Click Next.

11. If you don't need to support Windows NT Remote Access Service (RAS) on servers or assignment of Windows 2000 users to Windows NT resource server groups in a mixed-mode domain, select the Permissions Compatible Only with Windows 2000 Servers option. Otherwise, accept the default Permissions Compatible with Pre-Windows 2000 Servers option, which grants the Everyone group permissions for specific folders and other objects that ordinarily restrict access to members of the Authenticated Users group. Click Next.

TIP: Don't select the Permissions Compatible Only with Windows 2000 Servers option until you've upgraded all Windows NT resource servers to Windows 2000. Knowledge Base articles Q257988, "Description of Dcpromo Permissions Choices," and Q257942, "Error Message: Unable to Browse the Selected Domain Because the Following Error Occurred...," describe the consequences of selecting this option. You can't change the option you select in this dialog without demoting the DC and starting over.

12. In the Directory Services Restore Mode Administrator Password dialog, type and confirm the password to use to remove the domain or administer it with the Ntdsutil.exe command-line utility; click Next.

13. In the Summary dialog, review your settings and then click Next to start the AD installation and child domain creation process, which takes more than the advertised "several" minutes on moderate-speed servers.

14. Reboot the new DC for the child domain and log on with Enterprise Admins credentials.

15. Launch Active Directory Domains and Trusts, click to expand the parent domain node, right-click the child domain node, and choose Properties to open the *childdomain.parentdomain.ext* Properties dialog. The target (child) domain must run in native mode, so click Change Mode to make the domain ready for the move with ADMT.

16. Install ADMT on the DC for the child (target) domain. Download instructions are in the "Easing Restructure and Migration with ADMT" section of Appendix C.

17. On the child DC, launch the Domain Security Settings snap-in from Administrative Tools and navigate to and select the Windows Settings\Security Settings\Local Policies\Audit Policy node.

18. Double-click the Audit account management policy to open the Security Policy Settings dialog. Mark the Define These Policy Settings, Success, and Failure check boxes and click OK to apply the policy.

19. Repeat steps 17 and 18 on the parent domain DC. Account management auditing is required for ADMT operations on user accounts in both domains.

Adding a child domain automatically adds a Dynamic DNS (Active Directory-integrated, DDNS) primary forward lookup zone for the child domain to the parent domain's DNS server. When users move to the child domain, DHCP doesn't need to assign their Primary DNS Server to the child domain server's IP address.

Preparing the Domains for the Intraforest Move

Before you begin the migration process, in the parent domain add a Security Group containing all members of each OU you want to move, if such groups aren't present. Then add OUs in the child domain to contain the migrated Global groups and their users. For this example, the five sub-OUs of the Students OU (Freshmen, Sophomores, Juniors, Seniors, and Computers) don't have associated security groups, but you need only the four academic-year groups to define OU membership. ADMT requires Security Groups to place user accounts in designated OUs. You use the temporary groups discussed in the later section "Moving Groups and Their Users to Designated OUs" to regenerate OU membership by adding the user accounts based on group membership. After you complete group and user migration, you move all computers from the Students, Computers OU to the default Computers container of the child domain.

To add selected users to a temporary Security Group in the parent domain, do this:

1. Right-click the *domainname* node or any OU that doesn't have objects that duplicate the group names you create and then choose New, Group to open the New Object - Group dialog.

2. Type the name of the group in the text box, accept the default Global and Security options, and click OK to add the new group.

3. Select the OU to display its members and then multiselect all user objects only; don't include OU's or groups.

4. Right-click the selection, choose Add Members to a Group to open the Select Group dialog, type or scroll to and select the temporary group name, and click OK to perform the addition.

TIP: If the OU doesn't include objects other than users, right-click the OU node in the tree-view pane and choose Add Members to a Group. After you specify the group name, a message box opens to request confirmation that you want to add all users. Click Yes to All and wait for "The Add to Group operation was successfully completed" message to appear; then click OK. There is no user feedback during the Add to Group process.

5. Repeat steps 1 through 4 for each temporary group you created.

6. Add the OU to hold the other security groups for the user accounts being moved (Major Subject Groups).

To verify temporary group membership, right-click the *GroupName* node, choose Properties to open the *GroupName* Properties dialog, and click the Members tab.

NOTE: If you use student accounts created by GroupPol in these procedures, delete the Students Domain Local group before the migration. This group is applicable only to a single domain.

Adding Target OUs in the Child Domain

After you've added the necessary temporary groups, do the following to create required OUs in the child domain:

1. Log on to any DC or workstation that has ADMT installed with your Enterprise Admins account.

2. Launch Active Directory Users and Computers, right-click the domain name node, select Connect to Domain to open the dialog of the same name, type or browse to the child domain, and click OK.

3. Right-click the domain name node again, choose New | Organizational unit to open the New Object-Organizational Unit dialog, type the name of a first-level OU in the text box, and click OK. Repeat this step for each first-level OU for the first domain.

NOTE: For this example, the second-level OUs of the parent domain's Student(s) OU (Freshmen, Sophomores, Juniors, Seniors) become first-level OUs in the child domain, because only student accounts exist in the child domain. There's no need to have a Student OU in a domain named Students.

4. If you have second-level OUs, add them to the first-level OUs you created in the preceding step.

5. Also add an OU for migrating the first set of groups without user accounts. For this example, a Major Subject Groups OU will hold copies of the 14 Global groups, which contain student accounts by major subject.

Copying the First Set of Groups

When you migrate groups without their user accounts, ADMT copies the groups from the source to the target domain. Copying prevents users being denied access to these groups' resources while the migration is in process. Do the following to copy groups without their user accounts:

1. Launch ADMT, right-click the Active Directory Migration Tool node, and choose Group Migration Wizard. Click Next to bypass the Welcome dialog.

TIP: Appendix C has detailed instructions for using the Group Migration Wizard, including figures showing the wizard boxes. There are differences between the interforest migration from a Windows NT domain to a Windows 2000 domain and an interforest move between Windows 2000 domains, but most of the steps are similar.

2. In the Test or Make Changes dialog, select the Migrate Now? option if you want to perform the move without testing. If you select the Test the Migration Settings and Migrate Later option, you must repeat all migration steps to effect the migration. Click Next.

3. In the Domain Selection dialog, select the NetBIOS names of the source and target (child) domains (OAKMONTU and STUDENTS for this example) and click Next.

4. In the Group Selection dialog, click add to open the Group Selection dialog and double-click each Global group to which the users you're migrating belong, but *not* the groups that correspond to OU memberships. For instance, don't add the temporary security groups you added in the preceding set of steps. You add these groups later along with their users. For this example, you add the 14 *DepartmentName Majors* groups, but not the temporary Freshmen, Sophomores, Juniors, and Seniors groups (see Figure 2-15). Click OK to add the groups to the Group Selection dialog's list and then click Next.

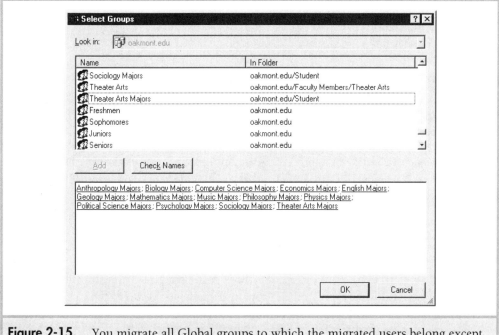

Figure 2-15. You migrate all Global groups to which the migrated users belong except those groups that you use to move user accounts from source OUs to target OUs.

5. In the Organizational Units dialog, click Browse to open the Browse for Container dialog, select the special OU you created for groups or the domain container, and click OK to add the full LDAP path to the group in the Target OU text box. For this example, the path is LDAP://STUDENTS/OU=Major Subject Groups,DC=students, DC=oakmont,DC=edu. Click Next.

6. In the Group Options dialog, accept the defaults and click Next.

7. In the User Account dialog, type your Enterprise or Domain Admins credentials for the child domain, change the downlevel domain name for your account, if necessary, and click Next.

8. In the Naming Conflicts dialog, accept the defaults and click Next.

9. In the Completing the Group Account Wizard dialog, click Finish to open the Migration Progress dialog and begin the group migration process.

10. When the Status value in the Migration Progress dialog changes to Completed, click View Log to open the Migration log for the groups (see Figure 2-16).

11. Close the Migration log and click Close in the Migration Progress dialog to return to ADMT's snap-in.

Moving Groups and Their Users to Designated OUs

The process of migrating groups with users to the child domain OUs you created previously is quite similar to that for copying groups without users. To migrate groups and users by copying accounts, do this:

1. Repeat steps 2 and 3 of the preceding section. In step 3, the Wizard adds the fully qualified DNS names of the source and destination domains you originally specified with NetBIOS names.

2. In the Group Selection dialog, click Add and type or select the group to move in the Select Group dialog (the temporary Freshmen group for this example). Click OK to return to the Wizard; then click Next.

3. In the Organizational Unit dialog, click Browse to open the Browse for Container dialog, select the OU in the source (parent) domain that contains the users you want to migrate, and click OK to add the full LDAP path of the OU to the Target OU text box (LDAP://STUDENTS/OU=Freshmen,DC=students,DC=oakmont,DC=edu for this example). Click OK.

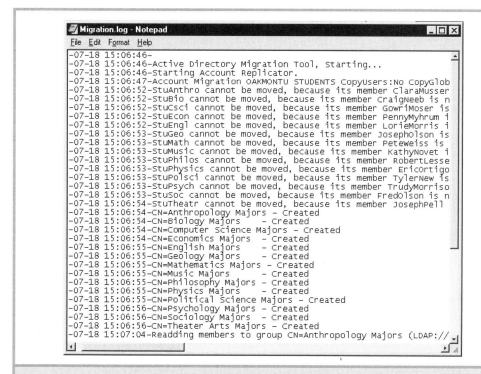

```
Migration.log - Notepad                                          _□×
File  Edit  Format  Help
-07-18 15:06:46-
-07-18 15:06:46-Active Directory Migration Tool, starting...
-07-18 15:06:46-Starting Account Replicator.
-07-18 15:06:47-Account Migration OAKMONTU STUDENTS CopyUsers:No CopyGlob
-07-18 15:06:52-StuAnthro cannot be moved, because its member ClaraMusser
-07-18 15:06:52-StuBio cannot be moved, because its member CraigNeeb is n
-07-18 15:06:52-StuCsci cannot be moved, because its member GowriMoser is
-07-18 15:06:52-StuEcon cannot be moved, because its member PennyMyhrum i
-07-18 15:06:52-StuEngl cannot be moved, because its member LorieMorris i
-07-18 15:06:53-StuGeo cannot be moved, because its member JosephOlson is
-07-18 15:06:53-StuMath cannot be moved, because its member PeteWeiss is
-07-18 15:06:53-StuMusic cannot be moved, because its member KathyNovet i
-07-18 15:06:53-StuPhilos cannot be moved, because its member RobertLesse
-07-18 15:06:53-StuPhysics cannot be moved, because its member EricCortigo
-07-18 15:06:53-StuPolsci cannot be moved, because its member TylerNew is
-07-18 15:06:53-StuPsych cannot be moved, because its member TrudyMorriso
-07-18 15:06:53-StuSoc cannot be moved, because its member FredOlson is n
-07-18 15:06:54-StuTheatr cannot be moved, because its member JosephPell
-07-18 15:06:54-CN=Anthropology Majors - Created
-07-18 15:06:54-CN=Biology Majors     - Created
-07-18 15:06:54-CN=Computer Science Majors - Created
-07-18 15:06:54-CN=Economics Majors   - Created
-07-18 15:06:55-CN=English Majors      - Created
-07-18 15:06:55-CN=Geology Majors      - Created
-07-18 15:06:55-CN=Mathematics Majors - Created
-07-18 15:06:55-CN=Music Majors        - Created
-07-18 15:06:55-CN=Philosophy Majors   - Created
-07-18 15:06:55-CN=Physics Majors      - Created
-07-18 15:06:55-CN=Political Science Majors - Created
-07-18 15:06:56-CN=Psychology Majors   - Created
-07-18 15:06:56-CN=Sociology Majors    - Created
-07-18 15:06:56-CN=Theater Arts Majors - Created
-07-18 15:07:04-Readding members to group CN=Anthropology Majors (LDAP://
```

Figure 2-16.   The Migration log for the first set of groups detects that user accounts haven't been migrated and copies (instead of moves) the groups. StuAnthro, StuBio, and other Stu... entries are the downlevel names of the groups assigned by GroupPol.

4. In the Group Options dialog, mark the Update User Rights and Copy Group Members check boxes and accept the default Do Not Rename Accounts option. Click Next. A message warns you that if Global groups weren't migrated previously, users lose their membership in the unmigrated groups. Click OK.

5. Repeat steps 7 through 11 of the preceding section.

6. Launch Active Directory Users and Computers on the child domain DC and verify migration of the groups and user accounts (see Figure 2-17). Also check the Members page of the Properties dialog for each Security Group you migrated to verify that the group contains the appropriate user accounts.

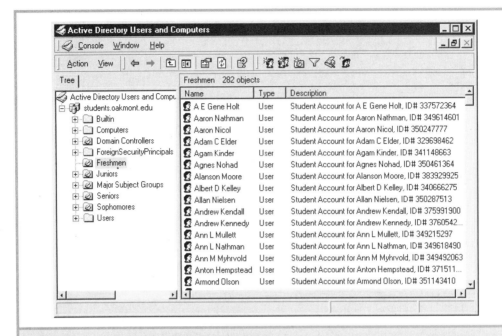

Figure 2-17. Active Directory Users and Computers running in the child domain verifies that user accounts you move based on their group membership migrate to the designated OU.

TIP: If the child domain's Active Directory Users and Computers snap-in was open during the migration process, choose View | Refresh to update its contents. If you don't see migrated objects, close and reopen the snap-in.

Migrating Computer Accounts

ADMT's Computer Migration Wizard lets you move Windows 2000 and NT computer accounts between domains. During the migration process, ADMT dispatches "agents" to automatically change the domain affiliation of the computer accounts and reboot the computer after a specified interval. One potential hitch in the process when migrating non-owned computer accounts is that the account you use to generate the computer migration agents must be a member of the local Administrators group of the client machines. The Domain Admins group of the source domain is a member of the local Administrators group of Windows 2000 clients, but using an Enterprise Admins account is the safer option. The "Migrating Computer Accounts" section of Appendix C shows you how to move computer accounts to a new domain.

Chapter 3

Designing Security Group Structures for Group Policy Filtering

After you've settled on your initial Windows 2000 domain topology, the next step is to plan a Security Group structure to control user access to local PC and networked resources and to govern the application of specific Group Policy objects to various categories of users and computers. The "simpler is better" rule of domain design also applies to your Windows 2000 Security Group structure. One of the primary objectives of Security Group design is to minimize the number of groups required to filter GPOs and control user access to resources. Filtering GPOs lets you selectively apply a GPO to members of a specific set of groups or exempt particular groups from application of a GPO.

NOTE: This book's conventions capitalize "Security Group," "Domain Local," "Global," and "Universal" when referring to Windows 2000 groups and use lowercase for Windows NT "security groups," and "local" and "global" groups. Similarly, Windows 2000 "Group Policy" is capitalized, and Windows NT and 9x "system policy" isn't. The objective of these conventions is to avoid confusing the names of Windows 2000 and NT objects.

Securing Windows 2000 Networks

A full description of the security features of Windows 2000 is beyond the scope of this book, but the following sections provide a brief description of the most common terms used when discussing Security Groups.

Security Principals

Security principals (SPs) are objects to which Windows 2000 assigns a unique security identifier (SID). Only users, groups, and computers have SIDs. If you delete a security principal and then re-create the account with the same name, the account receives a new SID. You must reestablish all group memberships when re-creating a security principal because of the SID change.

SIDHistory is an attribute found only in Windows 2000 native-mode domains; the "Domain Restructure or Consolidation" section of Chapter 2 discusses SIDHistory in the context of cloning Windows NT SPs in a Windows 2000 domain.

Well-known Security Principals

Well-known security principals have SIDs that are assigned by the system during Windows 2000 installation. You were introduced to well-known SPs in the "Registry Entries for Policies" section of Chapter 1.

Windows 2000 generates an S-1-1-0 SID for the generic Everyone group; other systemwide SIDs are S-1-5 for the NT Authority, and S-1-5-18 for the Local System service account. Builtin groups, which are discussed later in the "Comparing Windows NT and 2000 Security Groups" section, also have systemwide SIDs that start with S-1-5-32-544 (Administrators group) and end with S-1-5-32-552 (Replicators group for Windows NT domains only).

Appendix E of the *Windows 2000 Server Resource Kit's Distributed Systems Guide* lists all well-known SPs. You can't delete accounts for well-known SPs.

Security Principal Names

Security principal names (SPNs) are names assigned to SPs that are unique within a domain, but need not be unique from SPNs in other domains. The SPN for a user commonly is called the logon ID or username. SPNs and downlevel NetBIOS names are equivalent.

User Principal Names

User principal names (UPNs) consist of the user's SPN, followed by an ampersand and a UPN suffix in e-mail address format (*SPN@somewhere.ext*). By default, the UPN suffix is the user's fully qualified domain name (FQDN), but admins can assign alternate suffixes.

Each UPN must be unique within the entire Windows 2000 network. A UPN with the default suffix is considered (but not implemented as) the standard for Windows 2000 users and is equivalent to a full downlevel logon ID in *DOMAIN\username* format. The primary difference between a user logon with a UPN or an SPN is that the UPN must be resolved by a Global Catalog server. By default, the Windows 2000 logon dialog uses the SPN and the downlevel domain name, which can be resolved by any DC in the user's domain.

Access Control Lists

Access control lists (ACLs) are elements of an object's security descriptor. Discretionary ACLs (DACLs) contain access control entries (ACEs) with the SID of each SP having some form of access to the object, and the SP's permission for manipulating the object.

System ACLs (SACLs) contain ACEs for auditing security events triggered by designated users or groups.

TAKE COMMAND

You can use Cacls.exe at the command line to display a list of the names and permissions of users and groups who have ACEs in the DACL of a file or folder. The syntax for this use of calcls.exe is **cacls** *foldername | filename*. Cacls.exe also lets you add, edit, and remove ACEs.

Security Groups

Security Groups are SPs that can contain ACEs for computers, users, and other groups. Windows 2000 automatically adds Windows NT and 2000 computers to the Domain Computers security group when the computer joins the domain. Disjoining a computer from the domain by demoting it to a workgroup member removes its account in the domain. Rejoining the domain creates a new SID for the computer. When you promote a member server to a DC, the account moves from the Domain Computers to the Domain Controllers group.

Comparing Windows NT and 2000 Security Groups

Windows NT has only two types of groups: local and global. Membership in local groups grants users specific access permissions for a particular computer and its resources, such as shared folders and printers. Thus, local groups commonly are called *permission* or *resource groups*. Global groups contain user accounts only from the global group's domain and so are referred to as domain *user* or *account groups*. Rather than adding specific user accounts to local groups, you nest global groups within local groups to minimize the number of entries in local groups. Windows NT's nontransitive trusts let you add global groups from trusted account domains to local groups of resource domains. You can't nest local groups within global groups.

Windows 2000 has two classes of groups, Security and Distribution, and five types of groups, Local, Builtin Local, Domain Local, Global, and Universal. Distribution groups, which can be Global or Universal (not Local) in scope and don't support permissions, are intended only for creating e-mail lists from user accounts. Distribution groups aren't subject to Group Policy, so they aren't covered in this book. Table 3-1 compares the availability and behavior of Security Groups in mixed-mode and native-mode domains.

In a mixed-mode domain, you can convert a Domain Local group to a Universal group if the Domain Local group isn't a member of another Domain Local group. Similarly, you can convert a Global group to a Universal group if it isn't a member of another Global group. To convert a Global group to a Domain Local group or vice versa, you must first convert the source group to a Universal group.

Security Group Type	Mixed-Mode Domains	Native Mode Domains
Local	Corresponds to the Windows NT local group on workstations and member servers. Not present on DCs.	Same as mixed mode.
Builtin Local	Set of local groups to contain existing user accounts when upgrading from Windows NT Server. Member groups can't be deleted. Present only on DCs.	Same as mixed mode.
Domain Local	Corresponds to Windows NT local group on DCs only. Members can come from any domain in the forest or other explicitly trusted forests. Not present on member servers. Can contain users and Global groups. Can't contain other Domain Local groups.	Same as mixed mode, but available on DCs and member servers. Also can contain Universal and other Domain Local groups (supports nesting of Domain Local groups). Can be upgraded to a Universal group.
Global	Corresponds to Windows NT global group. Membership limited to users in the group's domain and contacts from its own and other domains. Can't contain other Global groups.	Same, but can nest other Global groups to limit the number of users in a group (to improve performance). Can be upgraded to a Universal group.
Universal	Not available. (Universal Distribution Groups can be created.)	Can contain user accounts and Global groups from any domain. Can nest other Universal groups. Used as an intermediary when converting Domain Local groups to Global groups or vice versa.

Table 3-1.   Availability and Characteristics of Windows 2000 Security Group Types in Windows 2000 Mixed- and Native-Mode Domains

Default Groups and Their Membership

Local groups of Windows 2000 workstations and member servers duplicate those of Windows NT: Account Operators, Administrators, Backup Operators, Guests, Power Users, Replicators, and Users. Windows 2000 adds a WINS Users group, which has read-only permissions for the WINS administrative snap-in. The Local Users and Groups node of the Computer Management snap-in has subnodes that list Local groups and users (see Figure 3-1). Properties dialogs for Local groups and users are simplified versions of those for similar objects opened in Active Directory Users and Computers, because the Security Account Manager (SAM) database, not Active Directory, stores Local groups. Windows 2000's SAM database is essentially identical to Windows NT's.

NOTE: All Windows 9x users accounts become members of the Local Administrators group when you upgrade Windows 9x clients to Windows 2000 Professional. You must manually move users you don't want to have full Administrators rights to the appropriate Local group, such as Users or Power Users.

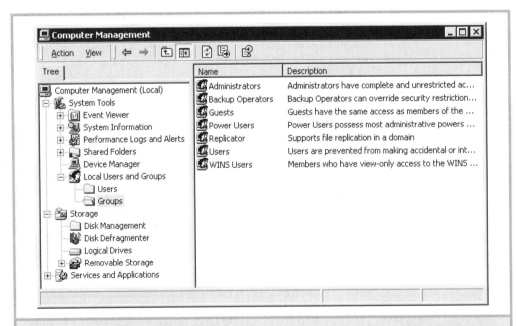

Figure 3-1. Windows 2000 workstations and member servers have nodes for managing Local accounts in the Computer Management snap-in. The Local Users and Groups node is disabled after you promote a member server to a DC.

Builtin Local group membership of DCs is identical to Local group membership with the following exceptions:

✦ The Power Users and WINS Users groups are missing.

✦ A Pre-Windows 2000 Compatible Access group is added.

Promoting a server to a DC moves the Local groups and users to the Builtin Local group and Users container, respectively. If you specify relaxed security during the AD upgrade to accommodate Remote Access Service (RAS) on Windows NT BDCs or member servers, the Everyone group is a member of the Pre-Windows 2000 Compatible Access group. Knowledge Base articles Q257988, "Description of Dcpromo Permissions Choices," and Q257942, "Error Message: Unable to Browse the Selected Domain Because the Following Error Occurred...," mentioned in Chapter 2, describe the consequences of selecting the wrong permissions choice.

CODE BLUE

If you didn't specify relaxed security during the AD upgrade and you need to support Windows NT resource and RAS servers in the domain, you can partially recover by adding the Everyone group to the Pre-Windows 2000 Compatible Access group. You can't perform this feat in Active Directory Users and Computers, because Everyone doesn't appear in the Select Users, Contacts, Computers, or Groups dialog. Instead, run the following instruction at the command prompt:

```
net localgroup "Pre-Windows 2000 Compatible Access" everyone /add
```

After running the preceding command, verify that the Everyone group appears as a member of the target group. Running the preceding command, however, doesn't fully solve authentication problems for downlevel severs and their trusts with Windows 2000 domains. If it's at all feasible, delete and re-create the domain if you need relaxed security.

The Users container holds a collection of default user accounts (Administrator, Guest, and krbtgt, the Kerberos key distribution account), three Domain Local groups (DnsAdmins, RAS and IAS Servers, and WINS Users), and eight Global groups. The initial root domain (the first domain you create on your network) has additional Enterprise Admins and Schema Admins Global groups with the Administrator of the initial root domain's DC as their only default member. AD's database stores all groups in the Users container.

NOTE: Enterprise Admins and Schema Admins become Universal groups when you upgrade the domain from mixed to native mode.

Following are descriptions of default Global groups in the Users container that play a role in Group Policy administration and filtering.

Domain Admins

Domain Admins have unlimited authority (Full Control permissions) for almost all objects within the domain, with the exception of GPOs. This group is a member of the Builtin Local Administrators group, and its authority is the same in Windows NT and 2000. By default, Windows 2000 Domain Admins don't have Delete All Child Objects and Apply Group Policy permissions on any GPOs. Their administrative workstation accounts receive the Computer Configuration settings of the Default Domain Security GPO, because Computer Configuration settings are applied before the user logs on.

CODE BLUE

The Security page of the Default Domain Policy Properties dialog has the Allow Apply Group Policy check box cleared by default for members of the Domain Admins and Enterprise Admins groups. Members of both groups have Default Domain Policy applied, however, because everyone logged on to the domain is a member of the Authenticated Users group, which has the Allow Apply Group Policy check box marked. If you want to exempt members of these two (or any other groups) from the User Configuration policies of the Default Domain Policy, you must mark the Deny Apply Group Policy check box, which overrides the Authenticated Users setting. The "Filtering the Application of Group Policy Objects" section of Chapter 1 mentions limiting the use of Deny permissions. This is one of the few cases in which setting Deny permissions is advisable.

Domain Computers

Domain Computers contains every Windows NT and 2000 computer account in the domain, except Windows 2000 DCs. Otherwise, Domain Computers membership corresponds to the Windows NT Server Manager's list with the View | All toggle selected.

Computer Configuration settings of the Default Domain Policy GPO and other domain-level GPOs apply to all Windows 2000 workstations and member servers in this group.

Domain Controllers

Domain Controllers holds computer accounts for all DCs in the domain, which is similar to the Windows NT Server Manager's list with the View | Servers toggle on (if you disregard Server Manager entries for member servers).

When you promote a member server to a DC, its computer account moves from Domain Computers to the Domain Controllers group and from the Computers container to the Domain Controllers OU. Computer Configuration settings of the Default Domain Policy and Default Domain Controllers Policy GPOs apply to these computers.

DCs deserve special security precautions. Placing DCs and member servers in a secure location, applying Securedc.inf as the default domain policy, and not logging on locally to servers are recommended methods for increasing server security. Renaming the local Administrator account of DCs to a nonobvious combination of letters and numerals also aids security. You can't apply a special security policy with stricter password security to the Domain Controllers OU or computers in any other OU, because you can have only one set of Account Policies for the entire domain.

Domain Users

Domain Users holds all user accounts in the domain, including the default Administrator account. The User Configuration settings of the Default Domain Policy and other policies added at the domain level apply to all members of this group, unless exempted by membership in a Global group. For instance, the Administrator account is exempt from application of Default Domain Policy by its membership in the Domain Admins group, which does not have Apply Group Policy permission.

Enterprise Admins

Enterprise Admins have the same privileges as Domain Admins in all AD domains. Like Domain Admins, Enterprise Admins can add, edit, and delete GPOs. In addition to Domain Admins privileges for GPOs, Enterprise Admins have the Delete All Child Objects permission. Only the Administrator account of the initial root domain is a member of Enterprise Admins by default.

Enterprise Admins gain object permissions on domains and their containers through inheritance. If you have only a single domain, you don't need to be concerned with the Enterprise Admins group.

Don't use Universal groups to filter GPOs. Membership in Universal groups is stored only on Global Catalog (GC) servers and requires a GC query to determine permissions for the GPO. GPO permissions for Universal groups must be replicated between GCs, which can greatly increase replication traffic. Avoid using the Enterprise Admins group to filter GPOs because in native mode this group is a Universal group.

Group Policy Creator Owners

Group Policy Creator Owners is a Global group with permissions to create new GPOs. The Local Administrator account is the only default member. By default, only Enterprise Admins, Domain Admins, and Group Policy Creator Owners can create new GPOs. To delegate creation of new GPOs to users who aren't administrators, you add them to the Group Policy Creator Owners group. The "Delegating Management of OU Group Policy" section of Chapter 7 describes the delegation process.

Schema Admins

Schema Admins, a Universal group, is the most dangerous of all Windows 2000 Security Groups. Schema Admins have the ability to alter the schema (AD structure) of the entire forest. The Administrator account of the initial root DC is the sole default member. Making changes to AD's schema is beyond the scope of this book.

Upgraded Windows NT Groups

Upgrading a Windows NT PDC to Windows 2000 Server, which promotes it to a DC for the initially mixed-mode domain, preserves all groups, users, and user group memberships in the Windows NT domain.

Trust relationships with other Windows NT domains are preserved as downlevel trusts, as mentioned in the "Domain Restructure or Consolidation" section of Chapter 2. If you use ADMT to create a new Windows 2000 native-mode domain from a Windows NT domain, as described in Appendix C, users, groups, and user group membership are imported intact.

Default, Imported, and Delegated Object Permissions

Like Windows NT, Windows 2000 Server applies a default set of permissions to all local objects created during a clean installation. Upgrading a Windows NT PDC to a Windows

2000 DC preserves all existing Windows NT group and user rights for the domain and permissions for all local objects of the PDC, such as printers and shared folders.

Windows NT's flat domain namespace doesn't have an AD container counterpart, so User Manager's User Rights Policy settings determine group permissions for domainwide operations. Settings you've applied in the User Rights Policy dialog of a PDC or BDC migrate to Group Policy's \Computer Configuration\Windows Settings\Security Settings\Local Policies\User Rights Assignment settings.

Windows 2000 uses a consistent UI for setting group permissions on all objects. The layout of the Security page of the Properties dialog for drives, folders, files, and printers is essentially identical to that for AD containers, groups, users, and computers. Only inheritance options at the bottom of the page change, depending on the type of object and its location within the object hierarchy. Of course, the contents of the Name and Permissions lists change for each object class.

The Security Configuration Manager (SCM) included in Windows NT's SP 4 and later adds some new Windows 2000 security features for drives, folders, and files by a change to the inheritance infrastructure of Windows NT 4.0's NTFS volumes. SCM replaces the Security page of the properties dialog for NTFS file system objects with a version almost identical to that of Windows 2000 and adds an Access Control Settings for *FileSystemObject* dialog. For more information on SCM running under Windows NT, read Knowledge Base article Q195509, "Installing Security Configuration Manager from SP4 Changes Windows NT 4.0 ACL Editor."

The *domainname* container at the top of the AD hierarchy establishes group permissions for the entire domain. The groups and their default permissions for the *domainname* container are as follows:

✦ **Administrators**   Read, Write, Create All Child Objects, Add GUID, Add/Remove Replica in Domain, Change PDC, Manage Replication Topology, Replicating Directory Changes, and Replicating Synchronization

> **NOTE:** Child objects are nested objects, such as a Global group contained in another Global group or an OU under another OU. Technically, AD doesn't have PDCs; Change PDC should be named Change PDC Emulator. The Replication and Replicating permissions apply to the Active Directory Sites and Services tool.

✦ **Authenticated Users**   Read, which applies List Contents, Read All Properties, Read Permissions (advanced permissions)

NOTE: Advanced permissions don't appear in the Security page's Properties list. You must click Advanced to display the Access Control Settings dialog to view advanced permissions, which the next section covers.

+ **Domain Admins**   Same as Administrators

+ **Enterprise Admins**   Full Control—Administrators/Domain Admins permissions, plus Delete All Child Objects

+ **ENTERPRISE DOMAIN CONTROLLERS**   Manage Replication Topology, Replicating Directory Changes, and Replicating Synchronization

+ **Everyone**   List Contents (advanced permission) for domains with Permissions Compatible with Pre-Windows 2000 Servers applied during promotion to a DC; otherwise, Everyone has only Read Properties permission

TIP: You can hide an AD object from members of a group by revoking its List Contents permission for the object.

+ **Pre-Windows 2000 Compatible Access**   List Contents (advanced permission), List Contents, Read All Properties, and Read Permissions for User Objects and Group Objects (special), and Read Permissions for This Object Only (special).

+ **SYSTEM**   Full Control

Windows 2000 defines membership in the Authenticated Users, ENTERPRISE DOMAIN CONTROLLERS, and Everyone groups. For example, the NT AUTHORITY adds each logged-on user account to the Authenticated Users group and removes the user account on logoff. The SYSTEM account is unrelated to the System container. There also are three "special" groups with predefined members: Interactive (the user logged on to the computer), Network (all users accessing the computer via the network), and Terminal Server User (users logged on to Terminal Services in application, not administrative, mode).

To explore permissions for container objects, right-click the *domainname* node in Active Directory Users and Computers, choose Properties, and click the Security tab. All groups having permissions for the domain appear in the Name list in alphabetical order (see Figure 3-2). Items following Full Control in the Permissions list are sorted in approximate order of frequency of use. For instance, granting Read permission is more common than granting Write permission.

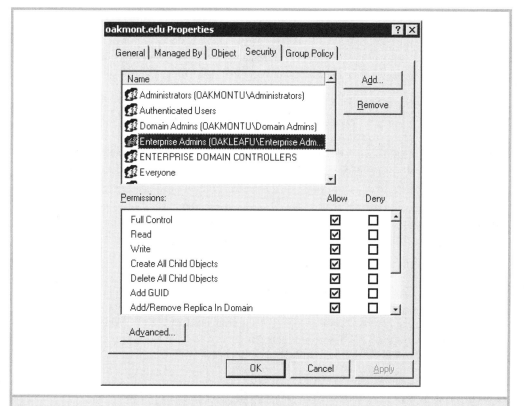

Figure 3-2.   Enterprise Admins have default Full Control Permissions for objects at the domain level. Some permissions, such as Change PDC, apply to methods (behavior) of the object.

CODE BLUE

If you don't see the Object and Security tabs, you forgot to choose View | Advanced Features to turn on the Advanced Features toggle.

NOTE: At lower levels of the AD container hierarchy, the Security page has an Allow Inheritable Permissions from Parent to Propagate to This Object check box. The domain is the top of the AD hierarchy, so it has no parent container.

The "Delegating Management of OUs" section of Chapter 2 introduced you to the procedures for setting permissions for OUs whose administration you delegate to users who aren't members of the Domain Admins or the local Administrators group of a DC.

You can use this Wizard to delegate control of any Active Directory container except Builtin and LostAndFound. For instance, at the domain level you can delegate to the Everyone group the Join a Computer to the Domain privilege, if you're so inclined. The Wizard's Tasks to Delegate list changes or doesn't appear, depending on the container from which you start the Wizard. There are no common tasks specified for delegation of the Computers and Users containers. When no common tasks are present, the Wizard takes you directly to the Active Directory Object Type dialog.

NOTE: The Join a Computer to the Domain privilege is the same as the Add Workstations to Domain policy under the Group Policy Editor's\Computer Configuration\Windows Settings\ Security Settings\Local Policies\User Rights Assignment node. This privilege also is the same as Windows NT's Add Workstations to Domain user right.

Inherited and Advanced Group Permissions

Object-oriented programming (OOP) is a technology for creating modular software components (object classes) having a defined set of characteristics (properties) and behavior (methods). Property inheritance is one of the most important features of objects; by default, subclasses of objects inherit the parent object's properties.

AD doesn't fully comply with commonly accepted OOP standards, but it does support inheritance. When you apply permissions to an AD object, you can specify the permissions as Applies to This Object and All Child Objects (inheritable) or Applies to This Object Only (not inheritable). Permissions not inherited are called *explicit permissions*; explicit permissions override inherited permissions. Inherited, explicit, and advanced object-specific group permissions provide Windows 2000 administrators with much finer-grained object permission sets than Windows NT offers.

To determine whether a group's security property is inheritable, click the Advanced button of the Security page for the object to display the Access Control Settings dialog. Each group has one or more Permissions Entries for Allow permissions on the object. The Apply To column specifies whether the permission entry is inheritable or not (see Figure 3-3). For the *domainname* node, one entry for the Administrator group and the only entry for the Enterprise Admins group have inheritable permissions; most other entries don't.

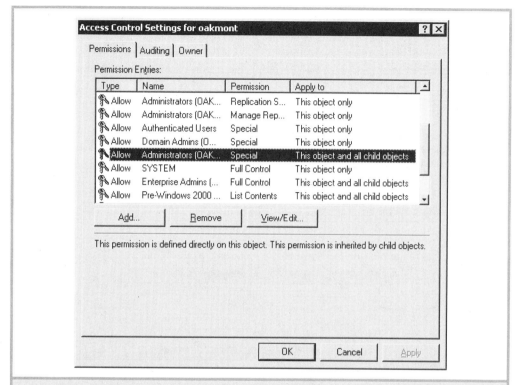

Figure 3-3. The Access Control Settings dialog contains a list of all permission entries applicable to an object. Special in the Permissions column indicates entries having multiple permissions.

The Auditing page of the Access Control Settings dialog lets you specify individual SACLs for auditing purposes. A simpler approach is to specify AD-related events to audit in the Group Policy Editor's\Computer Configuration\Windows Settings\Security Settings\ Local Policies\Audit Policy node.

NOTE: This chapter discusses permissions for groups but not users. You can set permissions for individual users, but doing this isn't common. Best practices dictate that you grant object permissions only to groups, even if the group has only a single member.

To view advanced permissions, double-click the entry in the Access Control Settings dialog to open the Permission Entry for *ObjectName* dialog, which displays the list of advanced permissions on the Object page. The selection This Object and All Child Objects on the Apply Onto list specifies inheritable permissions. Depending on the number of directory-enabled applications you've installed, such as Exchange 2000 and SQL Server 2000, the domain-level list might contain more than 100 entries. Enterprise Admins have the Allow right for every permission in the list; Administrators have the Allow right for most permissions (see Figure 3-4).

NOTE: The Permissions Entry for *ObjectName* dialog's Properties page controls Read and Write permissions for individual object properties. In the ordinary course of Security Group management, you don't need to modify these settings.

You can permit or prevent permission inheritance to child objects, such as users in an OU, by selecting This Object and All Child Objects or This Object Only from the Apply

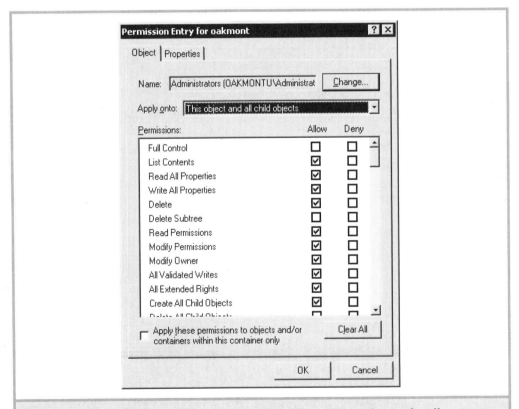

Figure 3-4. The Administrators group has inheritable Allow rights set for all permissions except those for deleting objects. Only Enterprise Admins have default inheritable Delete *ObjectName* rights.

Onto list. You can prevent inherited permissions from applying to a child object by clearing the Allow Inheritable Permissions from Parent to Propagate to This Object check box on the Security page of the child object. When you clear this check box, a message box offers you the options of replacing inherited with explicit permissions (Copy) or deleting the inherited permissions (Remove). Microsoft calls objects that prohibit permission inheritance *protected child objects*.

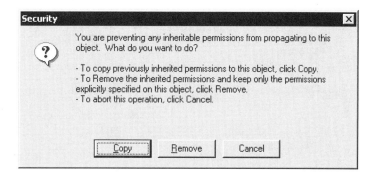

Preventing permission inheritance by clearing the Allow Inheritable Permissions from Parent to Propagate to This Object check box has an effect similar to marking the Block Policy Inheritance check box on the Group Policy page. You can override inherited permissions with explicit permissions; unlike Group Policies, object permissions don't have a No Override option. Neither action is recommended as an ordinary practice, because keeping track of the effective permissions for deeply nested objects with combinations of inherited and overriding explicit permissions is very difficult.

CODE BLUE

Don't change any permission entries for the Administrators or Domain Admins group unless you have a very good reason and fully understand the consequences of the action. Making the wrong change to the Domain Local Administrators group can permanently prevent AD administration on a DC.

Inherited permissions appear as disabled (gray) check boxes for objects lower in the AD hierarchy (see Figure 3-5). Enterprise Admins' Full Control permissions are explicit at every domain level and are inherited by all objects in every domain. Domain Admins gain explicit Read, Write, Create All Child Objects, and other permissions on their domain objects by default, because inheritable permissions aren't specified for this group.

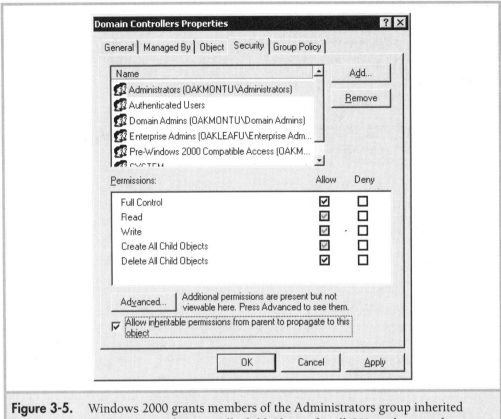

Figure 3-5. Windows 2000 grants members of the Administrators group inherited Read, Write, and Create All Child Objects for all OUs and most other containers within a domain. Marking the Allow Full Control check box adds explicit Delete All Child Objects permission.

Integrating Account and Permission Security Groups

It's a common practice to establish one or more account security groups to contain all user accounts within the enterprise. The recommended maximum size of Windows NT's SAM database is 80 MB, which translates to 60,000 or fewer user accounts per domain. Computer accounts also require SAM database records, so larger organizations use resource domains to hold Windows NT computer accounts and let the account domains hold a larger number of user accounts.

NOTE: Knowledge Base article Q130914, "Number of Users and Groups Affects SAM Size of Domain," recommends 40 MB as the maximum size of a SAM database, which corresponds to about 27,500 users, the approximate total number of user records in GroupPol's database.

Microsoft claims Windows 2000's AD can hold "millions of objects" but recommends constraining Security Group membership to 5,000 or fewer for better replication performance. AD stores the group membership list in a multivalue attribute, so each change to group membership requires replication of the entire list between DCs. Replication issues, especially over WANs, dictate dividing a large enterprisewide Windows 2000 Security Group into subgroups.

Another incentive for creating account subgroups is delegation of administration of group membership and user rights. If you design your OU structure for administrative delegation, such as by division and department or business unit, the account subgroup structure duplicates the OU hierarchy. Maintaining the same OU and group hierarchy simplifies user account management.

Under Windows NT and mixed-mode Windows 2000, you're limited to a two-level hierarchy; moving to native mode permits unlimited nesting of Global and Domain Local groups and lets you take advantage of Universal groups in multiple-domain topologies. Another benefit of the OU-based group structure is the ability to filter Group Policy applied at higher levels of the OU hierarchy by lower-level groups.

Mirroring OU and Security Group structures lets you assign read permissions for specific shared folders and their files by the same account groups you use to filter Group Policy. However, only users at a particular authority level in the division, department, or business unit should have Modify, Write, or Full Control permissions for such shares and their files. Thus, you need another set of role-based permission groups that reflect rank or job classification within the OU to assign additional file-system permissions.

You also use job classification, and to a lesser-degree rank, to filter group policies. As discussed in the section "An Example of Single-Domain Topology" in Chapter 2, it's far more efficient to filter Group Policy by Security Group than to add duplicate subordinate OUs, such as Department Managers, Supervisors, and Clerk-Typists, to each department or business unit OU. Filtering by permission groups lets you apply the Run Only Allowed Windows Applications policy to the Clerk-Typists group but not to the Department Managers or Supervisors group.

Applying Computer and User Configuration Policies by OU

The sample Faculty Members divisional OU described in Chapter 2 has a set of sub-OUs that, when generated by the GroupPol application, have 14 Global department-based account groups and 5 Global rank-based permission groups: Deans, Chairpersons, Professors, Lecturers, and Teaching Assistants. The department-level groups are nested in the Domain Local Faculty Members group. Each department has the same job classification levels for its members, so the Faculty Members OU has a homogenous permission structure, and a single set of permission groups applies to all account groups. Figure 3-6 illustrates account and permission groups of the Faculty Members OU. GroupPol doesn't add the Clerk-Typists, Network Admins, Software Developers, and System Admins groups from the Non-Faculty Staff division; the section "Filtering Group Policy Objects and Linking GPOs" later in this chapter discusses these four groups.

NOTE: GroupPol adds a folder and file for each department under the employees' share, which you specify when running GroupPol the first time. You can use these shared folders and files to test the application of file-system security by department and job classification. By default, the Everyone group has full permissions for the share and its objects.

If your top-level OUs are site-based and sub-OUs are department-based, you're also likely to be able to use common permissions groups across all sites. For instance, the Dallas site's Sales group is likely to have the same job classifications as the Sales groups in San Francisco, Atlanta, and New York City. Thus, members of the Sales groups at all sites can be members of a common set of permissions groups, such as Area Directors, Regional Directors, Managers, and Salespersons. Minimizing the number of permission groups simplifies group management operations, including policy filtering.

Using Loopback Policy Processing

Most User Configuration policies override Computer Configuration policies, because Windows 2000 processes computer-based policies during the boot process and user-based policies upon logon. In some cases, such as classroom or kiosk-type computers, you might want to apply Computer Configuration policies regardless of the user who logs on.

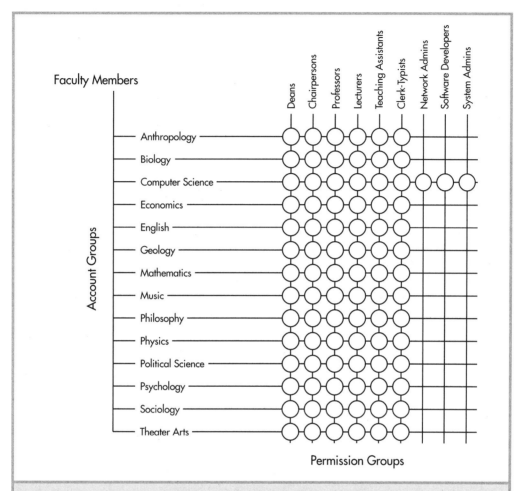

Figure 3-6.   Faculty Members department-based account groups hold user accounts for each academic department. The basic set of five rank-based permission groups applies to members of all account groups.

Enabling the User Group Policy loopback processing mode policy of the Computer Configuration\Administrative Templates\System\Group Policy node lets you choose between the following two modes:

- *Replace mode* disregards the User Configuration settings for the logged-on user and applies only Computer Configuration settings.

- *Merge mode* combines Computer Configuration and User Configuration settings. Computer Configuration settings override any conflicting User Configuration settings.

In the case of the 50 computer accounts GroupPol adds to the Lab Computers OU, you might consider using loopback processing. A better approach, however, is to add a GPO to the Lab Computers OU that applies appropriate policies for student use of the machines. Use a filter to apply the GPO only to the Students group; this permits members of other groups, such as Faculty Members, to use the machines with less restrictive policies applied.

Designing a Test for Group Policy Filtering

One of the principles of successful deployment of any new operating system feature is application of a test regimen similar to that for pharmaceutical products: conduct screening tests on lab animals (servers, clients, and testers in the deployment lab) before you run clinical trials on humans (selected production user groups).

TIP: If you have a major time and effort investment in your test domain configuration, run a System State backup before you make major modifications to your DCs.

Testing group policy filtering in a lab environment requires the following steps:

1. Use ADMT to clone your existing Windows 2000 or NT domain groups and user accounts (but not computer accounts) in the Windows 2000 lab domain. Disconnect the lab computer from the production network after you complete the cloning process. Alternatively, use GroupPol to quickly create a set of AD objects that you can rename or reorganize to mirror your current or anticipated domain design. Add 1,000 Employee Users with GroupPol to obtain a representative number of users in each security group and OU.

2. Apply Default Domain Security policies consistent with the security level you want for your test domain, unless you're using GroupPol. See the "Getting Acquainted with Group Policy Management" section of Chapter 1 for information on applying the appropriate security configuration template.

TIP: If you have more than one DC in your test domain, make policy changes only on the PDC emulator. Policies are replicated between DCs at the same site at five-minute intervals, so the changes you make on one DC don't appear immediately on other DCs.

3. Display detailed status messages during the computer startup and user logon process. These messages add a bit of entertainment during the repeated reboots and logons required to test GPO application. Open the Default Domain Security Policy in the Group Policy Editor (GPE), navigate to the Computer Configuration\Administrative Templates\System node, and enable the Verbose vs. Normal Status Messages policy. You can avoid the annoyance of the Welcome dialog's appearance for each new user account you test by enabling the Don't Display Welcome Screen at Logon policy under the \User Configuration\Administrative Templates\System node.

4. If you move test client computer accounts to OUs or use GroupPol to add computer accounts to OUs, provide a method for easily identifying the level in the domain hierarchy at which computer policy is applied, edit the Default Domain Policy to add a logon message title (type **Group Policy Test** as the value of the Message Title for Users Attempting to Log On policy) and text (type **Default Domain Computer Policy** as the value for the Message Text for Users Attempting to Log On policy). Both policies are located under the Computer Configuration\Windows Settings\Security Settings\Local Policies\Security Options node.

5. Prevent the appearance of the logon message when rebooting the DC. Apply empty (null) values to the two logon message policies in the Default Domain Controllers Policy; define the policy, but don't enter text. Security Options policies don't have an Enable/Disable choice, but the undocumented application of null values prevents the message box from opening when the DC is rebooted.

6. Authorize additional groups you want to be able to add workstations to the domain; the default is Authenticated Users only. (See the section "Issues with the Default Domain Controllers Policy's Add Workstation to Domain User Right" later in this chapter for comments on this subject.) With the Default Domain Controllers Policy in the GPE, click the ...\Local Policies\User Rights Assignment node, and double-click the Add Workstations to Domain entry to open the Security Policy Setting dialog, which displays Authenticated Users in its list box. Click Add to open the Add User or Group dialog and then click Browse to open the Select Users or Groups dialog. Type the names of the groups to add, such as Account Operators and role-based groups of the appropriate authority level. Domain and Enterprise Admins have this user right by default, so you don't need to add them to the list. Click Check Names, which prefixes the group name with the downlevel domain name, and click OK twice to add

the groups to the Security Policy Setting list. The downlevel domain prefix for Domain Local groups doesn't appear in the list.

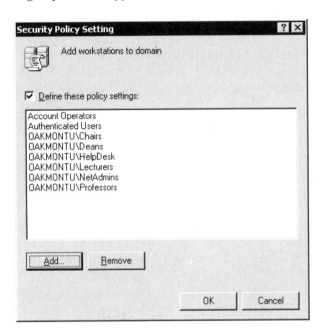

NOTE: Each change you make to policies under the \Computer Configuration\Windows Settings\Security Settings node adds a Security Configuration Editor Client (SceCli) ID 1704 "Security policy in the Group policy objects are applied successfully" (sic) event to the Application log.

7. To obtain a list of all security policy changes you make, enable the Audit Policy Change policy under the Default Domain Controllers Policy's\Computer Configuration\ Windows Settings\Security Settings\Local Policies\Audit Policy node. If you've applied the Securedc.inf security configuration template, this policy is already enforced. Otherwise, mark both Success and Failure check boxes to add entries to the Security log. Event ID 608 entries describe the security policy change; accompanying ID 617 Kerberos Policy Changed entries (with no changes indicated by two hyphens in the last line of the Description) are spurious. The audit policy of the Default Domain Policy doesn't apply to DCs, so you must enable auditing on each top-level OU whose security policy changes you want to track. Audit log events don't appear for nonsecurity-related changes, such as those to policies under Administrative Templates.

8. Add new User Configuration GPOs to at least one or two OUs at each hierarchy level. To add a new GPO to an OU, click New on the Group Policies page of the *OUName* Properties dialog to create a New Group Policy Object. Rename the GPO to indicate its association with the OU and then click Edit to open the Group Policy Editor with the new GPO active.

NOTE: You receive a "Windows cannot open template file" message when adding a new GPO and clicking the Security Settings node. A security template file for the GPO is generated only if you make changes to one or more of the Security Settings policies.

9. For each user-related GPO you add, provide a means of confirming its application. Unfortunately, there are no post-logon message box policies. In the GPE, navigate to the User Configuration\Administrative Templates\Start Menu & Taskbar node and enable one of the policies that removes a Start menu choice (see Figure 3-7). The first five rows of Table 3-2 list the policy changes for GPO identification used for this example. Note that the Network and Dial-up Connections choice is in \Start Menu\ Settings. If you're using GroupPol, it's not necessary to add all 10 GPOs at this point; one or two sub-OUs for Faculty Members and Non-Faculty Staff are sufficient.

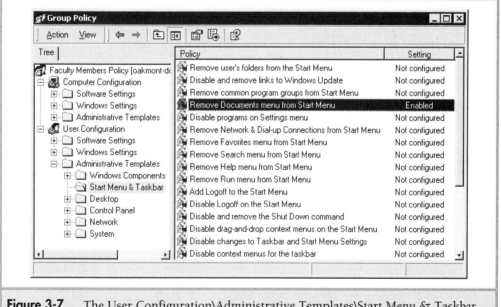

Figure 3-7. The User Configuration\Administrative Templates\Start Menu & Taskbar node has six policies to remove menu choices from the Start menu.

NOTE: Changes you make to GPOs in the GPE take place immediately on the DC that you're using. There's no "Save changes?" message when you exit the GPE.

10. For each user-related GPO, remove the Computer Configuration settings of the policy to improve performance. Close the GPE to return to the Group Policy page of the *OUName* Properties dialog, right-click the GPO's entry in the Group Policy Object Links list to open the General page of the *PolicyName* Properties dialog, mark the Disable Computer Configuration Settings check box (see Figure 3-8), and acknowledge the warning message.

11. If your computer accounts are in OUs, add a new GPO to each computer OU. Change the logon message text ("Faculty Computers Policy" for computer accounts in the Faculty members OU for this example) to identify the computer OU. Mark the Disable User Configuration settings check box in the General page of the *OUName* Properties dialog (refer to step 6).

OUs versus Security Groups for Computer Accounts

Placing your computer accounts within an OU structure makes feasible selective application of Computer Configuration policies by division or even department. You can

OU or Sub-OU	Start Menu & Taskbar Policy Enabled
Faculty Members	Remove Documents menu from Start menu
Anthropology	Remove Favorites menu from Start menu
Computer Science	Remove Search menu from Start menu
English	Remove Help menu from Start menu
Physics	Remove Run menu from Start menu
Non-Faculty Staff	Remove Network and Dial-up Connections from Start menu
Administrative Staff	Remove Favorites menu from Start menu
Financial Staff	Remove Search menu from Start menu
Human Resources	Remove Help menu from Start menu
Information Technology	Remove Run menu from Start menu

Table 3-2. Combinations of Missing Start Menu Choices That Let You Identify the GPO Applied When a User Logs On

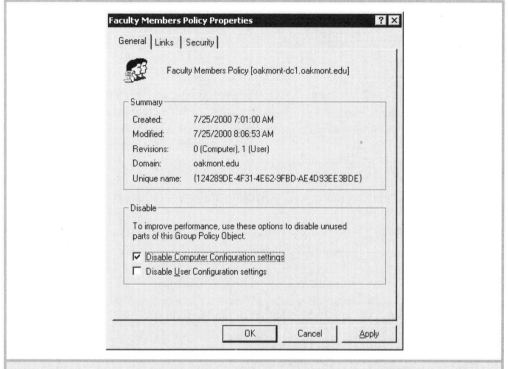

Figure 3-8.   If the GPO doesn't apply Computer Configuration policies, improve Group
Policy performance by marking the Disable Computer Configuration
Settings check box, and vice-versa.

exempt particular sets of users from restrictive division or department policies by filtering
GPOs with role-based permission groups. The alternative, placing computers in security
groups for filtering, isn't practical for large numbers of computers, unless you use scripts
or an application like GroupPol to precreate computer accounts having Security Group
membership. The inability to multiselect filtered or sorted computer accounts in an AD
container for addition to a Security Group is a serious Active Directory Users and
Computers design flaw.

   If you have a few hundred Windows 2000 computers on your network, you can add the
computers to a Security Group a few at a time by clicking the Add button on the Members
page of the *GroupName* Properties dialog to open the Select Users, Contacts, Computers, or
Groups dialog. Manual assignment of computers to security groups is a laborious process,
because the dialog lists almost every AD object, and computer accounts appear in the order

in which they were added to AD. Typing or pasting a comma-separated list of computer names in the text box usually is the best approach. Clicking Check Names runs an LDAP query on your list. The list and query combination is more efficient than the browsing process when your domain has a large number of computer accounts.

Another drawback of using security groups to filter GPOs for computer accounts is the need to manually change group membership when you reassign a computer to another user. The GroupPol application classifies computer accounts in the Faculty Members, Computers OU by membership in the Network Computers and Remote Computers Security Groups. This method of classification is appropriate for filtering GPOs that establish remote access policies. Reassignment of computer accounts between these two groups is infrequent.

Issues with the Default Domain Controllers Policy's Add Workstation to Domain User Right

Giving only members of the Authenticated Users group the Add Workstations to Domain right is an odd choice by Microsoft developers for the following reasons:

◆ Membership in the Authenticated Users group is dynamic; NT AUTHORITY adds a user account to the group for each logged-on user and removes the account when the user logs off. The user of the account specified in the dialog to authorize the joining of the domain must be logged on to the network. If NT AUTHORITY hasn't added the account to Authenticated Users, an "Access denied" message appears when the user attempts to use a precreated or add a new computer account.

NOTE: The ForeignSecurityPrincipals container holds the well-known NT AUTHORITY\ Authenticated Users group (S-1-5-11), which is linked to the Builtin Users group. This group's Properties dialog doesn't have a Members page, so you can't determine its membership in the UI.

◆ The objective of letting Authenticated Users add computer accounts to the domain purportedly is to permit users of new workstations to use a precreated computer account or add to the domain a new account for their out-of-the box Windows 2000 computer. After connecting the PC to the network and powering up, the user must log on with the default client Administrator account to enable the options of the Network Identification page of the System Properties dialog in order to change the computer name and specify the domain. The computer isn't yet joined to the domain, so the only method that the user can employ to become a member of Authenticated Users is to log on to another workstation in the domain. If another workstation isn't close by, the user is out of luck.

✦ Allowing any member of Authenticated Users to add any workstation to the domain isn't a good practice, especially if you precreate computer accounts. If the user mistypes the computer name, the error places an orphaned account in the Computers container instead of the proper OU. These errors are reasonably easy for admins to catch, if the Computers container doesn't hold a large number of accounts. A single disgruntled user having client Administrators permissions and the Add Workstations to Domain right can make up to 10 spurious changes to computer account names for any machine to which he or she has access before the right expires.

✦ You can at least partly overcome the preceding problem by permitting only the computer's user to add the computer. When manually precreating computer accounts for the domain, specify the user of the computer's account as having the authority to add the workstation to the domain. You must write complex scripts to precreate computer accounts with a specific user having Full Control privileges for the computer object. Restricting account addition to a specific user prevents typographical computer name errors, because the user receives an "Access denied" message for an incorrect account. Unless you replace the Authenticated Users group with Domain Users in the Add Workstations to Domain policy's list, the Authenticated Users problem remains. You can improve security by substituting specific role-based groups for Domain Users.

NOTE: Microsoft Knowledge Base article Q222525, "Automating the Creation of Computer Accounts in Windows 2000," provides a sample script for precreating a computer account that specifies a user account having Full Control privileges for the account, and thus the ability to add the account to the domain. Simple modifications to the script let you add the account to an OU you specify and add the computer as a member of a security group, if desired.

✦ Account Operators have the default authority to administer domain groups and user accounts, but not computer accounts. Logic dictates that if Account Operators have Full Control permissions for the Builtin Users container, they also should have Full Control of the default Computers container and have the Add Workstations to Domain right. You must assign the right and permissions explicitly.

Microsoft addresses problems with users joining computers to domains in Knowledge Base articles Q224676, "Enabling Authenticated Users to Join Computers to a Domain with No Administrative Intervention," and Q251335, "Users Cannot Join Workstations or Servers to Domain." Neither of these articles, however, deals with the inability of users to gain Authenticated Users membership without logging on at another workstation.

Performing an Initial Test of the GPOs with Workstations

Now that you have your user and computer GPOs in place and have precreated a few computer accounts, do the following to test them on a client running Windows 2000 Professional:

1. Right-click My Computer, choose Properties to open the System Properties dialog, click the Network Identification tab, and click Properties to open the Identification Changes dialog.

2. If the workstation currently is a member of the domain, disjoin it. Select the Workgroup option, type a temporary workgroup name, acknowledge the "Welcome to the *TEMPNAME* workgroup" and reboot messages, click OK on the Network Identification page, and reboot. Disjoining the workstation, which requires Administrator privileges on the workstation, disables the workstation's computer account in the domain. Repeat step 1.

3. Type the precreated account name in the Computer Name text box, select the Domain option, and type the FQDN of the domain to join in the Domain text box. If you're using GroupPol accounts, see Table 3-3 for some valid accounts for computers in the Faculty Members and Non-Faculty Staff OUs. This example uses the GaryAlmgren user account and the existing FAC389726594 computer account.

 NOTE: You must add a minimum of 1,000 employee user accounts to create all of the user accounts shown in Table 3-3.

4. Click OK to open the Domain User Name and Password dialog. Type the logon ID and password for an account with the right to add users to a domain, as discussed in the previous section. Click OK to close the dialog. After a few seconds, the "Welcome to the *DomainName* domain" message appears. Click OK and acknowledge the reboot message; then click OK to close the System Properties dialog and reboot the computer.

5. After closing the Welcome to Windows dialog, verify that the message box opens with the message indicating that the Computer Configuration policy came from the appropriate OU—Faculty Members for this example. If the message box doesn't appear, check the computer account name you typed in step 3. If the computer account name is correct, review the two message policies you added to the GPO for the computer's OU.

Logon ID	Computer ID	OU	Security Group
GaryAlmgren	FAC389726594	Anthropology	Chairpersons
CliftonHart	FAC407731574	Computer Science	Professors
DavidMckee	FAC418892874	English	Lecturers
JaneLoomis	FAC416405259*	Physics	Teaching Assistants
JillAyers	NFS390726090	Administrative Staff	Budget Analysts
EricBarnum	NFS391342657*	Financial Staff	Accountants
FredBarry	NFS391392887	Human Resources	Clerk-Typists
GaryAcres	NFS389115434*	Admissions Staff	Data Entry Operators
JeffAxe	NFS390700636*	Information Technology	Helpdesk Technicians
KateAverill	NFS390666607*	Information Technology	Network Administrators
LisaAhrens	NFS389333099	Information Technology	Software Developers
UshaAnderson	NFS390006119*	Information Technology	System Administrators

* Indicates that you must manually enable the computer account

Table 3-3. User Accounts That Verify Application of GPOs and Confirm Filtering by Security Group Membership

6. Log on with the precreated account for the computer's user—GaryAlmgren for this example. The password for GroupPol user accounts is "password" with the recommended password settings for GroupPol. If you created the accounts with complex passwords required, the password is empty, and you must specify a complex password. Verify that the menu choices used to identify the user's parent OU and sub-OU are missing from the Start menu (refer to Table 3-2). For GaryAlmgren (Faculty Members, Anthropology), the Documents and Favorites choices don't appear.

7. On a DC for the domain, use the Active Directory Users and Computers' Find dialog to locate the client's computer account. Right-click the account and choose Manage to open the Computer Management console for the user's computer. The ability of Domain Admins to remotely manage users' computers is a powerful feature of Windows 2000 Server, and many network admins new to Windows 2000 aren't aware of this capability. Adding a workstation to a domain automatically adds Domain

Admins to the local Administrators group. Domain Admins can add other Security Groups, such as Helpdesk Technicians, to enable remote workstation management.

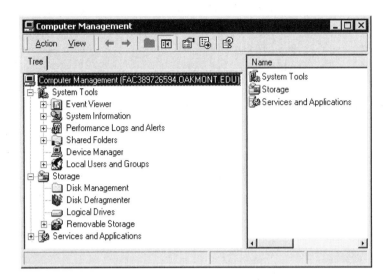

8. If you have only one test workstation available, change its membership to another computer account OU (Non-Faculty Staff, Computers, for example) and repeat steps 3 through 6. To change the domain computer name of a workstation, you must demote the computer to a temporary workgroup and then rejoin the computer with its new name to the domain. Computer accounts have a GUID that's independent of the name. If you attempt to rename a domain workstation to another precreated account without going through the demotion process, you receive an error message stating that the computer can't be renamed because it has an existing account.

CODE BLUE

Demoting a workstation to workgroup membership triggers an MrxSmb error, Event ID 8003 in the System log, relating to an attempt by the workstation to become the domain master browser. You can disregard these events, because they apply to the workgroup.

Setting up a sample OU infrastructure and iteratively testing the application of Computer Configuration and User Configuration policies to precreated accounts is laborious. One benefit of this exercise is gaining confidence that simple OU-based policies behave (almost exactly) as documented and becoming adept at adding and editing new policies. Another benefit is that you have a good starting point for testing GPO filtering by Security Group membership.

Filtering Group Policy Objects and Linking GPOs

Gaining maximum return on investment from upgrading your network servers and client workstations to Windows 2000 requires centralized configuration and management of workstations. Desktop/laptop lockdown and other restrictions, such as Run only Allowed Windows Applications, are suited to clerical workers and data-entry operators, but not for help desk folks and software developers. All employees might be assigned automatic installation of and upgrades to Microsoft Office 2000+, but users in some roles need only the basic Office members (Word, Excel, and Outlook), and others require assigned (mandatory) or published (optional) special-purpose applications. If you design your permission-based Security Groups correctly, as described in the earlier section, "Integrating Account and Permission Security Groups," you can use the same groups to filter GPOs by role.

Designing GPO Filters Based on Software Requirements

Figure 3-9 illustrates a sample set of role-based permission groups for members of Oakmont U's Non-Faculty Staff OU. Unlike the Faculty Members OU shown in Figure 3-6, the Non-Faculty Staff sub-OUs more closely resemble those of a conventional business organization and don't share an identical set of groups. The first task in assigning GPOs by role is to classify groups by their common denominators, one of which for many organizations is the type of Microsoft Office installation. Table 3-4 lists Office installation types, assigned special software, and the degree to which the users' desktops are locked down. Office installation is assigned (A) or published (P), depending on the user's role. To minimize the number of GPOs required to accomplish the organization's desktop/laptop management goals, start with a worksheet similar to Table 3-4 and add columns as necessary to accommodate policy. As you refine the worksheet, policies that apply to multiple groups become evident.

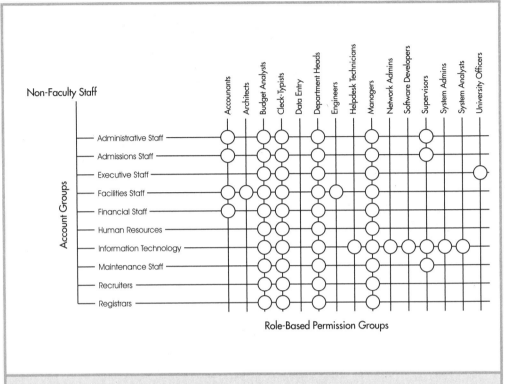

Figure 3-9. The Non-Faculty Staff OUs require more role-based permission groups than do Faculty Members.

The Office Installation column of Table 3-4 has four installation types: Standard, Standard less PowerPoint, Professional less Publisher and Small Business Tools, and Premium less Small Business Tools. Thus, you must add four GPOs to the Non-Faculty Staff OU to accommodate different Installer packages or transforms. You also can use the Office installation GPOs for the Faculty Members OU by linking the GPO to the Faculty Members OU. Deans and Department Chairs need Premium's FrontPage to manage their department Web sites. Professors get Professional, Lecturers receive Standard, and Teaching Assistants receive Standard less PowerPoint. Assigning and publishing special software and restricting users from reconfiguration of their computers (lockdown) requires additional filtered GPOs. The next chapter shows you how to generate and publish or assign software packages.

Security Group	Office Installation	Special Software	Lockdown
Accountants	Standard less PowerPoint (A)	Accounting	Moderate
Architects	Standard (A)	CAD	Limited
Budget Analysts	Professional less Publisher and Small Business Tools (A)	Custom Excel worksheets for each sub-OU	Moderate
Clerk-Typists	Standard less PowerPoint (A)	Time card entry	Total
Data Entry	None	Database front-ends by OU, time card entry	Total
Department Heads	Standard (A)	HR Level 2	Limited
Engineers	Professional less Publisher and Small Business Tools (A)	CAD	Limited
Helpdesk Technicians	Standard less PowerPoint (P)	Helpdesk workflow	Limited
Managers	Standard (A)	HR Level 1	Moderate
Network Admins	Standard less PowerPoint (P)	Adminpak.msi	Minimal
Software Developers	Premium less Small Business Tools (P)	Visual Studio 6.0 Enterprise	None
Supervisors	Standard less PowerPoint (A)	HR Level 0, time card summary	Total
System Admins (Domain Admins)	Standard (A)	Adminpak.msi, Resource Kit	None
Systems Analysts	Professional less Small Business Tools (P)	Mainframe apps	None
University Officers	Premium less Small Business Tools (P)	HR Level 3	None

Table 3-4   Microsoft Office Installation (A=assigned, P=published), Special-Purpose Published Software, and Degree of Desktop Lockdown for Members of the Non-Faculty Staff OU

TIP: If you intend to add Windows Installer packages (.msi files) for Office or other applications to \User Configuration\Software Settings\Software Installation, be sure to enable the Always Install with Elevated Privileges policy and mark the check box to enforce the setting. You must enable the policy in the \Administrative Templates\Windows Components\Windows Installer node of *both* Computer Configuration and User Configuration.

Adding the Software Installation GPOs and Setting the Filters

The procedure for adding GPOs to be filtered by Security Group membership is identical to that for OU-based GPOs, with the exception of specifying the groups to which the policy applies. For initial tests of GPO filtering, you don't want to be interrupted by a long hiatus while Office installs, but you need a method of identifying the policy in effect, similar to the disappearing menus of the earlier examples. The only policy that lets you directly enter text to identify the GPO in force is \User Configuration\Windows Settings\Internet Explorer Maintenance\Browser User Interface\Browser Title. The text you enter appears after "Microsoft Internet Explorer provided by." Figure 3-10 shows the four Office installation GPOs added to the Non-Faculty Staff GPO of the Non-Faculty Staff OU. Each of these GPOs has the Disable Computer Configuration Settings check box marked.

Apply Filters to the New GPOs

To filter each GPO by Security Group, do this:

1. Right-click the GPO link in the list, choose Properties, and click the Security tab.

2. With Authenticated Users selected in the Name list, clear the Apply Group Policy check box to prevent application of the policy to everyone who logs on.

3. Click Add to open the Select Users, Computers, or Groups dialog and type a semicolon-separated list of the groups to which the GPO applies: **Architects;Department Heads;Managers;System Admins** for the Office Standard installation in this example. Click Check Names to verify your typing; then click OK to add the groups to the Names list.

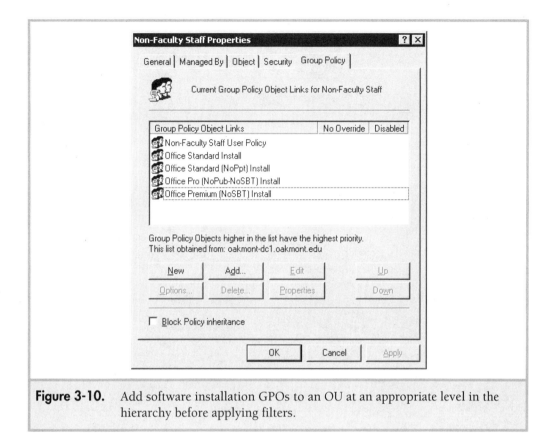

Figure 3-10. Add software installation GPOs to an OU at an appropriate level in the hierarchy before applying filters.

4. Select each of the groups you added in sequence and mark the Allow Apply Group Policy check box. Allow Read is marked by default (see Figure 3-11).

5. Repeat steps 1 through 4 for each GPO you added.

Test the Filters After You Apply Them

Test your filtered GPO application as you did for GPO-based groups in the earlier section, "Performing an Initial Test of the GPOs with Workstations." If you're using the GroupPol

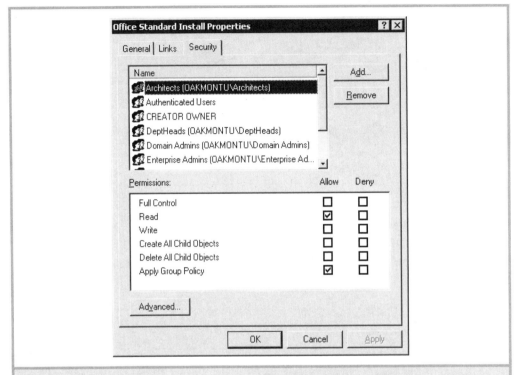

Figure 3-11.   To apply the GPO to members of the selected Security Group, mark the Allow Read and Allow Apply Group Policy check boxes.

application, log on at a client with one of the precreated Non-Faculty Staff user accounts that's a member of the group you want to test (refer to Table 3-3). Otherwise, you must add a user account to each of your filter groups. When you log on as a user in the filter group and have verbose status messages enabled, an "Applying Internet Explorer Branding Policy" message flashes briefly. Figure 3-12 shows IE 5.0's window for the JillAhrens account, a member of the Software Developers group.

TIP: An alternative is to specify for each GPO an individual user login script with a text message followed by a Pause command to identify the GPO applied when the user logs on. Temporarily branding IE is the easier method of identifying whether a particular policy is applied when you're troubleshooting Group Policy problems.

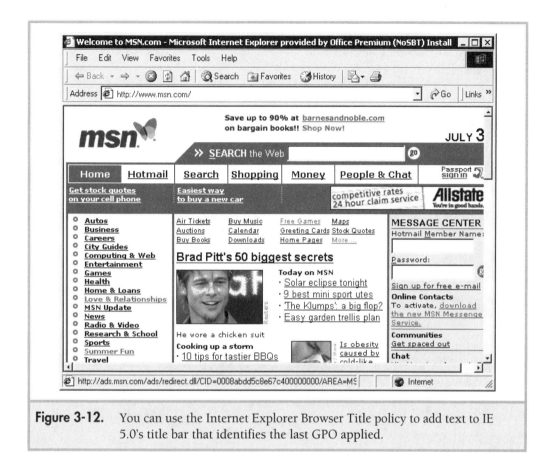

Figure 3-12.   You can use the Internet Explorer Browser Title policy to add text to IE
5.0's title bar that identifies the last GPO applied.

Link Policies to Other OUs

You can apply a GPO to multiple OUs by linking; using GPO links streamlines Group Policy
management by minimizing the number of policies in force. In the case of Oakmont U,
faculty members also receive automated Office installations, as mentioned in the earlier
section, "Designing GPO Filters Based on Software Requirements." To link a GPO from one
OU to another, do this:

1. On the Group Policy page of the *OUName* Properties dialog, click Add to open the
   Add a Group Policy Object Link dialog and then click the All tab to display a list of
   all GPOs in the domain.

TIP: If you have more than one domain, you can add cross-domain links by selecting the other domain in the drop-down list, but cross-domain links can cause a significant performance hit when users log on. Even multiple links to GPOs in the same domain can cause a slight decrease in performance.

2. Select the GPO you want to link to *OUName* (see Figure 3-13) and click OK to add the link to the Group Policy Object Links list. You can't multiselect GPOs in the Add a Group Policy Object Link dialog.

3. Click Properties to open the General Page of the *LinkedGPO* Properties dialog, verify the Disable settings, and click the Security tab.

4. Add the group(s) to which the policy applies to the Name list, marking the Allow Apply Group Policy check box for each group.

5. Repeat steps 2 through 4 for each GPO you want to link; then click OK to close the *OUName* Properties dialog to apply the links you established.

6. Test the links as described in the preceding section.

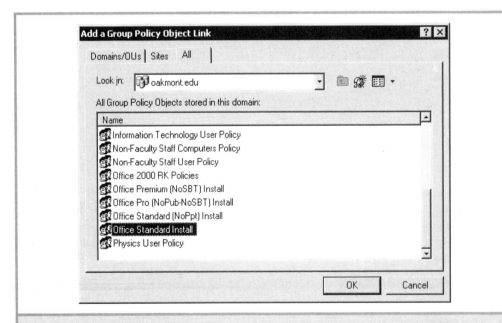

Figure 3-13. Add links to GPOs in other OUs with the Add a Group Policy Object Link dialog.

Organizations with complex OU and group hierarchies often have a very large number of linked GPOs. The Links page of the Properties dialog for a GPO provides a list of all sites, domains, and OUs that link the GPO (see Figure 3-14). Clicking the Find Now button populates the list from the Domain list selection.

Take Advantage of the Office 2000 Resource Kit

The Office 2000 Resource Kit (O2RK) includes a common set of Administrative Templates for customizing Office installation for Window 9*x*, NT, and 2000. If you're considering using Group Policy (or system policy) to install and update customized versions of Office 2000, the O2RK tools make the process much simpler than rolling your own packages.

O2RK is included with Microsoft's Universal MSDN subscription, or you can download its Core Tool Set, which includes an updated version of Poledit.exe for Windows NT and 9*x*, from http://www.microsoft.com/office/ork/2000/appndx/toolbox.htm. Installing O2RK adds

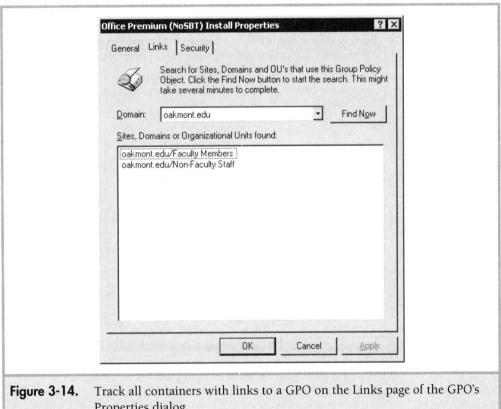

Figure 3-14.   Track all containers with links to a GPO on the Links page of the GPO's Properties dialog.

Access9.adm, Clipgal5.adm, Excel9.adm, Frontpg4.adm, Instlr1.adm, Office9.adm, Outlk9.adm, Ppoint9.adm, Pub9.adm, and Word9.adm for Office itself, the components of Office Premium, and Windows Installer. The size (1 kB to 61 kB) of these templates is quite small compared to System.adm's 717 kB, so adding these templates doesn't greatly affect replication traffic or substantially increase the size of Registry.pol files. However, the impact of most policies (except those for Outlook 2000) on users is minimal; the policies are very low level (see Figure 3-15). The O2RK templates don't have text on the Explain page, because Microsoft designed the .adm files to be compatible with Group Policy and Windows NT and 9x security policies. Poledit.exe doesn't accommodate explanatory text.

For this example, a GPO named Office 2000 RK Policies (refer to Figure 3-13) in the Non-Faculty Staff OU includes all O2RK .adm templates under the User Configuration node. Templates aren't added to the Computer Configuration node, because configuration depends on the logged-on user, and Computer Configuration is disabled.

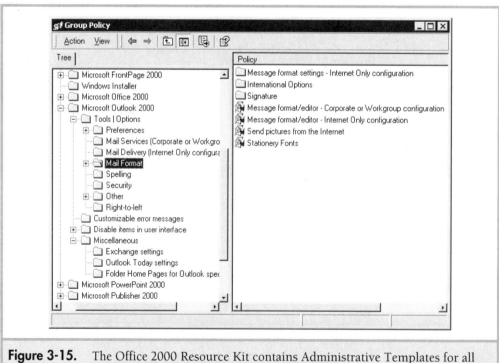

Figure 3-15. The Office 2000 Resource Kit contains Administrative Templates for all members of Office 2000 and Windows Installer.

Chapter 4

Supporting IntelliMirror Features

Microsoft uses the term "IntelliMirror" to describe a set of Windows 2000 Change and Configuration Management (CCM) services that are intended to reduce costs associated with managing networked clients running Windows 2000 Professional. The fall 1996 Zero Administration Windows (ZAW) initiative, described in Chapter 1, in the section "Comparing Group Policy with Windows NT System Policy," set the goals for basic IntelliMirror features. This chapter covers policy-managed Windows 2000 CCM features for Windows 2000 Professional clients.

Managing Change and Configuration with Group Policy

You can use local settings and policies to enable some IntelliMirror features, but using Group Policy to govern CCM for Windows 2000 clients is far more efficient and flexible. The problem, of course, is that most networks host a mix of 32-bit (and even some 16-bit) Windows clients. Downlevel clients must rely on the Zero Administration Kit (ZAK) to gain a subset of IntelliMirror features.

User Data Management

User data management employs folder redirection to store users' My Documents and, optionally, other folders on central servers. It's a common practice to encourage users to store originals or copies of important documents in home directories or other server shares for recovery from local hard disk crashes. Unfortunately, users often fail to follow network admins' recommendations, often with dire consequences. The My Documents folder is Microsoft's recommended location for all user documents and is the default location for new documents created with Microsoft Office and all recent applications that sport "Designed for Windows *Whatever*" or similar Microsoft-licensed logos. My Documents is the path of least resistance, so administratively controlled redirection of this folder to a network share is more likely to be successful than the voluntary home directory approach for storing important user documents on servers.

Windows 2000's new offline folders feature eliminates the need for mobile users to download many large files at every logon. The offline folders feature generates a local (cached) copy of redirected folders for use while disconnected from the network. Synchronization Manager updates the server copy of locally modified files when the mobile user reconnects to the network. Synchronization Manager has a manual conflict resolution dialog that handles multiple offline changes to redirected files.

The two primary benefits of user data management are assured backup of all user documents and the ability to quickly recover from catastrophic failure of a client computer. The downside is the amount of server disk space required to store all user documents generated by thousands of clients. Although you can limit the amount of disk space allocated to each client with Windows 2000's new disk quota management feature, insufficient quotas for redirected user files defeats the objectives of user data management.

User Settings Management

User settings management provides users with a consistent desktop or laptop look and feel, and lets you restrict users' ability to alter the configuration of their computers. Configuration restrictions range from limiting users' ability to manipulate Network and Dial-up Connections to total desktop lockdown. You also can set policies to redirect the contents of the user's Application Data, Desktop, and Start Menu subfolders of the \Documents and Settings*UserName* folder. The Application Data folder stores user data for applications that have been updated to Windows 2000 standards. Storing Desktop and Start Menu settings isn't necessary for users who can't modify them, but the amount of server space required for these settings isn't significant.

Roaming user profiles store the entire contents of users' \Documents and Settings*UserName* folder, except the Local Settings folder and other special folders excluded by Group Policy, on a server. Roaming profiles enable, for example, help desk technicians who log on at any user's machine as a member of the local Administrators group to temporarily download their standard desktop settings, preferences, and diagnostic executables and then automatically remove them at logoff. Roaming profiles delay each logon by the amount of time needed to download the profile, excluding the contents of the My Documents folder, from the server. The local My Documents folder points to the server share, but a current copy remains on the workstation for use in case of inability to connect to the server. Users who commonly log on to multiple machines are the primary candidates for roaming profiles.

NOTE: A user with local and domain accounts has two profiles. In this case, domain-based profiles append the downlevel domain name to the user name, such as \Documents and Settings\GaryAlmgren.OAKMONTU.

Windows NT also supports mandatory profiles, which are intended to lock down users' workstations to a specific configuration. The need for Windows NT–style roaming or mandatory profiles diminishes in all–Windows 2000 networks, because you can accomplish similar objectives with User Configuration policies. If you decide to implement roaming profiles, you must consider the impact of the size of the profiles in the storage planning process. Profiles include the Ntuser.dat file that holds Registry entries that are applied to the HKEY_CURRENT_USER (HKCU) hive after user logon. Ntuser.dat can become quite large; one of the workstations used in this book's examples has a 600 kB Ntuser.dat file. Group Policy's folder redirection doesn't store Ntuser.dat on the server; the folder redirection feature makes the assumption that GPOs determine users' HKCU settings.

TIP: The History, Local Settings, Temp, and Temporary Internet Files folders aren't included in roaming profiles to minimize storage space and logon/logoff time. You can add folders to exclude from the profile by enabling the Exclude Directories in Roaming Profile policy under the User Configuration\Administrative Templates\System\Logon/Logoff node. Add the folder names, separated by semicolons, to the text box's default list.

The location of user profiles on the workstation depends on the type of Windows 2000 Professional installation. For new installations and upgrades to Windows 9x with user profiles disabled, the profile location is that shown previously in this section: \Documents and Settings. Upgrading from Windows NT 3.51 or 4.0 and Windows 9x with user profiles enabled places profiles in the \Winnt\Profiles and \Windows\Profiles folders, respectively, for backward compatibility. After installation of Windows 2000 Professional, you can't change profile location. If necessary, you can use the following Unattend.txt switch for unattended setup to specify the legacy location for local user profiles in new installations:

```
profilesdir = "%systemroot%\profiles"
```

Software Installation and Maintenance

Software installation and maintenance uses Windows Installer to assign or publish applications, as briefly described in the section "Designing GPO Filters Based on Software Requirements" in the preceding chapter. Assigning an application adds a choice to the Start or Programs menu and, optionally, a desktop icon for the application. The application isn't installed until the user first starts the application.

Publishing an application adds an entry to Control Panel's Add/Remove Programs tool for optional installation. If an assigned or published application has a document association, such as .doc with Microsoft Word, the application is installed when the user first attempts to open a document that has the associated file extension. Some applications, such as GroupPol, are installed in multiple stages. Installation of GroupPol doesn't complete until you click OK in the startup dialog to display the program's main window, which is a Visual Basic form containing several thousand lines of compiled code.

Remote Installation Services

Remote Installation Services (RIS) isn't an official IntelliMirror member, but it's listed as a subtopic of IntelliMirror in the Windows 2000 Server online help file. RIS is a contender to replace disk imaging with Symantec Ghost and similar applications, or Unattended or SysPrep installation of Windows 2000 Professional. With an add-on from 3Com Corporation, you can use RIS to install other Windows operating systems and applications on clients.

RIS requires clients to have a network card that implements the Preboot eXecution Environment (PXE). Windows 2000 supports all PXE version 2 NICs, but only a limited number of NICs with the original PXE implementation. RIS automatically formats the entire C:\ drive with NTFS 5.0 and installs Window 2000 Professional in the \Winnt folder, so you can't use RIS to perform upgrades. RIPrep extends RIS to enable customization of the installation image to corporate standards. Microsoft recommends using Windows Installer, rather than RIPrep images, to load assigned and published productivity and special-purpose applications. Following this advice minimizes the number of different client images you need to store on your RIS server(s).

Associating Policies with IntelliMirror Features

Group policy doesn't have an IntelliMirror node that gathers all policies relating to IntelliMirror features under the Computer Configuration and User Configuration nodes. This is partly due to their implementation by different Group Policy Extensions. You won't find a single policy with "IntelliMirror" in its name. Similarly, a search for "IntelliMirror" in the .adm files of a DC returns no hits. Thus, you need a roadmap to the location of policies that enable and configure IntelliMirror features on clients.

NOTE: Appendix A provides detailed descriptions and, where applicable, Registry key value names for the policies described in this chapter.

User Data Management Policies

Group Policy enforces user data management with policies established by the following nodes of the Group Policy Editor (GPE):

✦ **My Documents**, a subnode of User Configuration\Windows Settings\Folder Redirection, a user-based policy, sets the network location and other properties of the user's \Documents and Settings*LogonID*\My Documents folder and optionally allows storage of its My Pictures folder on the server as a subfolder of My Documents. You can choose to store all folders under one network share or specify different servers, shares, or both for members of individual security groups (see Figure 4-1).

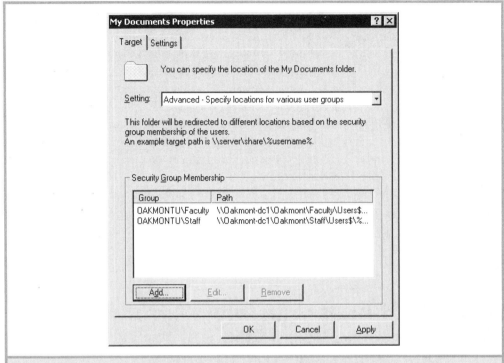

Figure 4-1. You can specify different server shares to hold redirected folders for members of Security Groups. The location is the UNC path to the group's share with a %username% environmental variable suffix.

◆ **My Pictures**, a subnode of My Documents, lets you choose whether to store contents of users' My Pictures folders on the server. Unless the user's responsibility involves graphic arts, it's not a good practice to redirect this subfolder. Users with digital cameras have a tendency to fill My Pictures with personal photo files.

◆ **Offline Files**, under the \Administrative Templates\Network nodes of Computer Configuration and User Configuration, determines whether offline files are enabled for the computer and how the feature is configured for the user. Twelve policies are identical for computers and users; if conflicts between these common policies exist, computer policies prevail. Five computer-based policies apply to all users: Enabled; Default Cache Size; Files Not Cached; At Logoff, Delete Local Copy of User's Offline Files; and Subfolders Always Available Offline.

✦ **Disk Quotas**, under the Computer Configuration\Administrative Templates\System node, has six policies that determine if and how the system manages disk quotas for individual volumes on the local computer, which can be the user's workstation, servers, or both, depending on the scope of the OU. For instance, you can apply disk quotas to volumes on member servers if you create a Domain Servers OU and move the member server accounts from Computer to the OU. Consider applying disk quotas only to workstations that have multiple users. Figure 4-2 shows a 100 MB (default) hard limit and 90 MB warning point set on all local volumes for new users who don't already own files on the volumes.

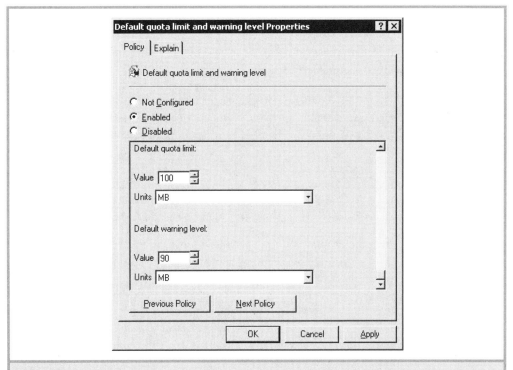

Figure 4-2.   The Default Quota Limit and Warning Level policy overrides local quota settings, if any, for new users of a workstation or server. The settings don't apply to individual users who have special quotas set by per-user Disk Manager entries.

Folder redirection and offline files are independent features. It's a common practice to assign folder redirection and Offline Files policies to mobile users and telecommuters. It's assumed that desktop users have a reliable, high-speed connection to the network, so these users don't need to cache network files locally.

User Settings Management Policies

The following subnodes of User Configuration\Windows Settings\Folder Redirection hold policies that determine implementation of user data management by Group Policy:

✦ **Application Data** redirects users' local \Documents and Settings*UserName*\ Application Data folder to a specified server share.

✦ **Desktop** redirects users' local \Documents and Settings*UserName*\Desktop folder to a specified server share.

✦ **Start Menu** redirects users' local \Documents and Settings*UserName*\Start Menu folder to a specified server share.

Like My Documents and My Pictures, you can use a common server share for all users or designate specific servers and shares by group membership. This feature eliminates the need for multiple GPOs that you filter by group membership to specify particular servers and shares.

TIP: Don't redirect the Desktop and Start Menu folders for users whose computers have been totally locked down. In this case, Desktop and Start Menu folders don't change.

As mentioned early in the chapter, Windows 2000 supports Windows NT–style roaming profiles. The following nodes contain policies that apply to roaming user profiles:

✦ **Logon** under \Computer Configuration\Administrative Templates\System has eight policies that affect the way roaming profiles behave when any user logs on and off the computer. Many of these policies relate to how the system handles roaming profiles with slow network connections, which are detected when the computer boots onto the network.

✦ **Logon/Logoff** under \User Configuration\Administrative Templates\System has two profile policies: Limit Profile Size (on the local computer) and Exclude Directories in Roaming Profile.

Software Installation Policies

The policies that affect software installation are scattered throughout computer and user GPEs. The following policies affect software installation by Windows Installer:

+ **Software Installation**, under the Software Settings node of Computer Configuration and User Configuration, lets you specify Windows Installer packages (.msi files) and conventional Setup.exe installations (augmented by .zap files) to be assigned or published based on computer or user group membership, respectively. A .zap file is a text file that specifies a "friendly name" for the application, such as Admin911: GroupPol and the UNC path to and the filename of the setup program, typically *servername**sharename*\Setup.exe.

+ **Windows Installer**, under \Computer Configuration\Administrative Templates\ Windows Components, offers 13 policies that apply to all computers within the scope of the policy, regardless of which user logs on. Chapter 6 discusses issues regarding the location of servers delivering installer files for domains with multiple sites.

+ **Windows Installer**, under \User Configuration\Administrative Templates\Windows Components, has four policies that are determined by user logon. User Configuration shares two policies, Always Install with Elevated Privileges and Disable Rollback, with Computer Configuration.

TIP: If you intend to take advantage of Windows Installer for all Windows 2000 clients, enable and mark the check box of the Always Install with Elevated Privileges policy under both the Computer Configuration and User Configuration nodes of the Default Domain Policy GPO. The two policies must be enabled to install packages on computers whose users don't have local Administrators privileges.

+ **Windows File Protection**, under \Computer Configuration\Administrative Templates\System, lets you set policies that determine parameters for ensuring that rogue packages don't permanently overwrite critical Windows 2000 system files.

Remote Installation Services Policy

RIS has only one policy setting, Choice Options under the User Configuration\Windows Settings node. The Choice Options Properties dialog determines the menu choices users or installation support personnel see when booting the client from the network or from a

RIS boot disk. Options you set in this Properties dialog also apply to RIPrep and installation of other operating systems with the 3-Com Menu Editor that you can download from http://www.3com.com/technology/key_net/dynamic/ris_overview.html. The 3Com Menu Editor lets you add new choices to the Automatic Setup or the Maintenance and Troubleshooting menus of the Client Installation Wizard for RIS or RIPrep images.

Planning a Server Infrastructure to Support IntelliMirror Features

The primary issues facing system admins contemplating a move to CCM with IntelliMirror is server capacity for storage of users' My Documents folders and network performance when many users attempt to open or save multimegabyte documents simultaneously. Users accustomed to multigigabyte local drives probably will adopt undesirable workarounds when given a 100 MB limit on server-stored My Documents folders. If network congestion or disk I/O limitation impedes the loading or saving of documents, users will store their documents locally, not on the server. If you can't immediately solve network performance problems, you can implement Offline Files policies for Windows 2000 desktop users.

If your domains span multiple sites, you must provide storage capacity for users at each site. In this case, you use site-level My Documents and Application Data and, optionally, Desktop and Start Menu policies to specify the local servers that hold redirected folders. This is one of the few cases in which you're likely to employ site-level policies. Plan on using Windows 2000 Server's File Replication Service (FRS) to accommodate users with roaming profiles who regularly log on at computers at different sites. You should provide Windows Installer files for assigned and popular published applications at each site; installing Microsoft Office, for instance, over a slow WAN link consumes most or all of the link's bandwidth and frustrates the recipients. You can use FRS to automatically replicate .msi files between sites, but you must use site-based policies to point to the appropriate server name in the path to the .msi file. RIS and RIPrep images require per-site installation, but RIS and RIPrep automatically find the client's closest RIS server.

In-Place Upgrades

Many large Windows NT networks now store user home directories, provide roaming profiles, implement system policies, have a complement of custom logon scripts for users, or perform various combinations of these functions. If you have a major infrastructure investment in the preceding accouterments, in-place upgrade of your PDCs, BDCs, and member servers to Windows 2000 is the fastest and least-effort route. When you upgrade

Windows 9x and NT clients to Windows 2000, users retain their previous settings. The only change users encounter is that to Windows 2000, which probably is all most help desk support groups can handle during a large-scale desktop and laptop upgrade.

Windows NT Server doesn't support disk quotas, but Windows 2000 Server adds disk quota management by file or folder ownership. If you have a third-party disk quota management application running on your server(s), contact the vendor to determine whether quota management survives the Windows 2000 upgrade. You can't retroactively apply Windows 2000 disk quotas to existing home directories or profiles for users whose SIDs change as a result of creation of a new user account. You can indirectly manage quotas for users who have roaming profiles by enforcing the Limit Profile Size policy mentioned earlier in the chapter. The advantage of this approach is that you can establish different size limits based on users' group membership.

After the deluge of trouble tickets subsides, move users into OUs and reorganize your Security Group structure. Then you can implement Group Policy on a predetermined schedule for members of specific OUs and role-based Security Groups, as discussed in the preceding chapter. You add server storage for My Documents at each site to accommodate the OUs, groups, or both, that implement folder redirection. Network-attached storage (NAS), which is optimized for file sharing, is a convenient method for incrementally increasing LAN storage space without upgrading existing servers. For example, Compaq Computer Corporation offers its TaskSmart N-Series NAS appliances, which run an embedded version of Windows 2000 and start at about $35,000 for 72 GB of storage. This translates to a cost of about $50 per user for 100 MB of My Documents storage, not counting the cost of a high-speed, high-capacity backup system.

Incremental Migration with Domain Restructure

Incremental migration to Windows 2000 Professional with domain restructure involves designing and implementing a Windows 2000 infrastructure that ultimately replaces your existing Windows NT servers. Incremental migration of user and computer accounts to a new Windows 2000 domain gives both users and network admins a fresh start without their suffering the accumulated detritus of an aging network infrastructure designed and implemented by long-departed system admins.

In this scenario, shared folders to which you redirect My Documents replace traditional home directories. Setting Folder Redirection policies eliminates the need to specify a profile path, logon script, or home folder path for individual users. If users are accustomed to home directories mapped to logical drive letters, you can write group-based logon scripts and assign them with Scripts (Startup/Shutdown) or Scripts (Logon/Logoff) policies for each group. Assigning home directories, however, compromises a Store All User Documents in Subfolders of My Documents policy for Windows 2000 users.

For networks with a substantial number (in the 50 or more range) of clients that redirect My Documents to a server or have roaming profiles, its a good practice to install at each site a member server optimized for sharing of user files from a high-performance RAID 5 subsystem. You optimize DCs for application serving to improve AD performance, which decreases file-sharing performance. NAS is an economical alternative to the use of member servers if you need more than about 30 GB of user file storage.

Setting Group Policy for Folder Redirection and Offline Files

The first consideration in determining a Group Policy design to support IntelliMirror services is whether you intend to employ roaming profiles or redirect appropriate subfolders of \Documents and Settings*UserName* to file server(s). You can't use group policy to designate roaming profiles for a group of users; you must specify the path to the profile location for each user on the Profile page of Active Directory Users and Computer's *UserName* Properties dialog. The sections that follow cover folder redirection; the section "Configuring Roaming User Profiles," later in this chapter, briefly discusses how to set up Windows NT–style roaming profiles.

Redirecting My Documents to a Common Share

Redirecting My Documents involves the following basic steps:

1. Share a folder to hold the redirected files for users. By tradition, the folder is named Users($) shared as Users$; the $ share name suffix hides the share. The GroupPol application used to create the examples for this chapter generates *ServerName**ShareName**DivisionName*\Users$ subfolders on a specified DC for each user division: Faculty Members, Non-Faculty Staff, and Students. The $ suffix doesn't hide the folder; it is present to identify the folder as containing individual *UserName* folders.

2. Set Folder Redirection\My Documents policy in an existing GPO for all users except Domain Admins (Default Domain Policy), or for OUs containing user accounts. Alternatively, create a new GPO specifically for folder redirection and, optionally, Offline Files policies. A separate GPO linked to multiple OUs makes it easier to disable folder redirection if you later decide not to implement redirection. You can filter application of the GPO by user groups, as described in the preceding chapter.

NOTE: The offline files feature isn't available to Terminal Server clients.

3. Test folder redirection by logging on and off at a workstation as a user to which the policy applies.

To use a common My Documents redirection folder for all members of an OU and its sub-OUs, if any, do this:

1. Create on the server the share to hold the folders to store the redirected files of each user in the OU and its sub-OUs. Set initial share permissions that give Domain Admins and Domain Users Allow Full Control rights. Users need Allow Full Control share permissions to create folders with exclusive access. Set folder permissions to give Domain Admins Allow Full Control and to give Domain Users Allow Modify rights. For this example, the folder is \Oakmont on Oakmont-dc1 shared as Oakmont. Users must have Allow Modify permissions on the Users$ folder to create their My Documents folder and add or delete files and subfolders on the server.

TIP: If users don't have Allow Modify permissions on the share to contain their My Documents folder, folder redirection fails silently. Adding the required permission and having the user log on again doesn't reenable redirection; you must reboot the workstation to reapply the policy successfully. You might need to log off and log on as the user again to cause redirection to succeed.

2. Create a new redirection GPO in one of the OUs to which it is to apply and use the Up button to move it to the top (highest priority) of the Group Policy Object Links list. This example uses a new Folder Redirection Policy created in the Faculty Members GPO. In the GPE, navigate to the User Configuration\Windows Settings\ Folder Redirection\My Documents node. Right-click the node and choose Properties to open the Target page of the My Documents Properties dialog.

3. Select Basic - Redirect Everyone's Folder to the Same Location in the Setting list to designate a single shared folder for all members of the OU and its sub-OUs.

4. Click Browse to open the Browse for Folder dialog. Navigate through My Network Places to the target share and subfolder: ...\Oakmontu\Oakmont-dc1\Oakmont\ Faculty\Users$ for this example. Select the subfolder and click OK to add the UNC path (\\Oakmont\Faculty\Users$) to the share in the Target Folder Location text box.

Don't specify a local path to the folder under My Documents. If you do, you receive a warning message that the path won't work; believe the message.

5. Add the required \%username% environment variable suffix to the UNC path in the text box (see Figure 4-3). If you don't add this suffix, users who have the policy applied encounter an error message when logging on and off.

6. Click the Settings tab. By default, only the user and the SYSTEM account have permissions for the My Documents folder and its files. Clear the Grant the User Exclusive Rights to My Documents check box during testing to make it easy to delete the folders later. In a production environment, mark this check box to ensure privacy of users' My Documents contents.

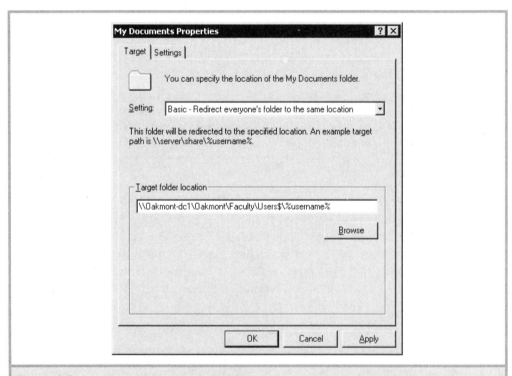

Figure 4-3. When you specify Basic redirection, add the UNC path to the share and, if applicable, the subfolder for My Documents storage; then add the \%username% environmental variable.

TIP: If you change the Grant the User Exclusive Rights to My Documents setting after some users log on and off, permissions for those users folders don't change. You must manually change the permissions.

CODE BLUE

Don't clear the Move the Contents of My Documents to the New Location check box, which is marked by default. If you clear this check box and later remove the GPO that redirects My Documents to the server, only the folder (not its contents) returns to users' computers. Users lose access to all of the files in My Documents and its subfolders.

7. Select the Redirect the Folder Back to the Local User Profile Location When Policy Is Removed option to ensure that users retain access to their documents on their local computer if you later change your decision to redirect My Documents folders. The section "Disabling or Changing Folder Redirection" later in this chapter describes the steps required to change the policy for all users.

8. Select the Do Not Specify Administrative Policy for My Pictures option to prevent users from filling your servers with family photo albums (see Figure 4-4). Specifying this option adds to the redirected My Documents folder a shortcut to the My Pictures subfolder on the workstations' local drive.

NOTE: Once you prevent My Pictures redirection and apply the policy, the My Picture Preferences options are disabled. If you change your mind, open the My Pictures Properties dialog and choose the redirection option you want from the Setting list.

9. Click OK to apply the policy to the OU.

10. Close the GPE and the *OUName* Properties dialog to ensure that the policies are applied.

Redirecting My Documents to Multiple Servers

If you want to specify different servers to store users' redirected folders, add the GPO at the domain level, and in step 3 in the preceding section, specify Advanced - Specify Locations for Various Users Groups in the Setting list of the *FolderName* Properties dialog; this adds a

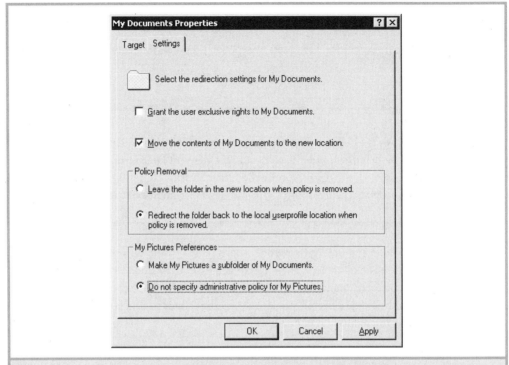

Figure 4-4. Specify folder redirection options on the My Documents Properties dialog's Settings page. Don't grant users exclusive rights to My Documents when testing folder redirection.

Security Group Membership list (refer to Figure 4-1). You can take advantage of Security Groups to designate alternate locations on a server or to share the redirected folders and roaming profiles load among member servers. This approach is much more efficient than creating individual GPOs that point to a single server and then filtering the GPOs by group membership.

To change the GPO you added in the preceding section to multiple locations with precreated Users$ shares, do the following:

1. Remove the link to the GPO from the OU and add a link to the GPO under the Default Domain Policy GPO.

2. With Advanced selected in the Setting list, click Add to open the Specify Group and Location dialog.

3. In the Security Group Membership frame, click the Browse button to open the Select Group dialog, type the name of the group (Faculty Members) in the Name list, and click OK to add the downlevel name of the group (OAKMONTU\Faculty) to the text box. If you mistype the group name, you receive an error message.

CODE BLUE

The Security Group you specify for each location must be a Global or Universal group. If you specify a Domain Local group in the name list, the Folder Redirection Policy appears to apply to group members, because the user's folder is present in the ...\Users$ share after the user logs on. However, specified folders don't redirect to the share. For example, GroupPol's Faculty Members, Non-Faculty Staff, and Students groups are Domain Local, because GroupPol must run on Windows NT and Windows 2000 in mixed mode, neither of which permit nested Global groups. Department-level groups (for instance, Anthropology and Information Technology) that contain user accounts are nested within Domain Local Groups (Faculty Members and Non-Faculty Staff, respectively). If you're using GroupPol, you must change the Faculty Members and Non-Faculty Staff groups from Domain Local to Universal and then change them to Global groups for folder redirection to work. Don't use Universal groups unless you have a specific need to do so.

BUG ALERT: When you change a Domain Local to a Global or Universal group that contains nested groups with user accounts, the Member Of page of the *UserName* Properties dialog doesn't display the user's membership in the group whose type you changed. Running Gpresult.exe on the user's workstation, however, displays the group membership correctly. Using Gpresult.exe is the subject of the section "Troubleshooting Policy Application on Workstations" later in this chapter.

4. In the Target Folder Location frame, click the Browse button to open the Browse for Folder dialog, navigate to the Users$ share, and click OK to add it to the text box. Append the %username% suffix to the UNC path to the share. Click OK to return to the My Documents Properties dialog and add the entry to the Security Group Membership list.

5. Repeat steps 1 through 4 for each additional group to add: OAKMONTU\Staff and \\Oakmont-dc1\Oakmont\Staff\Users$\%username% for this example.

6. If you don't plan to apply Offline Files policies to computers with this GPO, you can mark the Disable Computer Configuration Settings check box in the GPO's Properties dialog.

7. Close the GPO and the *DomainName* Properties dialog.

If you have multiple sites, you can employ this feature to redirect user folders to a specific server at a site. For example, Oakmont U has four high-rise buildings: Administration (for Non-Faculty Staff), Computer Science, Science (Biology, Geology, Mathematics, and Physics), and Liberal Arts (all other departments). If the buildings are distant sites connected by a comparatively low-speed WAN, each contains member server(s) with shares for redirected folders and, if implemented, roaming profiles. In this case, you assign members of a department's Security Group to a local server share, rather than to the central \\Oakmont-dc1\ Oakmont\ shares as shown in Figure 4-1. If you don't have Security Groups that correspond to users' sites, create and populate them with user accounts in the OU to which you apply Folder Redirection Policy. Populating site-based Security Groups with user accounts is a tedious process unless you have an attribute value on which to filter the user list. If you have the required attribute value, you can use Active Directory Users and Computers or ADSI scripts to populate the site-based groups.

NOTE: Most user accounts created by GroupPol have an Office attribute (physicalDeliveryOfficeName) whose value starts with the building name. The value for off-campus users is "Delivery to home address only," which enables identification of users who have dial-up, DSL, or cable-modem connections to the network.

Testing Folder Redirection

Testing folder redirection requires logging on to a workstation with a user account that's within the scope of the GPO that you added or modified as described in the preceding section. To perform an initial test of folder redirection with offline files, do the following:

1. Log on to a Windows 2000 workstation as a domain user in the OU or its sub-OUs. With verbose status messages enabled, folder redirection messages appear briefly during the logon process. Very large files, such as the user's MP3 music collection, delay the logon process while the files are copied to the server.

2. If you log on to the workstation as a new user and create a new profile, log off and log on again as the new user. A local profile for the user must exist before folder redirection succeeds.

3. Open My Documents and verify that the files are redirected. Folders within My Documents display the UNC path to the folder in the title bar (see Figure 4-5, top). If the default Enable Web Content in Folders option is enabled, a "This folder is Online" message appears under the My Documents heading. My Pictures isn't redirected, so a shortcut to My Pictures replaces the conventional subfolder icon. Double-clicking the shortcut displays the local path to My Pictures (see Figure 4-5, bottom).

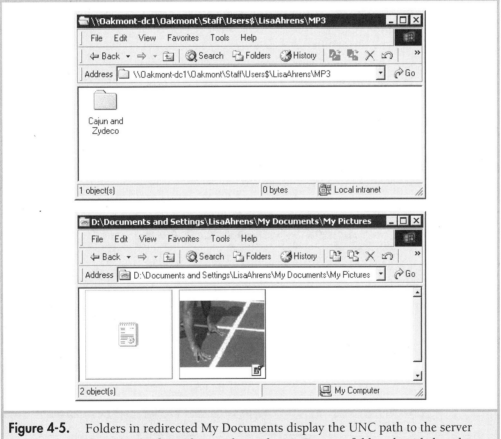

Figure 4-5. Folders in redirected My Documents display the UNC path to the server share (top). If you don't redirect the My Pictures folder, the title bar shows the path to the local drive (bottom).

4. Right-click My Documents and choose Properties to open the Target page of the My Documents Properties dialog. The Target text box contains the UNC path to the server-stored copy, which is read-only. The properties dialog also has General and Security pages.

NOTE: My Documents folders that aren't redirected or that the user redirects manually have a read-write Target text box and three buttons. The Restore Default button returns the location of the redirected folder to the local computer. Move lets the user place My Documents wherever he or she wants, and Find Target opens the folder on the server.

5. Choose Programs | Accessories | Synchronize to open Synchronization Manager's Items to Synchronize dialog, which displays entries for Offline Files and Offline Web Pages (see Figure 4-6). Offline file caching is enabled by default when you apply Folder Redirection Policy. Synchronizing Offline Web Pages requires that you be connected to the Internet and visit each site with offline files.

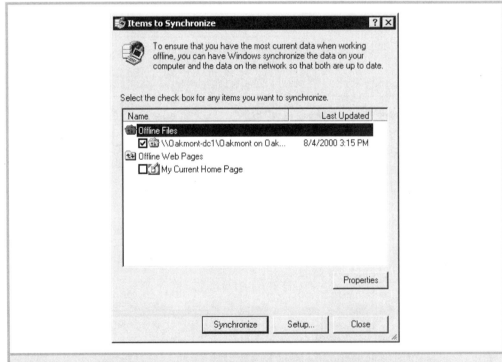

Figure 4-6. The Items to Synchronize dialog lets users perform an immediate synchronization of cached files with server-stored versions. Clicking Properties opens the Offline Files list.

6. Click Setup to open a tabbed dialog that lets the user perform an immediate synchronization, synchronize files while the computer is idle, or schedule periodic synchronization. Only one setting has a corresponding Offline Files policy: Synchronize all offline files before logging off.

7. Select the item with the check box and share path and click Properties to open the Offline Files Folder window that displays a laundry list of files under the control of Synchronization Manager (see Figure 4-7). Most offline files are Internet shortcuts to Microsoft's gratuitous IE 5+ Favorites entries, such as Links, Free Hotmail. The default Favorites choices are a primary incentive for network admins to lock down IE 5.0 with Group Policy. If multiple users have offline files, a user can see other users' files, but receive an "Access denied" message when attempting to open them in the Online Files window.

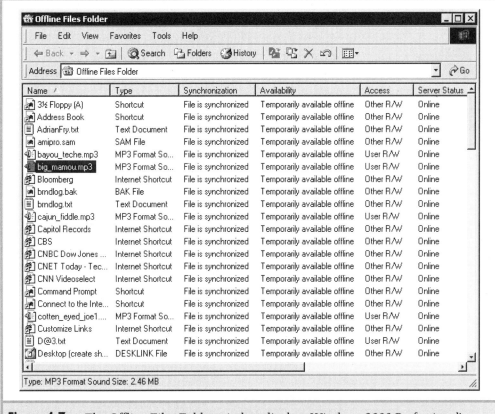

Figure 4-7. The Offline Files Folder window displays Windows 2000 Professional's default set of offline files, plus user files added to My Documents and its subfolders.

8. Log off the workstation. During the logoff process, Synchronization Manager dialogs flash briefly.

9. On the server, navigate to the Users$ share and open the *UserName* folder to verify folder permissions. If you gave the user exclusive rights to the folder, you receive a message indicating that you can only view permissions.

NOTE: During testing with offline files in use, you may receive spurious messages that say that the workstation is no longer connected to the server and is working offline. You can disregard these messages unless the connection icon in the tray has a red "X," which indicates a network failure.

Redirecting Application Data, Desktop, and Start Menu Folders

Applications that conform to Windows 2000 standards store personal settings and files, such as security certificates, for individual users in the Application Data folder. Thus, you should consider redirecting this folder to the same location as users' My Documents folders. If you must replace a failed workstation, the logon process recovers the user's personal configuration and data. Unfortunately, redirecting Application Data clutters the user's My Documents folder with the following two added folders:

✦ **Identities** contains an empty subfolder named for the GUID of the logged-on user, which is stored in HKCU\Identities\Default User ID. Identities are an element of public-key security, and users can have multiple identities defined by personal certificates.

✦ **Microsoft** is a system folder that contains Internet Explorer and SystemCertificates subfolders. Internet Explorer includes a QuickLaunch folder that defines the three default shortcuts (Show Desktop, Launch Internet Explorer Browser, and Launch Outlook Express) to the right of the Start button of the taskbar. If you applied Internet Explorer branding policy in the "Test the Filters After You Apply Them" section of the preceding chapter, Brndlog.txt, Brndlog.bak, and MSIMGSIZ.DAT files also appear. SystemCertificates contains a My subfolder with subfolders for storing CRLs (certificate revocation lists) and CTLs (certificate trust lists).

The preceding added folders undoubtedly will confuse most users, and Microsoft's developers should have hidden them. Application Data is a hidden folder in local and roaming user profiles, so logic dictates that Application Data be hidden when the folder is redirected. Users with default permissions can delete the QuickLaunch and SystemCertificates folders, although they receive a warning that SystemCertificates is a System folder. You can hide the Identities folder but not the Microsoft folder in the Microsoft Properties dialog; the Microsoft folder is a System folder, and the Hidden check box is disabled.

TAKE COMMAND

To hide the Microsoft folder and retain its System attribute and to hide the Identities folder, you must enter the following two instructions in the Command Prompt window:

```
attrib +s +h \path\microsoft
attrib +h \path\identities
```

These commands require that the user executing them have appropriate permissions for the user's share; if the user has exclusive access to the folder, executing the commands without permissions returns a "File not found" message. Only the user and the SYSTEM group have access.

Windows NT 4.0's Scheduler Service runs in the LocalSystem context, but Windows 2000's doesn't. You can open a Command Prompt window as LocalSystem and execute the instructions by following the instructions in Knowledge Base article Q238846, "How to Gain System Access to a Windows 2000–Based Computer." The process, which involves changing several Registry values, isn't simple.

TIP: Remember to clear the Grant User Exclusive Rights to *FolderName* check box when testing redirection of additional folders. Otherwise, you must take ownership of each user's folder on the server before deleting these folders or the parent folder.

As mentioned earlier, you don't need to redirect Start Menu and Desktop folders for users whose computer configuration is locked down by Group Policy. Start Menu and Desktop folders don't occupy much storage space or have a major effect on logon/logoff performance, but redirecting them can contribute to user confusion. Redirecting these two folders causes the following:

✦ **Start Menu** adds a Programs folder with a Startup subfolder to My Documents. By default, the two folders are empty, because Start menu items defined for all users aren't redirected.

✦ **Desktop** adds a desktop icon for each of the My Documents folders created by redirecting Application Data and Start Menu. If you hide the Application Data subfolders, the Identities and Microsoft icons don't appear on the desktop.

If you decide to redirect the Start Menu or Desktop folders, repeat steps 2 through 7 in the earlier section, "Redirecting My Documents to a Common Share," substituting the new folder name for My Documents in step 2. The Start Menu's Grant the User Exclusive Rights to Start Menu and Move the Contents of Start Menu to the New Location check boxes are disabled.

TIP: To save time and ensure that the target path is correct when applying Basic redirection to a single location, open the My Document Properties policy dialog and copy the contents of the Target Folder Location text box to the Clipboard. Paste it into the text box for the added folders.

Securing Redirected Folders

It's a common practice to create on servers a common Users folder shared as a hidden Users$ to hold all redirected folders, user profiles, and home directories. The examples in this book use a three-level hierarchy, \Oakmont*OUFolder*\Users$. In this case, the subfolders of Users$ are visible when browsing. A more serious security problem is users with Allow Full Control share permissions on Oakmont and inherited Allow Modify rights on the entire *OUFolder*. As mentioned earlier, Full Control share permissions are required for users to redirect folders with exclusive rights. Although you can disable permission inheritance on *OUFolder* to restrict user access and add required explicit permissions to Users$, a more secure approach is to establish a hidden share specifically for redirected folders that have the Grant the User Exclusive Rights to *FolderName* attribute set.

CODE BLUE

If you don't grant the users' Security Group Full Control share (not folder) permissions, the Grant the User Exclusive Rights to My Documents attribute fails silently, and all other users in the group have access to the contents of the newly redirected folder. The failure doesn't add an entry to the Application log. You can test whether users' redirected folders are user owned by attempting to open them on the server; folders with user-exclusive rights cause an "Access is denied" error. On the workstation, log on as the user, open the My Documents Properties dialog, click the Security tab, and verify that only the user and SYSTEM have Full Control permissions. The default Everyone group has no permissions. If the user doesn't have exclusive rights, permissions inherited from the share appear. To correct the problem, remove the inherited permissions, add the user, give the user Full Control permissions, and mark the Reset Permissions on All Child Objects... check box of the Advanced page.

If you want to delegate management of OUs and their members' redirected folders, create individual shares for the OUs, such as FacultyUsers$ and StaffUsers$, and use Security Groups to specify redirection to the appropriate share.

Users can't change the location of My Documents, but the policy doesn't prevent users from changing permissions on the Security page of the My Documents Properties dialog. Users can grant other groups or users access to their redirected folders, but doing so might contradict corporate confidentiality or security policy. You can remove the Security page from the user's My Documents Properties dialog by changing ownership of the folder from the user to the local Administrators group on the server and then removing the user's Read Permissions, Change Permissions, and Take Ownership rights. Administrators must have Allow Full Control permissions to delete unneeded *UserName* folders. Unfortunately, you must perform the preceding manual operation for each user folder.

Applying Offline Files Policies

The offline files feature is enabled by default on workstations and disabled on servers. To prevent users from disabling offline files on their workstations, you must explicitly enable the Computer Configuration\Administrative Templates\Network\Offline Files\Enabled policy.

CODE BLUE

Be sure the GPO in which you apply the Enabled setting for offline files doesn't have the Disable Computer Configuration Settings check box of its Properties dialog marked. It's a common practice to disable computer-based policies of GPOs you add to OUs, such as the Faculty Members Policy GPO or its equivalent that you added in earlier chapters.

If you disconnect the test workstation from the network and log on with the user's cached password, the only evidence of disconnection is an "X" across the Offline Files network connection icon at the right of the taskbar and a "This folder is Offline" message in the My Documents folder (if the default Explorer folder options are in effect). If you reconnect the workstation while logged on and then log off, a "Close open files" message appears, requesting that you close all open files and folders. Explorer has shut down at this point, so you can't perform the requested task. Click OK or Cancel (both buttons have the same effect) to continue the synchronization process.

You can further restrict users' online files options by applying the 16 additional policies in Computer Configuration\Administrative Templates\Network\Offline Files, the 12 policies in User Configuration\Administrative Templates\Network\Offline Files, or both. As was mentioned earlier, most of the Offline Files policies, with the notable exception of Enabled, can be applied to the computer or user. If you apply different settings to the same policy in the two locations, Computer Configuration policies prevail. The two "Offline Files" sections of Appendix A describe the effects of applying these policies.

Disabling Offline Files

You can disable the offline files feature on the workstation or by applying computer-based Offline Files policies. To disable offline files locally, in My Documents choose Tools | Folder Options, click the Offline Files tab, and clear all check boxes on the page.

Disabling offline files doesn't affect folder redirection; instead, user modifications to files in My Documents occur in real time on the server instead of being cached on the local drive and synchronized at logoff. If you disable offline files, users won't have access to redirected folders in the event of a network failure, and they won't be able to save changes to files in My Documents until their network connections are restored. To prevent users from caching offline files, disable the Computer Configuration\Administrative Templates\Network\Offline Files\Enabled policy. The workstation must be rebooted to apply the new policy. Disabling offline files makes other Offline Files policy settings moot.

Filtering Folder Redirection and Offline Files Policies

To exclude specific users from the use of folder redirection, offline files, or both, you need to create a separate GPO to manage these features. If the policies apply to users within a sub-OU of the OU to which the overall policy applies, for example Faculty Members, Computer Science, you can apply the GPO to the sub-OU. In this case, the policies you specify override those of the parent OU. Bear in mind that folder redirection is a user-based policy, but enabling or disabling offline files is computer based. If your computer accounts are contained in computer-class OUs, such as Desktops and Laptops, you can use computer-based policies to enable offline files when a user is working with a laptop and disable the feature when the user logs in on a desktop client.

If you don't have an appropriate OU structure for selective application of Folder Redirection and Offline Files policies, filter the GPOs by Security Group using the methods described in the preceding chapter. Here's another case where populating the groups with appropriate user and, especially, computer accounts is a tedious chore.

Disabling or Changing Folder Redirection

If you change the Target page's Setting value to No Administrative Policy Specified or alter the path to the redirected files, users' My Documents folders continue to be redirected to the original location on the server. There is no Disable Policy setting for folder redirection, and changing the location of the files on the server would result in users' not being able to find their My Documents folders.

To make changes to Folder Redirection policies, you must remove the link to the GPO that applies the settings to the Registry to return the redirected files to their original location on the workstation drive. Redirection entries appear in HKCU\Software\Microsoft\Windows\CurrentVersion\Explorer\Shell Folders\Desktop (if you redirected Desktop) and ...\Personal (the alias for My Documents). Identical value names appear under the HKCU\Software\Microsoft\Windows\CurrentVersion\Explorer\Shell Folders key. The entries repeat in HKEY_USERS*SID*\Software\Microsoft\Windows\CurrentVersion\Explorer\Shell Folders and ...User Shell Folders, where *SID* is the security ID of the user.

To disable folder redirection and return affected workstations to their original configurations, do the following:

1. If Folder Redirection policies are present in a GPO with other policies you want to retain, return the Setting selection of each folder you redirected to No Administrative Policy Specified. If you enabled Offline Files policies, reset these policies to No Administrative Policy Specified to return control of offline files settings to the user.

2. Remove the link to the GPO. Open the Properties dialog for the OU to which you applied the Folder Redirection Policy, select the GPO in the list, and click Delete. Accept the default Remove the Link from the List option, click OK, and click Close to close the Properties dialog. If you don't remove the GPO link, the redirection settings don't revert on the workstation.

3. Reboot the workstation and log on with an affected user's account. A few seconds' delay during the Applying Personal Document Settings period of the user logon process indicates that folders are being copied back to the user's local profile.

4. In the My Documents Properties dialog, verify that the Target value is the user's local profile. If My Documents remains redirected, log off and log on again.

5. After verifying that the local My Documents folder contains all the user's files, you can safely delete the copy of the folders on the server. If the user has exclusive rights to his or her folder, change ownership of the folder to the local Administrators group. Make sure to mark the Replace Owner on Subcontainers and Objects check box before you click OK.

6. If the GPO contains other policies that you want to continue to apply to users, re-create the links to the policies. The former policies are applied when users log on again, or when the Group Policy refresh interval expires.

CODE BLUE

If the user was a member of the Domain Admins group when you applied Folder Redirection policies, removing the GPO that established redirection doesn't remove the redirection entries from the workstation's Registry. Removing Domain Admins from the user's group memberships after applying the redirection GPO doesn't solve the problem. Changing folder security settings after redirection also can prevent removal of redirection entries. You must manually remove these tattooed settings on the workstation by searching for all instances of folder redirection for the user and manually changing the Registry entries to point to the local folder. For the examples in this chapter, you can find all instances of folder redirection by typing **Users$** in the Find What text box of Regedit.exe's Find dialog. The often undesirable alternative is to copy the contents of My Documents to a temporary folder, remove the user's profile from the workstation, create a new local profile, and copy the contents of the temporary folder back to My Documents.

Troubleshooting Policy Application on Workstations

The types of Group Policies you applied in earlier chapters are straightforward, and problems seldom occur with their application and removal. This isn't the case for Folder Redirection policies. If a user experiences problems while creating, updating, or synchronizing a redirected folder, the problem often adds a record to the Application log. Fortunately, you can read users' Event Viewer logs remotely by opening Active Directory Users and Computers, right-clicking the computer account, and choosing Manage to open the Computer Management snap-in. Typically, pairs of Folder Redirection (Event ID 101, 102, 106, or 401) and Userenv (Event ID 1000) errors appear in the Application log when users have problems with redirected folders. Figure 4-8 illustrates the properties for an "Access is denied" problem when the user attempted to save changes to a redirected folder. In many cases, you can solve the problem from the information in the Description text box. The description of Userenv problems typically is "The Group Policy client-side extension Folder Redirection was passed flags (0) and returned a failure status code of (1338)" or the like, which isn't very useful for troubleshooting unless you know what the status code means.

TIP: The Knowledge Base contains several articles for Userenv errors and a few for Folder Redirection Policy. A useful article to review is Q250842, "Troubleshooting Group Policy Application Problems."

The Userenv.log file in the workstation's \Winnt\Debug\UserMode folder might shed some light on the problem. Search for ProcessGPOs to display a terse description of the problem, such as "Folder Redirection ProcessGroupPolicy failed," and an inscrutable status code, such as 0x5. A much better Group Policy troubleshooting tool is the Windows 2000 Server Resource Kit's Gpresult.exe. Gpresult.exe, which you must install and run in the Command window of the affected workstation, provides a comprehensive list of user and computer attributes, including group membership and local user permissions.

When you're troubleshooting folder redirection problems with Gpresult.exe, the most useful topics are "The user is a member of the following security groups" and "The user received 'Folder Redirection' settings from these GPOs." If you don't see these sections, or if "*FolderName* is redirected to *ServerName**ShareName*[*Path*]" lines are missing, the workstation isn't receiving Folder Redirection Policy. The most common causes are errors in the group name or target folder you specify when setting multiple redirection folders based on group membership, and missing user accounts in a targeted Security Group. Following is

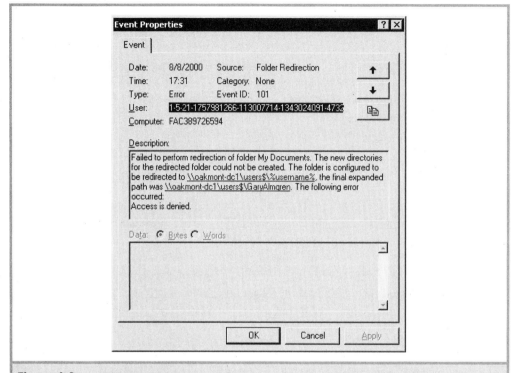

Figure 4-8.   Open the Computer Management snap-in of the user's computer to check the Application log for folder redirection problems. The user's name is replaced by his or her security ID when you manage a computer remotely.

most of the content from running Gpresult.exe /v (verbose mode) on a workstation with the GPOs added in this and the preceding chapter, less the Microsoft Office software installation GPOs:

```
Microsoft (R) Windows (R) 2000 Operating System Group Policy Result tool
Copyright (C) Microsoft Corp. 1981-1999
Created on Wednesday, August 09, 2000 at 9:25:27 AM
Operating System Information:
Operating System Type:      Professional
Operating System Version:   5.0.2195
Terminal Server Mode:       Not supported
############################################################
  User Group Policy results for:
  CN=Gary Almgren,OU=Anthropology,OU=Faculty Members,DC=oakmont,DC=edu
  Domain Name:     OAKMONTU
  Domain Type:     Windows 2000
  Site Name:       Oakland
```

```
   Roaming profile:  (None)
   Local profile:    F:\Documents and Settings\GaryAlmgren.OAKMONTU
   The user is a member of the following security groups:
      OAKMONTU\Domain Users
      \Everyone
      BUILTIN\Users
      OAKMONTU\Faculty
      OAKMONTU\Anthro
      OAKMONTU\Chairs
      \LOCAL
      NT AUTHORITY\INTERACTIVE
      NT AUTHORITY\Authenticated Users
   The user has the following security privileges:
      Bypass traverse checking
      Shut down the system
      Remove computer from docking station
############################################################
Last time Group Policy was applied: Wednesday, August 09, 2000 at 9:24:51 AM
Group Policy was applied from: oakmont-dc1.oakmont.edu
============================================================
The user received "Registry" settings from these GPOs:
   Default Domain Policy
        Revision Number: 9
        Unique Name:    {31B2F340-016D-11D2-945F-00C04FB984F9}
        Domain Name:    oakmont.edu
        Linked to:      Domain (DC=oakmont,DC=edu)
   Faculty Members Users Policy
        Revision Number: 42
        Unique Name:    {59FC7592-E6EB-4CD1-961B-E94925EEE141}
        Domain Name:    oakmont.edu
        Linked to:      Organizational Unit (OU=Faculty
Members,DC=oakmont,DC=edu)
                        Anthropology User Policy
        Revision Number: 1
        Unique Name:    {22AC8816-FDDF-4B01-975B-A2691C73E2F7}
        Domain Name:    oakmont.edu
        Linked to:      Organizational Unit (OU=Anthropology,OU=Faculty Members,
                        DC=oakmont,DC=edu)
   The following settings were applied from: Default Domain Policy
        KeyName:   Software\Microsoft\Windows\CurrentVersion\Policies\Explorer
        ValueName: NoWelcomeScreen
        ValueType: REG_DWORD
        Value:     0x00000001

        KeyName:   Software\Policies\Microsoft\Windows\Installer
        ValueName: AlwaysInstallElevated
        ValueType: REG_DWORD
        Value:     0x00000001

        KeyName:   Software\Policies\Microsoft\Windows\System
        ValueName: GroupPolicyRefreshTime
        ValueType: REG_DWORD
        Value:     0x00000090

        KeyName:   Software\Policies\Microsoft\Windows\System
        ValueName: GroupPolicyRefreshTimeOffset
```

```
        ValueType: REG_DWORD
        Value:      0x00000030
   The following settings were applied from: Faculty Members Users Policy
        KeyName:    Software\Microsoft\Windows\CurrentVersion\Policies\Explorer
        ValueName: NoRecentDocsMenu
        ValueType: REG_DWORD
        Value:      0x00000001
   The following settings were applied from: Anthropology User Policy
        KeyName:    Software\Microsoft\Windows\CurrentVersion\Policies\Explorer
        ValueName: NoFavoritesMenu
        ValueType: REG_DWORD
        Value:      0x00000001
=================================================================
The user received "Folder Redirection" settings from these GPOs:
   Folder Redirection Policy
        Revision Number: 6
        Unique Name:    {066B8FFE-3469-4B16-B7FB-33D1BA313BB5}
        Domain Name:    oakmont.edu
        Linked to:      Domain (DC=oakmont,DC=edu)
                        Faculty Members Users Policy
        Revision Number: 42
        Unique Name:    {59FC7592-E6EB-4CD1-961B-E94925EEE141}
        Domain Name:    oakmont.edu
        Linked to:      Organizational Unit (OU=Faculty
Members,DC=oakmont,DC=edu)
   My Documents is redirected to \\oakmont-dc1\facultyusers$\%username%.
##################################################################
   Computer Group Policy results for:
   CN=FAC389726594,OU=Computers,OU=Faculty Members,DC=oakmont,DC=edu
   Domain Name: OAKMONTU
   Domain Type: Windows 2000
   Site Name:   Oakland
   The computer is a member of the following security groups:
        BUILTIN\Administrators
        \Everyone
        BUILTIN\Users
        OAKMONTU\FAC389726594$
        OAKMONTU\Domain Computers
        NT AUTHORITY\NETWORK
        NT AUTHORITY\Authenticated Users
##################################################################
Last time Group Policy was applied: Wednesday, August 09, 2000 at 8:12:45 AM
Group Policy was applied from: oakmont-dc1.oakmont.edu
=================================================================
The computer received "Registry" settings from these GPOs:
   Local Group Policy
        Revision Number: 2
        Unique Name:    Local Group Policy
        Domain Name:
        Linked to:      Local computer
   Default Domain Policy
        Revision Number: 30
        Unique Name:    {31B2F340-016D-11D2-945F-00C04FB984F9}
        Domain Name:    oakmont.edu
```

```
        Linked to:        Domain (DC=oakmont,DC=edu)
   The following settings were applied from: Local Group Policy
        KeyName:    Software\Policies\Microsoft\SystemCertificates\EFS
        ValueName: EFSBlob
        ValueType: REG_BINARY
        Value:      Binary data.  Use the /S switch to display.
...
   The following settings were applied from: Default Domain Policy
        KeyName:    Software\Microsoft\Windows\CurrentVersion\Policies\System
        ValueName: VerboseStatus
        ValueType: REG_DWORD
        Value:      0x00000001
...

        KeyName:    Software\Policies\Microsoft\Windows\Installer
        ValueName: AlwaysInstallElevated
        ValueType: REG_DWORD
        Value:      0x00000001
================================================================
The computer received "Security" settings from these GPOs:
   Default Domain Policy
        Revision Number: 30
        Unique Name:      {31B2F340-016D-11D2-945F-00C04FB984F9}
        Domain Name:      OAKMONT.EDU
        Linked to:        Domain (DC=oakmont,DC=edu)
                          Faculty Computers Policy
        Revision Number: 3
        Unique Name:      {F68B7691-7BDF-4A24-B01C-4BB482FB6712}
        Domain Name:      OAKMONT.EDU
        Linked to:        Organizational Unit (OU=Computers,
                          OU=Faculty Members,DC=oakmont,DC=edu)
   Run the Security Configuration Editor for more information.
================================================================
The computer received "EFS recovery" settings from these GPOs:
   Local Group Policy
        Revision Number: 2
        Unique Name:      Local Group Policy
        Domain Name:
        Linked to:        Local computer
   Default Domain Policy
        Revision Number: 30
        Unique Name:      {31B2F340-016D-11D2-945F-00C04FB984F9}
        Domain Name:      oakmont.edu
        Linked to:        Domain (DC=oakmont,DC=edu)
   Additional information is not available for this type of policy setting.
================================================================
The computer received "Application Management" settings from these GPOs:
   Default Domain Policy
        Revision Number: 30
        Unique Name:      {31B2F340-016D-11D2-945F-00C04FB984F9}
        Domain Name:      OAKMONT.EDU
        Linked to:        Domain (DC=oakmont,DC=edu)
   The computer has been assigned the following applications:
        (None)
```

You also can run Gpresult.exe /s, which expands the binary blob data of user certificates and provides a bit more detail for some elements.

The Resource Kit also includes a Gpotool.exe application that you can use to check the health of your GPOs on DC(s). Run Gpotool with no arguments for a quick check. Following is the output of Gpotool.exe /verbose for the first and last policies of the server used for the examples in this and the preceding chapters.

```
Domain: oakmont.edu
Validating DCs...
oakmont-dc1.oakmont.edu: OK
Available DCs:
oakmont-dc1.oakmont.edu
Searching for policies...
Found 21 policies
============================================================
Policy {066B8FFE-3469-4B16-B7FB-33D1BA313BB5}
Policy OK
Details:
------------------------------------------------------------
DC: oakmont-dc1.oakmont.edu
Friendly name: Folder Redirection Policy
Created: 8/9/2000 12:03:55 AM
Changed: 8/9/2000 4:35:44 PM
DS version:      7(user) 0(machine)
Sysvol version: 7(user) 0(machine)
Flags: 0
User extensions: [{25537BA6-77A8-11D2-9B6C-0000F8080861}
    {88E729D6-BDC1-11D1-BD2A-00C04FB9603F}]
Machine extensions: not found
Functionality version: 2
------------------------------------------------------------
    ...
============================================================
Policy {FC5AD53A-9912-4921-8C33-A1AB7F438046}
Policy OK
Details:
------------------------------------------------------------
DC: oakmont-dc1.oakmont.edu
Friendly name: Administrative Staff User Policy
Created: 7/28/2000 11:59:27 PM
Changed: 7/29/2000 12:00:27 AM
DS version:      1(user) 0(machine)
Sysvol version: 1(user) 0(machine)
Flags: 2
User extensions: [{35378EAC-683F-11D2-A89A-00C04FBBCFA2}
    {0F6B957E-509E-11D1-A7CC-0000F87571E3}]
Machine extensions: not found
Functionality version: 2
------------------------------------------------------------
Policies OK
```

Chapter 25 of the Resource Kit's *Microsoft Windows 2000 Server Distributed Systems Guide*, includes "Group Policy Issues" and "User Data Management" sections. Most of the possible causes of redirection problems and their solutions are elementary; loss of server connectivity is the most common issue.

Configuring Roaming User Profiles

Compared to setting up and testing folder redirection, configuring roaming profiles for users is a piece of cake. The only hitch is that, as mentioned earlier, you must add the Profile Path attribute for each user, either manually or with a script. By default, roaming profiles copy the entire profile, including the contents of My Documents and My Pictures, to the server. The user has exclusive rights to the server-stored copy of the profile, so the same share and folder permissions required for user-exclusive redirected folders apply to roaming profiles. The workstation maintains a copy of the profile for use when the user is offline; thus, the offline files feature is disabled for user profiles. Unlike redirected folders, files that are hidden in the user's profile also are hidden in the roaming profile.

CODE BLUE
Roaming profiles don't support encrypted files because the user's encryption key is included in the profile's content. Redirected folders don't have this limitation, because the key is in the local user profile.

NOTE: The GroupPol application has an option that lets you automatically specify roaming profiles when you create new users. Launch GroupPol.exe, click Options, mark the Add Home Directory Paths for Employees and Add User Profile Paths for Employees check boxes, and click OK. The path is *ServerName**ShareName**OUName*\\Users$.

Setting Policies for Roaming Profiles

As with Folder Redirection policies, it's a good practice to create a separate GPO for roaming profiles that you can filter by Security Group. Make sure that users of roaming profiles aren't subject to GPOs that apply Folder Redirection policies.

The following two useful policies for roaming profiles are in User Configuration\ Administrative Templates\System\Logon/Logoff:

✦ **Exclude Directories in Roaming Profile** lets you exclude folders that are included in the user's profile by typing a semicolon-separated list of folders, based on the path to the folder's root. Excluded folders aren't stored on the network server, so they don't follow users to other computers. The default list is Local Settings;Temporary Internet Files;History;Temp. The suggested addition is My Documents\My Pictures;Templates;Favorites. Templates are particularly troublesome when you attempt to remove an obsolete profile from the server; sharing conflicts often occur with templates. Omitting the Favorites folder, which by default contains Microsoft marketing links, is a matter of user policy.

✦ **Limit Profile Size** lets you specify the maximum size, in kilobytes, of a roaming profile and the message that appears when a roaming user profile reaches the maximum size. By default, the space occupied by the Registry hive file (Ntuser.dat) isn't included in the quota. You also can set the interval between reminders to the user. If you enable the policy, the default maximum size is 30 MB; otherwise, the profile's size is unlimited unless you enforce disk quotas.

The following five policies in Computer Configuration\Administrative Templates\System\ Logon let you tune roaming profile operations, but apply to everyone who logs on to the computer unless you link them to an OU or filter the GPO:

✦ **Delete Cached Copies of Roaming Profiles** prevents saving of a copy of the user's roaming profile on the local computer when the user logs off. Apply this policy for occasional users of a machine and, especially, help desk technicians who use roaming profiles that include copies of diagnostic tools, such as Gpresult.exe, which are subject to per-location licenses. Deleting the local copy of the profile saves workstation disk space.

✦ **Wait for Remote User Profile** causes a wait for the remote copy of the roaming user profile to load, regardless of the speed of the connection. Enabling the Do Not Detect Slow Network Connection policy moots this policy.

✦ **Maximum Retries to Unload and Update User Profile** specifies the number of attempts made to unload and update Ntuser.dat for the profile. The default value is 60 retries in one minute; a 0 value prevents retrying of the operation after a failure. The retry rate is fixed at once per second.

✦ **Log Users Off When Roaming Profile Fails** automatically logs off users if the roaming user profile won't load, which is the same as creating an individual mandatory profile for the user. Otherwise, the local copy of the profile loads, if it is present; the default user profile loads when the server-stored copy isn't accessible.

✦ **Timeout for Dialog Boxes** lets you specify the length of time before the system applies a default response to a profile-related message box or dialog. The default timeout is 30 seconds.

Windows NT–style roaming profiles have been around for several years and thus are quite bulletproof. Policies that affect profiles are contained in Administrative Templates and so can be enabled or disabled, unlike Folder Redirection's missing "Disable this feature" setting. The "Contents of a user profile" topic in the Windows 2000 Server and Professional online help describes the new folders included in Windows 2000 profiles.

Removing Server-Stored Profiles

By default, users can disregard roaming profiles by right-clicking My Computer and choosing Properties to open the System Properties dialog. The User Profiles page has the user's roaming profile in the list. Selecting the profile and clicking Change Type opens the Change Profile Type dialog, where the user can select the Roaming Profile or Local Profile option. Users can't change their domain user account properties, other than passwords, so an administrator must remove the Profile Path entry from the Profiles page of the *UserName* Properties dialog. After the change, the user no longer has the option to create a roaming profile.

The user owns his or her server-stored roaming profile, so admins can't delete a profile without taking ownership of the folder and its contents, subfolders, and objects in subfolders. In most instances, marking the Reset Permissions on All Child Objects... check box when taking ownership of the folder lets you delete it. If you receive a "Cannot delete Launch Outlook Express.lnk; access is denied" or similar error message when attempting deletion, you must do the following:

1. Navigate to the Application Data\Microsoft\Internet Explorer\Quick Launch folder and select all three shortcuts.

2. Open the Security page of the Properties dialog for the multiple selection, add the Administrators group, and give the group Allow Full Control permissions on the shortcuts.

3. Delete the Quick Launch folder.

4. Navigate back to the *UserName* folder, multiselect the four Ntuser.* files, and repeat step 2 for these files.

5. Select the *UserName* folder and press Delete, which doesn't delete the folder. Press Delete again to finally get rid of it.

If you didn't exclude the Templates folder with the Exclude Directories in Roaming Profile policy, you might encounter a "Sharing violation" error when attempting to delete the folder. If so, the most expeditious method of deleting the folder is to reboot the server; a production alternative is to wait until after the next scheduled server shutdown to remove the folder.

Chapter 5

Enforcing Local Computer Policies

L ocal computer policies are the "low man on the totem pole" of Group Policy. All computers running versions of Windows 2000, ranging from Professional to Datacenter Server, have a default local security policy that's established when you perform a clean installation of Windows 2000 or upgrade a computer from Windows NT or 9x. Windows 2000 Professional has the same set of Administrative Templates as the Server versions. Thus, you can set a full gamut of local policies that apply until overwritten when the computer joins a domain that has customized Group Policy in effect and the user logs on with a domain account. The primary difference between local and AD-based Group Policy is that a single local policy applies to all users of the computer. The current version of Windows 2000 doesn't support multiple local GPOs that you can filter by group membership.

NOTE: Knowledge Base article Q218601, "Local Group Policy Objects Cannot Be Set on a Per-User Basis," states: "The ability to have multiple local group policy objects and have Access Control List (ACL) filtering for local group policy objects is being considered for inclusion in the next version of Microsoft Windows." Perhaps the forthcoming "Whistler" upgrade will support multiple local GPOs. In the meantime, disregard the article's recommendation to implement group-based Windows NT 4.0–style system policies for Windows 2000 clients.

Local GPO settings aren't of much consequence when you override them with GPOs applied at the site, domain, and OU level. But if you want to test Group Policy scenarios for specific users before you establish DC-delivered policies, setting local policies is an effective, albeit tedious, means of accomplishing test objectives. You must manually apply the local GPO settings to each test workstation. Combining domain-level security settings from Securews.inf or Securedc.inf with specialized local security settings lets you customize individual workstation or member server security.

CODE BLUE

Microsoft identified in late August 2000 a potential Windows 2000 security vulnerability, "Local Security Policy Corruption." A malicious network user with the ability to create an RPC connection to a workstation or server can send a series of commands that corrupt the local security policy database and remove the computer from the domain. An attack on a DC prevents the DC from processing logon requests, and recovery requires restoration of the DC from a known-good backup. If your Internet firewall is misconfigured and allows external RPC traffic to pass to your internal network, a hacker can mount an attack from the Internet and disable your entire network. The attacker doesn't need to be authenticated by the domain to take advantage of the vulnerability. Applying Windows 2000 Service Pack 1 or a hot-fix closes this security hole. Microsoft Security Bulletin MS00-062, available at http://www.microsoft.com/technet/Security/Bulletin/ms00-062.asp, provides additional information on the subject.

Using the Local Security Settings Console

The Local Security Settings console (Secpol.msc) is the primary tool for verifying the degree of local computer security. Secpol.msc is an extension snap-in for the Group Policy Editor (Gpedit.msc) that displays computer-based security settings in two columns: Local Setting and Effective Setting. The computer's local GPO generates the Local Setting entries, and GPOs at the site, domain, and OU level overwrite the Local Setting values to establish the Effective Setting entries. Figure 5-1 illustrates the default local policies for Windows 2000 Professional superceded by the Default Domain Policy GPO with the Securews.inf template applied. The Passwords Must Meet Complexity Requirements setting of Securews.inf has been disabled to accommodate GroupPol's use of "password" for user accounts.

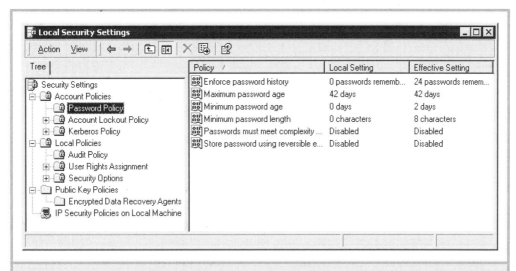

Figure 5-1. Secpol.msc displays the Local Security Settings console, which shows local and effective settings for each node except Encrypted Data Recovery Agents and IP Security Policies on Local Machine.

The shortcut to the Local Security Settings console is buried under Control Panel's Administrative Tools group. Members of the Domain Admins group have a Programs | Administrative Tools menu that includes a Local Security Policy choice. Ordinary local and domain users don't see the Administrative Tools menu; they can navigate to Control Panel's Local Security Policy shortcut, but they receive an "Access is denied" message if they try to open Secpol.msc. The same message appears when users attempt to open Secpol.msc from the Run dialog. The message "MMC cannot open the selected file" appears when users try to run mmc secpol.msc from the command prompt.

TIP: Hold SHIFT and right-click an MMC icon to open the Run As Other User dialog; type your user name, password, and domain in the text boxes; and click OK. Alternatively, use Runas in the Run dialog or at the command prompt to run Secpol.msc and other administrative tools on a workstation when you're not logged on with Administrators rights. For example, type **runas /user:administrator@***domain.ext* "mmc secpol.msc" and supply your password when requested.

If you remove the workstation from the domain by making it a member of a workgroup, only the security settings of the local GPO apply. Replacement of records in the security database accounts for much of the hiatus between the shutdown and startup processes when removing workstations from a domain. When you log on after the required reboot with the local Administrator account, the Programs | Administrative Tools menu is missing. You must navigate to Control Panel's Administrative Tools group to launch Secpol.msc or start it from the Run dialog. The values in Secpol.msc's Local Setting and Effective Setting columns are identical for workstations not joined to a domain.

Working with the Computer Management Console

Members of the local Administrators group and Domain Admins, if the workstation is a member of a domain, have full access to all of the functions of the workstation's Computer Management console (Compmgmt.msc). All users can run Compmgmt.msc by right-clicking My Computer and choosing Manage, navigating to Control Panel's Administrative Tools group and double-clicking Computer Management, or typing **compmgmt.msc** in the Open text box of the Run dialog. Domain Admins also have a Programs | Administrative Tools | Computer Management menu choice. Ordinary users have very limited rights to the extension snap-ins. Following are the extensions that return errors when an ordinary user clicks a node:

- **Event Viewer**   Security Log returns the message "A requested privilege is not held by the client."

- **Performance Logs and Alerts**   Returns a message indicating that the feature hasn't been installed, if the Administrator hasn't used the feature.

- **Shared Folders**   Shares, Sessions, and Open Files return the message "Access is denied."

- **Device Manager**   Returns a message indicating that the user can't modify device settings, but it permits driver information to be viewed.

- **Local Users and Groups**   Users and Groups return an "Access is denied" error message when users attempt to add new users or users to groups.

- **Disk Manager**   Returns the message "You don't have access rights to the service."

- **Disk Defragmenter**   Returns the message "You must have Administrator privileges to defragment a volume."

- **Logical Drives**   Returns the message "Media may be write-protected" when the user attempts to change a drive property value.

- **Services and Applications**   Services returns the message "Access is denied" when the user tries to alter Startup or other settings.

You can alter ordinary user access to a few of the preceding functions, such as the ability to view the Security log, on Secpol.msc's Security Settings\Local Policies\User Rights Assignment node. It's not a common practice, however, to modify local security policies for computers joined to a domain.

Adding Local Group Policy to a New Computer Management Console

The ability to display the contents of a remote workstation's Computer Management console from Active Directory Users and Computers is useful for diagnosing some computer problems, but the Computer Management console doesn't let Domain Admins view or edit the workstation's local GPO remotely. The workstation's local Group Policy

Editor (GPE) opens with the Local Security Settings extension snap-in and Administrative Templates for Computer Configuration and User Configuration. Although you can add the Group Policy snap-in to Compmgmt.msc, when you manage a workstation remotely, the added snap-in doesn't appear. Remote management uses the Remote Registry service to populate a local instance of Compmgmt.msc with values returned from the remote computer's Registry.

TIP: Use Terminal Services' Administrative mode, not Compmgmt.msc, to manage DCs and member servers.

Viewing the full complement of the local GPO remotely requires creation of a new snap-in that contains the Group Policy stand-alone snap-in and, optionally, the Computer Management snap-in. As a member of Domain Admins, you can create a snap-in on a server or your administrative workstation and specify a remote computer as the source of the snap-in data. Unfortunately, specifying a remote computer as the source of the local GPO doesn't include the Account Policies, Local Policies, or Public Key nodes under the Local Computer Policy\Computer Configuration\Windows Settings\Security Settings node. Its only subnode is IP Security Policies on Local Machine. You can, however, view and set all other policies except computer- or user-based Software Settings. If you apply security settings at the domain level, the missing Security Settings nodes aren't fatal to Group Policy test regimens.

NOTE: Microsoft's decision to prevent remote viewing and modification of workstations' security settings might be motivated by overall security concerns. The restriction requires physical access to the workstation by a person with administrative privileges for the machine to alter local security settings. Anyone with Domain Admins rights, however, can override the settings by modifying the Default Domain Policy.

To create a new Computer Management and Group Policy snap-in for a specific remote computer, do the following:

1. Log on to the local or administrative workstation with Domain Admins credentials and execute Mmc.exe from the Run dialog.

2. Choose Console | Add/Remove Snap-in to open the Standalone page of the Add/Remove Snap-in dialog, and click Add to open the Add Standalone Snap-in dialog.

3. Double-click the Computer Management item to open the dialog of the same name.

4. Select the Another Computer option and type the name of the computer, **FAC389726594** for this example, in the adjacent text box. Alternatively, click Browse to open the Select Computer dialog and double-click the computer name in the list to add its FQDN to the text box (see Figure 5-2).

NOTE: If you don't specify the remote computer name, Computer Management applies to the computer on which you run the console.

5. Mark the Allow the Selected Computer to be Changed When Launching from the Command Line check box; then click Finish and Close to return to the Add/Remove Snap-in dialog.

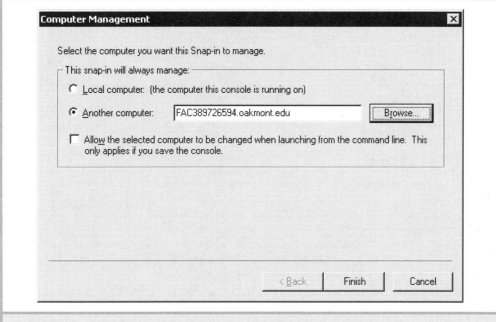

Figure 5-2.　Adding the remote computer name for the Computer Management snap-in from the Select Computer dialog appends the domain name to provide the FQDN of the computer account.

6. Select Computer Management in the Snap-ins Added to list and double-click the Group Policy item to open the Select Group Policy Object dialog.

7. Click Browse to open the Browse for a Group Policy Object dialog and click the Computers tab. Select the Another Computer option, click Browse to open the Select Computer dialog, and double-click the computer name in the list to add it to the Another Computer text box (see Figure 5-3).

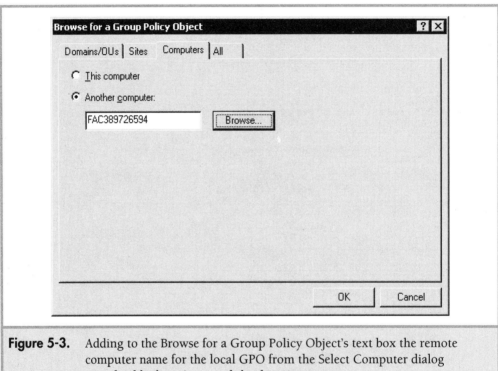

Figure 5-3. Adding to the Browse for a Group Policy Object's text box the remote computer name for the local GPO from the Select Computer dialog inexplicably doesn't append the domain name.

8. Mark the Allow the Focus of the Group Policy Snap-in to be Changed When Launching from the Command Line check box; then click Finish and Close.

9. Choose Console | Options to open the Options dialog, select User Mode - Full Access in the Console Mode list, and click OK. You can open the console in Author mode to make changes by right-clicking its file and choosing Author.

10. Click OK to close the Add/Remove Snap-in dialog and then choose Console | Save As. Type the computer name in the File Name text box and click Save to add the snap-in to the Administrative Tools subfolder of your Documents and Settings\Administrator folder. Saving the snap-in in this location adds a shortcut, FAC389726594.msc for this example, to your personal Programs | Administrative Tools menu.

Testing Operation of the Remote Console

To perform a quick test of the console you authored and verify that the two snap-ins return data from the specified computer, do this:

1. Choose Programs | Administrative Tools | *ComputerName*.msc to open the new snap-in in user mode and expand the *ComputerName* Policy nodes (see Figure 5-4). Unlike with Secpol.msc, the Policy list doesn't have Local Setting and Effective Setting columns; only the local policy configuration status appears in the Setting column.

NOTE: It's unfortunate that the designers of the GPE didn't provide Local Setting and Effective Setting columns for all policies. The feature would simplify confirmation of AD-based policy application, eliminating (at least in most cases) the need to run Gpresult.exe on the local computer.

2. Enable one of the more innocuous policies, such as Computer Configuration\ Administrative Templates\System\Verbose vs Normal Status Messages. On the remote workstation, run Gpedit.msc and confirm the change to the policy value. You don't need to restart the computer to see the policy value change, because the remote console operates directly on the remote computer's Registry. There's no Refresh choice on the Group Policy snap-in, so you must close and reopen Gpedit.msc to see the changes, reboot to apply local Computer Configuration changes, and log off and on to apply User Configuration changes.

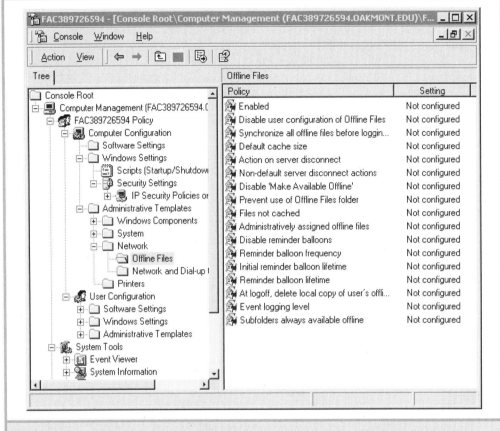

Figure 5-4. The expanded remote management console shows the Security Settings node without the Account Policies, Local Policies, and Public Key nodes. The Policy pane displays only local GPO settings.

3. Expand the System Tools | System Information node and click System Summary to verify that Compmgmt.msc points to the remote computer, not the computer on which you're running the console (see Figure 5-5). If you click Device Manager, you receive a warning that this element runs in read-only mode when opened on a remote computer.

If you need full remote control over all your workstations, including those running Windows NT and 9x, license Microsoft Systems Management Server 2.0 SP 2+ or

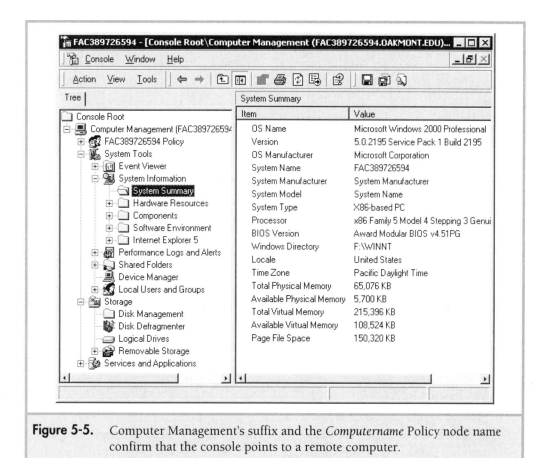

Figure 5-5.   Computer Management's suffix and the *Computername* Policy node name confirm that the console points to a remote computer.

remote control applications, such as Symantec pcAnywhere. For more information on Windows 2000 and SMS, check out *Admin911: Systems Management Server* by Rod Trent (Osborne/McGraw-Hill, 2001; ISBN 0-07-213022-9).

Using the Remote Console for Group Policy User Evaluation

One of the most productive uses of remote management consoles is to test user reaction to specific User Configuration\Administrative Templates policies before applying them with AD-based policies. Depending on the mode of the test, you can be up front or surreptitious when changing local user policies. User-based changes on the local machine take place immediately, not after the 60-minute to 90-minute delay that characterizes AD-applied policies with the standard refresh interval. The user must log off and on, however, for many local policy changes to be applied fully or at all. Changes to Computer Configuration require rebooting the machine and so aren't likely to be effective in surreptitious mode.

Applying Security Configuration Templates to Local Policy

The "Security Configuration Templates" section of Chapter 1 introduced the use of Windows 2000's built-in templates for setting security on workstations, member servers, and DCs. Applying the Securews.inf or Securedc.inf template to the Computer Configuration\ Windows Settings\Security Settings policies of your Default Domain Policy GPO assigns a setting to almost every important security policy. Following are the primary exceptions:

❖ **User Rights Assignment** isn't altered by any of the standard Basic??.inf, Secure??.inf, and Hisec??.inf security configuration templates. The Setup security.inf template establishes user rights for workstations and servers during Windows 2000 installation. The Professional and Server template versions differ slightly. The Server version adds rights for the anonymous IUSER_*SERVERNAME* and IWAM_*SERVERNAME* Internet user accounts when installing Internet Information Server 5.0, and the NetShowServices account if you add Windows Media Services to the server.

❖ **Security Options** are established by Setup security.inf, and the standard templates apply only a few changes. For example, applying the Securews.inf or Securesv.inf template to the Default Domain Policy alters the settings of only 11 of the 38 Security Options policies.

❖ **System Services** aren't modified by any standard template. Setup security.inf establishes the start mode and permissions for each service, which differ for workstations and servers.

❖ **Restricted Groups** are modified only by the Compatws.inf and Securews.inf templates, which prohibit adding users to the Power Users group. Setup security.inf adds Authenticated Users and the INTERACTIVE user account to the Users group.

❖ **Registry** and **File System** aren't modified by the standard templates. Setup security.inf establishes basic initial security on Registry keys and system files.

NOTE: System Services, Restricted Groups, Registry, and File System don't appear in the Local Security Settings snap-in, so you can't view changes applied by higher-priority GPOs to these settings.

Central management of workstation and server security policy by application of GPOs at the site, domain, and OU levels is the preferred practice. Central security policies make configuration management of large single domains practical, but require placing computer accounts in OUs and, in some cases, assigning computer accounts to Security Groups. Special Group Policy implementations, however, might require use of the Security Configuration Templates to upgrade the security of individual workstations or member servers. Following are a few conditions under which you might want to apply a template on an individual workstation or member server:

+ Member servers need increased security, but their computer accounts aren't in OUs or groups to which you can apply a domain-level GPO.

+ Individual member servers need special security policies, such as Restricted Group membership, based on the sensitivity of the resources they provide.

+ Particular Windows 2000 workstations must encrypt network communication with servers.

+ Workstations used by developers need special security privileges.

Bear in mind when contemplating modifications to local policies that you must decommission any security policies applied at the site, domain, or OU level that conflict with the local policy settings you want to apply. Setting higher-priority policies to Not Configured to accommodate local policy can compromise the security of your entire domain or individual OUs.

Adding Security Configuration Templates to a Console

It's a good practice to review the settings applied by security templates before applying them to the local computer. The Security Configuration snap-in lets you view the settings applied to the Computer Configuration\Windows Settings\Security Settings subnodes by every .inf file on the local workstation or server. Microsoft describes security templates as incremental, because applying a Secure??.inf template and then a Hisec??.inf template progressively increases the security level.

To create a new console containing Local Group Policy and Security Templates snap-ins, do this on a test workstation:

1. Run Mmc.exe to open a new console and add the Group Policy snap-in as described in the section "Adding Local Group Policy to a New Computer Management Console" earlier in this chapter.

2. Add the Security Templates snap-in.

3. Save the console in the default Administrative Tools folder to add an entry for it to your Administrative Tools menu.

4. Expand the Security Templates node to display the list of templates added to the console (see Figure 5-6).

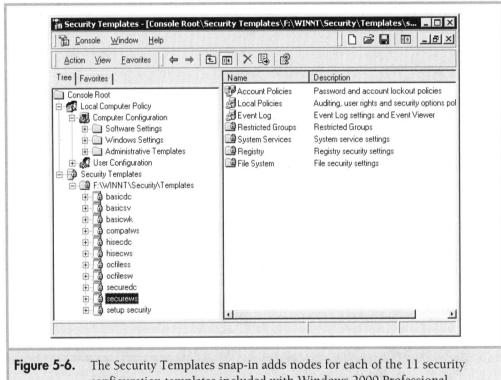

Figure 5-6. The Security Templates snap-in adds nodes for each of the 11 security configuration templates included with Windows 2000 Professional and Server.

When you expand the Local Group Policy's Windows Settings\Security Settings node, the System Services, Restricted Groups, Registry, and File System nodes that are present when you open an AD-based GPO on a DC are missing from local policies. The only way to alter these local settings is to modify the template you intend to apply to the workstation.

Creating Customized Security Configuration Templates

Modifying the standard templates isn't a good management practice, because you might want to revert local policy settings to a standard condition after a test. It's easy to forget which settings you modified, and unless you export the original and modified settings to a local file, documentation of template modifications can disappear. Another reason for maintaining the original templates is for use in validating security setting changes you make with the Security Configuration and Analysis Snap-in discussed later in the chapter.

The better approach is to create a new security information template by adding a new empty template to the console or copying an existing template within the \Winnt\Security\ Templates folder. In either case, you can edit the template and apply it to the \Computer Configuration\Windows Settings\Security Settings node. After testing, you can copy the new template and apply it to other workstations or member servers.

Adding a New Empty Template

You can use the following steps to add a new template in which all security settings are Not Configured:

1. Right-click the *D*:\Winnt\Security\Templates node and choose New Template to open the *D*:\Winnt\Security\Templates dialog.

2. Type a name for the template, such as **Customws**, in the Template Name text box, and add a brief comment on the purpose of the template in the Description text box.

3. Click OK to add the empty template to the list.

TIP: Right-click the name of any template and choose Set Description to open a dialog with a text box that displays the template's description. The terse descriptions written by Microsoft's standard template developers leave much to the imagination.

Copying an Existing Template

Copying a template that has settings that approximate those you want to apply to the workstation minimizes the number of manual changes you need to make. To add a copy of a template to the console, do this:

1. Navigate to \Winnt\Security\Templates and create a copy of a standard template: Securews.inf for this example.

2. Rename the copy to a descriptive file name: in this case, **CustomSecws.inf**.

3. On the console, right-click the D:\Winnt\Security\Templates node and choose Refresh to add the template copy to the templates list.

TIP: If you close the console and are prompted to save changes to any of the standard templates, don't. Save only changes to the console itself.

Modifying Custom Template Settings

The procedures for modifying security configuration templates don't vary significantly from the methods for making changes to security-related elements of the Local Computer Policy GPO. You can change most local security policies in the Local Computer Policy GPO, but Event Log, Restricted Groups, System Services, Registry, and File System aren't accessible. Event Log's Setting for Event Logs subnode uses conventional policy editing dialogs to alter settings. Policies under the other four nodes use specialized methods for setting values. If you want to give the upcoming Security and Configuration Analysis snap-in a full-scale trial run, make the changes described in the following four sections.

Restricted Groups

One of the most common reasons for customizing security templates is to restrict membership of groups, especially the local Administrators group, that have nearly unlimited user rights on the local machine. You restrict local group membership by doing the following:

1. Right-click the Restricted Groups node and choose Add Groups to open the dialog.

2. Type the name of the group to add, such as **Administrators**, in the text box, and click OK to add the group to the list.

3. Double-click the group you just added to open the Configure Membership for GroupName dialog, which opens with the default "<This group should contain no members>" and "<The groups to which this group belongs should not be modified>" messages.

4. Click the upper Add button to open the Add Member dialog, type the name of the user or group—**Administrator** in this case—and click OK to add the user.

TIP: To improve security, you should change the name of the Administrator account before restricting Administrators group membership.

5. Repeat step 4 for each additional user or group to add: **Domain Admins** for this example (see Figure 5-7).

6. If you want to modify the group's membership, click the lower Add button and repeat steps 4 and 5 for each group. Restricting group membership during this process isn't a common practice.

7. Click OK to close the dialog and add your selections to the Members column. If you restricted group membership in step 6, the groups appear in the Member Of column.

CAUTION: Make sure that you add at least one local account to a restricted group so you can continue to administer the computer after disjoining it from a domain.

System Services

If you have resource-challenged workstations, you might want to disable specific services, such as Fax Service and Indexing Service. Setup security.inf installs most unneeded services with Manual startup mode specified, although a few Manual-mode services, such as COM+ Event System, start by default. You might want to change the mode of some Manual services to Automatic. Applying a System Services policy prevents users with access to the Services and Applications element of Computer Management from changing the settings for a service.

To alter System Services settings, follow this drill:

1. Double-click the service you want to change to open the Template Security Policy Setting dialog and mark the Define This Policy Setting check box.

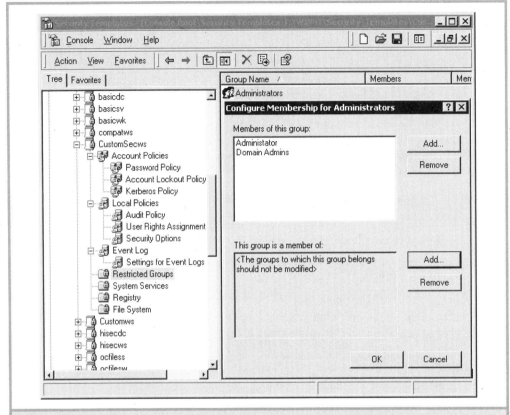

Figure 5-7. You can restrict membership in a local Administrators group to the default Administrator account and Domain Admins group, or to any other combination required to achieve your local security objective.

2. Select the service startup mode option, usually Disabled, which automatically opens the Security for *ServiceName* dialog. Strangely, by default Everyone has Allow Full Control privileges on the service.

3. Select the Everyone group, click Remove, and click Add to select a better choice, such as the local Administrators group, and assign Allow Full Control rights (see Figure 5-8).

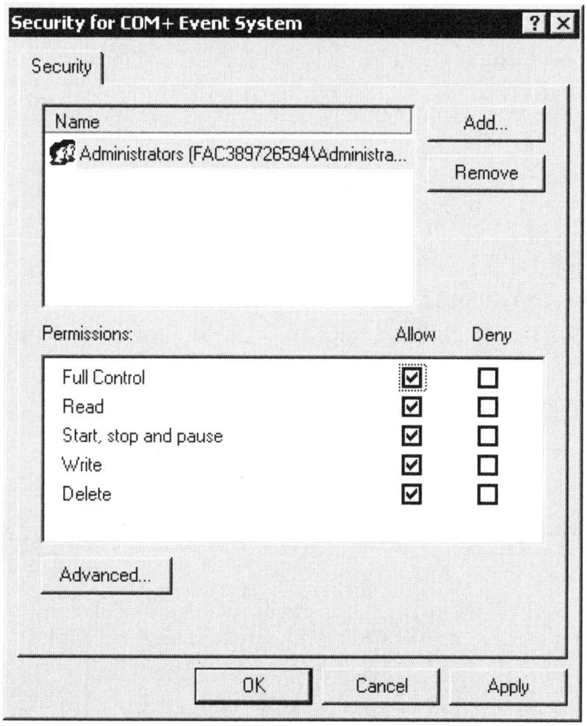

Figure 5-8.   Give the local Administrators group, not Everyone, Full Control
permissions on services you disable in the custom template.

4. Add any other groups that should have rights to the services; then click OK twice
to return to the console. The setting you selected in step 2 appears in the Startup
column, and the Permission column displays Configured.

Registry

There probably aren't many occasions to set security restrictions on individual Registry
keys, because removing nonadministrative users' access to the Registry editing tools is one

of the first domainwide policies you apply. Completeness, however, dictates the following procedure description:

1. Right click the Registry node and choose Add Key to open the Select Registry Key dialog.

2. Select and expand the hive in which the key you want to protect is located and select the key to add it to the Selected Key text box.

3. Click OK to open the Database Security for *KeyName* dialog.

4. Change the security on the key, as you did in steps 3 and 4 in the preceding section, and click OK to open another Template Security Policy Setting dialog in which to set the permissions that apply to the key and its subkeys.

5. Select Replace Existing Permissions on All Subkeys with Inheritable Permissions to change any explicit permissions that may have been applied to subkeys to inherited permissions (see Figure 5-9).

6. Click OK to return to the console. The policy you established adds the key name, Replace, and Replace to the Object Name, Permissions, and Audit columns, respectively.

File System

File System is another policy that you set only occasionally, but it's worth the minute or two required to exercise the Security Configuration and Analysis Snap-in. Ergo, do this:

1. Right-click the File System node and choose Add File to open the Add Folder or File dialog.

2. Navigate to and select a noncritical folder to secure, such as \Program Files\GroupPol or \Winnt\Repair, and click OK to open the Database Security on *PathToFolder* dialog.

3. Repeat the usual exercise, removing Everyone's permission and granting Full Control to the local Administrators group.

4. Click OK to open the same inheritance dialog as appeared for Registry security settings. Select the same option as in the preceding section and click OK twice to return to the console.

TIP: After you invest time in making your template modifications, it's a good practice to save the console, close it, save the changes to your custom template, and then reopen it.

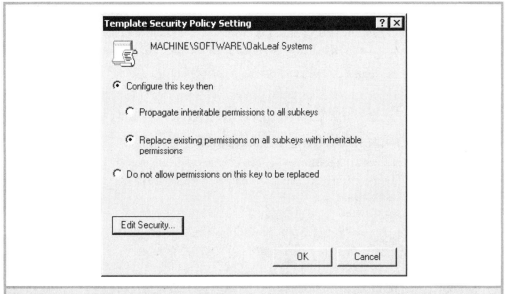

Figure 5-9. Specify inherited permissions for subkeys of the selected key. Running the GroupPol.msi Installer file adds an empty OakLeaf Systems key to the Registry.

Using the Security Configuration and Analysis Snap-in

The Security Configuration and Analysis snap-in adds the ability to compare the workstation's current security setting with those of a standard or custom template that acts as the baseline security standard for workstations or member servers. The basic process to highlight and correct security holes is as follows:

1. Create a new security database from the template that establishes baseline security.

2. Run a security analysis on the local computer.

3. Review the flagged policies that have differences between the database and computer settings.

4. Change settings that have differences that compromise security and rerun the analysis.

5. If the computer settings are based on a customized template, alter the template settings to conform to the changes you made in the preceding step.

6. Reapply the customized template and run a final analysis.

Adding the Security Configuration and Analysis Snap-in and Generating a Baseline

One of the better features of the Security Configuration and Analysis snap-in is the quick and easy process for generating a trial security database for comparison with your local computer's settings. Here it is:

1. Open the security templates console you created earlier in the chapter in Author mode, and add the Security Configuration and Analysis snap-in. When you select the node, instructions for opening or adding a database appear in the right pane.

2. Right-click the Security Configuration and Analysis node and choose Open Database to open the eponymous dialog.

3. Type a name for the database, **Securews** for this example, and click OK to open the Import Template dialog. Security databases use an .sdb extension.

4. Double-click the template from which to generate the database: Securews.inf in this case. The name of the database you created and simple instructions for configuring and analyzing the workstation appear in the console's right pane (see Figure 5-10).

Running and Examining the Initial Analysis

Running an analysis, viewing the results, and checking the resulting log file require the following simple operations:

1. Right-click the Security Configuration and Analysis node and choose Analyze to open the Perform Analysis dialog, which proposes to save a log file in a nonoptimal location.

2. Click Browse and navigate to your Administrator\Start Menu\Administrative Tools folder where you save console files.

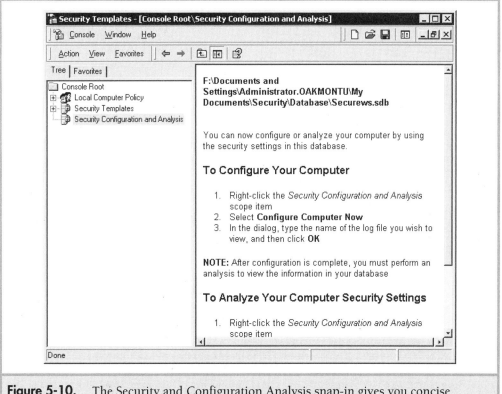

Figure 5-10. The Security and Configuration Analysis snap-in gives you concise instructions after you generate the baseline database, but the analysis step should precede configuration of your computer.

3. Click Open and OK to run the analysis, which adds a set of security configuration subnodes to the Security Configuration and Analysis node.

4. Expand each subnode in sequence to display security settings, which have Database Settings and Computer Settings columns. Policies with settings that conform to the baseline template have an icon with a circle containing a green check mark. Policies that are not configured in the database but are configured on the computer also get the green check mark. Nonconforming policies have a red "X" in the circle (see Figure 5-11).

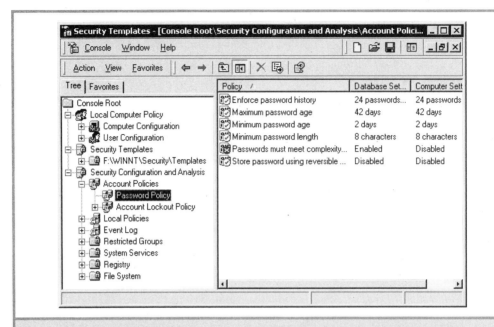

Figure 5-11. Current policy settings for the local computer that conflict with the baseline template display an icon with a red "X" in a circle, such as that shown for the Passwords Must Meet Complexity Requirements policy set by Default Domain Policy.

NOTE: The nonconforming Passwords Must Meet Complexity Requirements policy setting results from the Default Domain Policy having Securews.inf applied and the policy setting changed from Enabled to Disabled.

5. Open the log file, Securews.log for this example, and examine its contents. Lines preceded by "Mismatch" apply the red "X" icons (see Figure 5-12). The log file is of interest because it identifies policies that aren't configured by local or higher-priority GPOs.

TIP: You can open the log file in the snap-in's right pane by right-clicking the Security Configuration and Analysis node and choosing View Log.

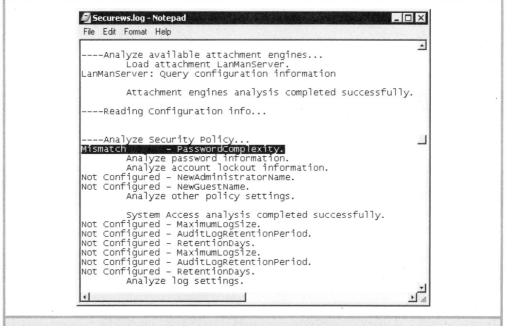

Figure 5-12.   Mismatch entries in the log file indicate conflicts in policy settings. It's often faster to run a search on "Mismatch" in the log than to navigate through the snap-in's nodes and subnodes.

Analyzing Your Modified Custom Template

Before you configure a computer with a custom security configuration template, it's a good practice to check the changes it applies to the computer's current configuration. If you added a customer template and modified its settings in accordance with the procedure described in the section "Modifying Custom Template Settings" earlier in this chapter, generate a database from it and check for mismatches with the current configuration. Here's how:

1. Right-click the Security Configuration and Analysis node, choose Open Database, type the database name, **CustomSecws** for this example, and select the corresponding custom template. Only one database can be open in the snap-in, so data from the new database replaces Securews.sdb.

2. Run the analysis and check each of the policies for red "X" icons. The modification you made to Restricted Groups appears in the right pane with a red "X" icon and "Investigate" in the Members column.

3. Double-click the entry to open the *GroupName* dialog, which displays the differences between the Database Setting and Computer Setting columns (see Figure 5-13). In this example, FAC389726594\Administrator is an AD user account, and Administrator is the local Administrator account that's used when the computer is disjoined from the domain. Thus, you should modify the template to include the domain-based Administrator account.

The modifications you made to System Services also get the red "X" treatment and "Investigate" in the Setting and Permissions columns. Registry and File System modifications display "Subitems Defined" until you navigate to the level of the modified key or folder, respectively.

After you reopen your custom template and make any fixes suggested by the Security and Configuration Analysis snap-in, you can safely import the new template to the \Computer Configuration\Windows Settings\Security Settings node.

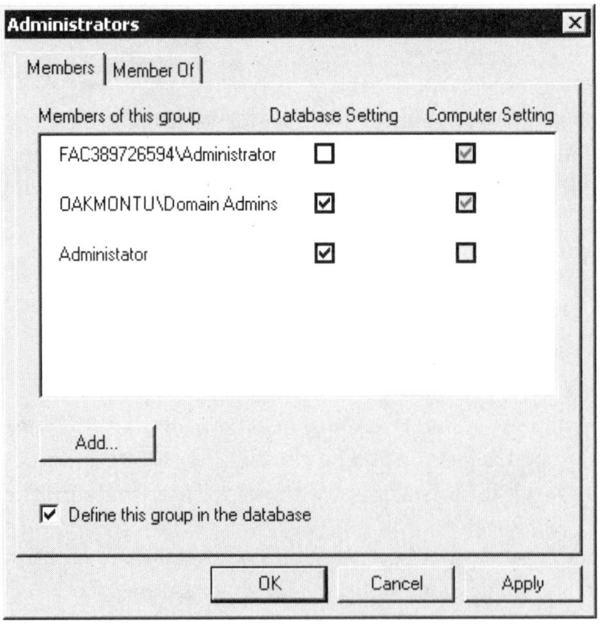

Figure 5-13. The domain-based Administrator account, prefixed with the computer name, is missing from the members of the restricted Administrators group.

Chapter 6

Applying Policies at the Site and Domain Levels

Earlier chapters of this book provide detailed examples of how to set domainwide Group Policy, so this chapter concentrates on how to establish policies for multisite domains. The primary use of site-based GPOs is to specify the location of servers that store users' redirected folders, roaming profiles, or both in a multisite environment. If you have only a single site, or if you implement child domains by geographical location, you needn't be concerned with applying policies at the site level, so you can skip to the section "Tuning Domain Security Policy" later in this chapter.

Applying Group Policies by Site

Figure 6-1 illustrates a simple two-site configuration for a single domain topology. The sites are defined by two private Class B subnets, 10.7.0.0 and 10.8.0.0, connected by routers that terminate a leased T-1 line. The Oakland and San Jose sites each have a pair of DCs to provide AD redundancy for local computer and user logon. Oakland's oakmont-dc1 server hosts the Global Catalog (GC) and handles the following FSMO roles: PDC Emulator (PDCE), schema master, domain naming master, and Relative Identifier (RID) master. The oakmont-dc2 server is the infrastructure master, acts as a backup (secondary) DNS server, and is the DHCP server for its subnet. San Jose's sjc-dc3 server maintains a copy of the GC for the site and a backup DNS server; sjc-dc4 is the DHCP server and another backup DNS server. At least one GC server is required at each site, because the Windows 2000 logon process checks a GC server to determine if the user is a member of one or more Universal groups.

Oakland handles all communication with remote users by a PPTP VPN and provides Internet connectivity to the site's clients. Windows 2000 clients can use L2TP over IPSec for greater security than PPTP, but PPTP, which all 32-bit Windows operating systems support, is adequate for most organizations. For simplicity, Oakland's hardware VPN appliance, firewall, and router are shown as a single unit. To keep client Internet traffic off the T-1 line between the sites, San Jose has its own DSL router/firewall that provides Internet services to clients.

Figure 6-2 shows AD Sites and Services displaying Servers and Subnet nodes for the Oakland and San Jose sites. Subnet IP addresses determine client computer site membership and, by inference, the site to which the user belongs. The second DC hasn't been added to the two sites illustrated by Figure 6-2.

Mapping Site Names and IP Addresses

DCs have explicit, persistent site assignments you store in AD when you move or add a DC to a site. Each Site object has an entry in AD's Configuration container; each Site object maps its associated IP subnet values to a collective in-memory structure. By default, running Dcpromo.exe to promote a member server to a DC adds the new DC to the site that

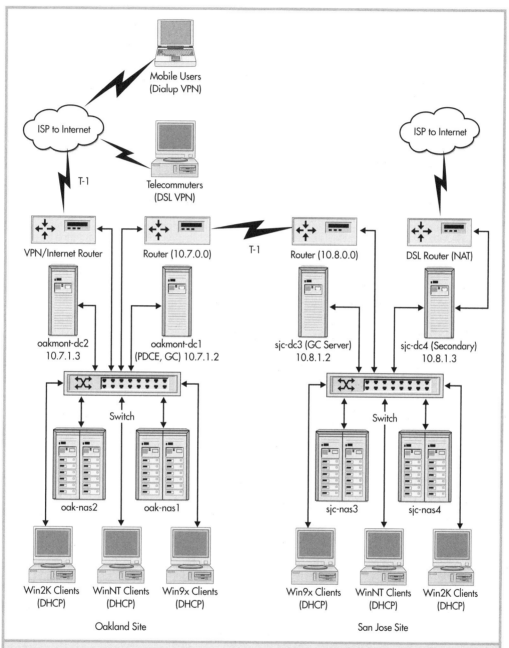

Figure 6-1. The sample Oakland and San Jose sites each have a pair of DCs and network-attached storage (NAS) file servers. Member servers aren't shown in this diagram.

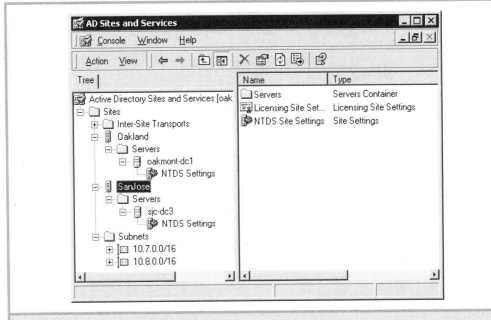

Figure 6-2. AD Sites and Services displays settings for the two sites used in site-based GPO examples that follow.

contains the PDCE. Unless you rename it, this site is *<default-first-site-name>*. You move the new DC to another site by right-clicking its *ServerName* node and choosing Move to open a dialog with a Site Name list. Double-clicking the desired site name moves the DC to its new site.

Client computers can move from site to site, so clients must confirm their site membership during the Net Logon process. Similarly, clients you add to the site must discover their site membership after obtaining an IP address lease from the site subnet's DHCP server. Following is a simplified version of the process by which clients determine their site membership:

1. When the Windows 2000 client boots, it receives a list of DCs and their IP addresses from the DNS server and queries a DC for site information by passing its IP address. AD-integrated Dynamic DNS's Service Location (SVR) records store pointers to the site's DC host records in the Forward Lookup Zones, *domain.ext*, _sites, *SiteName*, _tcp folder.

2. AD processes the query by finding the site subnet address that provides the closest match to the client's leased IP address and returns the site name to the client.

3. The client stores the site name in HKEY_LOCAL_MACHINE\SYSTEM\CurrentControlSet\ Services\NetLogon\Parameters in a value named DynamicSiteName.

If you want to force a client to a site for testing without reconfiguring IP addresses and DHCP scopes, you can tweak the Registry to assign the site. Navigate to HKEY_LOCAL_MACHINE\SYSTEM\CurrentControlSet\Services\NetLogon\Parameters and add a new REG_SZ data item named SiteName, with its value set to the appropriate site name. The SiteName value, if present, overrides the DynamicSiteName value. (If the computer can connect to the assigned site, no specific site name appears in the DynamicSiteName value.) One client reboot is needed to apply the newly assigned site and another reboot to load computer-based policies from the new site.

Don't forget to remove the SiteName value after you complete the tests. Otherwise, the client is forever bound to the site, whether or not the site exists. If the computer can't connect to a site, the Application log shows a UserEnv Event ID 1000 error: "Windows cannot connect to *domain.ext* with (0x0)." This is another example of an inscrutable UserEnv error description. The DC also generates Netlogon Event ID 5778 errors to indicate that the client can't find its designated site.

Windows 2000 clients connecting to Windows 2000 DCs use the IP/DNS-compatible Locator. Windows 2000 Server includes a Windows NT 4.0–compatible Locator to find the appropriate site DC for downlevel clients that pass the domain name as a NetBIOS name. Downlevel clients accept the first mail slot message received from a DC, which usually is a DC within the client's site.

Setting Server-Specific Site Policies

You can apply any computer- or user-based policy you want at the site level, but you can have only one domain-level security policy. The Default Domain Policy GPO usually determines security settings for the domain. You apply site-based policies only to operations that have the potential to generate heavy traffic loads on the intersite communication link. The primary traffic culprits are software installation, redirected folders, and roaming user profiles.

TIP: If you use RIS or RIPrep to install new copies of Windows 2000 Professional on clients, run the Remote Installation Service on a server in each site. RIS and RIPrep create very high traffic loads, but DHCP automatically finds the site's RIS server.

Setting Site-Based Software Installation Policies

Windows Installer (.msi) and .zap packages, which were mentioned in the "Software Installation Policies" section of Chapter 4 should run from a server in each site. Squeezing a 300 MB Microsoft Office installation through a T-1 line from one site to another isn't likely to leave much bandwidth for ordinary intersite communication, including AD replication. Intersite AD replication traffic is compressed, but normal IP traffic isn't. If you assign a large application to everyone after working hours, you can imagine users' consternation when they all log on to the network at the same time the next morning and click the menu choice for the newly assigned application. The GroupPol application has a relatively small (4.5 MB) Installer file that takes only about 30 seconds to download over a T-1 line with otherwise light traffic. If 100 users log on more or less simultaneously, the total execution time is a minimum of 50 minutes, during which the T-1 is totally clogged.

NOTE: Applications you assign with a GPO are advertised by adding a Start menu choice, such as Microsoft Access, and a file extension association with the application, if any. Windows Installer doesn't execute the full .msi file until the user clicks the Start menu choice or opens a file (*.mdb) with the association. Setup.exe files installed with .zap wrappers, however, execute the full installation operation at logon.

Each site that has clients subject to Software Installation policy requires a GPO to specify the UNC path to the .msi or .zap file on a local file server. The process of adding a GPO at the site level is almost identical to that for domains and OUs. In this case, however, you right-click the *SiteName* node in AD Sites and Services and choose Properties to open the *SiteName* Properties dialog, click the Group Policy tab, and click New. For this and the following site-based examples, the name of the GPO is San Jose Site Policy.

The section "Designing GPO Filters Based on Software Requirements" in Chapter 3 describes how to apply software installation policies for users in role-based security groups, but not how to specify the location and name of the Installer file to deliver. To set the default location for packages assigned or published by the San Jose site and assign a package, GroupPol.msi for this example, to all computers (including the site's DCs), do the following:

1. Expand the Computer Configuration\Software Settings node, right-click the Software Installation node, and choose Properties to open its Properties dialog.

2. On the General page, type or browse to the server share that holds the .msi and .zip files to assign. The entry in the Default Package Location text box must be the full UNC path to the folder, \\sjc-dc3\User Apps for this example (see Figure 6-3). The Authenticated Users group needs Read share permissions and the default Allow Read & Execute, List Folder Contents, and Read folder permissions.

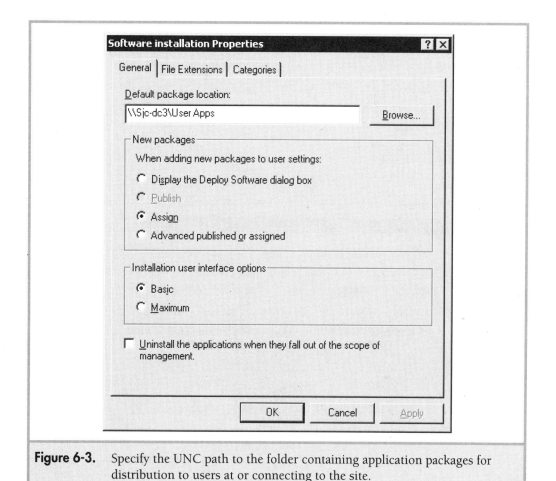

Figure 6-3.   Specify the UNC path to the folder containing application packages for distribution to users at or connecting to the site.

NOTE: You can only assign, not publish, applications to computers. Navigate to the User Configuration\Software Settings\Software Installation node to assign or publish applications when users log on.

3. If you want to create a default set of categories for types of assigned or published software in Control Panel's Add/Remove Programs tool, click the Categories tab, click Add to open the Enter New Category dialog, fill in the blank, and click OK. You can add as many categories as you like. Click OK when you're done.

4. Right-click the right pane of the Group Policy Editor (GPE), choose New | Package to open the Open dialog for the default folder, and double-click the name of the .msi or .zap file to open to add the first package to the list in the right pane.

5. Double-click the added entry to open its Properties dialog. You can make only limited changes to the default settings on the Deployment page. The Categories page lets you assign the application to one of the categories you added in step 3 (see Figure 6-4). Click OK to close the dialog.

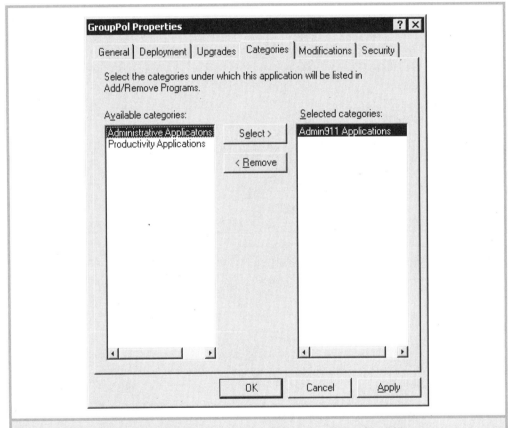

Figure 6-4. After you've added a set of software categories for the Add/Remove Programs tool, you can assign individual packages to one or more categories.

TIP: Reboot the DC to test the site-based Software Installation policy; the menu choice appears, and new software categories are added to the Categories list of the Add/Remove Programs tool's Add New Programs page. To verify that the policy applies only to the site, reboot a DC in another site and confirm that the .msi file you specified in step 2 doesn't run and that the Categories list doesn't include the new categories.

If you've added computer accounts to security groups, you can exempt particular sets of computers from the policy. DCs and member servers, for example, shouldn't receive packages intended for users. Thus, you should create a Domain Servers security group and add the DC and member server accounts to it. You also might want to exempt remote computers from the policy. The GroupPol application creates two computer security groups for faculty computers: Network Computers and Remote Computers.

When implementing group-based software installation policies, you must generate a set of filtered GPOs for each site, because the GPOs need a pointer to the appropriate distribution folder in the site for each Installer file. For example, you can link the five Microsoft Office installation policies described in Chapter 3 to either the Oakland or San Jose site, but not both. In this case, you set the default package policy and add packages under the \User Configuration\Software Settings\Software Installation node.

CODE BLUE

If you decide to link the GPO to a new site, for instance by removing the links to the default Oakland site of the example GPOs in Chapter 3 and adding new links to the San Jose site, you must change the value in the Default Package Location text box to point to the new server. You also *must* delete and re-create each package in the Name list. Changing the value of the Default Package Location text box on the General page of the Software Installation Properties dialog doesn't make retroactive changes to the UNC paths of the existing packages in the list.

To further complicate the problem, the UNC path to the .msi or .zap file doesn't appear on any page or secondary dialog of the *AppName* Properties dialog. If you store Installer files in more than one folder, there's no direct way to confirm the UNC paths to the files. The only safe way to confirm a path is to delete the package entry in the list and re-create it.

There's no simple mechanism for making copies of complete GPOs that you can add to other sites and then edit as necessary. When you generate a copy of a GPO, it gets a new GUID and doesn't have an association with a friendly name (the DisplayName attribute) in AD. It's unfortunate that Microsoft didn't add copy-and-paste GPO duplication capabilities to the Group Policy page of the Properties dialogs for sites, domains, and OUs. You can, however, copy and paste values for all subnodes of the Security Settings node, except Public Key Policies and IP Security Policies, from one GPO to another.

NOTE: Microsoft Knowledge Base article Q198722, "Copying and Renaming Group Policy Object Disables Policy," briefly discusses the GUID change issue.

BUG ALERT: If you change the location of the package, remove a workstation from a domain, or change domains before completing installation of a package assigned to a computer, rebooting the workstation runs the Windows Installer service, attempts to find the package, fails, and opens a "where is it?" dialog. If the package exists and the user knows where to find the package, the user can type the UNC path in the dialog's text box and click OK. Clicking Cancel and acknowledging the error sometimes kills the Installer, but about half the time the Installer goes into an endless loop until the user clicks Cancel in the initial Installer message box, not the "where is it?" dialog. After the Installer is killed in the current Windows instance, the Installer reruns after each reboot when the user logs on. Members of the local Administrators group can use Control Panel's Add/Remove Programs tool to remove the assigned program, but ordinary users can't. An expensive trip by a help desk technician usually is required to solve the problem.

Redirecting Folders to Site Servers

As with software installation, folder redirection GPOs must specify a share on a file server that's in the same site as the clients to avoid clogging the site interconnection. Users' redirected My Documents folders are likely to be huge, either initially or as they grow over time. Caching redirected folders with the offline files feature reduces or eliminates the simultaneous logon problem, because the redirected and local cached copies should be identical at logon. If a large number of Windows 2000 Professional users who've made recent changes to large files log off simultaneously, the result can be a tsunami of network traffic. Unlike for roaming user profiles, there are no slow link detection policies for folder redirection.

CAUTION: Don't turn on folder redirection simultaneously for all Windows 2000 users in a site, if you can avoid it. When a multitude of users boot up and log on simultaneously, sending everyone's contents of My Documents at once to a file server can easily saturate the server's disk I/O capacity and network hubs, if you don't use switches. Instead, progressively apply Folder Redirection policies in GPOs at the OU level.

The "Setting Group Policy for Folder Redirection and Offline Files" section in Chapter 4 includes detailed procedures for specifying attribute values of the Folder Redirection policy at the domain or OU level. In a multisite environment, the basic process for implementing folder redirection is as follows:

1. On a site file server, create a new folder with a name that includes the site code, such as SJC-Users.

2. Share the folder as hidden (SJC-Users$) and grant the Authenticated Users group Full Control privileges for the share. Users need Full Control privileges on the share to generate UserName folders with Allow Full Control privileges.

3. In the primary GPO for the site (San Jose Site Policy), navigate to User Configuration\Windows Settings\Folder Redirection\My Documents.

 TIP: If you redirect the files of some users and others have roaming profiles, create a Security Group for each class of user and use a separate GPO to apply Folder Redirection policy. Filter the Folder Redirection GPO so it applies only to the group that doesn't use roaming profiles.

4. Right-click the My Documents node to open the Target page of the My Document Properties dialog and select the type of administrative policy to apply: Basic - Redirect Everyone's Folder to the Same Location or Advanced - Specify Locations for Various User Groups. For the Basic option, type the UNC path to the share in the Target Folder Location text box. If you select the Advanced option, refer to the "Redirecting My Documents to Multiple Servers" section in Chapter 4 for instructions.

5. Click the Settings tab and accept the default Grant the User Exclusive Right to My Documents and Move the Contents of My Documents to the New Location settings. In the Policy Removal frame, select the Redirect the Folder Back to the Original Location When Policy Is Removed option. If you don't want to consume server space with family photo albums, select the Do Not Specify Administrative Policy for My Pictures option.

6. Click OK to close the My Documents Properties dialog.

7. Repeat steps 3 through 6 for other folders to redirect, if any.

Setting Offline Files Policy

It's a common practice to use the offline files feature to cache server-based folders on the local drive of mobile users' laptops and telecommuters' desktop PCs. For this chapter's two-site example, mobile and telecommuting users connect only to the Oakland site. If you don't want to enable the offline files feature for network-attached computers, you can set Offline Files policies at the site level. There's little or no benefit, however, to setting a site-level policy in this case, because you must categorize computers by their connection type. There's no "Disable Offline Files if Slow Link Detected" policy.

You can classify computers by connection type by placing the computer accounts in two OUs, such as Network Computers and Remote Computers. In this case, you explicitly enable or disable the \Computer Configuration\Administrative Templates\Network\Offline Files\ Enabled policy with individual GPOs for the two OUs. Alternatively, you can filter a pair of GPOs by computer Security Group membership. Thus, Offline Files policy is better set at the domain level, regardless of site topology, for remote users.

Specifying Roaming Profile and Home Folders

As mentioned in Chapter 4, in the section "Configuring Roaming User Profiles," many policies apply to roaming profiles, but assigning their location and that of home folders requires specific operations for each user account. You can write an ADSI script to add or change the Profile Path and home folder logical drive letter and location attribute values, but you need an LDAP attribute value to filter application of the script to determine each user's site assignment. If you populated the User Principal Name attribute of the computer account, you can find the user's computer and then use the Remote Registry service to return the client's HKEY_LOCAL_MACHINE\SYSTEM\CurrentControlSet\Services\ NetLogon\Parameters\DynamicSiteName value. Writing such a script isn't a walk in the park and is well beyond the scope of this book.

Whether you manually edit or script the roaming profile, home folder, or both locations or use a script, the better location for profile policies is at the domain level. Remember to exempt users employing My Documents redirection from roaming profile assignment.

Changing the Intersite Replication Interval

You can add and edit the GPO for any site on any DC with a connection to the site. If you use an out-of-site DC, changes to the GPO ordinarily don't occur on the target DC until the intersite replication interval expires and all DC's ...\SYSVOL folders are updated with the change. The default replication interval is every three hours. When you're testing site-based policies, you undoubtedly want faster replication between the sites.

NOTE: If you use the HKEY_LOCAL_MACHINE\SYSTEM\CurrentControlSet\Services\ NetLogon\Parameters\SiteName Registry hack described in the earlier "Mapping Site Names and IP Addresses" section to avoid resubnetting your test environment, this section doesn't apply.

The minimum intersite replication interval is 15 minutes, regardless of any lower number you might specify for this value. If you want to force immediate replication, do this:

1. In AD Sites and Services, expand the node of the target site to which you want to replicate your policy changes. For this example, changing policies on a DC in the Oakland site makes San Jose the target site.

2. Click NTDS Settings to display the <automatically generated> replication link in the right pane.

3. Right-click the link entry and choose Replicate Now to force the replication.

4. Acknowledge the message that says that replication between sites is not immediate.

TIP: The General page of the NTDS Settings Properties dialog has a check box that lets you specify whether or not a site DC is a GC server. This check box is cleared by default for all but the first GC of the domain.

To make a persistent change to the replication interval, do the following:

1. Navigate to the NTDS Settings node of a server in the target site (San Jose), right-click the <automatically generated> link in the Name list, and choose Properties to open the General page of its Properties dialog.

2. Click Change Schedule to open the Schedule for *LinkGUID* dialog.

3. Block the days and hours during which you want a 15-minute replication interval by clicking the upper-left day/hour rectangle and dragging to the lower-right rectangle to highlight the selection.

4. Select the Four Times per Hour option (see Figure 6-5) and click OK to apply the change.

5. Optionally, type what you believe will become a friendly name for the connection in the Description text box; then click OK.

6. Click Yes in the message box that asks if you want to remove the <automatically generated> attribute.

The name of the connection changes to its GUID; if you typed a description in step 5, it appears in the Description column. Why the GUID, rather than a friendly name, appears in the Name column is Yet Another Windows 2000 Mystery (YAW2KM).

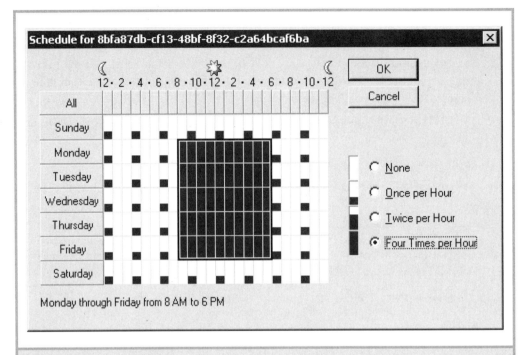

Figure 6-5. Drag a rectangle around the days and times during which you want to change the replication frequency and select one of the four interval options.

Moving Computers (and Their Users) Between Sites

If you don't use roaming user profiles or folder redirection, moving a computer and its user to a new site requires nothing more than releasing the computer's DHCP IP address lease by running ipconfig /release_all at the command line, disconnecting the computer, and then reconnecting it to the network at the new site. AD and Dynamic DNS handle the workstation's IP address change. It's a good practice to verify that the computer is a member of the new site by checking the HKEY_LOCAL_MACHINE\SYSTEM\CurrentControlSet\ Services\NetLogon\Parameters\DynamicSiteName value at the computer or with the Remote Registry service.

Users who have a roaming profile should change to a local profile by opening their workstation's System Properties dialog; clicking User Profiles, selecting their profile, if more than one exists; clicking Change Type; and selecting Local Profile. If you set the new path to a roaming profile before the user changes to a local profile, the user receives an error message when logging on. In this case, only the Local Profile option is available in the Change Type dialog.

If the user has a home folder mapped to a logical drive letter, it's a good practice to copy the folder's contents to the local drive. If the user has or will have a roaming profile, or if you implement folder redirection at the new site, an even better practice is to copy the home folder's contents to the user's My Documents folder and eliminate the home folder at the new site.

Moving a user's computer between sites is simple if the client has folder redirection and offline files enabled. The section "Disabling or Changing Folder Redirection" in Chapter 4 describes the problems with returning the My Documents and other redirected folders to the client's local drive. In this case, you can't remove the Folder Redirection policy because doing so affects all users within the scope of the policy. The Target Folder Location text box in the folder's Properties dialog is read-only, so you can't manually return the location to a local My Documents folder.

The simplest solution is to right-click the folder and choose Make Available Offline, if offline files aren't already in use. Use the Offline Files Wizard to cache the folder on the user's drive. When the computer is reconnected at the new site, the new site policy is applied, and the folder is redirected to the target folder of a share on a server in the site. If the Offline Files policy is disabled in the new site, Group Policy overrides the local Make Available Offline setting.

The simple solution without offline files in place requires a user who can follow instructions, an administrator with the ability to remotely control the workstation, or a technician at the computer. If none of these choices is available, you can create a temporary OU for the user and computer accounts, add a GPO to the OU that has the Offline Files policy enabled, and have the user reboot the computer and log on. Remember to move the accounts back to their original locations after the user logs off for the last time at the old site.

Tuning Domain Security Policy

Prior chapters discuss application of domain-level security policy in detail, as mentioned at the beginning of the chapter. The following sections offer suggestions for enhancing domain policy management and troubleshooting problems you're likely to encounter as you create and test policies prior to placing them in production.

Retaining a Pristine Default Domain Policy GPO

Default Domain Policy is the most common GPO in which to specify domainwide security policy. There's no hard-and-fast rule, however, that you set security policy in this GPO. An alternative is to add a new GPO at the domain level to set security and other policy. One of the advantages of applying domain security policy in a second GPO is that you can delete the link to the policy and add a new GPO with a different security configuration template. Deleting the link but saving prior GPOs lets you maintain a history of your policy changes. If you add a GPO to set security policy, make sure to move the policy above Default Domain Policy in the Group Policy Object Links list; otherwise, Default Domain Policy settings prevail.

NOTE: Adding a GPO at the domain level gives the impression that any member of Enterprise or Domain Admins can remove the link to Default Domain Policy and even delete the GPO itself, because the added GPO inhibits the error message you receive when attempting the deletion with only the Default Domain Policy present. When you close and reopen the GPE for domain-level policy, the Default Domain Policy reappears.

Another precaution to observe at the domain (and OU) level is not overwriting important site-level policies. For instance, if you add links to software installation or folder redirection GPOs at the site level, it's easy to forget to delete the corresponding links at the domain level.

Resolving Security Configuration Template Issues

The primary purpose of Group Policy is control and configuration management of workstations. Logic dictates that the appropriate security template for the Default Domain Policy GPO would be Securews.inf. The only alternative secure template that accommodates all operating systems is Securedc.inf, which is used in all preceding chapters. The primary difference between the two template files is audit policy: Securews.inf generates many more audit entries than Securedc.inf. You must modify the settings applied by either template before you put the Default Domain Policy GPO in production.

Fixing Errors Caused by Applying Securews.inf

Applying the Securews.inf template generates a pair of UserEnv errors and SceCli warnings in the Application log, which reoccur every five minutes. The description for UserEnv Event ID 1000 is "The Group Policy client-side extension Security was passed flags (17) and returned a failure status code of (1332)," which isn't the least bit helpful. SceCli Event

ID 1202 delivers the following description: "Security policies are propagated with warning. 0x534: No mapping between account names and security IDs was done. Please look for more details in TroubleShooting section in Security Help." Following this advice leads to a "Security Policy is not propagating properly" troubleshooting topic, which recommends adding an ExtensionDebugLevel REG_DWORD Registry entry with a value of 2 to the HKEY_LOCAL_MACHINE\SOFTWARE\Microsoft\Windows NT\CurrentVersion\ Winlogon\GPExtensions\{827D319E-6EAC-11D2-A4EA-00C04F79F83A} key. What the topic fails to mention is that you must run secedit /refreshpolicy machine_policy /enforce at the command line to generate the detailed Winlogon.log file in the \WinNT\Security\Logs folder after adding the new Registry value.

TIP: Consider adding the preceding Registry value, regardless of whether you're currently experiencing UserEnv errors and SceCli warnings. If you encounter errors in production, a quick review of the verbose Winlogon.log usually identifies their source. The verbose log file adds some system overhead, so once replication proves to be reliable, delete the Registry value.

Inspecting Winlogon.log uncovers the following error:

```
----Configure Group Membership...
   Configure *s-1-5-32-547.
Error 1332: No mapping between account names and security IDs was done.
   No system mapping is found for *s-1-5-32-547.
   Group Membership configuration completed with error.
```

S-1-5-32-547 is the well-known SID for Power Users, a Windows NT legacy Security Group that isn't present in the Active Directory Users & Computers' Builtin container of DCs. The errant group membership entry appears in the \Computer Configuration\Windows Settings\Security Settings\Restricted Groups policy. To correct the problem, do the following:

1. Delete the S-1-5-32-547 entry in Restricted Groups policy.

2. Close the GPE and click Yes in the Save Security Template dialog to save your changes. If you don't save the template changes, the remaining steps don't work.

3. Run **secedit /refreshpolicy machine_policy /enforce** at the command line.

4. In Event Viewer, right-click the Application Log node and choose Refresh.

5. Verify that a SceCli Information entry (Event ID 1704) confirms that security policy objects are now being applied successfully.

Microsoft's omission of the Power Users group in the DC's Builtin group is unfortunate, because the ability to restrict membership in workstations' Power Users group is a potentially useful policy. A local Power Users group is present on DCs; opening the Local Security Settings snap-in of a DC and navigating to the User Rights Assignment node displays Power Users in the Local Setting column of the Change the System Time and Log On Locally policies.

NOTE: Knowledge Base article Q247482, "Security Policies Are Propagating with Warning 0x534," includes the instruction to run the Secedit command, but states that the problem occurs because the User Rights policy has a reference to a deleted account, not a reference to a nonexistent group in the Restricted Groups policy.

Tweaking the Result of Applying Securedc.inf

If you apply the Securedc.inf template to avoid the exercise required to make Securews.inf behave, you'll discover a Securedc.inf gotcha that requires a fix to accommodate Windows 2000 legacy device drivers. Windows 2000's Drivers.cab file contains signed drivers for a multitude of video adapters and other common hardware devices. The probability that all your workstations and servers have hardware that's handled by drivers on the Windows 2000 installation CD-ROM is very low. If you don't change the device driver installation policy, you won't be able to install most third-party drivers for video adapters, sound cards, and other specialized hardware after Windows 2000 Professional or Server setup.

The Securedc.inf template sets the Computer Configuration\Windows Settings\Security Settings\Local Policies\Security Options\Unsigned Driver Installation Behavior policy to Do Not Allow Installation, and the Unsigned Non-driver Installation policy to Warn, but Allow Installation. Change the Unsigned Driver Installation Behavior policy to Warn, but Allow Installation and, optionally, the Unsigned Non-driver Installation policy to Silently Succeed. These two settings are the defaults for the Securews.inf template.

Diagnosing Other Sources of UserEnv Errors and SceCli Warnings

Another source of UserEnv Event ID 1000 errors and SceCli Event ID 1202 warnings is the existence of one or more unresolved user accounts in the Computer Configuration\ Windows Settings\Security Settings\Local Policies\User Rights Assignment policies. The Q247482 Knowledge Base article noted earlier addresses this problem, which usually is caused by not clearing workstation policy settings prior to moving a computer between domains or, in a test environment, re-creating a domain by running Dcpromo.exe twice on the last DC in the domain. You also can encounter this problem if you demote a secondary DC to a member server and then promote it to a DC in the same or another domain without clearing existing policies.

TIP: When you move a workstation or member server between domains or regenerate a test domain, demote the workstation or server to a workgroup member, preferably while connected to its original domain so the computer account is deleted. Demoting removes all policies except those applied by the local GPO. You can use any workgroup name (typically TEMP) in the demotion process.

You can determine if you have User Rights Assignment detritus by searching for unresolved group names that begin with S- in the User Rights Assignment list. Most, but not all, S- entries appear at or near the beginning of the list. For workstations and DCs or member servers, open the Local Security Policy and navigate to User Rights Assignment. Double-click each entry that has an S- group to open the Local Security Setting dialog and clear the Local Policy Setting check box for each S- entry. On DCs, double-click the User Rights Assignment entry to open the Security Policy Setting dialog, select the S- entry in the list, and click Remove.

If, after making the changes and running secedit /refreshpolicy machine_policy /enforce at the command line, you still see the UserEnv Event ID 1000 errors and SceCli Event ID 1202 warnings in the Application log, check the verbose version of Winlogon.log for any unresolved group names you missed.

NOTE: A DC with an invalid or empty ...\SYSVOL folder also can cause the preceding errors, but the causes described in the preceding three sections are the most common.

Setting Passwords for User Accounts Added Programmatically

Manually adding user accounts to AD is a tedious process, especially if you populate AD's added LDAP attribute values for User objects. Most admins write Visual Basic scripts to add user accounts and their attribute values by taking advantage of the Active Directory Service Interfaces (ADSI). JScript is an alternative language, but Microsoft ADSI script examples use VBScript. You must use scripts to precreate computer accounts that are contained in OUs or that you want to associate with a particular user by specifying the userPrincipalName attribute value. If you're a Visual Basic programmer, you can easily translate VBScript examples into VB 6.0 code; compiled Visual Basic programs let you use an Excel worksheet or database to add user accounts and attribute values. Conventional Visual Basic code, however, behaves differently from VBScript when dealing with Password Policies.

You *must* set the Computer Configuration\Windows Settings\Security Settings\Account Policies\Password Policies\Minimum password length value to 0 characters for programmatic addition of user accounts with Visual Basic 6.0 SP3+ and ADSI version 2.5 when you early-bind ADSI objects with statements such as Dim adsUser As IADSUser. Early binding is the standard for conventional Visual Basic projects, and the GroupPol application uses early binding exclusively. If you don't allow 0-length (null) passwords, you encounter error 80072035: "Automation error. The Server is unwilling to process the request." The problem doesn't occur, however, if you are running VBScript from Cscript.exe or Wscript.exe, or if you import and run unmodified VBScript user addition code in Visual Basic. VBScript supports only late binding, which substitutes the CreateObject method for Dim *objName* as [New] *objClass*.

If your VBScript assigns a simple temporary password, such as "password," to new users, however, you must disable the Passwords Must Meet Complexity Requirement policy. Otherwise, you receive error 800708C5, which is missing a description in VBScript, but offers the following explanation when run in Visual Basic: "The password does not meet the password policy requirements. Check the minimum password length, password complexity and password history requirements." GroupPol bypasses this error with an On Error Resume Next instruction and generates a null password for each user. Processing the error slows GroupPol's addition of users by a factor of about five, and the null password requires you to add and remember a complex password when you log on with a GroupPol user account.

NOTE: Microsoft defines a complex (strong) password as having a combination of seven or more uppercase and lowercase letters, numerals, and punctuation symbols. The password can't contain the user's logon ID or components of the user's name.

Following is a simple VBScript code example that adds a new user account, populates a few of its attributes, and adds a simple password:

```
Set adsOU = GetObject("LDAP://OU=Anthropology,OU=Faculty
Members,DC=oakmont,DC=edu")
Set adsUser = adsOU.Create("user", "CN=Andy Albrecht")
adsUser.Put "samAccountName", "AndyAlbrecht"
adsUser.Put "userPrincipalName", "AndyAlbrecht@oakmont.edu"
adsUser.Put "sn", "Albrecht"
adsUser.Put "givenName", "Andy"
adsUser.Put "telephoneNumber", "(510) 555-1212"
adsUser.Put "title", "Teaching Assistant"
adsUser.SetInfo
adsUser.SetPassword "password"
adsUser.AccountDisabled = False
adsUser.SetInfo
```

If you run the preceding code as a VBScript or in Visual Basic in a domain with complex passwords required, executing the adsUser.SetPassword "password" instruction returns the 800708C5 error. To avoid the problem, delete or comment out this instruction to create an empty password, delete the disabled user account, and rerun the script or subprocedure, which sets a null (empty) password for the user. When the user logs on to a workstation with the new account and an empty password, the message "Your password has expired and must be changed" appears. Specifying a simple password in early-bound Visual Basic code results in the same message. Clicking OK changes the Logon to Windows dialog to the Change Password dialog that includes Old Password, New Password, and Confirm Password text boxes. Instruct users to clear the Old Password text box, type and confirm a complex password, and click OK to acknowledge the "Your password has been changed" message.

NOTE: Knowledge Base article Q230750, "Basic User Account Creation with ADSI Scripting," from which the preceding code example is derived, and other Microsoft code examples for adding user accounts fail to mention the problem with complex password issue. The "secret***!" password in the example doesn't meet Microsoft's complexity requirements.

Assigning User Rights for Workstations

Local Security Settings prevail when you apply Securedc.inf or Securews.inf, because \Computer Configuration\Windows Settings\Security Settings\Local Policies\User Rights Assignment policies are set to Not Configured by default. At the minimum, remove the Guest account from the Log on Locally policy at the domain level. The Guest account is disabled by default, but someone might enable it. Remove the Everyone group assigned to the Access This Computer from the Network policy, unless you have users in trusted Windows NT domains who need access to resources shared by the workstation. The User Rights Assignment policies you set at the domain level apply to workstations and member servers. The next chapter discusses the application of user rights to member servers.

NOTE: Don't define the Log On Locally policy if your workstations have local Power Users who aren't members of the local Users group and need to log on to the local computer with this privilege. As mentioned in the section "Fixing Errors Caused by Applying Securews.inf" earlier in this chapter, you can't add the well-known Power Users group to a policy.

Adding individual groups or users to each of the policies you want to change is a tedious process. If you define a User Rights Assignment policy, you must add every group to which the policy applies, unless you add the Everyone group. For safety, add the Administrators group first to each policy you define.

TIP: Export the User Rights Assignment policies of a workstation's Local Security Settings to a tab-separated list. Print the list to use as a reference when you define new user rights.

To change User Rights Assignment policies—Access This Computer from the Network and Log On Locally for this example—do the following:

1. In the User Rights Assignment Policy pane, double-click the Access This Computer from the Network policy to open the Security Policy Setting dialog.

2. Mark the Define These Policy Settings check box and click Add to open the Add User or Group dialog.

3. Click Browse to open the Select Users or Groups dialog and type **Administrators;Authenticated Users** in the text box.

4. Click Check Names to verify your typing. Downlevel OAKMONTU\ and NT AUTHORITY\ prefixes are added to the two group names.

5. Click OK twice to add the groups without the prefixes to the Security Policy Setting dialog (see Figure 6-6) and click OK to add the policy to the list.

6. Double-click the Log On Locally entry and repeat steps 2 through 5. In step 3, type the following group names: **Administrators;Users;Domain Users;Backup Operators**. The Domain Users group retains the OAKMONTU\ prefix.

You must add Domain Users to the Security Policy Setting list if you define the Log On Locally policy, because users who log on to a domain don't have a local user account.

Test the Log On Locally policy by rebooting and logging on to a workstation with any domain user account that isn't a member of the Domain Admins group. Open the Local Security Settings snap-in to verify that the user rights changes you made appear in the Effective Settings column of the User Rights Assignment list.

TIP: If the new user rights don't appear, run secedit /refreshpolicy machine_policy /enforce at the command line of the workstation or DC and reboot the computer. It's a good practice to run this command every time you change a security-related policy.

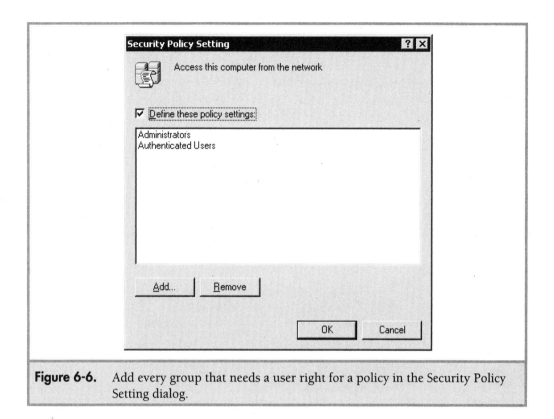

Figure 6-6. Add every group that needs a user right for a policy in the Security Policy Setting dialog.

Test the Access This Computer from the Network policy for Administrators by connecting to it in the Computer Management snap-in. Right-click the Computer Management (Local) node, choose Connect to Another Computer, and type or browse to the computer name in the Select Computer dialog.

Chapter 7

Customizing Policies
at the OU Level

E arlier chapters of this book describe the design of OU hierarchies and Security Group structures for selectively applying Group Policy to sets of workstations and their users. This chapter concentrates primarily on policies that apply to OUs containing DCs and member servers, with emphasis on establishing and maintaining server security through Group Policy. The chapter describes how to create a customized, restricted version of the Active Directory Users and Computers MMC console for use by operators rather than administrators. Remote access policy for member servers running the Routing and Remote Access Service also is covered. RAS security policy is Registry based and isn't under the control of Group Policy.

Increasing the Security of Domain Controllers

Domain controller security should be one of your first priorities as a system admin. All DCs hold confidential employee-related information in AD's newly added user account attributes. Every Global Catalog server contains enterprisewide data that, if compromised, could deal a serious blow to your organization's competitive position and future success.

The Account Policies you specify in the Default Domain Policy, or a higher-priority policy you add at the domain level, determine the password, account lockout, and Kerberos policies for the entire domain, including DCs. Thus, you can't establish by Group Policy a stricter level of password security for DCs. Whether or not you specify complex eight-character or longer passwords as the domain-level security policy, your organization's IT policy should require all Domain and Enterprise Admins to use long, complex passwords for their administrative user accounts. Limit members of the Enterprise and Domain Admins groups to as few persons as possible and allow only members of these two groups to gain unaccompanied access to DCs in locked server closets or enclosures.

The three sections that follow describe additional, specific steps that you can take to improve security for your DCs.

Running IIS 5.0 on Domain Controllers

As a matter of policy, don't run IIS 5.0 on a DC unless it's absolutely necessary. If you must run IIS 5.0 on a DC, make sure to disable anonymous access. All users connecting to your internal Web servers should be authenticated by the domain. Member servers deserve security precautions similar to DCs, so don't run IIS 5.0 with anonymous access on a member server inside your firewall. Even if you don't encounter reports of IIS 5.0 security breaches, there's a small possibility that determined hackers might dig a security tunnel between your Web server and AD.

To disable anonymous access on the IIS 5.0 Web server, do this:

1. Launch the Internet Services Manager console, right-click the Default Web Site node (or whatever you renamed it), and choose Properties to open the Web server's properties dialog.

2. Click the Directory Security tab and then click the Edit button in the Anonymous Access and Authentication Control frame to open the Authentication Methods dialog.

3. Clear the Anonymous Access check box and accept the default, Integrated Windows Authentication. Integrated Windows Authentication doesn't work with HTTP proxy connections (see Figure 7-1).

4. If members of Domain Users must be able to access the site through a proxy server or firewall, mark the Digest Authentication check box.

NOTE: Digest Authentication requires AD to store encrypted clear-text copies of user passwords, so the physical security of DCs is even more important if you enable this authentication option. You must enable the Store Passwords Using Reversible Encryption for All Users policy in the domain policy of the Password Policy node if you use Digest Authentication.

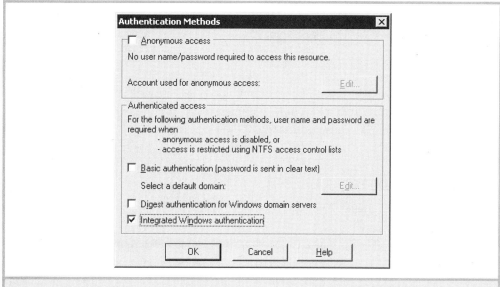

Figure 7-1.   Clear the Anonymous Access check box and mark the Integrated Windows Authentication check box to increase the security of IIS 5.0 running on a DC.

5. Click OK twice to open the Inheritance Overrides dialog, click Select All to apply your authentication settings to all child nodes of the Web server, and click OK to return to Internet Services Manager.

6. In the Active Directory Users and Computers' Users container, disable the IUSR_*ServerName* account and verify that network users can access the Web site. After a trial period, delete the IUSR_*ServerName* account from the container and remove the account from the User Rights Assignment node's Log On Locally and Log On as a Batch Job policies.

NOTE: IIS 5.0 runs under the IWAM_*ServerName* user account, so don't disable or delete this account. IWAM_*ServerName* is a member of the Domain Users and Builtin Guests groups.

FTP requires transmission of clear-text logon IDs and passwords, unless you permit anonymous connections, so FTP definitely doesn't belong on DCs. You disable anonymous access for SMTP and NNTP servers by clicking the Access tab of their properties sheets and clicking the Authentication button to open an Authentication (Methods) dialog. Authentication choices for SMTP and NNTP virtual directories are the same as for those for Web servers.

NOTE: IIS 5.0 components are required to enable the Internet Connection Server feature of Routing and Remote Access (RRAS). If you're providing Internet Connection Server services on a DC and remove IIS 5.0, clients attempting to use this feature can't open Web pages.

If you need only Web services, don't install FTP, SNMP, or NNTP services. You can delete a previously installed Default FTP Site, but you can't delete the Default SNMP or NNTP Virtual Server. If you don't need these three services, use Computer Management's Services tool to set the Startup Type property of the FTP Publishing Service, Network News Transport Protocol (NNTP), and Simple Mail Transport Protocol (SMTP) services to disabled.

Restricting User Rights

You gain additional security for DCs by modifying the security policies that *can* differ from those specified at the domain level. Unlike Default Domain Policy, the Default Domain Controllers Policy defines settings for every user rights policy that applies to all persons logging on to the DC, either locally or with a Terminal Services client. Policies with an empty Computer Column entry specify that only the system has permissions for the policy.

Many of the default settings give important user rights on all DCs to members of Builtin Local groups, including Account Operators, Backup Operators, Print Operators, and Server Operators. With the exception of Backup Operators, these groups are present only on DCs.

If you upgrade or clone a Windows NT PDC for a large domain, the Builtin Local groups commonly have user accounts. If these accounts are for users having current management responsibilities, you should alter the user rights for the Builtin Local groups to increase DC security. In a new domain, create OU(s) and corresponding Domain Local groups to hold user accounts for persons to whom you want to grant nonadministrative management permissions on DCs. In either case, following are guidelines for User Rights Assignment on DCs:

✦ **Domain Admins** and **Enterprise Admins** need Log On Locally rights to DCs, which they gain by membership in the Administrators group. DCs should not be physically accessible to anyone but members of the DC's Administrators group, but maintaining DCs and member servers in separate cages might not be practical. The Administrators group should hold only the renamed Administrator account and the Domain and Enterprise Admins groups. Only members of the Administrators group have the default right to log on to a server running Terminal Services in Remote Administration mode.

> **NOTE:** If you run Terminal Services as an application server on a DC, which isn't a recommended practice, you must add Authenticated Users to the Log On Locally policy's group list.

✦ **Server Operators** should be permitted to perform management duties on member servers, not DCs. Members of this group have default permissions to add and delete shares, shut down DCs remotely and locally, back up and restore files, and even format local drives. In domains with more than a few hundred users, DCs shouldn't do double duty as file or print servers.

✦ **Account Operators** must have authority to run the Active Directory Users and Computers console from a workstation, unless your policy is to use scripts only for user account management. Account Operators don't need any other management privileges on a DC, such as privileges to run the GPE. Account Operators have default, explicit permissions to create, modify, and delete User, Computer, or Group objects in all appropriate AD containers except the Builtin container, the Domain Controllers OU, and the Administrators, Domain Admins, and Enterprise Admins groups. Only Domain and Enterprise Admins should have the authority to add or delete Security Groups.

✦ **Backup Operators** need the ability to run backup operations on DCs, but only in the event that automated backup software fails and manual intervention is necessary. By default, this group has backup and restore permissions for all files on the DC through the Back Up Files and Directories policy and isn't subject to file or folder ownership restrictions for these operations. Restore permissions on DCs should be reserved to Administrators, because restoring the wrong version of critical files can incapacitate a DC.

✦ **Print Operators** can manage printers and document queues. DCs shouldn't be used as print servers, so Print Operators should have management authority only on member servers.

NOTE: The "Well-Known Security Identifiers" topic of early versions of the Resource Kit's Books Online incorrectly states that the Domain Users group is a member of the Print Operators group. The Print Operators group has no default members.

Modifying the Domain Controller OU's User Rights Assignment Policies

If you decide to follow the preceding guidelines, you can modify the Default Domain Controllers Policy or add a new GPO to the Domain Controllers OU. The latter alternative lets you quickly revert to the original default policy by deleting the GPO link, in case you encounter problems with the user rights changes.

TIP: Use the Browse button to open the Select Users and Groups dialog to add groups to User Rights Assignment policies instead of typing the group names. Group names you type in the Add User or Group dialog's text box aren't checked against AD for validity, and you can inadvertently add invalid groups to the policy's list.

Following are recommended security-related changes to the Default Domain Controllers Policy or settings to define in a new GPO added to the Domain Controllers OU:

✦ **Access This Computer from the Network** Administrators, Authenticated Users, ENTERPRISE DOMAIN CONTROLLERS, and if IIS 5.0 is running on the DC, IWAM_*ComputerName*. You don't need to modify this setting if the IUSR_*ComputerName* account isn't present. You must retain the default Everyone group if *any* user accounts require authentication by a Windows NT PDC or BDC, because trusting Windows 2000 domains validate users in trusted Windows NT domains as members of Everyone. The Everyone group also is required for replication between DCs upgraded from Windows NT PDCs and BDCs, unless you add the ENTERPRISE DOMAIN CONTROLLERS group to the policy, because the Authenticated Users group doesn't include computer accounts.

NOTE: Knowledge Base article Q249261, "Replication Does Not Work After Upgrading to Windows 2000," describes the replication issue with DCs upgraded from PDCs and BDCs in which the Everyone group didn't have Access This Computer from the Network rights.

✦ **Add Workstations to Domain**   Administrators. If you want users to be able to add computer accounts to the domain, add the Domain Users group. Alternatively, add individual Security Groups containing the members of specific OUs you want to have this right.

✦ **Back Up Files and Directories**   Administrators, Backup Operators

✦ **Change the System Time**   Administrators

✦ **Force Shutdown from a Remote System**   Administrators

✦ **Log on as a Batch Job**   IWAM_*ComputerName*, if IIS 5.0 is running on the DC

✦ **Log on Locally**   Administrators

✦ **Restore Files and Directories**   Administrators

✦ **Shut Down the System**   Administrators

Figure 7-2 illustrates the first 20 User Rights Assignment policy settings for a GPO, Oakmont DC Policy for this example, added above Default Domain Controllers in the Group Policy Links list. The Default Domain Controllers Policy defines rights shown as Not Defined in the Computer Setting column.

TAKE COMMAND

After making the User Rights Assignment changes to a second GPO, run the following two commands on the DC to verify its application to the DC:

```
secedit /refreshpolicy machine_policy /enforce

gpresult
```

Verify that the added GPO is the last policy in Gpresult.exe's "The computer received 'Security Settings' from these GPOs" list. Gpresult returns the following for a domain having two GPOs at the domain level and a GPO added to the Domain Controllers OU:

```
Local Group Policy
Default Domain Policy
Oakmont Domain Policy
Default Domain Controllers Policy
Oakmont DC Policy
```

Even after running the secedit command, it takes a few minutes for the updated Group Policy to apply. Make sure that the Last Time Group Policy Was Applied time is equal to or greater than the system time at which you ran secedit.

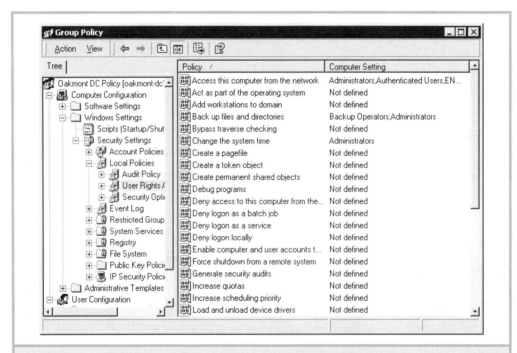

Figure 7-2. Adding a second GPO to the Domain Controllers OU with a priority higher than that of the Default Domain Controllers GPO lets you customize the policy without making changes to the original GPO.

After confirming that the altered policy has been applied to the DC, launch the Local Security Policy snap-in and check each altered user right in the Local Security Policy Setting dialog to verify that the Effective Policy Setting is what you intended (see Figure 7-3).

Setting Local Security Options for DCs

Security Options policies applied at the domain level with the Securedc.inf template applied to the Default Domain Policy or a domain-level GPO with a higher priority than Default Domain Policy are, for the most part, adequate for DCs. Securedc.inf sets all but Rename Administrator Account, Rename Guest Account, and Secure System Partition (for RISC platforms only). Windows 2000 doesn't support RISC platforms, so the last policy isn't of significance.

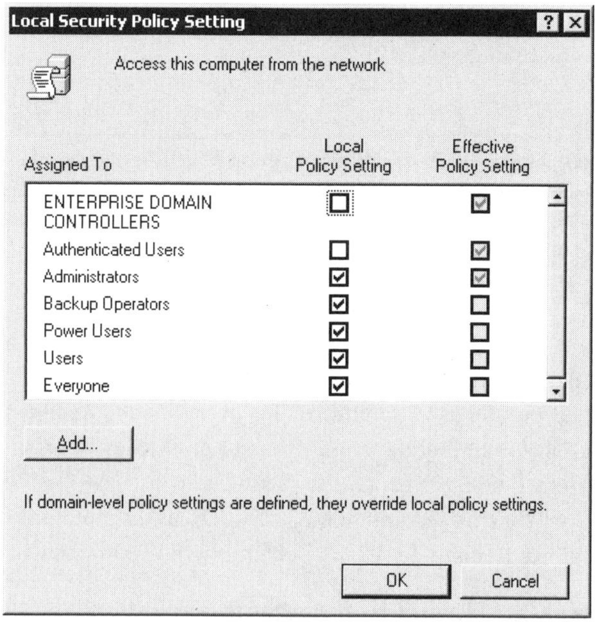

Figure 7-3. The read-only Effective Policy Setting check boxes reflect changes to the DC's Local Security Policy made by a GPO added to the Domain Controllers OU.

Following are recommendations for improving the security of DCs with \Security Settings\Local Policies\Security Options policies when Securedc.inf has been applied at the domain level:

✦ **Audit Use of Backup and Restore Privilege**   Enabled. Enabling this policy generates a log of DC backup operations.

✦ **Do Not Display Last User Name in Logon Screen**   Enabled. This policy prevents unauthorized persons from determining the administrative account name from the Windows Logon dialog, but doesn't prevent them from seeing the account name in the Windows Security or Shut Down Windows dialog.

After you've made the changes, verify their application to the DC's local security policy following the procedure in the previous section.

The following Security Options policies set at the OU level don't apply to DCs:

✦ Automatically Log Off User When Logon Time Expires

✦ Rename Administrator Account

✦ Rename Guest Account

NOTE: Knowledge Base article Q259576, "Group Policy Application Rules for Domain Controllers," gives Microsoft's reason for exempting DCs from the three options: DCs can be moved from the Domain Controllers OU, to which different settings might apply, in which case users would not "have a consistent experience regardless of which domain controller they use to log on."

The lack of ability to change the Administrator account name for DCs from that specified at the domain level isn't a major issue, because DCs don't have a local SAM database. The local Administrator account is used only in AD Recovery mode. Members of Enterprise and Domain Admins should use individual logon IDs and passwords to provide an audit trail of their DC management activities. Type a difficult-to-discover name for this account and store the name and password for this account, along with the diskettes containing your certificate copies, in secure onsite and offsite locations, preferably in fireproof safes.

Restricting the Membership of Builtin Groups

You can't delete Builtin groups, so it's a good administrative practice to add each of the Builtin groups to the Restricted Groups list of a GPO at the domain level to prevent users other than Administrators from adding or removing members. Administrators must alter the Restricted Groups list to change membership. If the Builtin groups have members and you want to preserve the groups and their membership for compatibility with existing Windows NT servers, add these user accounts to the Restricted Group's Members of This Group list in the Configure Membership dialog. Otherwise, accept the list's default value, which is no members.

Providing Account Operators with a Custom Administrative Console

Account Operators need to run the Active Directory Users and Computers snap-in, but they don't need, and therefore shouldn't have, the other administrative tools installed by Adminpak.msi. Unfortunately, Adminpak.msi lacks a "Custom Installation" option to specify particular tools to install; the present version is an all-or-nothing process.

It's equally unfortunate that you can't just install a copy of Dsa.msc on the computers of members of the Account Operators group. The Active Directory Users and Computers snap-in, which includes three extensions, requires a primary DLL and several helper DLLs that Adminpak.msi installs and registers on workstations. Attempting simply to run a copy of Dsa.msc on an Account Operators' computer throws "Snap-in failed to initialize" errors.

Enabling Account Operators to add, move, change, and delete user accounts without granting them unneeded privileges is a multistep process. Following is a brief description of the procedure:

1. Create a shared folder on the DC or a member server for distributing the console, DLL, and optional help files to Account Operators or the equivalent Domain Local group.

2. Fabricate a custom console that contains the stand-alone Active Directory Users and Computers snap-in without the Group Policy, RAS Dialin - User Node, and Terminal Services - Extension elements.

3. Copy the console and its DLL to a test workstation on which you haven't run Adminpak.msi and test the console with a temporary user account in the Account Operators group.

4. Alter security settings on critical OUs, such as Domain Controllers and Member Servers, to prevent Account Operators from seeing them. Optionally, hide other OUs and containers to which Account Operators don't need access. Create test user and computer accounts and verify that Account Operators have the permissions they need to perform their designated duties.

5. Install the snap-in and support files on Account Operators' computers and register the snap-in's DLL.

Providing the Required Files for Account Operators

To create the Account Operators' console, ADUC.msc for this example, do this:

1. On a DC or administrative workstation with Adminpak.msi installed, run mmc to open a new Console 1 in Author mode.

2. Choose Console | Add/Remove Snap-in to open the Standalone page of the Add/Remove Snap-in dialog; click Add to open the Add Standalone Snap-in dialog.

3. Double-click Active Directory Users and Computers in the list and click Close.

4. Click the Extensions tab, clear the Add All Extensions check box, and then clear the check boxes of the three extensions, which aren't required for administering user and computer accounts (see Figure 7-4). Click OK to close the dialog and add the bare-bones snap-in.

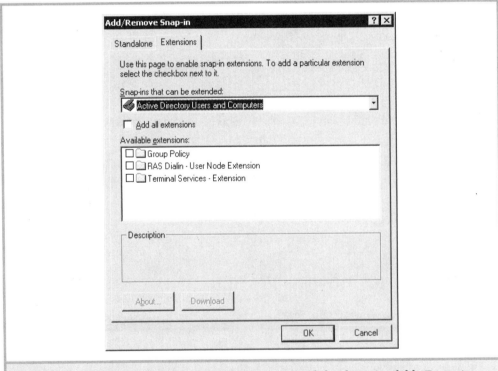

Figure 7-4. You must clear the Add All Extensions and the three Available Extensions check boxes to eliminate snap-in elements that require extension DLLs.

5. Expand the nodes to verify that the console works as expected. Rename the Console Root node to **Account Operators** or the applicable group name. For simplicity, Account Operators is used in this and the following procedures.

6. Choose Console | Options to open the Options dialog. Replace Console 1 with the name of the console, **Active Directory Users and Computers (Account Operators)** for this example.

7. Change the Console Mode to User Mode - Full Access and click OK.

8. Choose Console | Save As and save the console file with an appropriate name, **ADUC.msc** for this example, in the distribution file share (AcctOps).

To complete the distribution file set and prepare for the test, do the following:

1. Copy Dsadmin.dll from your \Winnt\System32 folder to the share.

2. Add a temporary test member, AccountOp for this example, to the Account Operators group.

NOTE: Copying the Dsadmin.chm and Dsadmin.hlp files to the user's \Winnt\Help folder doesn't enable online help for ADUC.msc, because the ADUC help files require installation of other support files by Adminpak.msi.

Testing the Console and Setting Security Options

On a workstation that's never run Adminipak.msi, do the following to install and run a test copy of the console:

1. Add the temporary member's account to the workstation's Administrators group, so you can copy the files to protected folders, and then log on as the test member.

2. Open the distribution share and copy and paste the console file (ADUC.msc) to the user's desktop.

3. Copy Dsadmin.dll to the \Winnt\System32 folder.

4. Choose Start | Run, type **regsvr32 dsadmin.dll** in the Open text box, and click OK. Acknowledge the message that registering the DLL succeeded.

5. Launch the console from the desktop to verify connectivity with the DC.

6. Choose View | Advanced Features, right-click the domain node, and verify that the Properties dialog seen by Account Operators has only General, Managed By, Object, and Security pages. The Group Policy page is missing because the Group Policy extension isn't present.

7. Click the Security tab and acknowledge the message that Account Operators have permission only to view security settings.

At this point, Account Operators have access to all OUs in the domain. To protect DCs, member servers, and other OUs to which Account Operators should not have access, do the following:

1. Open the Active Directory Users and Computers snap-in as a member of Domain Admins on an administrative workstation or the DC.

2. Right-click the Domain Controllers OU, choose Properties, and click the Security tab of the Domain Controllers Properties dialog.

3. If the Account Operators group isn't present, click Add and add Account Operators from the Select Users, Computers, or Groups dialog to the Name list.

4. With Account Operators selected on the Security page, mark the Deny Full Control check box to prevent the group from seeing or gaining any type of access to the Domain Controllers OU.

NOTE: Earlier chapters of this book recommend against applying Deny permissions. In this case, explicit Deny permissions simplify your security structure.

5. If the Domain Controllers OU is visible in the console of the test workstation, click the OU and acknowledge the message that the OU no longer exists or isn't accessible. Removing permissions for the OU superimposes an exclamation point (!) over the OU icon after you click it and while it remains visible.

NOTE: Pressing F5 to refresh the UI doesn't remove the Domain Controllers node. You must close and reopen the console to verify its disappearance. In some cases, new security settings might not apply until you open and close the console. In this case, the message mentioned in the preceding step doesn't appear.

6. Repeat steps 2 through 5 for each container or OU you want to exclude from management by Account Operators. Candidates for exclusion are OUs that contain accounts for member servers, OUs containing administrative accounts, and most containers that aren't OUs, typically Built-in, ForeignSecurityPrincipals, System, and Users. You can't apply Deny permission to Account Operators on the LostAndFound container. Figure 7-5 illustrates the appearance of the ADUC.msc snap-in with most of the containers hidden.

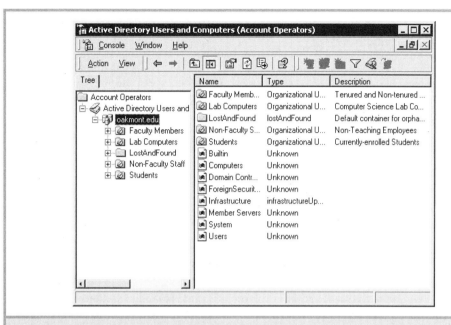

Figure 7-5.   The Account Operators' snap-in hides unnecessary nodes in the tree-view pane, but not in the Name list. Double-clicking an entry for an Unknown type opens a Properties dialog with the message "The Active Directory object could not be displayed."

TIP: Don't allow Account Operators to place user accounts in the Users container; all user accounts should be in OUs. If you place computer accounts in OUs, which this book recommends, hide the Computers container, too.

7. Verify with the temporary user account on the test workstation that you can add, delete, and move user and computer accounts and add accounts to security groups.

8. If you don't want Account Operators to have the authority to add and delete groups in the OUs to which members have access, open the Properties dialog for the OU, click the Security tab, click Advanced to open the Access Control Settings for *OUName* Properties dialog's Permissions page, select the Create/Delete Group Objects permission for Account Operators in the Permission Entries list, click View/Edit to open the Permission Entry for *OUName* dialog, and change the permissions for Create Group Objects and Delete Group Objects from Allow to Deny. Denying the Create Group Objects permission removes the New | Group choice from the OU's context menu.

9. Account Operators automatically receive explicit Allow Full Control privileges on all Security Groups, so you also must clear the Full Control and Write check boxes of each group. This is no small chore in a domain with a larger number of groups.

If you permit Account Operators to create new groups, the group becomes the creator-owner of each group added and has Full Control permissions for the group.

TIP: Create your own AccountOps or similarly named Domain Local group and assign the group appropriate privileges and user rights to add user accounts. Move the members of the Builtin Account Operators to the new group. Creating a new group and moving Account Operators to it is easier than removing Account Operators privileges from a large number of Security Groups.

Distributing the Files to Account Operators

If you have a large number of Account Operators, consider creating (or having a developer produce) a Windows Installer file that you can publish or assign to group members. Alternatively, you can script installation of the files. Manual installation, following the procedure described near the end of the earlier "Providing the Required Files for Account Operators" section, is a satisfactory alternative for a few Account Operators. The user who installs the custom console must be a member of the local Power Users or Administrators group.

Establishing OUs and Adding GPOs for Member Servers

Adding a member server to the domain places its account in the default Computer container to which you can't apply Group Policy. Member servers deserve security policies similar to but not necessarily as restrictive as those specified for DCs. Default Domain Policy (with or without Securedc.inf applied) doesn't establish a default set of User Rights Assignment policy settings. All User Rights Assignment settings are Not Configured, so the servers' local user rights settings apply. Placing member servers in their own OU(s) gives you the opportunity to create a single GPO for all member servers or GPOs for specific server types, such as file, print, Web, database, mail/messaging, and so on. Account Operators do their work on DCs, so they don't need access to member server OUs.

User Rights Assignment policies usually differ by server type. For instance, Print Operators need user rights only for managing print servers, and only database administrators (DBAs) should be permitted to restore files on database servers. One of the first Domain Local groups you add should be for DBAs. Model User Rights Assignment policies for member servers on those for DCs, with minor exceptions specified by the type of server.

> **NOTE:** Knowledge Base article Q242955, "Overview of Windows 2000 Server Roles," has additional information on typical roles of member servers, including their use as proxy servers running Microsoft Proxy Server 2.0. You must upgrade Proxy Server 2.0 with the Windows 2000 Update Wizard for Microsoft Proxy 2.0, which is available from http://www.microsoft.com/proxy/support/win2kwizard.asp.

As mentioned earlier, Securedc.inf sets all but a few inconsequential Security Options for the domain. The recommendations in the "Setting Local Security Options for DCs" section of this chapter apply equally to member servers.

Copying DC Local Policies to Member Server GPOs

You can copy all the Local Policy settings you define for the DC and paste the policy settings to your GPOs for member servers. You need to edit only a few of the settings to establish an effective set of user rights for member servers. To copy and paste the full set of Local Policies, which include Audit Policy, User Rights Assignment, and Security Options, do this:

1. Open the Default Domain Controllers GPO in the GPE and navigate to the Computer Configuration\Windows Settings\Security Settings\Local Policies node.

2. Right-click the node and choose Copy. The CTRL+C shortcut key isn't available in the GPE.

3. Open your member server GPO and navigate to the ...\Local Policies node.

4. Right-click the node and choose Paste. The Paste choice is disabled for all Security Settings subnodes except Local Policies.

5. Edit the User Rights Assignment and, if necessary, Security Options policies to reflect those appropriate for member servers.

Exploring the IIS 5.0 Security Templates for Web Servers

The Windows 2000 Server Resource Kit's CD-ROM includes two security templates, SecureInternetWebServer.inf and SecureIntranetWebServer.inf. Installing the Resource Kit places the templates in the \Program Files\Resource Kit folder. The "Using the Security Templates" section of the Resource Kit's Books Online describes the purpose of the templates. Your initial use of the templates should be as the source of a test database for an initial security audit of your intranet servers with the Security Configuration and Analysis snap-in. Performing local security audits on member servers is the subject of the "Using the Security Configuration and Analysis Snap-in" section of Chapter 5.

To add these two templates, plus a mysterious Cmdhere.inf template having no policies defined, to your Security Templates console and review their settings, do the following:

1. Open the console to which you've added the Security Templates snap-in and right-click New Template Search Path to open the Browse for Folder dialog.

2. Navigate to the \Program Files\Resource Kit folder of the machine on which you installed the Resource Kit files and click OK to add the templates to the console.

3. Expand the SecureIntranetWebServer node to display the template's Security Policies. The settings for Password Policy differ significantly from those applied by Securedc.inf. For instance, the Store Password Using Reversible Encryption for All Users in the Domain policy is enabled, presumably to support Digest authentication (see Figure 7-6). Account Lockout Policy settings also differ markedly from those of Securedc.inf.

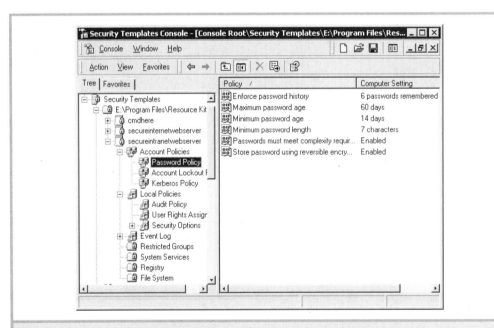

Figure 7-6. The Resource Kit's SecureIntranetWebServer.inf template has Security Policy settings that arbitrarily differ from those of the standard Securedc.inf template.

4. To run a quick audit of a member Web server or DC against the template, follow the instructions in Chapter 5, but substitute SecureIntranetWebServer.inf for Securews.inf for the baseline template. Figure 7-7 illustrates only a fraction of the nonconforming security elements reported by the audit.

The SecureIntranetWebServer template illustrates the difficulties of attempting to design a universal template for local security audits of servers. The snap-in's audit report simply displays differences as nodes with a superimposed red circle and white "X." Every policy value difference is reported, regardless of whether the policy in effect increases or decreases the security of the server when compared with the template. A more useful report would be one that flags only the differences in policy settings that might compromise security.

Regardless of the limitations of the Security Configuration and Analysis template, it's a good policy to run frequent security audits on DCs and member servers. After you've set up

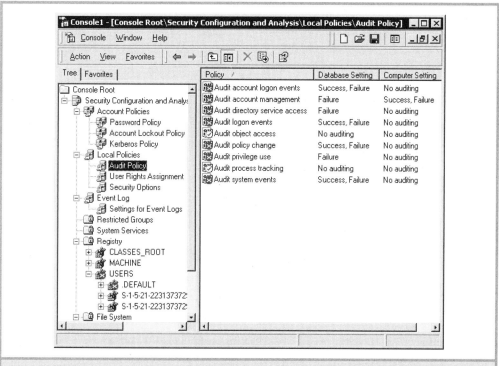

Figure 7-7.   An audit by the Security Configuration and Auditing tool displays a large number of differences between the SecureIntranetWebServer template and a member Web server in a domain with Securedc.inf applied.

and tested initial security for DCs and member servers, edit one of the templates to the point where no (or acceptably few) differences occur during the local audit process. Save the template(s) for use in periodic security audits of all your servers.

Configuring Internet Explorer on Clients

Windows 2000 Professional users must have Administrator or Power User rights to run the Internet Connection Wizard and manually configure Internet Explorer 5+ on their computers. When users join the domain with precreated user and computer accounts, they have no local account on the workstation. Clicking the Connect to the Internet icon displays a detailed message stating that the user has insufficient privileges to run the Wizard. The user is instructed to right-click the Internet Explorer icon, open its Properties dialog, and configure the LAN settings. Ordinary domain users can't configure dial-up connections and should not be granted this permission. Mobile users have a local account with at least Power Users (usually Administrator) permissions, so this issue doesn't apply to road warriors.

If the default LAN connection parameter for IE 5+, Automatically Detect Settings, works in your network environment, users can simply click the Internet Explorer icon and connect immediately to the Internet and your organization's intranet. If automatic discovery of your proxy server doesn't work, you must provide instructions to users for completion entries in the Proxy Server frame of IE's Local Area Connection (LAN) Settings dialog. Unattended installation lets you specify a proxy server address, port, and other connection parameters. Group Policy, however, provides considerably greater flexibility in establishing connection parameters and lets you customize many other important IE settings. Following are a few of the IE-related Group Policies you should consider implementing at the domain or OU level:

✦ **User Configuration\Windows Settings\Internet Explorer Maintenance\Connection** policies let you customize IE connection settings, including proxy server addresses and port numbers. Automatically Detect Configuration Settings is enabled by default in the Automatic Browser Configuration dialog.

✦ **User Configuration\Administrative Templates\Windows Components\Internet Explorer\Internet Control Panel** policies' Disable the Connection page policy prevents users from altering the connection parameters you set.

✦ **User Configuration\Windows Settings\Internet Explorer Maintenance\URLs** policies let you override Microsoft's self-serving defaults, such as automatic connection to msn.com when the user opens the browser. Use the Important URLs policy to set the default opening page to a page of your organization's intranet and specify an online support URL. Consider specifying at the OU level a home page link to the department's site. The Favorites and Links policy lets you replace Microsoft's favorites with those of your organization.

✦ **User Configuration\Windows Settings\Internet Explorer Maintenance\Programs** has a dialog for importing from your computer and modifying the names of e-mail, newsgroups, calendar, contact list, and other programs used for Internet services.

Establishing Remote Access Policy

Remote access policy isn't a Group Policy, but this policy deserves inclusion in a discussion of policies applied to member servers running RRAS, with or without Internet Authentication Service (IAS) for RADIUS authentication. If you implement a Windows 2000 VPN server or provide direct dial-in access to your domain with a bank of modems or ISDN adapters, a default remote access policy named Allow Access If Dial-in Permission Is Enabled applies to the RAS or VPN server. This policy appears in the Remote Access Policies list of the Routing and Remote Access snap-in when you select the Remote Access Policies node for the server, regardless of the type of server you specify when enabling RRAS. If you specify authentication with IAS, the same policy is present in the Internet Authentication Service console and applies to all RAS and VPN servers that use the same IAS.

NOTE: The Dial-in page of the *UserName* Properties dialog determines the user's remote access settings for dial-up or VPN connections. The default dial-in option for user accounts added to a native-mode domain is Control Access Through Remote Access Policy, so you don't need to set this attribute for every user.

CODE BLUE

Most options of the Dial-in page of the *UserName* Properties dialog can't be set for mixed-mode domains. Specifically, the Control Access Through Remote Access Policy and Verify Caller ID options, Assign a Static IP Address and Apply Static Routes selections, and settings in the Static Routes dialog have no effect on user accounts in mixed mode. Mixed mode provides the same RAS client choices offered by Windows NT: Grant Dial-in Permission to User and callback properties in User Manager or the Remote Access Admin utility. User accounts added to a mixed-mode domain are set to Deny Access for dial-in. Knowledge Base article Q193897, "Dial-in Options Unavailable with Active Directory in Mixed Mode," covers this issue.

Enabling Remote Access for All Users

Selecting Remote Access Policies in the Routing and Remote Access snap-in and double-clicking the default policy opens the Allow Access If Dial-in Permission Is Enabled Properties dialog. The dialog has a single Day-and-Time-Restrictions condition in the Specify Conditions to Match list. The default condition is 24 hours per day, seven days per week, and the If a User Matches the Conditions option is Deny Remote Access Permission. The result of this combination is the reverse of the policy name; the default setting denies remote access permissions to everyone all the time.

To allow all users to have around-the-clock dial-in access, select the Grant Remote Access Permission option (see Figure 7-8). Selecting the default condition in the list opens a Time of Day Constraints dialog that's similar to that for setting intersite replication frequency (refer to Figure 6-5 in Chapter 6). The dialog lets you change combinations of days and hours for which users are permitted or denied remote network access.

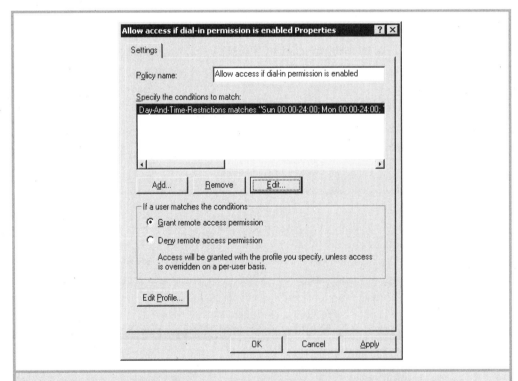

Figure 7-8. Users can't use RAS to connect to the domain until you select the Grant Remote Access Connection option in the Allow Access If Dial-in Permission Is Enabled Properties dialog.

Controlling Remote Access by Attribute Value

Unlike most Group Policies, RAS or IAS policies have numerous attributes of connections that you can test to determine if the remote user should be granted network access. Clicking the Add button opens a Select Attribute dialog with 13 attributes (see Figure 7-9).

The most useful of these attributes is Windows-Groups, which lets you restrict access by group membership. Select Windows-Groups and click Add to open the Groups dialog, and click Add to open the Select Groups dialog. Type the group names in the text box, click Check Names, and then click OK twice to return to the Properties dialog.

Editing the Dial-in Profile

Clicking the Edit Profile button opens the Edit Dial-in Profile dialog, whose Dial-in Constraints page is shown in Figure 7-10. Settings you apply in this dialog apply to all RAS users connecting to the server or all RAS servers if IAS is enabled. For example, if you allow only VPN connections, Windows NT and 9x users must use PPTP to connect. Windows 2000 clients can connect with PPTP or, if they have a computer certificate, L2TP over IPSec. A full discussion of RAS configuration is beyond the scope of this book. Fortunately, the online help for RAS is quite comprehensive.

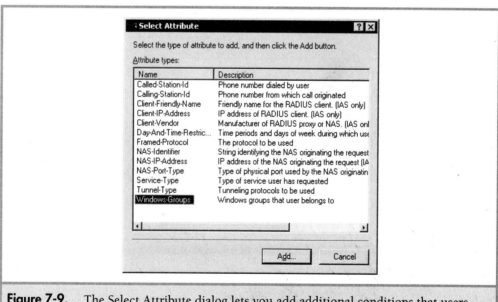

Figure 7-9. The Select Attribute dialog lets you add additional conditions that users must meet to enable a RAS connection.

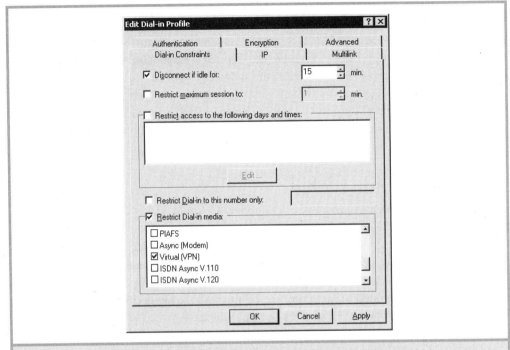

Figure 7-10. Remote access policy you set in the Edit Dial-in Profile dialog apply to all RAS users. The Dial-in Constraints page has optional dial-in media constraints for the type of RAS connection.

Setting Remote Access Account Lockout Policy

Unlike Group Policy, which lets you specify Account Lockout Policy under the GPE's Computer Configuration\Windows Setting\Security Settings\Account Policies node, you must enable the account lockout policy with Registry values set in the HKEY_LOCAL_MACHINE\SYSTEM\Current ControlSet\Services\RemoteAccess\ Parameters\AccountLockout key of the member server hosting RAS or, if you use RADIUS authentication, the server running IAS. Why these settings aren't present on a page of the

Edit Dial-in Profile dialog is a mystery. Following are the two required entries for account lockout:

- **MaxDenials** corresponds to the Account Lockout Threshold Group Policy, the maximum number of times a user can fail logging on before being locked out of the account. The default value is 0, which disables remote access account lockout. Setting a value of 1 or greater (commonly 5) enables lockout and specifies the number of invalid logon attempts allowed.

- **ResetTime (mins)** corresponds to the Reset Account Lockout Counter After Group Policy. The default value is 2,880 minutes (two days); a more appropriate value is in the range of 5 to 30 minutes.

Locking out a user adds a *DomainName:UserName* value to the key. To reset the user's account prior to expiration of the ResetTime value, you must manually delete this key on the server.

TIP: Set the MaxDenials and ResetTime values for all RAS servers. A marauder who makes a RAS connection to the server and knows or can generate a valid logon ID for the domain can disable a user's account by reconnecting and trying a different password until reaching the MaxDenials limit. The added protection of MaxDenials against password cracking outweighs potential user inconvenience.

Delegating Management of OU Group Policy

The "Delegating Management of OUs" section of Chapter 2 mentions that management of Group Policy links should be reserved for Domain Admins. If your organization decides to establish OUs with a high degree of administrative autonomy, you might want to grant administrative delegates additional rights to manage GPO links, create new GPOs, and edit existing GPOs. For example, you might want to delegate management of GPO links for Oakmont U's Faculty Members and Non-Faculty Staff OUs to members of the Non-Faculty Staff, System Administrators group. The Delegation of Control Wizard's Tasks to Delegate dialog lets you assign the Manage Group Policy Links task to a group or individual user.

Permission to manage links allows the delegates only to add or remove links in the *PolicyName* Properties dialog, but not create new GPOs or edit existing GPOs for the OU.

To extend the delegated permissions, you must add the delegates to the Group Policy Creator Owners Global group. If the group to which you want to grant Write, Create All Child Objects, and Delete All Child Objects GPO permissions is a Global group, which is the case for Oakmont U's Systems Administrators group, the domain must run in native mode to allow nesting Global groups. The workaround in mixed mode is to add individual user accounts to the Group Policy Creator Owners group. Only the delegated user or group that created the GPO can edit it. You must add the group to the Security page of a preexisting GPO and grant the group at least Allow Read and Write permissions.

Groups or users to whom you delegate GPO management must have an extended version of the Active Directory Users and Computers snap-in, not the limited-rights console described in the earlier section, "Providing Account Operators with a Custom Administrative Console." Fortunately, you can add the Group Policy extension to the basic Active Directory Users and Computers snap-in without having to copy additional DLLs to administrative workstations. Windows 2000 Professional includes the supporting files for the GPE. To create a custom console that includes access to GPOs and the GPE, follow the steps in that earlier section, but add the Group Policy extension in step 4.

Chapter 8

Conforming System Policies on Downlevel Clients

omogeneous networks having only Windows 2000 servers and clients are rare and will continue to be the exception rather than the rule for at least a few years after Windows 2000's release. Migration of Windows NT servers to Windows 2000 will accelerate as IT managers and system administrators gain confidence in Windows 2000's increased stability and improved performance. Client-side migration from Windows 9x and NT will progress at a much slower pace. Windows 2000's RAM requirements, hardware compatibility issues, licensing cost, and training expense are just a few of the impediments to establishing a fully managed all-Windows 2000 network. Migration from 16-bit to 32-bit Windows is a prime example of client upgrade inertia. Several years elapsed before Windows 95 displaced Windows 3.x on the majority of networked PCs, and even migration from Windows 95 to 98 remains a continuing process in many large organizations.

Much of the content of this chapter is a detailed cross-reference between Windows NT/9x system policies and Windows 2000 Group Policies. If you've established system policies for your downlevel clients and want to quickly locate their Group Policy counterparts, skip to the "Windows NT Computer Policy" or "Establishing Windows 9x Computer Policy" section. Sections that cover user-based system policy follow the sections for computer policy.

Avoiding Client Class Warfare

The vast majority of network administrators must continue to support Windows 9x and NT 4.0 clients together with new and upgraded workstations running Windows 2000 Professional. Except for domain-level password and account lockout policies, Group Policy doesn't apply to downlevel clients. Thus, Windows 9x and NT clients are exempt from the Change and Configuration Management features you implement for Windows 2000 workstations and laptops. Having two classes of network clients raises at least the following two issues:

◆ If you've already implemented CCM for downlevel clients with system policy, it's imperative to maintain consistency between Group Policy and system policy. Applying a more constrictive Group Policy than system policy causes users to complain about the loss of freedom to configure "their" new Windows 2000 computer. Hopefully, you can convince users that the benefits of Windows 2000 outweigh the newly imposed restrictions. The better alternative is to increase the level of desktop control imposed by existing system policy to that of Group Policy you apply or intend to apply to Windows 2000 clients.

✦ If you haven't applied system policy and want to maximize the economic payoff from CCM on Windows 2000 clients, consider implementing parallel system policies for Windows 9x and NT machines. A full understanding of Group Policy makes implementing system policy a relatively easy process for network admins. The political challenges of user desktop lockdown, however, are much more difficult to overcome. Users accustomed to years of desktop anarchy aren't likely to accept lockdown quietly, but implementing system policy smooths the path to Windows 2000's CCM.

NOTE: The Windows Millennium Edition (Me) installation CD-ROM doesn't include the System Policy Editor and administrative templates, and there is no Resource Kit for Windows Me.

Creating Windows NT System Policies

The System Policy Editor, Poledit.exe, uses a pair of administrative templates, Common.adm and Winnt.adm, to establish system policies for Windows NT clients. Installing Windows 2000 Server or running Adminpak.msi on a Windows 2000 workstation adds Poledit.exe to your \Winnt folder but doesn't add an Administrative Tools menu choice for the System Policy Editor. The \Winnt\Inf folder holds the Common.adm and Winnt.adm templates, which have a structure that's quite similar to Group Policy's .adm files. The "Administrative Template File Structure and Syntax" section of Chapter 1 describes the elements of .adm files. Common.adm stores policy templates that are identical for Windows NT and 9x; Winnt.adm has templates that apply to Windows NT only. The primary difference between system policy and Group Policy .adm files is system policy's lack of text for the policy dialog's Explain page. Like Group Policy, you can create custom .adm files for system policy, if you need special Registry settings and have the time to test your additions thoroughly.

NOTE: Windows 2000 installs version 5.0 of Poledit.exe. The only difference between version 5.0 and version 4.0, which is included with Windows NT and 98, is the ability of Poledit.exe version 5.0 to accommodate Unicode characters in templates. You can use versions 4.0 and 5.0 interchangeably.

Windows NT implements system policy by using an Ntconfig.pol file stored in the NETLOGON share of the logon server. Unlike Group Policy's Computer Configuration policies, system policy changes don't apply until the user logs on and the local or roaming profile makes its alteration to the HKEY_LOCAL_MACHINE (HKLM) and HKEY_CURRENT_USER (HKCU) Registry hives. System policy then adds or overwrites existing value entries in the HKLM and HKCU hives. System policies changes written to the Registry are persistent and saved to the user's profile in HKEY_USERS upon logoff.

Like Group Policy, you can filter system policy by user group membership, but Windows NT doesn't support group membership of computer accounts. Thus, all system policies, regardless of whether you filter by user group, apply during a single stage at the end of the logon process. System policy permits establishing policies for individual Windows NT computer and user accounts, but doing so isn't practical for more than a very few special computers and users. Setting per-computer policies, other than for servers, isn't practical, and per-user policies should be limited to very special users. Each policy collection you add to Ntconfig.pol increases its size, which increases network traffic and slows user logon.

CODE BLUE

Windows 2000 and NT support authoring of Ntconfig.pol files for Windows NT clients and servers, and for Windows 2000 clients and servers in some network configurations. Adminpak.msi installs the Windows.adm template that you use in combination with Common.adm to create the Window 9x's Config.pol system policy file. You can't create Windows 9x policy files on a Windows 2000 or NT machine. You must run Poledit.exe on a Windows 98 client to create Config.pol files, as described later in the section "Establishing Windows 9x System Policy."

System Policy Precedence

System policies apply throughout the domains containing user and computer accounts in the following order:

1. Computer policy for a computer account designated by its NetBIOS name, if present

2. Default Computer policy for computers that don't have a computer policy assigned by name

3. User policy assigned to a particular user account by its logon ID, if present

4. Default User policy, if present and the user hasn't been assigned a policy by logon ID

5. Group-based policy, if one is present, the user is a member of the group, and the user hasn't been assigned a policy by logon ID

You can specify the precedence of policies applied to users who receive group-based policy from more than one group.

System and Group Policy Applied to Windows 2000 Clients

Windows 2000 clients receive Windows NT-style system policy if their computer or user accounts are authenticated by Windows NT PDCs or BDCs. For example, if a Windows 2000 client's computer account is in a Windows NT resource domain and AD stores the user's account in a Windows 2000 domain, the client receives computer system policy from the resource domain and the User Configuration elements of Group Policy from the Windows 2000 domain.

When migrating from a network topology with resource domains that contain computer accounts, it's a good practice to migrate resource domains to Windows 2000 OUs or child domains as soon as possible after migrating account domains. Handling a mix of system policy and Group Policy on workstations can increase client support costs when computer and user policies conflict.

System Policies and Upgraded Windows NT PDCs

When you upgrade to a Windows 2000 DC from a Windows NT PDC in a domain that implements system policy for Windows NT and 9x clients, the Ntconfig.pol and Config.pol system policy files move from their original location (\Winnt\System32\Repl\Import\Scripts, the folder shared as NETLOGON by Windows NT) to Winnt\SYSVOL\Sysvol\domain.ext\ Scripts, Windows 2000's NETLOGON share. Windows NT's LANMan Directory Replication service (LMRepl) manages replication of the contents of the NETLOGON share between the PDC and BDCs of the domain to permit clients to download Ntconfig.pol or Config.pol files from any logon server, if you enable the Load Balancing feature of the Update policy described in the "Network" section later in this chapter. The conventional practice is to specify the PDC as the export server and add Ntconfig.pol and Config.pol to the \Winnt\ System32\Repl\Export\Scripts folder. Upgrading a PDC doesn't relocate the Export folder.

Windows 2000 replaces LMRepl with the File Replication Service (FRS), which replicates the contents of the default Windows 2000 NETLOGON share, Winnt\SYSVOL\Sysvol\ domain.ext\Scripts, between DCs. Before you upgrade a PDC that acts as a LMRepl export server, remove the export function from the PDC and assign a BDC as the export server.

To enable Windows NT BDCs in a mixed-mode domain to receive by replication changes to policies and other contents of the NETLOGON share from a Windows 2000 PDC Emulator upgraded from a Windows NT PDC, you use a script to replicate the contents of Winnt\SYSVOL\Sysvol\domain.ext\Scripts to the \Winnt\System32\Repl\Export\Scripts folder of the BDC that acts as the LMRepl export server. The Lmbridge.cmd script, which is installed as a component of the Windows 2000 Server Resource Kit, handles this chore with Xcopy.

NOTE: Knowledge Base article Q248358, "Windows 2000 Does Not Support Windows NT 4.0 Directory Replication (LMRepl)," provides additional information on this upgrade issue.

The System Policy Editor

Emulating Group Policy that differs for OUs, that's filtered by Windows 2000 Security Groups, or both requires applying individual system policy to specific user groups. If you don't have security groups for each OU that contain all the members of the OU, you must create the groups; only Default User policy applies to users who aren't members of a group for which you create a group-based policy.

TIP: If your domain runs in native mode, you have Domain Local groups that you can change to Global or Universal groups, and you want to establish group-based system policy for these groups, make the change before creating your initial system policies. For example, GroupPol's Faculty Members group is a Domain Local group that you can convert to a Global Group by first converting it to a Universal group. You can't convert a Domain Local group to a Global group by this method if the Domain Local group contains Global groups from other domains.

To prepare for creating a set of Windows NT system policies that parallel your Group Policies, do the following:

1. Run Poledit.exe to open the System Policy Editor (PolEdit) with an empty window.

2. Choose File | New Policy to add the Default Computer and Default User icons to the window.

3. Click the Add Computer button to open the Add Computer dialog. Type the NetBIOS name of the computer you want to exempt from application of the Default Computer policy, typically a Windows NT server. Alternatively, click Browse to open the Browse for Computer dialog, which displays only Windows NT computers under the domain node, and double-click the computer to add. Click OK to close the Add Computer dialog; then repeat this step for each additional computer you want to exempt from system policy.

4. Click the Add Group button to open the Add Group dialog, and click the Browse button to open the Windows NT version of the Add Groups dialog, which displays only the Global and Universal groups of Windows 2000 domains and the global groups of trusted Windows NT domains.

5. Select the group to add and click Add to add the group with its downlevel *DOMAIN/* prefix to the Add Names list. Repeat this step for each group to add.

6. Click OK twice to close the dialogs and add icons for the groups to PolEdit's window.

TIP: If you want to save the changes you've made at this point, save the policy file as Ntconfig.pol to a temporary share on the server. When you've completed configuring system policies for all computers and users, save it in the *ComputerName*\NETLOGON share.

Figure 8-1 illustrates computer icons for two Windows NT member servers and user icons for a few Faculty Members and Non-Faculty Staff groups added by the GroupPol application. PolEdit has a convenient copy and paste feature that lets you author a set of system policies for one group and apply them to other groups. You then edit the pasted policy settings as necessary to conform the policies to the Group Policy for the OU or group. Up to this point, use of PolEdit is identical under Windows NT and 9x, except that you can't browse for users and groups when you run PolEdit under Windows 9x.

Viewing Local Policy Settings

The default template setting for all system policies is unconfigured, in which case local policy settings apply, if enabled or disabled. You can determine local system policy settings by choosing File | Open Registry to open PolEdit with the Local Computer and Local User icons in its window. Double-click the Local Computer icon and expand all nodes to view the policy-related Registry keys that are present, indicated by a cleared or checked box, and read their default value item settings. For example, the Default Computer's Remote Update policy is enabled by default, and the Update Mode value is Automatic (Use Default Path), if a different system policy hasn't been applied to the computer. After system policy is applied, the effective system policy settings appear when you expand the Local Computer and Local User nodes. The Local Computer and Local User settings are analogous to those of the Effective Settings column in the right pane of the Windows 2000 Local Security Settings tool.

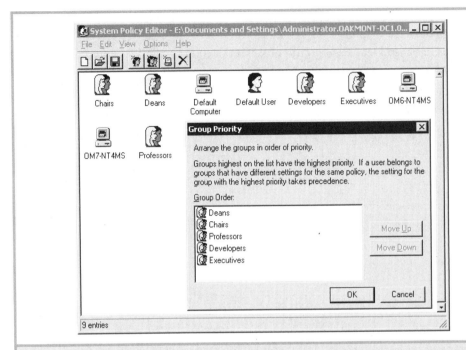

Figure 8-1. Add icons to PolEdit for individual computers you want to exempt from computer policy, groups that correspond to OUs that receive their own GPOs, and Security Groups that are exempted from application of specific GPOs. The Group Priority dialog lets you set the sequence of system policy application.

CODE BLUE

In Local mode, PolEdit is a variant of RegEdit that displays only the system policy Registry values. Changes you make to Local Computer and Local User settings add and alter Registry values if you save changes on closing PolEdit, or open a new policy or a saved Winnt.pol file. Make sure not to save changes to the local computer's Registry unless that's your specific intention.

Viewing a Remote Computer's Settings

You can inspect the Local Computer and Local User policy settings of a remote computer for which you have administrative privileges by doing this:

1. Choose File | Connect to open the Connect dialog.

2. Type the NetBIOS name of the remote computer in the text box and click OK to open the Users on Remote Computer dialog.

3. In the Users on *ComputerName* list, select the name of the account to administer, usually *DOMAIN*\Administrator to start, and click OK to change the Local Computer and Local User settings to those of the remote computer.

If you can't connect to the remote Registry, verify that the account you're using in Windows 2000 is a member of the Administrators group of the remote Windows NT computer. Windows 9*x*'s Remote Administration feature of Control Panel's Passwords tool must be enabled to permit inspecting a Windows 9*x* Registry. Remote registry administration requires user-level access control for shared folders.

Setting Policy Application Priority

If users belong to more than one group to which you apply system policy, you can set the precedence of policy application by choosing Options | Group Priority to open the Group Priority dialog (refer to Figure 8-1). If policy settings for groups to which the user belongs conflict, the settings for the group highest in the list apply to the user.

NOTE: Adding many policy settings that apply to individual groups greatly increases the size of the Ntconfig.pol file and slows user logon.

Windows NT Computer Policy

Double-clicking the Default Computer or a named computer icon opens the Properties dialog for setting computer policy. Expanding a few of the nodes displays tri-state check boxes that correspond to Group Policy's Not Configured (gray), Enabled (checked), and Disabled (cleared) options for Administrative Templates policy settings. Figure 8-2 shows the eight categories of computer systems policies, with the Network\System policies update\Remote update policy enabled and the \Network\System\Run policy unconfigured.

The following eight sections list the available policy settings for each Windows NT computer configuration category. The Registry value name appears parenthetically under the policy or control name in the first column of each table. Where a Group Policy corresponds

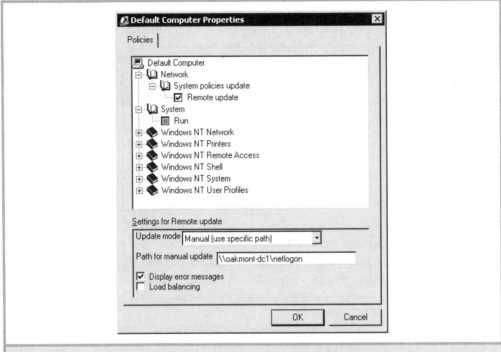

Figure 8-2. PolEdit uses a single-page dialog that combines a version of the GPE's tree view of the Administrative Templates node with the Policy page of the *PolicyName* Properties dialog.

directly to a system policy, the tables have a third column: Group Policy. To maintain consistency, don't enable or disable a computer system policy unless a corresponding Group Policy is available and you apply or intend to apply the corresponding Group Policy. Of the 33 computer system policies, only 10 have Group Policy counterparts.

NOTE: The Common.adm template specifies only two computer configuration system policies: Network\Remote update and System\Run. The remaining system policies are in Winnt.adm.

Network

The Network node has a single policy, Remote Update, stored in the HKLM\System\CurrentControlSet\Control\Update key. Remote Update has four parameters set by controls whose names appear in italic type. There's no Group Policy equivalent of Remote Update.

The User Configuration\Administrative Templates\System\Group Policy node's Group Policy Domain Controller Selection policy applies to the Group Policy Editor, not to the server from which the client obtains Group Policy updates.

System Policy/Control (Update)	Effect of Enabling Policy
Remote update	Enables the setting of the following four values:
Update Mode list (UpdateMode)	Automatic specifies automatic download from the DC that authenticates the client's logon; Manual requires typing of a UNC path to a specific server, share, and file name for the system policy.
Path for Manual Update text box (NetworkPath)	UNC path to specific server storing the Ntconfig.pol file, usually *ComputerName*\NETLOGON\Ntconfig.pol; you must include the name of the file.
Display Error Messages check box (Verbose)	Displays an error message if the updated Ntconfig.pol file can't be loaded.
Load Balancing check box (LoadBalance)	Enables the client to obtain system policy from any logon server having a replicated copy of Ntconfig.pol in the NETLOGON share.

TIP: If you don't enable the Load Balancing policy, clients check for the policy file only on the PDC Emulator DC for the domain, which can result in a performance hit when many downlevel clients log on simultaneously. Using load balancing requires setting the Update Mode value to Automatic. Refer to the earlier section "System Policies and Upgraded Windows NT PDCs" for replication issues in a mixed-mode domain.

System

The System node's Run policy stored in the HKLM\Software\Microsoft\Windows\CurrentVersion\Run key has a single text box that provides the Run value. The closest Group Policy match is a startup script that runs the applications called by the Computer Configuration\Windows Settings\Scripts (Startup/Shutdown) policy. The User Configuration\Administrative Templates\System\Logon/Logoff node's Run These Programs at User Logon policy is similar to the Run system policy, but it doesn't apply to all users unless specified at the domain level with no Security Group filtering.

System Policy/Control	Effect of Enabling Policy
Run	Enables the Show button, which opens the Show Contents dialog for Items to Run at Startup.
Value Name/Value (Application Text Name)	Runs the applications specified by a list of executable files you add to the Show Contents list.

NOTE: The templates of Windows NT 4.0 servers have an additional policy, SNMP, with values for Communities, Permitted Managers, and Public Community Traps. The SNMP policy isn't included in the templates installed by Windows 2000.

Windows NT Network

The single Sharing policy group stored in the HKLM\System\CurrentControlSet\Services\ LanManServer\Parameters key has two values, neither of which is set by default. Windows NT automatically creates the shares unless you disable the policies. There is no equivalent Group Policy.

System Policy (Sharing)	Effect of Enabling Policy
Create hidden drive shares (workstation) (AutoShareWks)	Creates an ADMIN$ share and D$ share(s) for each drive (D) of the client.
Create hidden drive shares (server) (AutoShareServer)	Same as above for Windows NT servers.

Windows NT Printers

The Windows NT Printers category stored in the HKLM\System\CurrentControlSet\ Control\Print key has three values, only one of which has a Group Policy counterpart. Scheduler Priority and Beep for Error Enabled have default values.

System Policy/Control	Effect of Enabling Policy	Group Policy
Disable browse thread on this computer spin box (DisableServerThread)	The print spooler doesn't notify other print servers of the computer's shared printers.	Computer Configuration\ Administrative Templates\ Printers\Printer browsing
Scheduler priority list (SchedulerThreadPriority)	Lets you select from Above Normal or Below Normal printing priority for the machine; the default is Normal.	None
Beep for error enabled check box (BeepEnabled)	Print servers emit a beep at 10-second intervals when a print job error occurs on a print server; the default is disabled.	None

Windows NT Remote Access

The Windows NT Remote Access policy category stored in the HKLM\System\ CurrentControlSet\Services\RemoteAccess\Parameters key has spin boxes to set four values. The default values listed are those that apply when the policy is enabled. Remote Access

Policy (the subject of the "Establishing Remote Access Policy" section in Chapter 7), not Group Policy, determines Windows 2000 RAS policies.

System Policy Spin Box	Effect of Enabling Policy
Max number of unsuccessful authentication retries (AuthenticationRetries)	Lets you specify the number of retries (1 to 10; defaults to 2) before locking out the account.
Max time limit for authentication (AuthenticateTime)	Lets you set the number of seconds (20 to 600; defaults to 120) allowed for authentication.
Wait interval for callback (CallbackTime)	Lets you set the number of seconds (2 to 12; defaults to 2) before the server calls a client that has callback enabled.
Auto Disconnect (AutoDisconnect)	Lets you set the idle time in minutes before logging off the user (0 or greater; defaults to 20).

NOTE: You can type numbers larger than the maximum values shown in the preceding table for the AuthenticationRetries, AuthenticateTime, and CallbackTime values, but larger values return to the listed maximum when you reopen the policy.

Windows NT Shell

The Custom Shared Folders policy group stored in the HKLM\Software\Microsoft\Windows\CurrentVersion\Explorer\UserShellFolders key has four values that you set in text boxes, each of which has a default value when enabled. The Common shared Startup folder duplicates the effect of specifying applications with the earlier Run policy. There is no direct Group Policy counterpart to this policy.

System Policy (Custom Shared Folders)	Effect of Enabling Policy
Custom shared Programs folder (Common Programs)	Lets you specify a UNC path to a folder containing folders, files, and shortcuts for all users' Start | Programs menu (Common) area. The default is the local %SystemRoot%\Profiles\All Users\Start Menu\Programs.
Custom shared desktop icons (Common Desktop)	Same as the preceding, except the specified folder contains desktop icons for all users. The default is the local %SystemRoot%\Profiles\All Users\Desktop.
Custom shared Start menu (Common Start Menu)	Same as the preceding, except the folder contains folders, files, and shortcuts for all users' Start menus. The default is the local %SystemRoot%\Profiles\All Users\Start Menu.
Custom shared Startup folder (Common Start Menu)	Same as the preceding, except the menu. The default is the local %SystemRoot%\Profiles\All Users\Start Menu\Programs\Startup menu.

Windows NT System

The Windows NT System category has two policy groups: Logon in HKLM\Software\
Microsoft\Windows NT\CurrentVersion\Winlogon and File System in HKLM\System\
CurrentControlSet\Control\FileSystem. The Group Policy equivalents of the Logon policies
are Security Options policies, which Windows 2000 stores in the security database
(Secedit.sdb), not the Registry. There is no Group Policy equivalent for any of the File
System policies, which are enabled or disabled by check boxes.

Numbers in parentheses in the Group Policy column specify the location of Group
Policies, as follows:

(1) Computer Configuration\Windows Settings\Security Settings\Local Policies\Security
Options node
(2) Computer Configuration\Administrative Templates\System\Logon node

System Policy (Logon)	Effect of Enabling Policy	Group Policy
Logon banner	Enables (by default) the following two text boxes:	The following two Group Policies apply:
Caption (LegalNoticeCaption)	Title bar text for pre-logon dialog (empty by default)	Message title for users attempting to log on option (1)
Text (LegalNoticeText)	Text box text for pre-logon dialog (empty by default)	Message text for users attempting to log on option (1)
Enable shutdown from Authentication dialog box check box (ShutdownWithoutLogon)	Allows all users to shut down the computer without first logging on by enabling the Shutdown button (disabled by default).	Allow system to be shut down without having to log on option (1)
Do not display last logged on user name check box (DontDisplayLastUserName)	Empties the Log On to Windows dialog's User Name text box.	Do not display last user name in logon screen option (1)
Run logon scripts synchronously check box (RunLogonScriptSync)	Requires logon scripts to complete execution before Explorer (or an alternate shell) starts.	Run Logon Scripts Synchronously (2)

NOTE: Use the Caption and Text values of the Logon Banner policy during the test phase to
verify that computer system policy has been applied to the client. If you don't add at least one
of the two text values, the Logon banner doesn't appear.

System Policy (File System)	Effect of Enabling Policy
Do not create 8.3 file names for long file names (NtfsDisable8dot3NameCreation)	Prevents generating 16-bit DOS-compatible aliases for files with names longer than eight characters or extensions longer than three characters.
Allow extended characters in 8.3 file names (NtfsAllowExtendedCharacterIn 8dot3Name)	If the preceding policy isn't enabled, allows the inclusion of characters in 8.3 file names that aren't supported by the current code page.
Do not update last access time (NtfsDisableLastAccessUpdate)	Increases file system performance by eliminating update of the last access time parameter if the file isn't modified.

Windows NT User Profiles

Values for the six Windows NT User Profile policies are stored in the HKLM\Software\ Microsoft\Windows NT\CurrentVersion\Winlogon key. None of these policies has a default value. The four equivalent Group Policies are located under the \Computer Configuration\ Administrative Templates\System\Logon node.

System Policy/Control	Effect of Enabling Policy	Group Policy
Delete cached copies of roaming profiles check box (DeleteRoamingCache)	Removes the local copy of roaming user profiles when the user logs off.	Delete cached copies of roaming profiles
Automatically detect slow network connections check box (SlowLinkDetectEnabled)	Uses an algorithm to detect a network connection slower than that of a 10BaseT LAN.	Do not detect slow network connections
Slow network connection timeout spin box (SlowLinkTimeout)	Number of seconds to wait for automatic detection to complete.	None
Slow network default profile operation list (SlowLinkProfileDefault)	Lets you select Download Profile or Use Local Profile.	None
Choose profile default operation list (ChooseProfileDefault)	Lets you select local or roaming user profiles as the default for all users.	None
Timeout for dialog boxes spin box (Show)	Sets the default time that the system waits for user input to profile dialogs.	Timeout for dialog boxes

Windows NT User Policy

Windows NT user system policy has much more in common with Windows 2000 User Configuration Group Policy than computer system policy and Computer Configuration Group Policy. The following seven sections list individual policies and their corresponding Group Policies for each user system policy category. Figure 8-3 illustrates PolEdit's Default User Properties dialog with a few policy groups expanded. The 49 Windows NT user system policies have 37 corresponding Group Policies. Thus conforming Windows NT user system policies with the more important User Configuration Group Policies is practical for most organizations.

NOTE: The Common.adm template specifies the following user configuration system policies: Control Panel\Display, Desktop\Wallpaper, Desktop\Color Scheme, Shell\Restrictions, and System\Restrictions. The remaining user system policies are in Winnt.adm.

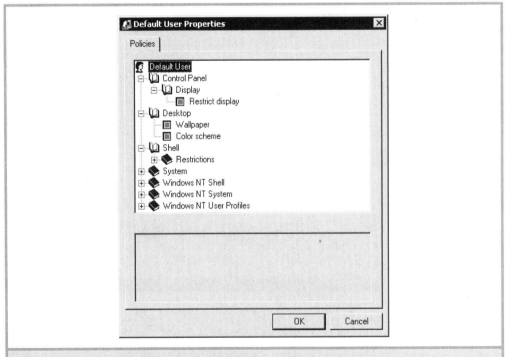

Figure 8-3. The Default User and *GroupName* Properties dialogs have seven user-related system policy categories.

Control Panel

The HKCU\Software\Microsoft\Windows\CurrentVersion\Policies\System key holds value entries for Control Panel category's single Display policy group, which doesn't have default local policy values. The User Configuration\Administrative Templates\Control Panel\ Display node contains the corresponding Group Policies.

System Policy (Display)	Effect of Enabling Policy	Group Policy
Restrict Display	Enables the following five policy check boxes:	
Deny access to Display icon (NoDisplCPL)	Removes the Display tool's icon from Control Panel's window.	Disable Display in Control Panel
Hide Background tab (NoDispBackgroundPage)	Removes the Background page from the Display Properties dialog.	Hide Background tab
Hide Screen Saver tab (NoDispScrSvrPage)	Removes the Screen Saver page from the Display Properties dialog.	Hide Screen Saver tab
Hide Appearance tab (NoDispAppearancePage)	Removes the Appearance page from the Display Properties dialog.	Hide Appearance tab
Hide Settings tab (NoDispSettingsPage)	Removes the Settings page from the Display Properties dialog.	Hide Settings tab

Desktop

The HKCU\ControlPanel\Desktop key holds value entries for the Desktop\Wallpaper policy, and HKCU\ControlPanel\Appearance has the value of the Color Scheme property, neither of which has default local policy values. The User Configuration\Administrative Templates\Desktop\Active Desktop node contains the Active Desktop Wallpaper policy. This Group Policy applies regardless of whether Active Desktop is enabled, because its Registry key is HKCU\Software\Microsoft\Windows\CurrentVersion\Policies\Explorer.

System Policy/Control	Effect of Enabling Policy	Group Policy/Control
Wallpaper check box	Enables or disables the following two controls for wallpaper attributes (not policies):	Active Desktop Wallpaper
Wallpaper Name text box (Wallpaper)	Lets you type a local or UNC path to a *Wallpaper*.bmp file. The default local value is (none).	*Wallpaper Name* text box
Tile Wallpaper check box (TileWallpaper)	Enables or disables tiling the *Wallpaper*.bmp image.	*Wallpaper Style* list (Center, Stretch, Tile)
Color Scheme list (Current)	Lets you select from a Scheme Name list; only Blue and Black or Blues (256) options are available for 8-bit (256-color) color depth.	None

Shell

The 11 value entries of the Shell Restrictions policy group are stored in the HKCU\Software\ Microsoft\Windows\CurrentVersion\Policies\Explorer key. The Effect of Enabling Policy column is missing, because the policies are self-descriptive. Numbers in parentheses in the Group Policy column specify the location of Group Policies, as follows:

(1) User Configuration\Administrative Templates\Start Menu & Taskbar
(2) User Configuration\Administrative Templates\
(3) User Configuration\Administrative Templates\Desktop

System Policy (Restrictions)	Group Policy
Remove Run command from Start menu (NoRun)	Remove Run menu from Start Menu (1)
Remove folders from Settings on Start menu (NoSetFolders)	Remove user's folders from the Start Menu (1)
Remove Taskbar from Settings on Start menu (NoSetTaskbar)	None
Remove Find command from Start menu (NoFind)	Remove Search menu from Start Menu (1)
Hide Drives in My Computer (NoDrives)	Hide specified drives in My Computer (2)
Hide Network Neighborhood (NoNetHood)	Hide My Network Places on desktop (2)
No Entire Network in Network Neighborhood (NoEntireNetwork)	No "Entire Network" in My Network Places (2)
No workgroup contents in Network Neighborhood (NoWorkgroupContents)	No "Computers Near Me" in My Network Places (2)
Hide all items on Desktop (NoDesktop)	Hide all icons on Desktop (2)
Remove Shut Down command from Start menu (NoClose)	Disable and remove the Shut Down command (1)
Don't save settings at exit (NoSaveSettings)	Don't save settings at exit (3)

System

The Disable Registry Editing Tools value entry of the System Restrictions policy group is stored under the HKCU\Software\Microsoft\Windows\CurrentVersion\Policies\System key. Run Only Allowed Windows Applications is located under HKCU\Software\Microsoft\ Windows\CurrentVersion\Policies\Explorer. Corresponding Group Policies are in the User Configuration\Administrative Templates\System node.

System Policy (Restrictions)	Effect of Enabling Policy	Group Policy
Disable Registry editing tools check box (DisableRegistryTools)	Prevents users from opening Regedit.exe or Regedt32.exe.	Disable registry editing tools
Run only allowed Windows applications text box (RestrictRun key)	Restricts users to a list of explicitly permitted applications you add to the List of Allowable Applications in the Show Contents dialog.	Run only allowed Windows applications

CODE BLUE

Don't enable the Disable Registry Editing Tools policy until you've thoroughly tested application of your policy by group membership. If you accidentally apply this policy to the local Administrators group, members of the group won't have access to the local Registry. Also, make sure that software developers don't have this policy applied to their accounts. Disabling the Registry editing tools, however, is one of the most important policies to impose on ordinary users.

Windows NT Shell

The Windows NT Shell category has three policy groups: Custom User Interface, Custom Folders, and Restrictions. The HKCU\Software\Microsoft\Windows NT\CurrentVersion\ Winlogon key stores the Custom Shell policy setting. The Custom User Interface Group Policy is in the User Configuration\Administrative Templates\System node.

System Policy (Custom User Interface)	Effect of Enabling Policy	Group Policy
Custom shell (Shell)	Lets you specify in a text box the name of a shell executable other than Explorer.exe.	Custom user interface

Custom Folders policies are stored in the HKCU\Software\Microsoft\Windows\ CurrentVersion\Explorer\UserShellFolders key, except the Hide Start Menu Subfolder policy, which is under the HKCU\Software\Microsoft\Windows\CurrentVersion\Policies\Explorer key. Custom Folders policies are similar to those of the Custom Shared Folders computer system policies but can be applied by user security group. As with the Custom Shared Folders group, there are Group Policies that correspond to Custom Folders system policies.

Neither of these system policy groups is included in Group Policy undoubtedly because of their lack of use by Windows NT system admins.

System Policy (Custom folders)	Effect of Enabling Policy
Custom Programs folder (Programs)	Lets you specify in a text box a UNC path to a file containing the user's (not Common) section of the Programs menu. The local default is %UserProfile%\StartMenu\Programs.
Custom desktop icons (Desktop)	Lets you specify in a text box the UNC path to a file containing the files for the user's custom desktop icons. The local default is %UserProfile%\Desktop.
Hide Start menu subfolders (NoStartMenuSubFolders)	Hides Start menu subfolders when you specify Custom Programs, Custom desktop, or both folders.
Custom Startup folder (Startup)	Lets you specify in a text box the UNC path to a file containing the files for the user's Programs	Startup menu. The local default is %UserProfile%\Start Menu\Programs\Startup.
Custom Network Neighborhood (NetHood)	Lets you specify in a text box the UNC path to a file containing the files for the user's desktop. The local default is %UserProfile%\NetHood.
Custom Start Menu (StartMenu)	Lets you specify in a text box the UNC path to a file containing Start menu shortcuts. The local default is %UserProfile%\Start Menu.

HKCU\Software\Microsoft\Windows\CurrentVersion\Policies\Explorer stores the value entries for the 12 system policies of the Windows NT Shell Restrictions group. Following are the Group Policy nodes corresponding to the parenthetical numbers following Group Policy names:

(1) User Configuration\Administrative Templates\Windows Components\ Windows Explorer

(2) User Configuration\Administrative Templates\Start Menu & Taskbar

(3) Computer Configuration\Administrative Templates\System

System Policy (Restrictions)	Group Policy
Only use approved shell extensions (EnforceShellExtensionSecurity)	Only allow approved Shell extensions (1)
Remove View->Options menu from Explorer (NoOptions)	Remove the Folder Options menu item from the Tools menu (1)
Remove Tools->GoTo menu from Explorer (NoGoTo)	None
Remove File menu from Explorer (NoFileMenu)	Remove File menu from Windows Explorer (1)

System Policy (Restrictions)	Group Policy
Remove common program groups from Start menu (NoCommonGroups)	Remove common program groups from Start menu (2)
Disable context menus for the taskbar (NoTrayContextMenu)	Disable context menus for the taskbar (2)
Disable Explorer's default context menu (NoViewContextMenu)	Disable Windows Explorer's default context menu (1)
Remove the "Map Network Drive" and "Disconnect Network Drive" options (NoNetDisconnect)	Remove "Map Network Drive" and "Disconnect Network Drive" (1)
Disable link file tracking (LinkResolveIgnoreLinkInfo)	Do not use the tracking-based method when resolving shell shortcuts (2)
Remove NT Security item from Start menu (NoNtSecurity)	Remove Security option from Start menu (Terminal Services only) (3)
Remove Disconnect item from Start menu (NoDisconnect)	Remove Disconnect item from Start menu (Terminal Services only) (3)
Prevent users from changing file type associations (NoFileAssociate)	None

Windows NT System

Windows NT System entries are scattered among HKLM\Software\Microsoft keys. The value items for Parse Autoexec.bat and Run Logon Scripts Synchronously are in HKLM\Software\Microsoft\Windows NT\CurrentVersion\Winlogon; Disable Logoff is in HKCU\Software\Microsoft\Windows\CurrentVersion\Policies\Explorer; Disable Task Manager, Disable Lock Workstation, and Disable Change Password are in HKCU\Software\Microsoft\Windows\CurrentVersion\Policies\System; and Show Welcome Tips at Logon is in HKCU\Software\Microsoft\Windows\CurrentVersion\Explorer\Tips.

Following is the key to the nodes in which the Group Policies are located:
(1) User Configuration\Administrative Templates\System\Logon/Logoff
(2) User Configuration\Administrative Templates\Start Menu & Taskbar
(3) User Configuration\Administrative Templates\System

System Policy	Effect of Enabling Policy	Group Policy
Parse Autoexec.bat (ParseAutoexec)	Adds environmental variables defined in Autoexec.bat to the user's environment.	None
Run logon scripts synchronously (RunLogonScriptSync)	Requires logon scripts to execute before running applications included in the Startup menu.	Run logon scripts synchronously (1)

System Policy	Effect of Enabling Policy	Group Policy
Disable Logoff (NoLogoff)	Prevents users from logging off the network.	Disable logoff on the Start menu (2)
Disable Task Manager (DisableTaskMgr)	Prevents users from running Taskman.exe.	Disable Task Manager (2)
Disable Lock Workstation (DisableLockWorkstation)	Prevents users from pressing CTRL+ALT+DEL and selecting Lock Computer.	Disable Lock Computer (2)
Disable Change Password (DisableChangePassword)	Prevents users from voluntarily changing their passwords; change is allowed only when requested by the system.	Disable Change Password (2)
Show Welcome Tips at logon (Show)	Displays the Welcome to Windows splash screen unless disabled.	Don't display welcome screen at logon (3)

Windows NT User Profiles

The Limit Profile Size system policy is stored under the HKCU\Software\Microsoft\ Windows\CurrentVersion\Policies\System, and Exclude Directories is in Software\Policies\ Microsoft\Windows\System. The two Windows NT User Profiles system policies have corresponding Group Policies, both of which are located in the User Configuration\ Administrative Templates\System\Logon/Logoff node.

System Policy/Controls	Effect of Enabling Policy	Group Policy
Limit profile size (EnableProfileQuota)	Enables the following five controls:	Limit profile size
Custom Message text box (Profile Quota Message)	Specifies a message warning users who have exceeded their profile size quota (a standard message is provided).	*Custom Message*
Max Profile size (kB) spin box (MaxProfileSize)	Sets the maximum size of the profile (the default is 30 MB).	*Max Profile size (kB)*
Include registry in file list check box (IncludeRegInProQuota)	Includes the HKLM and HKCU Registry hives from the profile size calculation.	*Include registry in file list*
Notify user when profile space is exceeded check box (WarnUser)	Displays the Custom message.	*Notify user when profile space is exceeded*

System Policy/Controls	Effect of Enabling Policy	Group Policy
Remind user every X minutes spin box (WarnUserTimout)	Sets the interval at which the Custom message appears (the default is 15 minutes).	*Remind User every X minutes*
Exclude directories in roaming profile text box (ExcludeProfileDirs)	Lets you specify a semicolon-separated list of folders to exclude from the profile.	Exclude directories in roaming profile

Establishing Windows 9x System Policy

If you're establishing Windows 9x system policy as a prelude to upgrading Windows 9x clients to Windows 2000 Professional and applying Group Policy for CCM, it's important to configure only policies that have Group Policy counterparts or that emulate the default behavior of Windows 2000 Professional. Like Windows NT system policies, relatively few Windows 9x policies have exact Group Policy counterparts. You can and should apply policies that increase network security, such as User-Level Access Control for folders shared by clients, which doesn't have a corresponding Group Policy.

Creating Config.pol files to implement Windows 9x group policy requires running Poledit.exe under Windows 9x with the Common.adm and Windows.adm templates. PolEdit isn't installed by Windows 9x Setup. You must install Poledit.exe and its related files from the distribution CD-ROM or a network share as follows:

✦ **Windows 95 OSR2**   Open Control Panel's Add/Remove Programs tool, click the Windows Components tab, click Have Disk, and navigate to the *d*:\Win95\OSR2\Admin\Apptools\Poledit folder. Accept the default Grouppol.inf file and click OK to open the Have Disk dialog. Mark the Group Policies and System Policy Editor check boxes and click Install to complete the installation.

✦ **Windows 98 SE**   Use the Windows 95 OSR2 installation process, but navigate to the *d*:\Win98_SE\Setup\Tools\Reskit\Netadmin\Poledit folder to find Grouppol.inf.

NOTE: The preceding file locations are those of the Microsoft Developer Network (MSDN) Platform Archive (32-bit) Disk 1 for Windows 95 and MSDN Development Platform Disk 5 for Windows 98SE. The location of the files vary with the distribution medium.

CODE BLUE

> If you intend to apply system policy by the user's Windows 2000 group membership, the Group Policies Windows component must be installed on all Windows 9x clients on the network. This inaptly named component has nothing at all to do with Windows 2000 Group Policies. Installing the Group Policies component is an often overlooked option during Windows 9x setup. When installing the Group Policies component on Windows 9x clients, make sure the System Policy Editor check box is cleared to prevent users from running Poledit.exe. Applying the Disable Registry Editing Tools policy doesn't affect user access to Poledit.exe.

The organization and individual system policies for Windows 9x differ from those for Windows NT, and there are differences in the nomenclature of Windows 95 and 98 system policies. The following sections describe Windows 98 system policies, which are backwardly compatible with Windows 95 policies. Windows 98 has two system policy categories for computers and users: Windows 98 Network and Windows 98 System. The corresponding Windows 95 policy categories are Network and System.

NOTE: There are minor differences between the Windows.adm template supplied with Windows 2000 and that installed when you add PolEdit to Windows 98. You use the Windows 98 version of the template for Windows 9x policies, so you can disregard any differences you notice.

Windows 98 Computer System Policy: Windows 98 Network

The Windows 98 Network category has 11 policy groups for computers, three of which apply only to NetWare networks. NetWare policies aren't within the scope of this book, so the Microsoft Client for NetWare, NetWare Directory Services, and File and Printer Sharing for NetWare Networks aren't included in the following eight policy group sections.

Access Control

The HKLM\Security\Provider key stores the Authenticator Name value. The Authenticator Type value (Mssp.vxd) for Windows NT Domain authentication is stored under the HKLM\System\CurrentControlSet\Services\VxD\MSSP key. There is no Group Policy equivalent to the User-Level Access Control policy, because Windows 2000 Professional computers with a domain account require user-level access control for shared resources.

System Policy/Controls	Effect of Applying Policy
User-level access control	Specifies that computers require user-level access control for resources shared by the client (Access Control page of the Network dialog) and enables the following two controls:
Authenticator Name text box (Provider)	Lets you specify the downlevel name of the Windows 2000 domain that provides the list of groups and users permitted access to the client's shared resources.
Authenticator Type list (StaticVxD)	Lets you select between a Netware 3.x or 4.x or Windows NT Domain.

CODE BLUE

Applying the User-Level Access Control policy to Windows 9x clients that currently share folders with share-level access removes the shares when the policy is first applied to the client. A similar removal of sharing properties occurs when changing from share-level to user-level access control (or vice-versa) on the Access Control page of Control Panel's Network dialog.

Logon

HKLM\Software\Microsoft\Windows NT\CurrentVersion\Winlogon stores the two Logon Banner values. HKLM\Network\Logon stores the remaining three values.

Numbers in parentheses in the Group Policy column specify the location of Group Policies, as follows:

(1) Computer Configuration\Windows Settings\Security Settings\Local Policies\ Security Options node

(2) Computer Configuration\Administrative Templates\System node

System Policy/Controls	Effect of Enabling Policy	Group Policy
Logon Banner	Enables the following two controls:	
Caption text box (LegalNoticeCaption)	Title bar text for pre-logon dialog (the default is "Important Notice").	Message title for users attempting to log on option (1)

System Policy/Controls	Effect of Enabling Policy	Group Policy
Text text box (LegalNoticeText)	Text box text for pre-logon dialog (the default is "Do not attempt to log on unless you are an authorized user").	Message text for users attempting to log on option (1)
Require validation from network for Windows access (MustBeValidated)	Requires user to be authenticated by Windows 2000 (or Windows NT or NetWare) to run Windows 9x.	None
Don't show last user at logon (DontShowLastUser)	Empties the Log On to Windows dialog's User Name text box.	Do not display last user name in logon screen option (1)
Don't show logon progress (NoProgressUI)	Hides the series of messages that appear during Windows 98 logon.	Similar to Verbose vs. normal status messages (2)

Password

The HKLM\Software\Microsoft\Windows\CurrentVersion\Policies\Network key holds values for password system policies. When logging on to a Windows 2000 domain, the domain-level password policies apply to Windows 9x users. If your domain-level policy doesn't specify a minimum password length or complex passwords, the system policy settings apply.

Numbers in parentheses in the Group Policy column specify the location of Group Policies, as follows:

(1) Computer Configuration\Windows Settings\Security Settings\Local Policies\Security Options node

(2) Computer Configuration\Windows Settings\Security Settings\Account Policies\Password Policy node

System Policy	Effect of Enabling Policy	Group Policy
Hide share passwords with asterisks (HideSharePwds)	Replaces share-level security passwords with asterisks when typed (enabled by default).	None
Disable password caching (DisablePwdCaching)	Prevents saving of passwords and use of the Quick Logon feature.	Similar to Number of previous logons to cache set to 0 (1)
Require alphanumeric Windows password (AlphanumPwds)	Requires a password containing a combination of letters and numbers.	Similar to Passwords must meet complexity requirements (2)

System Policy	Effect of Enabling Policy	Group Policy
Minimum Windows password length (MinPwdLen)	Length spin box sets the minimum length of the password.	Minimum password length (2)

Proxy Server

The HKLM\Software\Microsoft\Windows\CurrentVersion\Internet Settings key stores the single Proxy Server value for the browser. Group Policy's User Configuration\Windows Settings\Internet Explorer Maintenance\Connection node has related settings, but none are direct counterparts of the Disable Automatic Location of Proxy Server system policy.

System Policy	Effect of Applying Policy
Disable automatic location of proxy server (DisableProxyServerAutoLocate)	Prevents Windows 98 from checking the DHCP server for the presence and location of a proxy server.

Microsoft Client for Windows Networks

The HKLM\Network\Logon key holds the two Log On to Windows NT values, HKLM\System\CurrentControlSet\Services\VxD\VNETSUP stores the Workgroup value, and HKLM\System\CurrentControlSet\Services\VxD\VREDIR stores the Alternate Workgroup value. None of these policies has a Group Policy counterpart, because values set in the System Properties dialog's Network Identification page determine Windows 2000 client logon parameters.

System Policy/Controls	Effect of Enabling Policy
Log on to Windows NT	Enables the following three controls:
Domain name text box (Authenticating Agent)	Lets you specify the downlevel domain name for the DC that authenticates the user.
Display logon confirmation check box	Displays a "Welcome to the DomainName" message.
Disable caching of domain password check box (NoDomainPwdCaching)	Prevents saving of the network password (see the Disable Password Caching policy in the "Passwords" section earlier in this chapter).
Workgroup (Workgroup)	Lets you specify in a text box a Workgroup name for the client.
Alternate Workgroup (Workgroup)	Lets you specify in a text box the name of a Workgroup that has clients with Windows File and Printer Sharing for Microsoft Networks enabled, if the primary workgroup runs only File and Printer Sharing for NetWare.

File and Printer Sharing for Microsoft Networks

The HKLM\Software\Microsoft\Windows\CurrentVersion\Policies\Network key stores the two File and Printer Sharing values, which don't have Group Policy counterparts. You can prevent installation of File and Printer Sharing for Microsoft Networks by appropriate entries in the [Networking] section of the Unattend.txt file for unattended Windows 2000 Professional installation.

System Policy	Effect of Enabling Policy
Disable File Sharing (NoFileSharing)	Prevents users from sharing files over the network.
Disable Printer Sharing (NoPrintSharing)	Prevents users from sharing printers over the network.

Dial-Up Networking

The Dial-Up Networking group has a single policy that's stored under the HKLM\Software\ Microsoft\Windows\CurrentVersion\Policies\Network key. The policy applies only to clients that have modems installed. There is no corresponding Group Policy, but you can restrict user access to the Network and Dial-up Connections window with polices under the User Configuration\Administrative Templates\Network\Network and Dial-up Connections node.

System Policy	Effect of Enabling Policy
Disable dial-in (NoDialIn)	Prevents all users from allowing incoming modem connections.

Update

The Update group's Remote Update system policy template is in Common.adm, so Windows 9x's settings are the same as those of Windows NT, which are described in the "Network" section under the "Windows NT Computer Policy" heading earlier in this chapter.

Windows 98 Computer System Policy: Windows 98 System

The Windows 98 System category of computer system policies has six policy groups. The SNMP group is missing from Windows 2000's Winnt.adm template, and its policies are seldom implemented, so the SNMP group isn't covered in the five sections that follow.

User Profiles

User Profiles has a single policy, Enable User Profiles, whose value is stored in the HKLM\
Network\Logon key. There is no corresponding Group Policy, because user profiles aren't
optional for Windows 2000. For consistency with Windows NT and 2000 clients, consider
enabling user profiles and providing Windows 9*x* users with roaming user profiles, if you
implement them for Windows NT and 2000 users.

System Policy	Effect of Enabling Policy
Enable user profiles (UserProfiles)	Same as selecting the Users Can Customize Their Preferences and Desktop Settings option of the User Profiles page of the Password Properties dialog.

Network Paths

The HKLM\Software\Microsoft\Windows\CurrentVersion\Setup key stores the two Network
Paths policies. Providing the Setup path is convenient for users who are permitted to
change their computer configuration. There are no corresponding Group Policies.

System Policy	Effect of Enabling Policy
Network path for Windows Setup	Lets you specify in the Path text box the UNC path to the network share for the Windows 9*x* Setup folder.
Network path for Windows Tour	Lets you specify in the Path text box the UNC path to the network share for the Windows 9*x* Tour program. You must add \Discover.exe to the path to enable the Microsoft Tour.

Programs to Run

The HKLM\Software\Microsoft\Windows\CurrentVersion\Run, HKLM\Software\
Microsoft\Windows\CurrentVersion\RunOnce, and HKLM\Software\Microsoft\Windows\
CurrentVersion\RunServices keys hold the three value entries of the Programs to Run
group. Enabling a policy lets you open a Show dialog to enter the application file
name and another dialog to add parameters to the execution instructions. The Show
dialogs add sequentially numbered value items with the name of the executable file
as the value.

The Run system policy has related User Configuration Group Policies; Run Services is
related to the policies of the Computer Configuration\Windows Settings\Security Settings\
System Services node, which controls the Startup mode of installed Windows 2000 services.
The Run Once policy doesn't work as advertised, so it's seldom, if ever, enabled.

System Policy	Effect of Enabling Policy	Group Policy
Run	Same as the Windows NT Run system policy described in "System" section within the earlier "Windows NT Computer Policy" section.	See Run in the earlier "System" section
Run Once	Runs the list of programs every time the user logs on unless you disable the policy after you're sure all users have run the programs at least once.	None
Run Services	Runs the list of service items you specify at system startup.	Related to the System Services policies

Install Device Drivers

The HKLM\Software\Microsoft\Driver Signing key holds a policy value name with the value set by the Digital Signature Check list. The corresponding Group Policy is in the Computer Configuration\Windows Settings\Security Settings\Local Policies\Security Options node.

System Policy\Control	Effect of Enabling Policy	Group Policy
Install Device Drivers	Enables the following control:	Unsigned driver installation behavior
Digital Signature Check list (Policy)	Lets you select from Allow Installation of All Drivers, Block Installation of Non-Microsoft Signed Drivers, and Warn Installation of Non-Microsoft Signed Drivers.	Corresponding selections are Silently succeed, Do not allow installation, and Warn but allow installation

Windows Update

The Software\Microsoft\Windows\CurrentVersion\Policies\Explorer key holds the Disable Windows Update value; the remaining values appear under the Software\Policies\Microsoft\ Windows Update key. The Disable and Remove Links to Windows Update Group Policy is under the User Configuration\Administrative Templates\Start Menu & Taskbar node. There are no Group Policy counterparts to Override Local Web Page and Override Windows Update system policies, but the User Configuration\Windows Settings\Internet Explorer Maintenance\URLs has IE 5–related Group Policies.

System Policy/Control	Effect of Enabling Policy	Group Policy
Disable Windows Update (NoWindowsUpdate)	Removes Windows Update from the Start menu.	Disable and remove links to Windows Update
Override Local Web Page	Enables the following control:	None
Local Web Page text box (Local URL)	Points to the path of a local Web page that replaces the default Windows update URL.	

System Policy/Control	Effect of Enabling Policy	Group Policy
Override Windows Update Site URL	Enables the following control:	None
Site URL text box (Remote URL)	Points to the URL on your intranet or the Intranet for a Web page to replace the default Windows Update URL.	

Windows 98 User System Policy: Windows 98 Network

The user-based network system policy category has a single group: Sharing. The HKCU\ Software\Microsoft\Windows\CurrentVersion\Policies\Network key holds the two values. Group Policy has no counterpart to this system policy group.

System Policy	Effect of Enabling Policy
Disable file sharing controls (NoFileSharingControl)	Removes the Sharing page of all *FolderName* Properties dialogs.
Disable print sharing controls (NoPrintSharingControl)	Removes the Sharing page of all *PrinterName* Properties dialogs.

TIP: If you permit Windows 98 users to share folders, enable the User-Level Access Control policy described in the earlier "Access Control" section. Allowing users to share folders under Share-Level access control, with or without password protection, compromises network security.

Windows 98 User System Policy: Windows 98 System

Default User has four Windows 98 System categories: Shell, Control Panel, Desktop Display, and Restrictions. Most of the policy groups and policies of these categories are identical to or closely resemble those of their Windows NT counterparts.

Shell

The system policies of the Windows 98 Custom Folders group are identical to the Windows NT Custom Folders category described in the earlier "Windows NT Shell" section within the "Windows NT User Policy" section, with two exceptions: The Registry key that holds the paths to the custom folders for users is HKCU\Software\Microsoft\ Windows\CurrentVersion\Explorer\User Shell Folders, and no default values are provided for folder paths.

The Windows 98 Shell Restrictions policies and their value locations in the Registry are the same as those for Windows NT user policy listed in the "Windows NT Shell" section.

Restrictions

The 11 Windows 98 Restrictions policies are identical to those described in the earlier "Windows NT Shell" section within the "Windows NT User Policy" section, except for very minor changes to the policy names.

Control Panel

The Windows 98 Control Panel Display subgroup is identical to that described in the earlier Windows NT "Control Panel" section. As is the case with Shell Restrictions, Microsoft made minor changes to policy names, but no change to the value item names or Registry location.

The Network, Passwords, Printers, and System subgroups are specific to Windows 9x. Each subgroup contains only one system policy, and most of the settings have similar Group Policy counterparts. By default, ordinary Windows 2000 users can't change most Control Panel settings; enabling the Group Policies listed in the following tables precludes members of the local Administrators group from making the specified changes.

 NOTE: The User Configuration\Administrative Templates\Control Panel node has a Hide Specified Control Panel Applets policy that lets you create a list of .cpl files for the tools whose icons you want to remove from Control Panel's window. Adding a file to the list of the Show dialog is equivalent to enabling the corresponding Restrict *ToolName* Control Panel policy.

The HKCU\Software\Microsoft\Windows\CurrentVersion\Policies\Network Registry key holds the Restrict Network Control Panel value settings. Windows 2000's *ConnectionName* Properties dialogs for each LAN or dial-up connection replaces Control Panel's Network tool. Group Policies that control user access to LAN and dial-up connections are located under the User Configuration\Administrative Templates\Network\Network and Dial-up Connections node.

System Policy/Controls	Effect of Enabling Policy	Group Policy
Restrict Network Control Panel	Enables the following three controls:	
Disable Network Control Panel check box (NoNetSetup)	Removes the Network icon from Control Panel's window, so the following two controls have no effect.	Prohibit access to properties of a LAN connection
Hide Identification page check box (NoNetSetupIDPage)	Removes the Identification page from the dialog.	None
Hide Access Control page check box (NoNetSetupSecurityPage)	Removes the Access Control page from the dialog.	None

Restrict Passwords Control Panel values are stored under the HKCU\Software\Microsoft\ Windows\CurrentVersion\Policies\System key. Windows 2000 doesn't have a Passwords tool, but it does have a Disable Change Password Group Policy under the User Configuration\ Administrative Templates\System\Logon/Logoff node. Remote management of Windows 2000 computers is enabled by default and can't be disabled without restricting the groups specified in the Access This Computer from the Network policy of the Computer Configuration\Windows Settings\Security Settings\Local Policies\User Rights Assignment node. Windows 2000's System Properties dialog has the User Profiles page, and there's no Group Policy to prevent users from viewing the page or members of the local Administrators group from making changes to user profiles.

System Policy/Controls	Effect of Enabling Policy	Group Policy
Restrict Passwords Control Panel	Enables the following four controls:	
Disable Password Control Panel check box (NoSecCPL)	Removes the Passwords Properties dialog's icon from Control Panel.	Not applicable
Hide Change Passwords page check box (NoPwdPage)	Prevents users from changing their local passwords or their network passwords until requested by the system.	Disable Change Password
Hide Remote Administration page check box (NoAdminPage)	Prevents users from enabling or disabling Remote Administration.	Not applicable
Hide User Profiles page check box (NoProfilePage)	Prevents users from enabling or disabling user profiles.	Not applicable

The HKCU\Software\Microsoft\Windows\CurrentVersion\Policies\Explorer key holds the Restrict Printer Settings values. Two corresponding Group Policies are located under the User Configuration\Administrative Templates\Control Panel\Printers node.

System Policy/Controls	Effect of Enabling Policy	Group Policy
Restrict Printer Settings	Enables the following three controls:	
Hide General and Details pages check box (NoPrinterTabs)	Removes the General and Details pages from the *PrinterName* Properties dialog.	None

System Policy/Controls	Effect of Enabling Policy	Group Policy
Disable Deletion of Printers check box (NoDeletePrinter)	Prevents deletion of *PrinterName* icons from the Printers window.	Disable deletion of printers
Disable Addition of Printers check box (NoAddPrinter)	Removes the Add Printers icon from the Printers window.	Disable addition of printers

Restrict System Control Panel values are stored under the HKCU\Software\Microsoft\ Windows\CurrentVersion\Policies\System key. You can prevent users from opening the Device Manager extension snap-in of the Computer Management console by disabling the Device Manager policy under the User Configuration\Administrative Templates\Windows Components\Microsoft Management Console\Restricted/Permitted snap-ins\Extension snap-in node. The remaining system policies don't have corresponding Group Policies due to the lack of settings that control the visibility of pages and other elements of the Windows 2000 System Properties dialog.

System Policy/Controls	Effect of Enabling Policy	Group Policy
Restrict System Control Panel	Enables the following four controls:	
Hide Device Manager page check box (NoDevMgrPage)	Removes the Device Manager page from the System Properties dialog.	Device Manager
Hide Hardware Profiles page check box (NoConfigPage)	Removes the Hardware Profiles page from the System Properties dialog.	None
Hide File System button check box (NoFileSysPage)	Removes the File System button from the Performance page of the System Properties dialog.	None
Hide Virtual Memory button check box (NoVirtMemPage)	Removes the File System button from the Performance page of the System Properties dialog.	None

Desktop Display

The two Desktop Display policies, Wallpaper and Color Scheme, are nearly identical to those for Windows NT and described in the earlier "Desktop" section. A Display Method list with Center Wallpaper and Stretch Wallpaper choices replaces the Tile Wallpaper check box. The Color Scheme list offers different choices in 8-bit and higher color depths, but its function is identical to that of the Windows NT Color Scheme policy.

Restrictions

The Disable Registry Editing Tools and Run Only Allowed Windows Applications system policies are the same as those for Windows NT and are described in the earlier "System" section within the "Windows NT User Policy" section. Windows 98 adds two system policies that apply to the MS-DOS window and DOS applications. The User Configuration\Administrative Templates\System node holds the Disable the Command Prompt Group Policy.

System Policy/Controls	Effect of Enabling Policy	Group Policy
Disable MS-DOS prompt	Prevents users from gaining access to the Programs I MS-DOS menu choice.	Disable the command prompt
Disable single-mode MS-DOS applications	Prevents users from running DOS applications in MS-DOS mode.	None

Applying System Policies to Test and Production Domains

System policy, like Group Policy, requires thorough testing to ensure that users don't experience problems with their Windows NT and 9x clients after the initial system policy application. You can correct problems caused by incorrect Group Policy settings simply by altering the errant GPO and instructing all Windows 2000 Professional users to reboot their clients. Because of the Registry tattooing problems described in the "Central Administration and Lockdown" section of Chapter 1, you must reverse the settings of the offending system policy. If users receive multiple system policies as a result of membership in two or more groups having group-specific system policies, changing a group's policy from enabled to disabled might have undesirable side effects for other group-based policies. Unlike Group Policy, changing a system policy from enabled or disabled to not configured has no effect on users' Registry settings.

CODE BLUE

Tattooing of the Registry by system policy can cause misleading test results when you change and retest system policies or use the same client to test application of security policy by Security Group membership. To return a client's Registry to an approximation of its initial, "clean" status, you must reverse every policy you applied to the client. Disabling a previously enabled policy, however, retains many of the value entries under the Registry keys listed in the preceding tables; the values of REG_DWORD entries, for example, change from 1 to 0 when you disable a previously enabled policy. The better approach is to back up the entire Registry of your test clients prior to application of system policy and then restore the Registry from the backup copy prior to each test operation.

After you've completed your Windows NT and 98 system policy settings, save the policy file as Ntconfig.pol or Config.pol, respectively, to the NETLOGON share of a DC in a test domain for initial evaluation. Policies you set under Windows 98 also work with Windows 95 clients; Windows 95 ignores unsupported Windows 98 policies. Once you've confirmed that your system policies deliver the expected results for members of each group for which you've specified user-based policies, copy Ntconfig.pol and Config.pol to the NETLOGON share of a DC in your production domain.

Before placing system policy in production, be sure to notify users that their client PCs will undergo behavior changes. This is especially important if you apply policies that affect user logon, such as Windows 9*x*'s Require Validation from Network for Windows Access, or a policy that makes file-system changes, such as User-Level Access Control.

Configuring Internet Explorer 5+ for Downlevel Clients

Microsoft recommends using the User Configuration\Windows Settings\Internet Explorer Maintenance Group Policy for configuring IE 5.0, which is installed by default on all Windows 2000 systems. These Group Policies emulate the installation configuration files generated by the Internet Explorer Administration Kit (IEAK) 5.0. IE 5.5 was the current version when this book was written. No changes are required to the version 5.0 Group Policies to accommodate the new features of version 5.5.

> **NOTE:** You can download the latest English version of the IEAK from http://www.microsoft.com/windows/ieak/en/default.asp. The downloaded IEAK runs only in demonstration mode until you enter a license key, which you can obtain via e-mail at no charge from Microsoft by clicking the Get Customization Code button in the third Wizard dialog and completing a Licensing & Registration form.

You can customize the IE 5+ installation for downlevel clients by running the Customization Wizard with your license key. Choices you make in the Wizard dialogs are very similar to those you make in the Browser User Interface, Connection, URLs, Security, and Programs subnodes. Many of the .adm files that the IEAK Setup program installs in the \Program Files\IEAK5_5\En\Policies folder, such as Inetres.adm, Inetcorp.adm, and Inetset.adm, are identical to those installed by Windows 2000. The Wizard uses the .adm files to generate the Install.ins file that defines the custom installation. The IEAK offers customized installation options for Outlook Express that aren't available as Group Policies.

TIP: When you run the Customization Wizard to establish a standard IE 5+ installation package for your organization, print copies of the exported Group Policy settings of the four Internet Explorer Maintenance subnodes for reference.

After you complete the initial configuration, you can open the Install.ins installation file in the Profile Manager, change the installation settings as necessary, and save the changes as group-specific *GroupName*.ins and associated *GroupName*.cab files. For example, data-entry operators might receive a bare-bones browser, while corporate officers get an installation with all IE 5+ bells and whistles.

Chapter 9

Deploying Group Policies to Production Domains

T he majority of the content of this book is devoted to establishing optimal strategies for deploying Group Policy and determining the effects of applying GPOs to Windows 2000 clients in test domains. Developing an effective Group Policy for your organization is similar to writing a Windows application, such as GroupPol.exe: 10 percent of the project hours are devoted to writing code; the remaining 90 percent of the effort is testing internal alpha and limited-release beta versions of the application.

Once you're satisfied that the set of GPOs that you apply at the site, domain, and OU levels meet IT management's Group Policy objectives for TCO reduction, the question remains how to move the GPOs you created from the test to the production domain. Windows 2000's Administrative Tools don't include the capability to copy GPOs from one domain to another, nor can you back up and restore GPOs as individual files. If you document your final GPO collection adequately, you can construct a duplicate set of GPOs in the production domain. Full documentation of your GPOs is essential for recovery from a system failure. Following are just a few of the problems you're likely to encounter when you re-create GPOs for a production domain:

+ Re-creating GPOs manually in a new domain is a time-consuming and costly process, especially when system or network admins must be assigned to the task.

+ Policies apply incrementally to groups and users as you generate the GPOs for the production domain. You can enable the User Configuration\Administrative Templates\System\Group Policy's Create New Group Policy Object Links Disabled by Default policy and then enable all policies you've added. This technique, however, isn't a cure for incremental policy application, and there's no equivalent Computer Configuration policy.

+ Entry errors often occur when referring to onscreen or printed GPO documentation that you generate by exporting tab-separated text files from individual nodes in the GPE and importing the files into a worksheet.

+ GPOs must be linked to the same sites, domains, and OUs as those of your test versions. The GPE can't export link information, so you must document and re-create the links along with the GPOs. Here's another chance for errors to occur.

It's unfortunate that Microsoft didn't provide the capability to copy GPOs from one domain to another. On the other hand, omission of such features creates a market opportunity for independent software vendors to provide missing Group Policy tools.

Moving GPOs from Testing to Production with FAZAM 2000

FullArmor Corporation's Zero Administration for Windows (FAZAM) 2000 application is a suite of tools for creating, duplicating, managing, and archiving Windows 2000 GPOs. FAZAM 2000 builds on the company's FAZAM 6 toolset for Windows NT system policy and has qualified for Microsoft's Certified for Windows 2000 logo. FullArmor's primary customers are Fortune 1000 corporations, but any organization with more than a few hundred Windows 2000 clients is a candidate for a FAZAM 2000 license. FullArmor's Web site at http://www.fullarmor.com has additional information on FAZAM 2000.

One of FAZAM 2000's most useful features is the ability to back up and restore your entire collection of GPOs for a domain in a few minutes. During the testing process, you can maintain snapshots of previous Group Policy versions and quickly revert to the last-known good set if necessary. When restoring GPOs to the domain from which you created the backup, the operation preserves GPO links and Security Group filters.

NOTE: Versions 1.0 and 1.2 of FAZAM 2000 don't handle site-level and local GPOs. FullArmor has scheduled adding these extensions for a future version.

You also can restore or import GPOs from the backup to any other domain for which you have administrative rights. This feature enables fast Group Policy migration from the test (source) to the production (target) domain and eliminates the problems described in the preceding section. FAZAM 2000 version 1.0 doesn't restore GPO links or Security Group filters in a different target domain, so you must re-create the original GPO links and filters manually. GPO links and filters are dependent on AD object GUIDs that differ between the test and production domains. Version 1.2 has a six-dialog GPO Replication Wizard that automatically handles links and filters for source and target domains that have identical OU and Security Group structures.

FAZAM 2000's setup process runs a Microsoft Installer file from the distribution CD-ROM. Installation adds FAZAM 2000.msc to the Programs menu and a Jet 3.51 (Access 97) Fazam.mdb database to store GPO data. In most cases, you run FAZAM 2000 on an administrative workstation, but you also can run the application on a member server or DC.

Backing Up Domain GPOs

Opening the FAZAM 2000.msc snap-in displays a console with two nodes in the tree-view pane: FAZAM 2000 Administrator and FAZAM 2000 Policy Analysis. To back up GPOs in the test domain, do the following:

1. Create a backup folder, **GPO Backups** for this example, in any location you want.

2. Right-click the FAZAM 2000 Administrator node and choose Connect to Domain to open the eponymous dialog. Type the FQDN of the domain in the text box, **oaktest.edu** for this example, or click Browse to open the Browse for Domain dialog; then select the domain and click OK. Click Finish to add the domain's node under the Administrator node.

3. Expand the nodes to display FAZAM 2000's variation on Active Directory Users and Computers' tree-view pane, which adds nodes for each GPO linked to the domain and its OUs in their priority order. Each GPO node has Filters and Settings items (see Figure 9-1).

4. Right-click the domain node and choose All Tasks | Backup to open the Backup Group Policy Object(s) dialog, which displays a list of all GPOs linked to the domain and its OUs. Type an optional description of the backup set in Comments text box.

5. Click the Backup Directory's browse button to open the Browse for Folder dialog, navigate to the folder you created in step 1, and click OK. The Backup Directory list displays the path to the folder with a \ suffix (see Figure 9-2).

6. Select the GPO to back up and click Backup to create the GPO backup file. A GPO Backup message confirms successful backup. Repeat this step for each GPO you want to restore, import, or merge to the target domain.

NOTE: If you retain unmodified Default Domain Policy and Default Domain Controllers Policy GPOs and add custom GPOs with a higher priority, you don't need to back up the two default policies.

7. Click Done to dismiss the Backup Group Policy Objects(s) dialog.

The backup process creates a subfolder of the backup folder named for the domain, which contains subfolders identified by the GUID of each policy you back up. Each {GUID} folder holds seven .sec files and two .dat files, plus a GPO subfolder with a Gpt.ini file and ADM, Machine, and User subfolders.

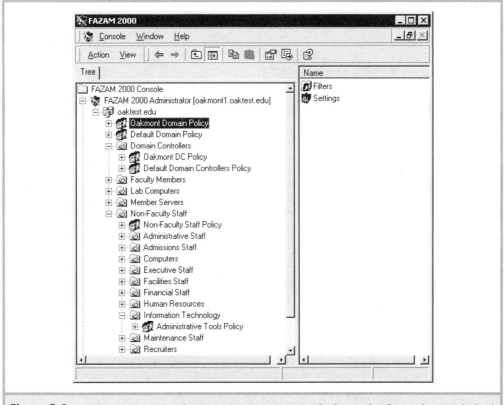

Figure 9-1. FAZAM 2000's Administrator tree view includes nodes for each GPO linked at the domain and OU levels.

Copying Backed-Up GPOs to a Production Domain

Using Restore is the simplest method of copying policies from one domain to another, because it mirrors the backup process. To copy policies from the source (oaktest.edu) backup folder to the target (oakmont.edu) domain using FAZAM 2000 version 1.0, do the following:

1. With the source domain open in the FAZAM 2000 Administrator node, right-click the domain name node and choose All Tasks | Restore Group Policy to open the Restore Group Policy Object(s) dialog.

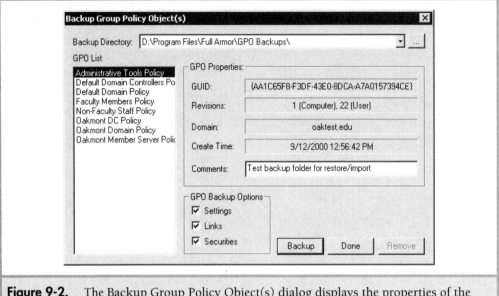

Figure 9-2. The Backup Group Policy Object(s) dialog displays the properties of the GPO selected in the GPO list.

2. If the Backup Directory list is empty or doesn't point to the correct folder, click Browse and navigate to the GPO backup folder you created in step 1 of the procedure in the preceding section.

3. Select the Multiple Target option to enable copying of GPOs to target domains. Selecting Multiple Target disables the Links and Securities option in the GPO Restore options frame.

4. Select the GPO to copy, click Restore to open the Choose Domains dialog, which has a list of candidate downlevel domain names, and select the target domain, OAKMONTU for this example (see Figure 9-3).

5. Click OK to copy the GPO to the target domain. There's no hourglass mouse cursor or other visual feedback during the restoration process, so wait for and acknowledge the Restore GPO message before proceeding.

6. Repeat steps 4 and 5 for each GPO to restore to the target domain.

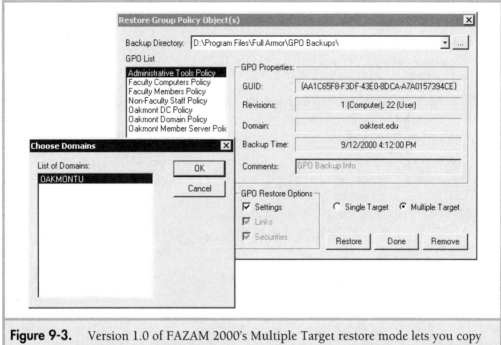

Figure 9-3.   Version 1.0 of FAZAM 2000's Multiple Target restore mode lets you copy
GPOs, but not GPO links or Security Group filter data from the backup to
the target domain.

Linking and Filtering GPOs with FAZAM 2000 Administrator

FAZAM 2000 offers expedited access to most of the capabilities of Active Directory Users
and Computers' Group Policy page through the Administrator node. To link the imported
policies in the target (production) domain, do this:

1. Right-click the FAZAM 2000 Administrator node, choose Connect to Domain, type
   or browse for the production domain, and click Finish.

2. Right-click the target domain name node, choose Link Group Policy to open the
   Select Group Policy Object to Link dialog, and select an additional policy to link at

the domain level. Figure 9-4 illustrates use of unmodified Default Domain Policy in the production domain and application of changes to domain-level policy by an additional GPO: Oakmont Domain Policy for this example. Policies you add at the domain or OU level have precedence in the reverse order of addition; the last GPO you add has the highest priority.

3. Verify the addition of the GPO link under the domain name node and its priority by selecting the Administrator node and pressing F5 to refresh the console. The GPO you add appears above the Default Domain Policy for this example.

4. Repeat steps 2 and 3 for each GPO to link at the OU level. In step 2, right-click the appropriate OU node instead of the domain name node.

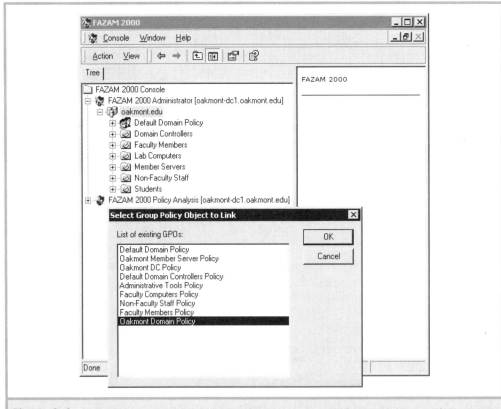

Figure 9-4.   Multiple-target restore mode disables copying of GPO linking and Security Group filtering data, but lets you copy individual GPOs from the test domain's backup file to the production domain.

5. Prepare to apply Security Group filtering to OU-level policies that duplicates the filters applied in the test domain by right-clicking the OU node and choosing Adjust Filter to open the dialog of the same name. The list on the left shows user accounts, downlevel names of groups, and computer accounts within the OU container. By default, the Authenticated Users group has the Allow Apply Group Policy privilege enabled, so this group appears in the Current Filters list.

6. Select the Authenticated Users group and click the left arrow button to remove the group from the Current Filters list, unless you want the GPO to apply to all members of the OU.

7. Select a group to receive the policy and click the right arrow button to add the group to the Current Filter list (see Figure 9-5). Repeat this step for each group to receive the GPO and then click OK to close the dialog.

FAZAM 2000's convenience of applying GPO filters to AD containers under the Administrator node has a minor drawback. The only Security Groups that appear in the Adjust Filters list are those in the currently selected container. Using GroupPol's Faculty

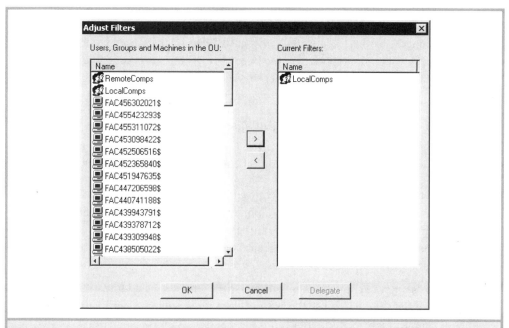

Figure 9-5.   FAZAM 2000's Adjust Filters dialog lets you apply Security Group filtering to GPOs applied at the domain or OU level.

Members collections as an example, you can't filter GPOs applied at the department level, such as Anthropology, by faculty role groups, such as Deans or Chairpersons. The Faculty Members OU contains the role-based groups, so they don't appear in the Adjust Filters dialog's list. You must use the Security page of Active Directory Users and Computers' *GPOName* Properties dialog to filter GPOs by out-of-OU groups.

Taking Advantage of FAZAM 2000's Other Features

FAZAM 2000 offers several additional features that are difficult or impossible to accomplish with the GPE. These added features are especially useful for admins who are responsible for creating and managing complex GPOs with a large number of policy settings or AD containers to which multiple, filtered GPOs are applied. Policy Analysis is a unique tool for troubleshooting unexpected behavior of your Group Policy designs, and the Policy Diagnostics component runs on workstations, so these feature are described in the section "Using FAZAM 2000's Analysis and Diagnostics Tools" later in this chapter.

Viewing and Saving GPO Documentation

Selecting the Settings item under a GPO node renders a scrollable HTML page with a list of the GPO's policies and their settings. Figure 9-6 illustrates the display of most of the Local Policies settings for the Oakmont DC Policy GPO.

Right-clicking the Settings item and choosing All Tasks opens a context menu with choices to print the page as a report, save the page as an HTML or Jet .mdb file, open the GPE to edit GPO settings, and delegate authority to modify ADM files. The Jet 3.51 database file has SecurityInfo, PolicyData, IEAKData, and SoftwareInstall tables that hold policy settings.

Copying, Importing, and Merging Policies

In addition to backing up and restoring policies, FAZAM 2000 has the following features to speed creation of GPOs having policy settings in common with existing GPOs:

- ✦ **Copy** lets you use the Clipboard to copy and paste the contents of one GPO into another GPO in the same domain. All policy settings, except Software Settings and IP Security Policies, overwrite existing settings, if any, in the target GPO. The GPE's copy and paste feature supports Clipboard operations only on Computer Configuration\Security Settings subnodes.

- ✦ **Merge** is similar to copy, but emulates policy inheritance by adding settings for policies except those that use the last-written values, such as User Rights Assignment. For example, merging adds applications and scripts from the source GPO to the Software Installation and Scripts (Startup/Shutdown) or Scripts (Logon/Logoff) list.

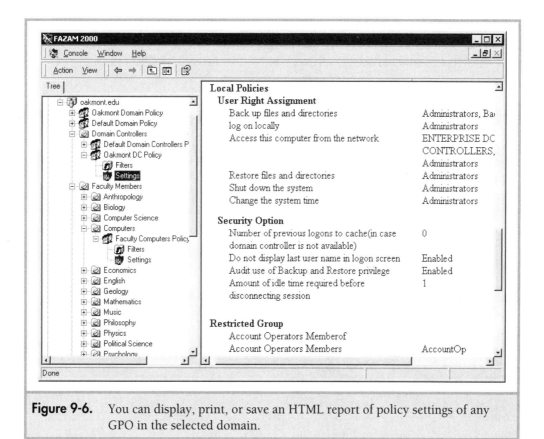

Figure 9-6.   You can display, print, or save an HTML report of policy settings of any GPO in the selected domain.

✦ **Import** uses a backed-up GPO as the source of the settings to apply to an existing GPO. Like restore, importing a GPO permits copying of a GPO's settings from another domain's backup folder. Unlike copying, importing a GPO includes Software Settings and IP Security Policies.

Delegation of Group Policy Administration

FAZAM 2000 offers an alternative to the Delegation of Control Wizard that you access from the Adjust Filters dialog (refer to Figure 9-5). Selecting a group or user in the Current Filters list and clicking the Delegate button delegates control of the GPO to the user or group. If the user or group has delegated authority, selecting its icon changes the Delegate button's caption to Undelegate.

You also can limit the authority of delegates to settings contained in the GPO's Administrative Templates: Conf.adm, Inetres.adm, and System.adm. You open the Delegate ADM Files dialog from the context menu of the Settings item of the GPO.

Troubleshooting Group Policy Problems

On the whole, Group Policy is a stable, reliable Windows 2000 feature. Most of the problems you're likely to encounter with previously tested GPOs in production are symptomatic of more fundamental troubles, such as AD or SYSVOL replication failure between DCs, incorrect client DNS settings, or missing well-known Security Groups. These types of problems usually affect multiple Windows 2000 services, but you often find the initial symptoms logged in a workstation's or DC's Event Viewer as Group Policy errors.

Clearing the Usual Suspects

Chapter 12, "Troubleshooting Change and Configuration Management," of the Windows 2000 Resource Kit's *Distributed System Guide* has nine Group Policy troubleshooting topics. The "Possible Causes" lists for the problems addressed in the section include obvious items, such as the network is down, the client can't connect to a domain controller, or the affected workstation isn't running Windows 2000. Network connectivity to a DC is a fundamental Windows 2000 Professional requirement; if the domain can't validate the computer and user accounts, Group Policy won't be applied.

If your test domains include only Windows 2000 servers and your production domain has trusted/trusting Windows NT domains, Group Policies might exhibit unexpected behavior. Problems with application of Computer Configuration policies occur if the production domain has workstations that receive authentication from Windows NT resource domains. Instead, computer system policy, if implemented, applies each time the user logs on. Similarly, users authenticated by Windows NT domains receive user system policies, if any, not User Configuration policies. The only solution for these issues is to expedite upgrading of all Windows NT domains to Windows 2000.

Using the Resource Kit's Group Policy Tools

The Windows 2000 Resource Kit's Gpresult.exe and Gpotool.exe are the basic command-line tools for troubleshooting Group Policy problems. Run Gpresult on workstations, member servers, and DCs to determine the Computer Configuration and User Configuration policies in effect. Gpotool.exe runs a recursive test on all DCs in a domain to verify the consistency of replicated policies in SYSVOL folders. The "Troubleshooting Policy Application on Workstations" section in Chapter 4 describes how to use these two diagnostic tools in the context of troubleshooting folder redirection policies.

Using Telnet to Run Gpresult.exe on Workstations

You can use the Telnet service to run a local copy of Gpresult.exe or any other locally installed diagnostics tool on workstations and display the output in Telnet's command window or write the results to a local log file. Create a Gpresult.msi or Gpresult.zap file for Gpresult.exe and add the program to the Computer Configuration\Software Settings\ Software Installation policy's deployment list for ordinary workstations on your LAN. A Microsoft Installer file is the better choice, because you can only publish (not assign) .zap files.

Windows 2000 Setup installs Telnet.exe on workstations, but the default service startup mode is Manual. You can start the service on the workstation with Computer Management's remote connection feature. If you start the Telnet service manually, the Everyone group has Allow Full Control permissions for Telnet sessions to the computer while the administrative session is running. If you neglect to stop the service, anyone with the Access This Computer from the Network privilege can run a Telnet session until someone reboots the workstation.

CODE BLUE

A potential security hole in the Windows 2000's Telnet service was identified in August 2000. The single-logon feature of the Telnet service stores a hashed copy of the user's logon ID and password, which makes the service vulnerable to hackers. A document, such as an e-mail message, having an attachment that runs Telnet reportedly permits a hacker to gain access to users' hashed logon IDs and passwords. A patch for this security vulnerability is available from http://www.microsoft.com/ security as "Windows 2000 Telnet Client NTLM Authentication." Even with the patch applied, it's a good security practice not to enable the Telnet service on servers and especially on DCs. Use Terminal Services' Remote Administration mode to manage servers.

A more secure alternative to manually starting Telnet is to use Group Policy to enable Telnet as a service on all machines in OUs containing computer accounts on the LAN and to permit only members of specified security groups to open a Telnet session. Following is the procedure:

1. With the GPO for the OU containing the desired computer accounts open in the GPE, navigate to the Computer Configuration\Windows Settings\Security Settings\ System Services node.

TIP: If you've established separate Security Groups for local and remote computers, such as the Local Computers and Remote Computers groups generated by the GroupPol application in the Faculty Members, Computers OU, consider adding a new GPO to the OU to enable Telnet and install Gpresult.zap. Filter the GPO so that it applies only to LAN-attached computers.

2. Double-click the Telnet policy in the Service Name list to open the Security Policy Setting dialog, mark the Define This Policy Setting check box, and select the Automatic option.

3. Click the Edit Security button to open the Security for Telnet dialog, select the default Everyone group, and click Remove.

4. Click Add to open the Select Users, Computers, or Groups dialog, add the groups you want to have permission to run Telnet on the client, and click OK.

5. Set permissions for each group you added in the preceding step. For the sample oakmont.edu domain, Enterprise and Domain Admins have Allow Full Control permissions, and Helpdesk Technicians and Network Administrators have Read; Start, Stop, and Pause; and Write permissions. Click OK twice to close the dialogs and apply the settings.

6. Test the added policy on a workstation with a computer account in the OU.

NOTE: The End-User License Agreement for the Microsoft Windows 2000 Server Resource Kit CD lets you install an unlimited number of copies of the software "on computers physically residing at a single geographical location." This language indicates that you must have a separate Resource Kit license for each site at which you install Gpresult.exe or other Resource Kit utilities. The location restriction makes it economically impractical to install Gpresult.exe on remote machines.

Verifying Local Security Policies

Gpresult.exe is effective for diagnosing most Group Policy problems, but doesn't enumerate Security Settings. Run the Local Security Policy snap-in on the client to verify that the computer is receiving the correct Account Policies, Local Policies, and if applicable, Public Key Policies and IP Security Policies. You also can run the Security Configuration and Analysis tool on the workstation to verify that its local security configuration corresponds to the standards of the security template for domain computers and, if applicable, the OU that stores the computer account. The "Using the Security Configuration and Analysis Snap-in" section in Chapter 5 describes how to set up and run this snap-in.

Verifying Group Policy History on Clients

If it isn't convenient to run Gpresult.exe on a workstation that exhibits Group Policy problems, you can review Registry entries that hold policy-related values with Regedit.exe. Windows 2000's Registry maintains a record of the last application of Group Policy to computers and users. Each client-side extension stores a Version value for every GPO that uses the extension. A Netlogon subprocess checks the Version number of the GPOs on the DC against that of the client's last-applied GPOs. If the version number differs, the extension processes the updated policy with data from the DC's SYSVOL share and updates the local version number.

You can verify application of Group Policy to clients by inspecting the contents of subkeys under the following Registry keys:

✦ HKLM\Software\Microsoft\Windows\CurrentVersion\Group Policy\History for GPOs applied to the computer

✦ HKCU\Software\Microsoft\Windows\CurrentVersion\Group Policy\History for GPOs applied to the currently logged-on user

NOTE: You can read the HKLM values of a remote workstation with Regedit.exe's remote Registry feature, but the HKCU hive isn't accessible remotely. The only value in the HKEY_USERS*UserSID*\Software\Microsoft\Windows\CurrentVersion\Group Policy\History key is DCName, which points to the default DC for the user's domain.

Successive application of Group Policies creates serially numbered subkeys under each client-side extension key. For example, if you maintain computer accounts in OUs and apply a GPO with Computer Configuration settings, subkeys 0, 1, and 2 appear under the {*ExtensionGUID*} keys. The numbered subkeys represent the local, domain, and OU computer policies, respectively. Knowledge Base article Q201453, "Group Policy History Stored in Registry," explains the value names that appear under the subkeys.

Enabling Verbose Logging of UserEnv Events

You can troubleshoot Group Policy application problems of a particular workstation remotely by adding Registry values to increase the amount of detail logged for UserEnv events in the Userenv.log file and Event Viewer's Application log. In most cases, enabling verbose logging for Userenv.log is the most expeditious approach. Searching hundreds of individual UserEnv events in the Application log to locate the source of a Group Policy application problem is a tedious process, because problems, such as the inability to find a GPO on the DC, aren't identified by warning or error icons.

Expanding the Detail of Userenv.log on Workstations

By default, the Userenv.log file in the Winnt\Debug\UserMode folder contains rows for errors and warnings only. You can add a Registry value, UserenvDebugLevel, to the HKLM\Software\Microsoft\Windows NT\Current Version\Winlogon key to enable or disable verbose logging, which tracks all changes and settings applied to the computer and the logged-on user. For verbose logging, the REG_DWORD value is hexadecimal 3002 (0x00030002), decimal 196610. Hexadecimal 3001 sets normal logging, and 3000 disables UserEnv logging. Figure 9-7 shows a few of the rows for Computer Configuration policies added to Userenv.log as a result of enabling verbose logging; the computer account that generated the log is located in the Faculty Members, Computers OU.

Use the hidden administrative share of the remote workstation, usually C$, to open \Winnt\Debug\UserMode\Userenv.log on your administrative workstation.

Enabling Event Viewer Logging of Detailed UserEnv Activity

You can add value items to a HKLM\Software\Microsoft\Windows NT\CurrentVersion\ Diagnostics Registry key to enable verbose logging of UserEnv events in Event Viewer's Application log. This key isn't present, so you must add an empty Diagnostics key to HKLM\Software\Microsoft\Windows NT\CurrentVersion. Then add to the Diagnostics key one or more of the following value names, a REG_ DWORD value type, and a value of 1 to log events:

✦ **RunDiagnosticLoggingGlobal** adds verbose entries to the log for all UserEnv events. This mode generates a very large number of entries and is overkill for diagnosing most Group Policy problems.

✦ **RunDiagnosticLoggingGroupPolicy** enables logging of UserEnv events for Group Policy application only. This is a better choice than RunDiagnosticLoggingGlobal, because it limits the Event log entries to those that apply specifically to Group Policy.

✦ **RunDiagnosticLoggingIntelliMirror** enables logging of UserEnv events relating only to IntelliMirror features.

✦ **RunDiagnosticLoggingAppDeploy** logs events for Software Installation policy.

Using FAZAM 2000's Analysis and Diagnostics Tools

FAZAM 2000 includes two troubleshooting tools: Policy Analysis and Diagnostics. These components, accessed from the context menu of the FAZAM 2000 Policy Analysis node, provide more detailed and useful information on policies that should be and are applied, respectively, to computer and user accounts.

Figure 9-7.   Enabling verbose logging of the Userenv.log on a workstation experiencing Group Policy application problems usually tells you more than you want to know about Netlogon's processing of GPOs.

Analyzing the Resultant Set of Policies for a User and Computer

The FAZAM 2000 Policy Analysis node lets you specify a combination of user and computer accounts to return a Resultant Set of Policies (RSoP) for a particular user logged on to a specified Windows 2000 workstation. The RSoP report lists the combined Computer Configuration and User Configuration policy settings on an HTML page having the same format as that for documenting individual GPOs. Unlike Gpresult.exe's output, the Policy Analysis report includes Security Policies settings.

Following is the process for creating a typical RSoP report:

1. Right-click the FAZAM 2000 Policy Analysis node and choose Perform Analysis to open the dialog of the same name.

2. Click the upper Browse button to open the Select User dialog, type the name of the user to emulate, **Bryan Brewer** for this example, and click OK.

3. Click the lower Browse button to open the Select Computer dialog, type the computer name for the user you added in the preceding step, **FAC393931724** in this case, and click OK.

4. Click OK to start the RSoP analysis process, which takes a minute or two, depending on the speed of your workstation, DC, and network. When the dialog closes, the RSoP process adds a *UserName* at *ComputerName* node, Bryan Brewer at FAC393931724 for this example, under the *domain.ext* node.

5. Expand the nodes to display the Group Policy hierarchy for Computer Configuration and User Configuration policies and select the Settings item under the Resultant Policy node to display the RSoP report's HTML page. Figure 9-8 shows part of the Security Options policy settings for the selected computer.

The Perform Analysis dialog has a What-If Analysis list to which you can add conditions to emulate the effect of making changes to the OU and Security Group membership of a user, computer, or both. What-If scenarios let you verify the Group Policy setting changes that will occur before you alter user and computer objects' OU and group membership in Active Directory Users and Computers.

Running the Diagnostics Utility on Workstations

FAZAM 2000 includes an executable utility, Fadiag.exe, that you run locally on the workstation to create a local diagnostic (.dgn) file. Typically, you install Fadiag.exe in the workstation's \Winnt folder and run it at the command prompt with a **fadiag** *userid***.dgn** instruction to create a *userid*.dgn file in the current folder. Fadiag.exe runs very quickly, so

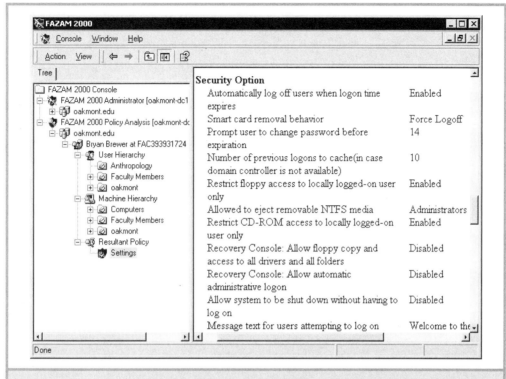

Figure 9-8. The Resultant Policy node for a selected user and computer combination displays all policy settings that should be applied to the machine after the user logs on.

you can specify a logoff script that runs fadiag faculty.dgn every time the user logs off. Alternatively, you can run the command in a Telnet session.

NOTE: FAZAM 2000 version 1.2 replaces the Fadiag.exe utility with a Remote Diagnostics feature that uses Windows Management Instrumentation (WMI) technology to diagnose GPO problems on workstations.

Once you've generated the .dgn file on the workstation, right-click the *domain.ext* node under the FAZAM 2000 Policy Analysis node, choose Import Diagnostics, and navigate to the location of the workstation's .dgn. Opening the file in FAZAM 2000 and expanding diagnostics nodes results in a tree view similar to that shown in Figure 9-9. The example in the figure is for

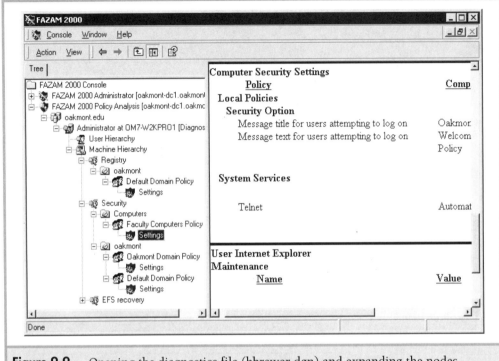

Figure 9-9. Opening the diagnostics file (bbrewer.dgn) and expanding the nodes provides access to an HTML report of the settings applied to the computer by the GPOs that apply Computer Configuration policies.

Fadiag.exe executed while Byran Brewer was logged on to the FAC393931724 computer. Default Domain Policy, Oakmont Domain Policy, and Faculty Computers policy applies to the computer. The report pane shows the Telnet service setting (Automatic) discussed in the earlier "Using Telnet to Run Gpresult.exe on Workstations" section.

Solving Problems Caused by System Configuration Changes

Thorough testing of GPOs on an isolated lab network or with a test domain running on your production network doesn't guarantee that the copies of the GPOs created will operate correctly in the production domain. Differences in the network configuration of test and production DCs, as well as workstations, can prevent successful deployment of Group Policy. You also can encounter Group Policy problems when modifying network topology, such as changing client network segments or reassigning the use of network adapters on DCs.

Multihomed DCs

Using DCs as routers isn't a recommended practice in large networks, but smaller organizations might have hardware limitations that dictate use of a DC to provide DSL or T-1 Internet connectivity to clients. This configuration sometimes is used in small branch office sites that have only one or two servers, both of which are configured as DCs. Regardless of the type of firewall installed on the Internet connection, it's a standard security practice to disable the Client for Microsoft Networks and File and Printer Sharing for Microsoft Networks components on the NIC that's connected to the Internet.

Depending on the initial setup process or later changes to adapter use assignment, the Internet NIC becomes the primary network adapter on the DC. This condition occurred in the process of diagnosing a DSL connectivity problem during the writing of this book. Client Internet, file share, and printer access to the DC was unaffected by exchanging the use of the two NICs, but the Application log filled with UserEnv 1000 "Windows cannot access the registry information at ..." and SceCli 1001 "Security policy cannot be propagated" errors when working with the GPE.

The solution to this problem, as outlined in Knowledge Base article Q258296, "Unbinding File and Printer Sharing from Primary Network Adapter in Multihomed Domain Controller Causes Policy Problems on the Domain Controller," is to alter the access order of the NICs in the seldom-used Advanced Settings dialog of the Network and Dial-up Connections window. If you encounter the error messages described in the preceding paragraph, check the NIC priorities as follows:

1. Right-click My Network Connections and choose Properties to open the Dial-up and Network Connections window.

2. Choose Advanced | Advanced Settings to open the Advanced Settings dialog.

3. If the NIC connected to the LAN isn't the first entry in the Connections list, select it and click the up-arrow button to move it to the top of the list (see Figure 9-10). Verify that the File and Printer Sharing for Microsoft Networks check box and its Internet Protocol (TCP/IP) check box are marked. File and printer sharing and the Client for Microsoft Networks and Internet Protocol (TCP/IP) are enabled by default during Windows 2000's network setup phase.

4. Click OK to close the dialog and apply the new NIC priorities.

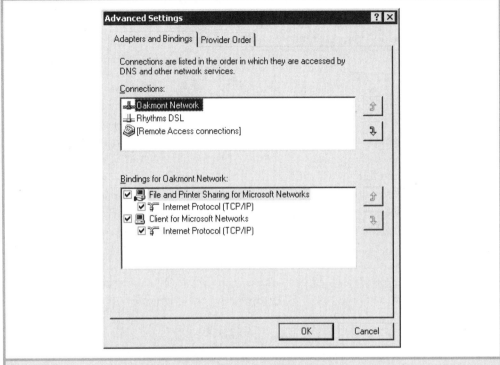

Figure 9-10. The Dial-up and Network Connection window's Advanced Settings dialog displays the priority of NICs installed on a multihomed DC. Make certain the NIC connected to your LAN is at the top of the Connections list and has File and Printer Sharing for Microsoft Networks enabled.

Client DNS Problems

Knowledge Base article Q246108, "Windows 2000 Client May Not Apply Group Policies," advises that clients don't receive Group Policies if their Preferred DNS Server or Alternate DNS Server entries are misconfigured. Incorrect DNS Server addresses can occur as a result of incorrect options entries for the DHCP scope that applies to the workstation or local DNS Server settings that override correct DHCP-assigned addresses. Running Gpresult.exe on a workstation with misconfigured DNS Server addresses displays "LookupAccountSid failed with 1789" errors. Incorrect DNS Server addresses, of course, affect more than just Group Policy application on clients. Run Ipconfig.exe on the workstation to determine its current DNS Server address list.

Appendix A

Group Policy Reference

W indows 2000 Group Policies replace Windows NT and 9x System Policies that you create with the System Policy Editor (PolEdit.exe) running under Windows NT or 9x, respectively. System Policies underlie Microsoft's Zero Administration for Windows (ZAW) initiative and the Zero Administration Kit (ZAK) for Windows NT 4.0. System Policies are intended to implement desktop lockdown by means of Registry entries on user workstations.

NOTE: You can download this appendix as a Microsoft Word file from http://www. admin911.com. Use that file to search for policy names and/or Registry items as you work with Group Policy on your own system.

Windows 2000 Group Policies extend the concept of System Policies by providing administrators with much more granular control of computer and desktop configuration and user rights. There are a total of about 230 policies that apply to computers and 320 policies for users. The actual number of policies applicable to computers and users varies a bit, depending on the level at which you apply the Group Policy Object (GPO) container: local computer, site, domain, or organizational unit (OU).

Group Policies are divided into two classes: Computer Configuration and User Configuration. This appendix lists each policy for computers and users and provides a brief explanation of the purpose of and the effect of applying each policy. The default values given in the text are those for a Domain Controller (DC) that has the Default Domain Policy and Default Domain Controllers Policy installed during promotion from a member server to a DC, without security configuration templates having been applied. Windows 2000 Server with Service Pack 1 applied was used to write and verify this list. Instructions show you how to add items to initially empty policies, such as Registry and File System. The lists are ordered in the top-to-bottom sequence of their appearance in the tree view pane of the Group Policy Editor. The majority of the Group Policies are Not Configured, which means that the policy isn't defined and thus isn't applied to any computer or user.

TIP: Be judicious when applying policies to computers and users. The more computer policies you add, the longer it takes clients to boot when receiving the policies, and many user policies delay the initial logon process. Once computers and users receive their policies, AD sends only Group Policies that have changed since the last boot or logon.

Domain and Domain Controller Security Policies

The Administrative Tools menu offers Domain Controller (DC) Security Policy and Domain Security Policy choices that open an abbreviated variant of the standard Group Policy

Editor snap-in, Gpedit.msc. Choosing Domain Controller Security Policy opens a snap-in of the same name (see Figure A-1) that lets you apply policies to the domain's DCs. Similarly, Domain Security Policy opens a snap-in for applying domainwide policies. Domain Controller Security Policies override conflicting Domain Security Policy settings, because DCs are contained in the Domain Controllers OU, and policies for OUs apply after local, site, and domain policies.

The purpose of these two Administrative Tools is to provide a shortcut for setting important domain-based security-related policies, so only the Computer Configuration\Windows Settings\Security Settings nodes and subnodes appear in these two views. Jump to the "Security Settings" topic for descriptions of the policies you apply with these Administrative Tools. It's not a common practice to apply policies other than those under the Security Settings nodes to DCs.

Computer Configuration Policies

Computer Configuration policies apply to the computer account and load when the computer boots onto the network, which makes these Group Policies independent of the

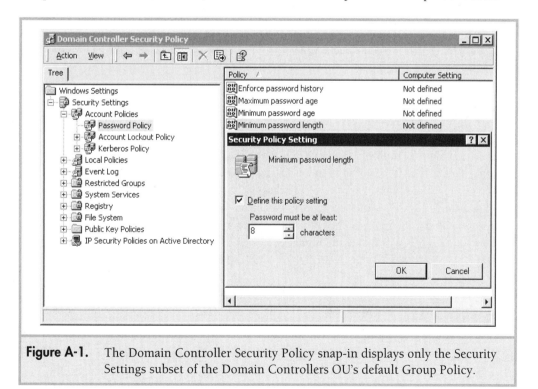

Figure A-1.   The Domain Controller Security Policy snap-in displays only the Security Settings subset of the Domain Controllers OU's default Group Policy.

user who logs on to the computer. Some User Configuration policy settings override conflicting Computer Configuration policies when set at the same level of the policy application sequence (local, site, domain, OU, called LSDOU).

TIP: If you want Computer Configuration to override User Configuration policy settings, enable the User Group Policy Loopback Processing Mode policy of the Computer Configuration\ Administrative Templates\System\Group Policy node. Select Merge in the Mode list to make Computer Configuration settings override User Configuration settings. Select Replace to apply only Computer Configuration settings, regardless of what user logs on.

The Computer Configuration node has three subnodes: Software Settings, Windows Settings, and Administrative Templates. Figure A-2 shows the Group Policy Editor displaying the Computer Configuration nodes and subnodes for the Software Settings and Windows Settings categories of the Default Domain Policy. AD stores the Group Policy settings for these two policy categories.

NOTE: To open the Group Policy Editor for a domain or OU, launch Active Directory Users and Computers, right-click the domain or OU node, choose Properties, and click the Group Policy tab in the *ObjectName* Properties dialog. For a site, open Active Directory Sites and Services, right-click the site name node, choose Properties, and click the *SiteName* Properties dialog's Group Policy node.

Software Settings

Location: Computer Configuration\Software Settings

Software Settings has only one policy, Software Installation, which lets you specify assigned software installation packages as Windows Installer (.msi) or Zero Administration Windows (ZAW) downlevel application packages (.zap) files. Unlike with the User Configuration\Software Settings policy, you can assign but not publish packages to computers. Newly assigned packages are installed during the boot process. The Registry stores pointers to assigned packages as data for the policies value of the \HKEY_LOCAL_MACHINE\ Software\Microsoft\Windows\CurrentVersion\Group Policy\AppMgmt key.

To add an assigned package, do this:

1. Right-click the Software Settings node, choose New | Package, and double-click the .msi or .zap file in the Open dialog.

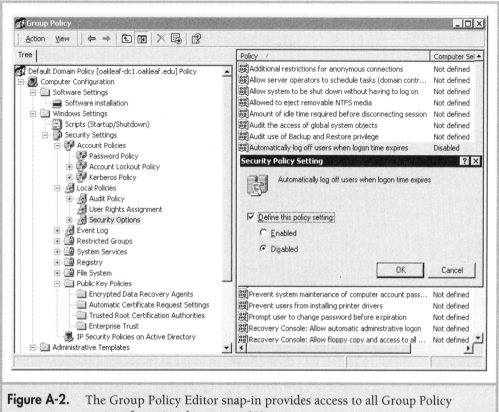

Figure A-2. The Group Policy Editor snap-in provides access to all Group Policy settings for a site, domain, or OU.

2. If the .msi file isn't located in a shared folder, you receive an error message. Click Yes if you want to share the folder at a later time or click No to abandon the process.

3. In the Deploy Software folder, select the Assigned or Advanced Assigned option and click OK. If you select Assigned, the package and its properties appear in the Names list, and you're done.

4. If you select the Advanced Published or Assigned option, the *PackageName* Properties dialog opens to let you modify the properties of the package. You also can open this dialog by double-clicking an existing entry (see Figure A-3). Click OK after making the changes you want to the package name, deployment, upgrades, categories, modifications, and security attributes. The package data appear in the Names list.

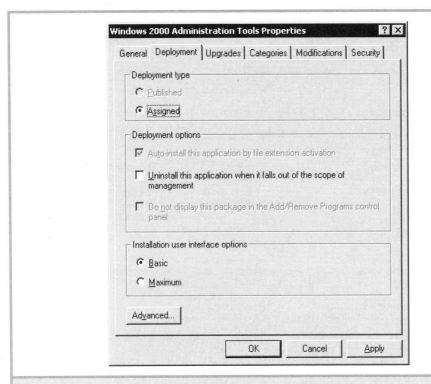

Figure A-3. Double-click an entry for an assigned software package to display its properties dialog. Click Advanced to open a dialog that lets you ignore the installer's language options and remove previous installations that weren't installed by a policy.

TIP: Each administrator needs a copy of the server Administrative Tools on his or her workstation. If you place workstation accounts for administrators in an OU, such as Admins, assign a copy of the Administrative Tools (Adminpak.msi) that's located in a shared folder as an element of the Group Policy for the OU. When a computer in the OU boots, Adminpak.msi downloads and installs automatically.

Windows Settings

Location: Computer Configuration\Windows Settings

Windows Settings has two subnodes: Scripts (Startup/Shutdown) and Security Settings. Security Settings are the most important element of Group Policy, because they determine the level of security maintained in each domain of your Windows 2000 network.

Scripts (Startup/Shutdown)

Location: Computer Configuration\Windows Settings\Scripts (Startup/Shutdown)

Scripts (Startup/Shutdown) has the following two policies:

✦ **Startup** lets you specify a startup script (.bat and .cmd MS-DOS–style commands; .vbs VBScript, and .js JScript files) that runs when the computer boots onto the network. You must embed VBScript and JScript code in .bat files for Windows NT 4.0 and Windows 95 clients, unless the clients have the Windows Script Host (WSH) installed. Third-party suppliers offer other scripting languages that run under the WSH.

✦ **Shutdown** runs the specified script when the user shuts down the computer.

To add a script, double-click the Startup or Shutdown node to open the Properties dialog and click Add to open the Add a Script dialog (see Figure A-4). Type or browse for the script name, add script parameters, if required, and click OK to add the script to the list. If you have more than one script, you can alter the execution sequence in the list.

TIP: These two policies expect startup and shutdown scripts to be in the *DomainName*\Sysvol*DomainName*\Policies*GUID*\Machine\Scripts\Startup and \Shutdown shares, respectively, for replication between DCs. If the scripts aren't in the default location, you must specify the full UNC path to the shared folder that holds the scripts. Open the Browse dialog with its default Startup or Shutdown entry in the Look In list and click the down-arrow button at the right of the list to display the full path to the share.

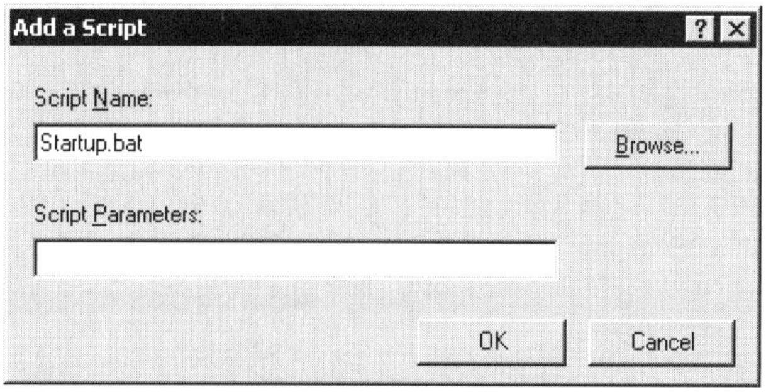

Add a Script [?] [X]

Script Name:
`Startup.bat`   Browse...

Script Parameters:

OK   Cancel

Figure A-4. Add startup or shutdown scripts in the *ScriptType* Properties dialog.

Security Settings

Location: Computer Configuration\Windows Settings\Security Settings

There are nine Security Settings subnodes: Account Policies, Local Policies, Event Log, Restricted Groups, System Services, Registry, File System, Public Key Policies, and IP Security Properties. You can add security to any of these areas by defining security settings in a policy that is associated with a site, domain, or OU, such as Domain Controllers. If you apply security templates, such as Securedc.inf or Securews.inf, to a server or workstation, respectively, many Security Settings policies in all subnodes change from the values listed in the sections that follow. When you upgrade a Windows NT 4.0 PDC to a Windows 2000 DC, the Security Policies of the PDC are enforced, not those of the installation security template.

NOTE: The Security Settings policies alter records in the affected computers' security database file, Secedit.sdb, which is located in \Winnt\System32\Security\Database folder. Security Settings policies don't appear in Regedit.exe's or Regedt32.exe's view of the computer's local Registry database.

Account Policies

Location: Computer Configuration\Windows Settings\Security Settings\Account Policies

Account policies apply to computers; there are no Account Policies in the User Configuration category. Account Policies has three subnodes: Password Policy, Account Lockout Policy, and Kerberos Policy. Password Policy and Account Lockout Policy applied at the Domain level applies to all users, regardless of whether they log on to the computer with a local account or with a Domain Users account. Kerberos Policy applies only to Windows 2000 workstations and servers. The Default Domain Policy sets default values for all Password policies.

Password Policies   Include the following six policies to specify password security:

✦ **Enforce password history** lets you specify the number of unique passwords that a user must utilize before a password can be repeated. The default value is 1 password remembered.

✦ **Maximum password age** lets you specify how long a password can be used on the computer before it must be changed by the user. You can set the number of days to 0, which lets users maintain their current passwords indefinitely. The default is 42 days. The initial change to this policy opens a dialog that suggests a change to the Minimum Password Age value.

◆ **Minimum password age** lets you specify the minimum amount of time a password can be used on the computer before the user can change it. You can set the number of days to 0, which will allow users to change passwords immediately. The password age must be less than the maximum password age. The default is 0 days.

◆ **Minimum password length** lets you specify the minimum number of characters a user's password may contain. You can set this length to any value between 0 and 14. A value of 0 specifies that no password is required and is the default value.

TIP: This is the first value you should set in the Default Domain Policy after promoting a server to the first DC in a production domain. Allowing use of empty passwords is a breach of security. Alternatively, apply the Securedc.inf security template to Default Domain Policy or another domain-level GPO. Securedc.inf sets a minimum password length of 8 characters and requires complex passwords. Don't apply either of these two policies, however, if you use the GroupPol application to add user accounts to a test domain. Adding user accounts with GroupPol requires zero-length, simple passwords.

◆ **Passwords must meet complexity requirements** lets you specify that all system passwords must meet Microsoft's specifications for strong passwords: Passwords must be seven characters or more and not include the user's logon ID or parts of the user's display name. Passwords also must contain at least three of the following four types of characters: Uppercase letters, lowercase letters, digits, and keyboard symbols, such as #, !, ?, % and the like. The default value is Disabled.

◆ **Store password using reversible encryption for all users in the domain** lets Windows 2000 store user passwords using reversible encryption. Most administrators don't enable this policy, because storing passwords using reversible encryption closely resembles storage of clear-text versions of the passwords. Enable this policy only if your application requirements, such as support for Macintosh clients or dial-in users requiring Challenge Handshake Authentication Protocol (CHAP), surpass the need for protected password information. The default value is Disabled.

Account Lockout Policy   Has the following three policies that control the result of failed user logons:

◆ **Account lockout duration** lets you set the number of minutes that an account is locked out. You can set the value between 0 and 99999. A 0 value specifies that the account be locked out until an administrator unlocks the account on the Account page of the *UserName* Properties dialog. Marking or clearing the Define This Policy Setting check box opens a dialog that suggests changes to the following two policy values.

✦ **Account lockout threshold** lets you set the number of failed logons a user can make before being locked out of an account. You can choose a number between 1 and 999. The Default Domain Policy sets this value to 0 invalid logon attempts.

✦ **Reset account lockout counter after** allows you to set the number of minutes that must pass before the bad logon attempt counter is reset to 0 bad logons. You can choose a number between 1 and 99999.

Kerberos Policy Applies only at the domain level, is set by Default Domain Policy, and has the following five policies and default values:

✦ **Enforce user logon restrictions** ensures that the Kerberos Key Distribution Center (KDC) validates every request for a session ticket against the user rights policy of the target computer. The default value is Enabled.

✦ **Maximum lifetime for service ticket** lets you set the maximum number of minutes that a user can submit a granted session ticket to access a particular service. This number must be higher than 10 and must be less than or equal to the setting for Maximum Lifetime for User Ticket. The default value is 600 minutes.

✦ **Maximum lifetime for user ticket** lets you set the maximum number of hours that a user's ticket-granting ticket (TGT) may be utilized. A new user's ticket can be requested, or the ticket can be renewed in the event that it expires. The default for this setting is 10 hours.

✦ **Maximum lifetime for user ticket renewal** lets you set the number of days for which a user's ticket-granting ticket (TGT) may be renewed. The default for this setting is 7 days.

✦ **Maximum tolerance for computer clock synchronization** lets you set the maximum number of minutes that Kerberos permits between a client's clock and the server's clock to consider the two clocks synchronous. This setting is important because Kerberos uses timestamps that require both clocks to be in sync to work properly. The default value is 5 minutes.

Local Policies

Location: Computer Configuration\Windows Settings\Security Settings\Local Policies

Technically, all Security Settings policies are "Local Policies," because they overwrite the default local security policy settings for workstations and servers. There are no Local Policies in the User Configuration category. To review the default local security settings on a server or workstation, open Control Panel, double-click Administrative Tools, and double-click Local Security Policy to open the snap-in of the same name. The Effective Settings column displays Local Setting values unless they are overwritten by policies set at the site, domain, or OU level. Figure A-5 illustrates a change made to the local Automatically Log Off Users

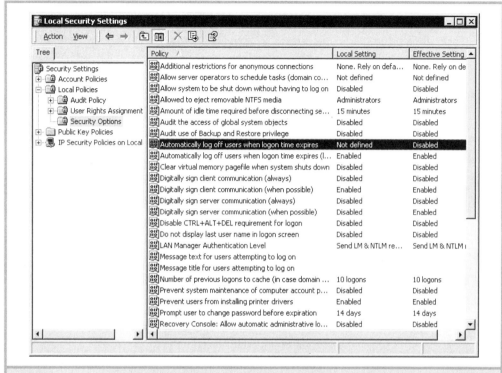

Figure A-5. Control Panel's Local Security Policy snap-in lets you review and change local policies of workstations and servers. Security Policies that you apply by Group Policy take precedence over local security policy.

When Logon Time Setting policy by the corresponding policy of the Default Domain Policy. The three Local Policies subnodes of Security Settings, Audit Policy, User Rights Assignment, and Security Options are no more or less local than the other Security Settings policies.

Audit Policy Determines what events appear in Event Viewer's Security Log on the local computer with the following nine policies, all of which are specified as Not Defined in the Default Domain Policy GPO:

✦ **Audit account logon events** controls auditing of instances of a user's logging on or logging off another computer when another computer validated the user's account. If you define this or any other Audit Policy, you have a choice of specifying whether to audit success, failure, or, by leaving the Success and Failure check boxes unmarked, not to audit the event type.

+ **Audit account management** controls auditing of account management events. An example of an account management event is the setting or changing of a password. If you use Microsoft's Active Directory Migration Tool (ADMT), you must mark the Success and Failure check boxes for this policy for the target DC. ADMT is the subject of Appendix C.

+ **Audit directory service access** controls auditing when a user accesses an Active Directory object that has specified its own system access control list (SACL).

+ **Audit logon events** controls auditing of instances of a user's logging on, logging off, or making a network connection to this computer.

+ **Audit object access** controls auditing of instances of a user's accessing an object (a file or folder, for instance) that has specified its own system access control list (SACL).

+ **Audit policy change** controls auditing of instances of changes to user rights assignment policies, audit policies, or trust policies.

+ **Audit privilege use** controls auditing of instances of a user's exercising a user right. Security log entries aren't created for user rights that have their own policies, such as Bypass Traverse Checking.

+ **Audit process tracking** controls whether or not the system audits detailed tracking information for events such as program activation, handle duplication, and indirect object access.

+ **Audit system events** controls auditing when a user restarts or shuts down the computer; or when an event has occurred that affects either the system security or the security log.

User Rights Assignment Policies   Determine which groups and users can perform specific actions on the computer. All policies are specified as Not Configured by the Default Domain Policy GPO. The Default Domain Controllers Policy defines (enables) all User Rights Assignment policies and establishes default values for most of them. Double-clicking the policy opens the Security Policy dialog with a list of users and groups that have permissions for the policy. Clicking Add opens the Add User or Group dialog that lets you browse AD with the Select Users or Groups dialog.

The default values for policies in this list are those of the Default Domain Controllers Policy. If a default value is missing, permission is granted only for most policies to the LocalSystem (SYSTEM) account, which doesn't appear in the Security Policy Setting list. Following are the 34 User Rights Assignment policies:

◆ **Access this computer from the network** controls which users and groups have permissions to connect to the computer over the network. Defaults are Administrators, Authenticated Users, Everyone, and domainwide Internet service (IUSR_ and IWAM_) accounts for each server running Internet Information Server.

◆ **Act as part of the operating system** enables a process to authenticate as any user, which lets the process gain access to the same resources as any user.

◆ **Add workstations to domain** controls the groups or users who can add workstations to a domain. This policy takes effect only when set on a DC. The default is Authenticated Users.

◆ **Back up files and directories** lets you specify which users can back up the system by circumventing file and directory permissions. The defaults are Administrators, Backup Operators, and Server Operators.

◆ **Bypass traverse checking** controls which users can traverse folder trees, even if users do not have permissions on the traversed folder. Users who don't have this permission can't list the contents of a folder. The defaults are Administrators, Authenticated Users, and Everyone.

◆ **Change the system time** lets you specify which users and groups can change the time and date on the internal system clock of the computer. The defaults are Administrators and Server Operators.

◆ **Create a pagefile** lets you specify which users and groups can create and change the size of a pagefile. The default is Administrators.

◆ **Create a token object** controls which accounts can be used by processes to create a token that can be used to gain access to local resources when the process uses NtCreateToken() or other token-creation APIs. The default is Administrators.

◆ **Create permanent shared objects** lets you specify which accounts can be used by kernel-mode processes to create a directory object.

◆ **Debug programs** lets you specify which users can use a debugging tool with any process. The default is Administrators.

◆ **Deny access to this computer from the network** lets you specify users who can't access the computer remotely.

◆ **Deny logon as a batch job** allows you to specify which accounts can't log on as a batch job.

✦ **Deny logon as a service** lets you specify which service accounts can't register a process as a service.

✦ **Deny logon locally** lets you specify which users can't log on at the computer.

✦ **Enable computer and user accounts to be trusted for delegation** lets you specify which users are able to set the Trusted for Delegation setting on a user or computer object. Users or objects must have write access to the account control flags on the user or computer object to utilize this privilege. The default is Administrators.

✦ **Force shutdown from a remote system** lets you specify which users can shut down a computer remotely. The defaults are Administrators and Server Operators.

✦ **Generate security audits** lets you specify the accounts that can be used by a process to add entries to the security log. You can use the security log to trace unauthorized access on your system.

✦ **Increase quotas** lets you specify which accounts can use a process that has write privileges for another process to increase the percentage of processor cycles assigned to the other process. The default is Administrators.

✦ **Increase scheduling priority** lets you specify which accounts can use a process that has write privileges for another process to increase the execution priority of the other process. The default is Administrators.

✦ **Load and unload device drivers** lets you specify which users can dynamically load and unload device drivers, which is necessary when installing drivers for Plug and Play devices. The default is Administrators.

✦ **Lock pages in memory** is obsolete because enabling this policy could adversely affect your system's performance.

✦ **Log on as a batch job** permits a user to be logged on through a batch-queue facility. The defaults are the domain's Internet service accounts.

✦ **Log on as a service** lets you specify which service accounts can register a process as a service.

✦ **Log on locally** lets you specify which users can log on at the computer. The defaults are Administrators, Server Operators, Account Operators, Backup Operators, Print Operators, and the Internet service accounts.

✦ **Manage auditing and security log** lets you specify which users can set object access auditing options for individual resources such as files and Active Directory objects. The default is Administrators.

✦ **Modify firmware environment variables** let you specify which users are able to modify system environment variables. The default is Administrators.

✦ **Profile single process** controls which users can use Windows NT's and Windows 2000's Performance Monitor (PerfMon) for nonsystem processes. The default is Administrators.

✦ **Profile system performance** controls which users can use PerfMon to monitor system processes. The default is Administrators.

✦ **Remove computer from docking station** lets you specify which users can undock a laptop computer. The default is Administrators.

✦ **Replace a process level token** lets you specify which user accounts can replace the default token for a running subprocess.

✦ **Restore files and directories** lets you specify which users can restore backed-up files and folders by circumventing file and folder permissions and can assign ownership of a directory object. Defaults are Administrators, Server Operators, and Backup Operators.

✦ **Shut down the system** lets you specify which users who are logged on locally to the computer can use the Shut Down command. The defaults are Administrators, Server Operators, Account Operators, Backup Operators, and Print Operators.

✦ **Synchronize directory service data** allows a process spawned by an application, such as Microsoft Exchange 2000, to provide Directory Synchronization Services (DSS).

✦ **Take ownership of files or other objects** lets you specify which users can take ownership of secure system objects. These objects include Active Directory objects, files and folders, printers, Registry keys, processes, and threads. The default is Administrators.

Security Options   Are the following 39 policies, most of which have default local security settings, that apply to all or particular accounts. Default Domain Policy and Default Domain Controllers Policy set only the Automatically Log Off Users When Logon Time Expires policy to Disabled; all other policies are specified as Not Configured. Thus, this list uses the default local security settings for a DC, which apply unless you change them with Group Policy.

✦ **Additional restrictions for anonymous access** lets you set security restrictions for anonymous users. The default local security setting is None (Rely on Default Permissions); other choices are Do Not Allow Enumeration of SAM Accounts and Shares, which is moderately secure, and No Access Without Explicit Anonymous Permissions.

◆ **Allow server operators to schedule tasks (domain controllers only)** lets members of the Server Operators group submit task-scheduled (AT) jobs on DCs. The default local security setting is Not Defined.

◆ **Allow system to be shut down without having to log on** specifies that users don't need to log on to Windows to shut down the computer. This policy adds the Shut Down choice to the logon dialog. The default local security setting is Disabled.

◆ **Allowed to eject removable NTFS media** enables selected users to eject removable NTFS media from the computer. The default local security setting is Administrator.

◆ **Amount of idle time required before disconnecting a session** lets administrators define when a computer disconnects an inactive Server Message Block (SMB) session. The default local security setting is 15 minutes.

◆ **Audit the access of global system objects** controls auditing of global system objects. System objects are created with a default system access control list (SACL) if this policy is enabled. Access to these system objects is audited when the Audit Object Access policy is also enabled. Enabling this policy quickly fills the System Event log. The default local security setting is Disabled.

◆ **Audit use of Backup and Restore Privilege** causes an audit of every exercise of user rights, including Backup and Restore. Enabling this policy also fills the System Event log rapidly. The default local security setting is Not Defined.

◆ **Automatically log off users when logon time expires** causes a client session with an SMB server to be forcibly disconnected when the client's logon hours have expired. The default local security setting is Not Defined; Default Domain Policy sets this value to Disabled (refer to Figure A-5).

◆ **Automatically log off users when logon time expires (local)** causes users to be restricted to their valid logon hours. If users attempt to access or continue access to the system outside of valid logon hours, they are forcibly disconnected. The default local security setting is Enabled.

◆ **Clear virtual memory pagefile when system shuts down** clears the virtual memory pagefile when the computer shuts down. This policy may be useful if your system multiboots other operating systems and you want to prevent unauthorized access to sensitive information in the pagefile. The default local security setting is Disabled.

◆ **Digitally sign client communications (always)** controls the computer's ability to digitally sign client communications. Enabling this policy ensures that client communications are always signed. This policy requires the SMB client to perform SMB packet signing. The default local security setting is Disabled.

◆ **Digitally sign client communications (when possible)** ensures that the SMB client performs SMB packet signing when communicating with an SMB server that is enabled or required to perform SMB packet signing. The default local security setting is Enabled.

◆ **Digitally sign server communications (always)** requires the SMB server to perform SMB packet signing. The default local security setting is Disabled.

◆ **Digitally sign server communications (when possible)** causes the SMB server to perform SMB packet signing. The default local security setting is Disabled. This policy is enabled by the Default Domain Controllers Policy.

◆ **Disable CTRL+ALT+DEL requirement for logon** eliminates the need for users to give the three-finger salute to log on. Enabling this policy creates a situation where the user's password might be intercepted by hackers. The default local security setting is Disabled.

◆ **Do not display last user name in logon screen** improves security by ensuring that the last user name accessed does not appear in the logon dialog. The default local security setting is Disabled.

◆ **LAN Manager authentication level** lets you choose the challenge/response authentication protocol that's used for network logons on your system. The options are various combinations of LM, NTLM, and NTLMv2 authentication. The default local security setting is Send LM & NTLM responses.

TIP: Review your options carefully, as the protocol you choose affects the level of the authentication protocol used by clients, the level of session security negotiated, and the level of authentication accepted by servers. Select Send LTLMv2 Response Only\Refuse LM if all computers on your network natively support or have been upgraded to support LTLMv2.

◆ **Message text for users attempting to log on** lets you specify a text message that is displayed to users when they log on. The default local security setting is an empty string (no message.)

◆ **Message title for users attempting to log on** lets you add the specification of a title that appears in the title bar of the window that contains the message text for users attempting to log on. The default local security setting is an empty string (no title.) If the values of this and the preceding policy are empty strings, the message dialog doesn't appear prior to user logon.

✦ **Number of previous logons to cache (in case domain controller is not available)** lets you specify the number of times a user can log on to a system utilizing cached information. Cached information is used if a domain controller is not available to provide the information. The default local security setting is 10 logons.

✦ **Prevent system maintenance of computer account password** eliminates the automatically generated computer passwords that Windows 2000 renews once a week by default. The computer retains its initial password indefinitely. The default local security setting is Disabled.

✦ **Prevent users from installing printer drivers** ensures that users aren't able to install printer drivers. In this case, users can't add printers that have previously installed printer drivers. The default local security setting is Enabled.

✦ **Prompt user to change password before expiration** lets you specify how far in advance users are warned to change their passwords. The default local security setting is 14 days.

✦ **Recovery Console: Allow automatic administrative logon** lets users log on to the Recovery Console without providing a password. The default local security setting is Disabled.

✦ **Recovery Console: Allow floppy copy and access to all drives and folders** enables the Recovery Console SET command, which lets you choose to enable or ignore four Recovery Console environment variables: AllowWildCards, AllowAllPaths, AllowRemovableMedia, and NoCopyPrompt. The default local security setting is Disabled.

✦ **Rename administrator account** lets you associate a different account name with the security identifier (SID) for the Administrator account. Renaming the Administrator account helps guard against hackers, who often search for Administrator accounts when attempting illicit access to your network. The default local security setting is Not Defined.

✦ **Rename guest account** lets you associate a different account name with the security identifier (SID) for the Guest account. The Guest account is disabled when you install Windows 2000. The default local security setting is Not Defined.

✦ **Restrict CD-ROM access to locally logged-on user only** makes CD-ROM drives accessible first to an interactively logged-on user. If there is no interactively logged-on user, the CD-ROM may be shared on the network. If this policy is disabled, the default value, local and remote users can access the CD-ROM simultaneously.

- **Restrict floppy access to locally logged-on user only** makes diskette drives accessible first to an interactively logged-on user. If there is no interactively logged-on user, the diskette drive may be shared across the network. If this policy is disabled, the default value, local and remote users can access the diskette drive simultaneously.

- **Secure channel: Digitally encrypt or sign secure channel data (always)** ensures that the system digitally encrypts or signs all outgoing secure channel traffic. Signing and encryption is negotiated if this policy is disabled, the default.

- **Secure channel: Digitally encrypt secure channel data (when possible)** ensures that the system digitally encrypts all outgoing secure channel traffic whenever possible. No encryption will take place if this policy is disabled. The default local security setting is Enabled.

- **Secure channel: Digitally sign secure channel data (when possible)** causes the system to sign all outgoing secure channel traffic whenever possible. No signing takes place if this policy is disabled. The default local security setting is Enabled.

- **Secure channel: Require strong (Windows 2000 or later) session key** requires a strong encryption key for all outgoing secure channel traffic. The key strength is negotiated if this policy is disabled. The default local security setting is Disabled.

- **Send unencrypted password to connect to third-party SMB servers** lets the Server Message Block (SMB) redirector send clear-text passwords to non-Microsoft SMB servers that don't support password encryption for authentication. The default local security setting is Disabled.

- **Shut down system immediately if unable to log security audits** causes the computer to down if it can't log a security audit. Only an administrator can restart the system in the event that this policy is enabled and a shutdown occurs. The default local security setting is Disabled.

- **Smart card removal behavior** lets you define what happens when a logged-on user removes a SmartCard from the reader. You can choose from three options: No Action, Lock Workstation, or Force Logoff. The default local security setting is No Action.

- **Strengthen default permissions of global system objects (e.g. Symbolic links)** controls nonadministrative access to the default discretionary access control list (DACL) for objects. If you enable this policy, nonadministrative users can read shared objects but not modify shared objects that they did not create. The default local security setting is Enabled.

- **Unsigned driver installation behavior** lets you specify how computers react to an attempt to install a device driver (with the Windows 2000 device installer) that hasn't been certified by Microsoft's Windows Hardware Quality Lab (WHQL). You can choose from three options: Silently Succeed, Warn but Allow Installation, and Do Not Allow Installation. The default local security setting is Not Defined. The Do Not Allow Installation setting prevents set up of hardware, such as video adapters, that don't have Windows 2000–compliant drivers.

✦ **Unsigned non-driver installation behavior** lets you specify what happens when an attempt is made to install software that isn't on the Certified for Windows 2000 list, other than device drivers, using the Windows Installer. The options are the same as for the previous policy. The default local security setting is Not Defined, because there were *very* few applications certified when Microsoft released Windows 2000.

TIP: For a current list of Certified for Windows 2000 Professional and Server applications, go to http://www.microsoft.com/windows2000/upgrade/compat/certified.asp.

Event Log

Location: Computer Configuration\Windows Settings\Security Settings\Event Log

The Event Log node has only a single subnode, which lets you set properties of Event Viewer's Application, Security, and System event logs. The other three server event logs, Directory Service, DNS Service, and File Replication Service, don't have associated policies. The default value of all Settings for Event Logs policies is Not Defined. Settings for Event Logs policies aren't present in local security settings, so they apply only when set by Group Policy.

Settings for Event Logs   Offer the following 13 relatively inconsequential policies:

✦ **Maximum application log size** lets you define the maximum size for the Application log, up to the 4 GB limit for log files. The default log size is 512 kB, but you can set values as low as 64 kB in the spin box.

✦ **Maximum security log size** does the same for the Security log.

✦ **Maximum system log size** does the same for the System log.

✦ **Restrict guest access to application log** prevents the Guest user from viewing the Application log. The Guest user account is disabled by default, so this policy is of interest only if you enable that account (not a recommended practice).

✦ **Restrict guest access to security log** does the same for the Security log.

✦ **Restrict guest access to system log** does the same for the System log.

✦ **Retain application log** lets you specify how long (in days) events should be retained in the Application log. The value overwrites that set in the Overwrite Events Older Than spin box of the Application Log Properties dialog's General page, which has a default value of 7 days. Set a maximum log size that can accommodate the number of events expected during the retention interval.

✦ **Retain security log** does the same for the Security log.

✦ **Retain system log** does the same for the System log.

✦ **Retention method for application log** lets you specify which of three wrapping methods to use for the Application log: Overwrite Events as Needed, Overwrite Events by Days, or Do Not Overwrite Events. Specify Overwrite Events by Days if you apply the Retain Application Log policy.

✦ **Retention method for security log** does the same for the Security log.

✦ **Retention method for system log** does the same for the System log.

✦ **Shut down the computer when the security audit log is full** duplicates another policy. Use the Shut Down System Immediately If Unable to Log Security Audits policy under the Security Options node to implement this policy.

Restricted Groups

This policy lets administrators define membership of security-sensitive groups, which include Builtin (predefined) Windows 2000 groups. To create a restricted group, right-click the Restricted Groups node and click Add Group to open the Add Group dialog. Type or browse for the name of the group you want to restrict and click OK to add the group to the list. Double-click the new entry in the list to open the Configure Membership for *GroupName* dialog, which has the following two list boxes:

✦ **Members** defines who belongs to the restricted group, which defaults to This Group Should Have No Members. Click Add to open the Add Member dialog and type or browse in the Select Users or Groups dialog to add groups or individual users.

✦ **Member Of** defines which other groups the restricted group belongs to and defaults to The Groups to Which This Group Belongs Should Not Be Modified (see Figure A-6). Click Add or open the Add Group dialog and type or browse in the Select Groups dialog to add groups.

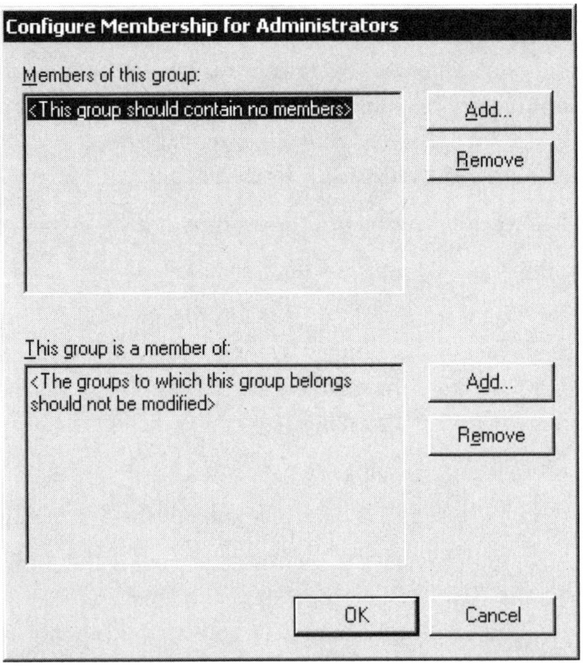

Configure Membership for Administrators

Members of this group:

<This group should contain no members>

[Add...]
[Remove]

This group is a member of:

<The groups to which this group belongs should not be modified>

[Add...]
[Remove]

[OK] [Cancel]

Figure A-6. The process of defining membership of a restricted group starts with a Configure Membership for *GroupName* dialog that has mysterious default values.

CAUTION: Be careful when restricting membership of Builtin groups and Domain Admins. If you don't include the appropriate users in the Members of This Group list, you might find that you've accidentally locked out accounts of administrators who need membership in these security-sensitive groups.

When a restricted Group Policy is applied, it deletes members of a restricted group that are not on the Members list. The policy adds Users on the Members list who are not currently members of the restricted group. Similarly, contents of the group's original Member Of list are made to conform to the contents of the restricted group's Member Of list.

System Services

Clicking the System Services node opens a laundry list of every installable service on a server. Defining a system service policy lets you specify a Start-up Mode (Manual, Automatic, or Disabled) and apply security to specify which groups and users have permissions to manage (Start, Stop, or Pause) the service. The default mode is Disabled, and the Everyone group gets Manage permissions, neither of which is likely to be your choice for most services. You might find setting System Services values useful for ensuring service consistency for a domain's DCs. You also can control which services run on domain workstations.

Registry

This policy lets you apply security to individual Registry hives or keys and subkeys. Right-click the Registry node and choose Add Key to open the Select Registry Key dialog. Navigate to the key you want to protect on all computers within the scope of the Group Policy (see Figure A-7.) When you click OK, the Database Security for *PathToKey* dialog opens with

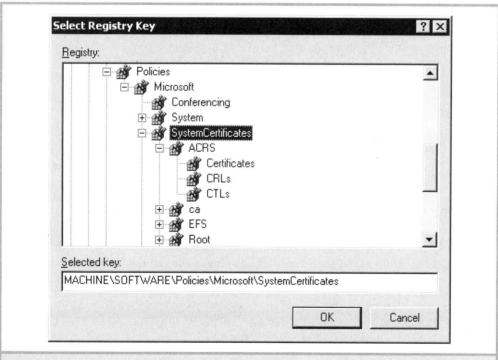

Figure A-7.   Set security on Registry keys and subkeys by selecting the key in the Select Registry Key dialog and clicking OK to open the Database Security for *PathToKey* dialog.

the Everyone group having Full Control permissions for the selected key. Set permissions for the groups permitted to alter key values and click OK. The Template Policy dialog opens with options for configuring inheritance of permissions on the key and its subkeys. Click OK to close the dialog. The key is added to the Names list.

File System

This policy is similar to the Registry policy. The File System policy lets administrators define access permissions (DACLs) and audit settings (SACLs) for file system objects that are common to all computers within the scope of the policy. Right-click the File System node and choose Add File to open the Add a File or Folder dialog. Navigate to the file system object to protect and click OK to open the Database Security for *PathToObject* dialog. After you set permissions for the object, clicking OK opens the Template Security Policy Setting dialog that offers inheritance options similar to that for Registry keys.

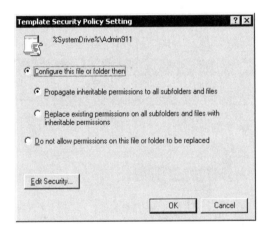

Public Key Policies

Public Key Policies has the following four policies for specifying PKI settings on computers within the scope of the policy. There is one Public Key Policies subnode (Enterprise Trust) in the User Configuration category, because individual users can establish their own Certificate Trust Lists.

✦ **Encrypted Data Recovery Agents** provide administrators with the capability of decrypting files encrypted by others with the Encrypting File System. The default certificate is issued to the Administrator of the server. Double-click the item in the

Issued To list to open the Certificate dialog to display its default trust status (not trusted). Right-click the node and choose Add to start the Add Recovery Agent Wizard or choose Create to start the Certificate Request Wizard.

✦ **Automatic Certificate Request Settings** let you add certificate requests by right-clicking the node and choosing New | Automatic Certificate Request to start the Automatic Certificate Request Setup Wizard.

✦ **Trusted Root Certification Authorities** let you import certificates from a file to a certificate store. Right-click the node and choose All Tasks | Import to start the Certificate Import Wizard.

✦ **Enterprise Trust** lets you add a certificate trust list to the computer. Right-click the node and choose New | Certificate Trust List to start the Certificate Trust List Wizard.

CAUTION: Don't set Public Key Policies unless you have a full understanding of Windows 2000's Public Key Infrastructure (PKI) and have your Enterprise Root Certificate server set up with the appropriate certificates for applications that require computer certificates, such as virtual private networks (VPNs). Setting incorrect values quickly fills your Security log.

IP Security Properties on Active Directory

This node has the following three unassigned policies for setting IP Security (IPSec) properties for secure network communication with AD:

✦ **Client (Respond Only)** allows unsecured (normal) clients to communicate with AD. Clients use the default response rule to negotiate security with servers that request IPSec. This setting secures only the requested protocol and port traffic with the server.

✦ **Secure Server (Require Security)** uses a Kerberos trust for all IP traffic with trusted clients only.

✦ **Server (Request Security)** requests a Kerberos trust with clients, but allows unsecured communication with clients that aren't set up for IPSec with Kerberos trust.

Double-click any of these policy entries to display the policyName Properties dialog. The General page provides a lengthy description of the effect of assigning the policy. Clicking the Rules page's Add button starts the Security Rule Wizard that lets you specify a tunnel endpoint, one of three Network Type options, an authentication method (Kerberos v5, certificate, or shared key), create an IP filter list, and specify filter actions. You also can edit the security methods, authentication methods, and connection types for existing rules. Obviously, you must be thoroughly familiar with IPSec to take advantage of these three policies.

CAUTION: Don't set IPSec policies unless you have IPSec running on your network and you've confirmed that the network is operating properly. Specifying incompatible IPSec policies and attributes can prevent DCs, member servers, and clients from communicating with one another and AD.

Administrative Templates

Location: Computer Configuration\Administrative Templates

Administrative Templates under the Computer Configuration category determine computer-related Registry key values on machines within the scope of the Group Policy. Administrative Templates are related to Windows NT System Policies and are intended primarily for managing Windows 2000 Professional workstations, not servers. Thus, it's an uncommon practice to apply Administrative Templates policies to DCs and member servers. For this reason, it's a good practice to place computer accounts for workstations in one or more OUs and apply Group Policies that implement Administrative Templates policies to the OUs, not at the site or domain level.

NOTE: Many Administrative Templates policies appear in both the Computer Configuration and User Configuration categories. In most cases of policy duplication, the Computer Configuration setting prevails over a conflicting User Configuration setting without using loopback processing. If the Computer Configuration prevails, this is noted in the policy description.

Unlike the Properties dialogs for the preceding AD-stored policies, the Properties dialog of each policy defined by Administrative Templates has an Explain page. Many of the explanations are quite lengthy; the following descriptions of the effects of configuring these policies as Enabled are abbreviated. All policies under the Administrative Templates node are set to Not Configured by default.

Registry key names with value names appended are included with policy descriptions; key and value names are abstracted from the Computers class of the appropriate template (.adm) files. All Computer Configuration Registry entries are in subkeys of the HKEY_LOCAL_ MACHINE (HKLM) hive. A typical entry is HKLM\Software\Microsoft\Windows\ CurrentVersion\Policies\System\VerboseStatus. VerboseStatus is the value name. Figure A-8

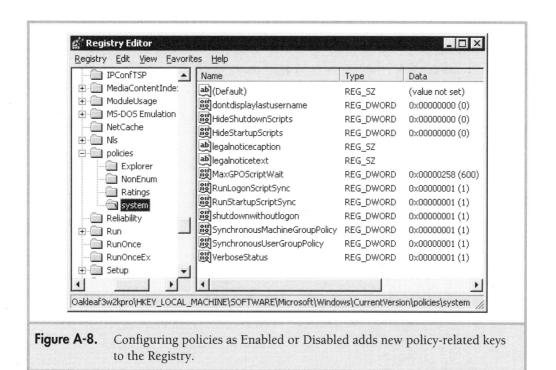

Figure A-8. Configuring policies as Enabled or Disabled adds new policy-related keys to the Registry.

shows RegEdit displaying the nine values added by policies configured in the Computer Configuration\Administrative Templates\System node, which are shown in Figure A-9. For a complete guide to the Windows 2000 Registry, purchase a copy of *Admin911: Windows 2000 Registry* by Kathy Ivens (Osborne/McGraw-Hill, 2000; ISBN: 0-07-212946-8).

TIP: You can use Regedit.exe (not Regedt32.exe) to troubleshoot issues with propagation of policies to computers and users. Choose Edit | Find to open the Find dialog and then type the value name to find, such as VerboseStatus, in the Find What text box. Start at the HKLM\Software\Microsoft key to speed the search. If you've configured the policy as Enabled, the corresponding computer Registry value should be present after a computer within the scope of the Group Policy reboots or after the Group Policy refresh interval (roughly 90 minutes by default) expires. User Configuration Registry values for enabled policies should be present after the next logon of a user to whom the Group Policy applies. Registry values for disabled policies appear when the default (Not Configured) value is Enabled.

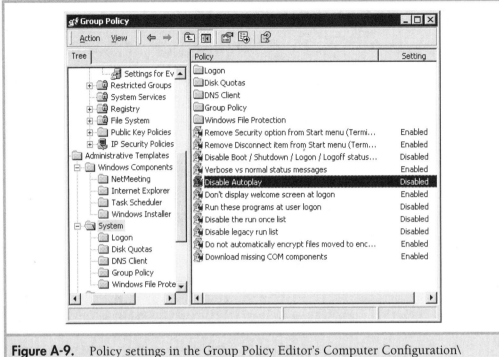

Figure A-9. Policy settings in the Group Policy Editor's Computer Configuration\
Administrative Templates\System node that created the Registry keys
shown in Figure A-8.

Windows Components

Location: Computer Configuration\Administrative Templates\Windows Components
   The Windows Components node has four subnodes: NetMeeting, Internet Explorer,
Task Scheduler, and Windows Installer.

NetMeeting

Location: Computer Configuration\Administrative Templates\Windows Components\
NetMeeting
   The NetMeeting node has only the following policy, which has Not Configured, Enabled,
and Disabled options:

✦ **Disable remote desktop sharing** prevents users from using the remote desktop
   sharing feature of NetMeeting, which prevents users from using this NetMeeting
   feature to remotely control affected computers. (HKLM\Software\Policies\Microsoft\
   Conferencing\NoSharingExplorer)

Internet Explorer

Location: Computer Configuration\Administrative Templates\Windows Components\
Internet Explorer

The Internet Explorer (IE) policies in the Computer Configuration and User Configuration
categories combine to provide features similar to those of the Internet Explorer Administration
Kit (IEAK). The Internet Explorer node has the following eight policies obtained from the
Inetres.adm template file, each of which has Not Configured, Enabled, and Disabled options:

◆ **Security Zones: Use only machine settings** causes all user changes to IE Security
Zones to apply to all users of the computer. IE's default is an individual set of
Security Zones for each user of the computer. (HKLM\Software\Policies\Microsoft\
Windows\CurrentVersion\Internet Settings\Security_HKLM_only)

◆ **Security Zones: Do not allow users to change policies** prevents all users from
changing the Security Zone settings established by an administrator. (HKLM\
Software\Policies\Microsoft\Windows\CurrentVersion\Internet Settings\Security_
options_edit)

◆ **Security Zones: Do not allow users to add/delete sites** prevents all users from
adding or removing sites from Security Zones. (HKLM\Software\Policies\
Microsoft\Windows\CurrentVersion\Internet Settings\Security_zones_map_edit)

◆ **Make proxy settings per-machine (rather than per user)** applies the same proxy
settings to all users of the computer. IE's default is an individual proxy setting for
each user. (HKLM\Software\Policies\Microsoft\Windows\CurrentVersion\Internet
Settings\ProxySettingsPerUser)

◆ **Disable Automatic Install of Internet Explorer components** prevents automatic
downloading and installation of IE components, but doesn't prevent all users from
clicking OK to save a downloadable component as a file or install it without saving
the file. (HKLM\Software\Policies\Microsoft\Windows\CurrentVersion\Internet
Settings\NoJITSetup)

◆ **Disable Periodic Check of Internet Explorer software updates** prevents periodic
notification from Microsoft of new IE version updates. (HKLM\Software\Policies\
Microsoft\Windows\CurrentVersion\Internet Settings\NoUpdateCheck)

◆ **Disable software update shell notifications on program launch** prevents all users
from receiving notification when an IE update is received from a software distribution
channel. Software distribution channels are a special type of the IE4+ Active Channel
that uses Open Software Distribution (OSD). (HKLM\Software\Policies\Microsoft\
Windows\CurrentVersion\Internet Settings\NoMSAppLogo5ChannelNotify)

◆ **Disable showing the splash screen** bypasses IE's startup window for all users. (HKLM\Software\Policies\Microsoft\Windows\CurrentVersion\Internet Settings\NoSplash)

NOTE: The System.adm template contains the definition of all remaining Computer Configuration\Administrative Templates policies.

Task Scheduler

Location: Computer Configuration\Administrative Templates\Windows Components\ Task Scheduler

The Task Scheduler node contains the following seven policies, each of which has only Not Configured, Enabled, and Disabled options:

◆ **Hide Property Pages** prevents all users from viewing or changing the properties of an existing scheduled task by disabling user access to the task's Properties dialog. If configured for both computers and users, the computer setting applies. (HKLM\Software\Policies\Microsoft\Windows\Task Scheduler5.0\Property Pages)

◆ **Prevent Task Run or End** prevents all users from starting or stopping scheduled tasks manually. If configured for both computers and users, the computer setting applies. (HKLM\Software\Policies\Microsoft\Windows\Task Scheduler5.0\Execution)

◆ **Disable Drag-and-Drop** prevents all users from using drag-and-drop or copy-and-paste methods to move or copy programs in the Scheduled Tasks folder. If configured for both computers and users, the computer setting applies. (HKLM\Software\Policies\Microsoft\Windows\Task Scheduler5.0\DragAndDrop)

◆ **Disable New Task Creation** prevents all users from adding new scheduled tasks. If configured for both computers and users, the computer setting applies. (HKLM\Software\Policies\Microsoft\Windows\Task Scheduler5.0\Task Creation)

◆ **Disable Task Deletion** prevents all users from removing scheduled tasks. If configured for both computers and users, the computer setting applies. (HKLM\Software\Policies\Microsoft\Windows\Task Scheduler5.0\Task Deletion)

◆ **Disable Advanced Menu** prevents all users from viewing or changing the properties of new tasks during their creation. This policy doesn't affect existing tasks (see the Hide Property Pages and Prohibit Browse policies). If configured for both computers and users, the computer setting applies. (HKLM\Software\Policies\Microsoft\ Windows\Task Scheduler5.0\Disable Advanced)

✦ **Prohibit Browse** restricts all users to Start menu items when creating new scheduled tasks and prevents them from changing existing tasks. If configured for both computers and users, the computer setting applies. (HKLM\Software\Policies\ Microsoft\Windows\Task Scheduler5.0\AllowBrowse)

Windows Installer

Location: Computer Configuration\Administrative Templates\Windows Components\ Windows Installer

All but the first and last of the following 13 policies have only Not Configured, Enabled, and Disabled options:

✦ **Disable Windows Installer** offers a choice of the following three installation policies: Never (No User Restrictions), For Non-managed Apps Only (Install Only Administrator-Assigned or -Published Applications), or Always (Disable Windows Installer). The most common setting for ordinary users is For Non-managed Apps Only. Windows Installer has no restrictions if you don't configure this policy. (HKLM\Software\Policies\Microsoft\Windows\Installer\DisableMSI)

✦ **Always install with elevated privileges** causes Windows Installer to use system permissions, instead of user permissions, when installing programs. If you enable Windows Installer for ordinary users, enable this policy. If configured for both computers and users, the computer setting applies. (HKLM\Software\Policies\ Microsoft\Windows\Installer\AlwaysInstallElevated)

✦ **Disable rollback** prevents saving of files required to reverse an interrupted or unsuccessful installation and revert to the computer's original configuration. If this policy is configured for both computers and users, the computer setting applies. Don't enable this policy for either computers or users. (HKLM\Software\Policies\ Microsoft\Windows\Installer\DisableRollback)

✦ **Disable browse dialog box for new source** prevents all users from searching for installation files when they add features or components to an installed program by disabling the Browse button in the Use Feature From list. HKLM\Software\Policies\ Microsoft\Windows\Installer\DisableBrowse)

✦ **Disable patching** prevents all users (not administrators) from installing patches (updates to individual files) with Windows Installer. Malicious patches can disable the computer. (HKLM\Software\Policies\Microsoft\Windows\Installer\DisablePatch)

✦ **Disable IE security prompt for Windows Installer scripts** prevents notification of all users when Web-based applications install software on the user's computer. By default, IE opens a warning dialog that permits users to accept or refuse the application. Enabling this policy jeopardizes security. (HKLM\Software\Policies\Microsoft\Windows\Installer\SafeForScripting)

✦ **Enable user control over installs** lets all users change installation options that are usually available only to system administrators. Enabling this policy also jeopardizes security. (HKLM\Software\Policies\Microsoft\Windows\Installer\EnableUserControl)

✦ **Enable user to browse for source while elevated** enables the Browse button when Installer runs with system privileges. It defeats the objective of enabling the Disable Browse dialog box for new source policy. (HKLM\Software\Policies\Microsoft\Windows\Installer\AllowLockdownBrowse)

✦ **Enable user to use media source while elevated** lets all users insert removable media, such as diskettes and CD-ROMs, to install programs. Be very judicious in your application of this policy. (HKLM\Software\Policies\Microsoft\Windows\Installer\AllowLockdownMedia)

✦ **Enable user to patch elevated products** defeats the objective of enabling the Disable Patching policy. (HKLM\Software\Policies\Microsoft\Windows\Installer\AllowLockdownPatch)

✦ **Allow admin to install from Terminal Services session** lets only Terminal Services administrators install and configure programs remotely. This Registry value is installed and set to true (value of 1) by default. (HKLM\Software\Policies\Microsoft\Windows\Installer\EnableAdminTSRemote)

✦ **Cache transforms in secure location on workstation** moves the location of locally saved Windows Installer transform files from the user's profile folder to a user-inaccessible folder. (HKLM\Software\Policies\Microsoft\Windows\Installer\TransformsSecure)

✦ **Logging** lets you specify in a text box a string of characters to specify the events that Windows Installer adds to the Msi.log file in the \Temp folder of the system volume. (HKLM\Software\Policies\Microsoft\Windows\Installer\Logging)

System

Location: Computer Configuration\Administrative Templates\System

Unlike most other third-level nodes, the System node contains 11 policies and the following five subnodes: Logon, Disk Quotas, DNS Client, Group Policy, and Windows File Protection. Following are descriptions of the 11 System policies, which (with one exception) have only Not Configured, Enabled, and Disabled options:

✦ **Remove Security option from Start menu (Terminal Services only)** requires all users to give the three-finger salute (CTRL+ALT+DEL) when logging on to a Terminal Services session. (HKLM\Software\Microsoft\Windows\CurrentVersion\Policies\Explorer\NoNTSecurity)

✦ **Remove Disconnect item from Start menu (Terminal Services only)** prevents all users from disconnecting from the Terminal Services server by the ordinary method. (HKLM\Software\Microsoft\Windows\CurrentVersion\Policies\Explorer\NoDisconnect)

✦ **Disable Boot / Shutdown / Logon / Logoff status messages** prevents all users from seeing the usual messages during these events. The purpose of this policy is obscure, at best. (HKLM\Software\Microsoft\Windows\CurrentVersion\Policies\System\DisableStatusMessages)

✦ **Verbose vs normal status messages** displays very detailed status messages during the preceding four processes. For example, all policy categories applied to the computer appear in the status list during the boot process. Not surprisingly, disabling status messages also disables this policy. (HKLM\Software\Microsoft\Windows\CurrentVersion\Policies\System\VerboseStatus)

✦ **Disable Autoplay** disables autostarting of CD-ROM setup programs and opening of CD Player or Windows Media Player when inserting an audio CD. You have the option of disabling CD-ROM drives or all drives. Administrators are likely to want this policy applied to their computers. If configured for both computers and users, the computer setting applies. (HKLM\Software\Microsoft\Windows\CurrentVersion\Policies\Explorer\NoDriveTypeAutoRun)

✦ **Don't display welcome screen at logon** hides the Getting Started with Windows 2000 dialog, which most users and administrators are likely to welcome. If configured for both computers and users, the computer setting applies. (HKLM\Software\Microsoft\Windows\CurrentVersion\Policies\Explorer\NoWelcomeScreen)

✦ **Run these programs at user logon** lets administrators type a list of applications to run or documents to open when any user logs on. If configured for both computers and users, the computer setting applies. To add a program to run or document to open, choose the Enabled option, click the Show button to open the Show Contents dialog, click Add to open the Add Item dialog, type the well-formed path or UNC path to the file, and click OK to add the item to the Show Contents list. (HKLM\Software\Microsoft\Windows\CurrentVersion\Policies\Explorer\Run subkey)

✦ **Disable the run once list** ignores a customized run-once list that executes one or more programs the next time the computer boots, but not thereafter. If configured for both computers and users, the computer setting applies. (HKLM\Software\Microsoft\ Windows\CurrentVersion\Policies\Explorer\DisableLocalMachineRunOnce)

✦ **Disable legacy run list** ignores the Windows NT 4.0 equivalent of the Run These Programs at User Logon policy's list. If configured for both computers and users, the computer setting applies. (HKLM\Software\Microsoft\Windows\CurrentVersion\ Policies\Explorer\DisableLocalMachineRun)

✦ **Do not automatically encrypt files moved to encrypted folders** changes the default behavior of the Encrypting File System (EFS) to not encrypt files all users move to a previously encrypted folder on the same volume. (HKLM\Software\Microsoft\ Windows\CurrentVersion\Policies\Explorer\NoEncryptOnMove)

✦ **Download missing COM components** enables the computer to search AD's Class Store for missing Component Object Model (COM and COM+) components required by an application. Enable this policy unless you have a good reason for doing otherwise. A missing COM or COM+ component can render an application unusable. If configured for both computers and users, the computer setting applies. (HKLM\ Software\Policies\Microsoft\Windows\App Management\COMClassStore)

Logon

Location: Computer Configuration\Administrative Templates\System\Logon

Logon policies determine how clients run logon scripts and handle roaming user profiles. Many of these policies apply to mobile users who are connected by a slow communication channel (such as a dial-up modem) to the network. Following are descriptions of the effect of enabling each of the 13 Logon policies:

✦ **Run logon scripts synchronously** causes logon script processing to complete before the user's desktop configuration appears. Long-running logon scripts delay the user's ability to start work. If configured for both computers and users, the computer setting applies. (HKLM\Software\Microsoft\Windows\CurrentVersion\Policies\System\ RunLogonScriptSync)

✦ **Run startup scripts asynchronously** causes multiple startup scripts to run simultaneously, rather than in the order specified in the Computer Configuration\ Windows Settings\Scripts (Startup/Shutdown) policy. (HKLM\Software\Microsoft\ Windows\CurrentVersion\Policies\System\RunStartupScriptSync)

✦ **Run startup scripts visible** causes the instructions of the script to appear in a command window so that users can view them. This setting is recommended for advanced users only. (HKLM\Software\Microsoft\Windows\CurrentVersion\Policies\ System\HideStartupScripts)

◆ **Run shutdown scripts visible** does the same thing for shutdown scripts. (HKLM\Software\Microsoft\Windows\CurrentVersion\Policies\System\HideShutdown Scripts)

◆ **Maximum wait time for Group Policy scripts** lets you set the total interval allowed for all startup and logon (or logoff and shutdown) scripts applied by Group Policy to complete execution. The default setting lets scripts run for a total of 10 minutes. (HKLM\Software\Microsoft\Windows\CurrentVersion\Policies\System\ MaxpolicyScriptWait)

◆ **Delete cached copies of roaming profiles** prevents saving of a copy of the user's roaming profile on the local computer's fixed disk when the user logs off. Don't enable this policy without enabling the next policy, because slow link detection requires a local copy of the roaming profile. (HKLM\Software\Policies\Microsoft\Windows\System\DeleteRoamingCache)

◆ **Do not detect slow network connections** disables the slow link detection feature that measures the speed of the connection to the network. Windows 2000 uses a sophisticated algorithm to detect a slow network link; the default is less than 500 kbps throughput for a slow link. (HKLM\Software\Policies\Microsoft\Windows\System\SlowLinkDetectEnabled)

◆ **Slow network connection timeout for user profiles** lets you change the threshold for slow link detection on IP networks where the default is 500 kbps or for other network protocols where the default is 120 milliseconds for a simple test of the server's file system. (HKLM\Software\Policies\Microsoft\Windows\System\SlowLinkTimeOut and \UserProfileMinTransferRate)

◆ **Wait for remote user profile** causes the system to wait for the remote copy of the roaming user profile to load, regardless of how long it takes. If you enable the Do Not Detect Slow Network Connection policy, this policy has no effect. (HKLM\Software\ Policies\Microsoft\Windows\System\SlowLinkProfileDefault)

◆ **Prompt user when slow link is detected** opens a dialog that lets users select whether to use a local copy of the user profile or wait for the roaming user profile to download. (HKLM\Software\Policies\Microsoft\Windows\System\ SlowLinkUIEnabled)

◆ **Timeout for dialog boxes** lets you specify the length of time for a user response to a dialog for a profile-related option before the system applies a default response. The default timeout is 30 seconds. (HKLM\Software\Policies\Microsoft\Windows\System\ ProfileDlgTimeOut)

◆ **Log users off when roaming profile fails** automatically logs off users if the roaming user profile won't load. Enabling this policy has the effect of making the user's profile mandatory. If this policy is not configured or disabled, the local copy of the profile loads, if present; if not, the default user profile loads. (HKLM\Software\Policies\ Microsoft\Windows\System\ProfileErrorAction)

◆ **Maximum retries to unload and update user profile** specifies how many attempts are made to unload and update the Registry component of a user's profile. The default value is 60 retries in one minute; a 0 value prevents retrying the operation after a failure. (HKLM\Software\Policies\Microsoft\Windows\System\ProfileUnloadTimeout)

Disk Quotas

Location: Computer Configuration\Administrative Templates\System\Disk Quotas

You can use Disk Quotas policies to enforce quota management policies on workstations that have multiple users, but it's unusual to apply Disk Quotas policies to file servers that store user profiles, redirected folders, and the like. Administrators normally manage file-server quotas directly. Following are the six Disk Quotas policies:

◆ **Enable disk quotas** establishes disk quota management on all NTFS volumes of computers within the policy's scope. If you enable this policy, be sure to enable the next two policies and set values for the Default Quota Limit and Warning Level. (HKLM\Software\Policies\Microsoft\Windows NT\DiskQuota\Enable)

◆ **Enforce disk quota limit** causes the quota limit and warning level you set in the next policy to become operative. (HKLM\Software\Policies\Microsoft\Windows NT\DiskQuota\Enforce)

◆ **Default quota limit and warning level** lets you set the default disk quota limit and the warning level for new users of each NTFS volume on the computer. The default values are 100 MB for both quota limit and warning level; you can change the numeric values with spin buttons and select units (kB, MB, GB, TB, PB, and EB) from drop-down lists. (HKLM\Software\Policies\Microsoft\Windows NT\DiskQuota\Limit, \LimitUnits, \Threshold, and \ThresholdUnits)

◆ **Log event when quota limit exceeded** causes an event to be added to the Application log when a user reaches the quota limit. The event appears regardless of the setting of the Enforce Disk Quota Limit policy. (HKLM\Software\Policies\Microsoft\Windows NT\DiskQuota\LogEventOverLimit)

◆ **Log event when quota warning level exceeded** does the same when a user reaches the warning level. (HKLM\Software\Policies\Microsoft\Windows NT\DiskQuota\ LogEventOverThreshold)

✦ **Apply policy to removable media** sets quotas for NTFS file system volumes on removable media. If this policy is not configured or disabled, quotas don't apply to removable media. (HKLM\Software\Policies\Microsoft\Windows NT\DiskQuota\ApplyToRemovableMedia)

DNS Client

Location: Computer Configuration\Administrative Templates\System\DNS Client
DNS Client has only the following policy:

✦ **Primary DNS Suffix** lets you specify the primary Domain Name System (DNS) suffix for all computers within the scope of the policy, so this policy usually is set at the domain level. If you enable and specify a DNS suffix (such as oakmont.edu), neither users nor local administrators can alter the suffix. The setting made in the Primary DNS Suffix of This Computer text box on the local computer is ignored. If enabled, this policy takes effect on the next reboot. (HKLM\Software\Policies\Microsoft\System\DNSclient\NV PrimaryDnsSuffix).

Group Policy

Location: Computer Configuration\Administrative Templates\System\Group Policy
The following 16 policies affect how Group Policies are applied to all computers within the current scope:

✦ **Disable background refresh of Group Policy** prevents group policy updates while the computer is in use. When the user logs off, computer and user updates occur immediately. It's not uncommon (but is a potential security breach) for users to remain logged on for an entire work week (or longer), in which case changes to Group Policies are delayed (sometimes indefinitely). Never apply this policy to member servers or, especially, DCs, because these computers (hopefully) run forever. (HKLM\Software\Microsoft\Windows\CurrentVersion\Policies\System\DisableBkGndGroupPolicy)

NOTE: A better option would be a range of hours (such as very early morning) during which background refresh is disabled. Providing a time window would prevent users from being disrupted by a change in policy while working at the computer, but not control application of Group Policy changes by reliance on users' periodically logging off their computers. A more draconian approach is to put a 24-hour timer on the circuits powering the workstations.

✦ **Apply Group Policy for computers asynchronously during startup** lets the computer display the logon dialog prior to completion of Group Policy updates. Unless Group Policy changes are frequent and substantial, there is little reason to apply this policy. (HKLM\Software\Microsoft\Windows\CurrentVersion\Policies\System\ SynchronousMachineGroupPolicy)

✦ **Apply Group Policy for users asynchronously during logon** lets the computer display the user's desktop configuration before user Group Policy updates are complete. This is another policy that you should apply only in exceptional cases. (HKLM\Software\Microsoft\Windows\CurrentVersion\Policies\System\ SynchronousUserGroupPolicy)

✦ **Group Policy refresh interval for computers** lets you set the frequency of Group Policy updates while the computer is in use. The default rate for updates is every 90 minutes, with a random offset of 0 to 30 minutes. You can set the maximum interval to 64,800 minutes (45 years) or 0 minutes; setting 0 results in a refresh interval of 7 seconds and a randomizing time interval of 0 to 1,440 minutes (24 hours). This policy doesn't apply to DCs. (HKLM\Software\Microsoft\Windows\CurrentVersion\ Policies\System\GroupPolicyRefreshTime)

✦ **Group Policy refresh interval for domain controllers** lets you set the Group Policy replication frequency between DCs and so is most commonly applied to the Default Domain Controllers Policy. The default value is 5 minutes, the frequency at which other AD settings are replicated between DCs in the same site. The interval and randomizing setting ranges are the same as for computers. (HKLM\Software\Policies\ Microsoft\Windows\System\GroupPolicyRefreshTimeDC)

✦ **User Group Policy loopback processing mode** causes Computer Configuration policies to override all (Replace option) or only conflicting (Merge option) settings made by User Configuration policies. Loopback processing mode with the Replace option set most commonly is used for computers in public or school computer lab environments. (HKLM\Software\Policies\Microsoft\Windows\System\ UserPolicyMode)

✦ **Group Policy slow link detection** is the Group Policy equivalent of the Slow Network Connection Timeout for User Profiles policy that's under the Logon node. (HKLM\Software\Policies\Microsoft\Windows\System\GroupPolicyMinTransferRate)

✦ **Registry policy processing** offers two options that affect processing of policies set in the Administrative Templates folder and a few other locations: Do Not Apply During Periodic Background Processing and Process Even If the Group Policy Objects Have Not Changed. Marking the first check box has an effect similar to specifying the

Disable Background Refresh of Group Policy policy, but affects only policies that make changes to the Registry. Marking the second check box causes a complete refresh of Registry-based properties, rather than the default incremental (changes-only) refresh operation. The latter option is useful for reinstating policy changes that the user has made by editing the Registry. (HKLM\Software\Policies\ Microsoft\Windows\Group Policy\{35378EAC-683F-11D2-A89A-00C04FBBCFA2}\ NoBackgroundPolicy and \NoGPOListChanges)

+ **Internet Explorer Maintenance policy processing** has the same effect as the preceding policy for IE maintenance settings. (HKLM\Software\Policies\ Microsoft\Windows\Group Policy\{A2E30F80-D7DE-11D2-BBDE-00C04F86AE3B}\ NoSlowLink, \NoBackgroundPolicy, and \NoGPOListChanges)

+ **Software Installation policy processing** offers two options for processing assigned and published software installation: Allow Processing Across a Slow Network Connection and Process Even If the Group Policy Objects Have Not Changed. Clearing the first check box prevents installation over a slow connection; marking the second check box causes installation to occur in the unlikely event that the user has altered the Registry in an attempt to prevent installation. (HKLM\Software\Policies\ Microsoft\Windows\Group Policy\{C6DC5466-785A-11D2-84D0-00C04FB169F7}\ NoGPOListChanges and \NoSlowLink)

+ **Folder Redirection policy processing** lets you apply the same two options as in the preceding policy to folder redirection policies. (HKLM\Software\Policies\Microsoft\ Windows\Group Policy\{25537BA6-77A8-11D2-9B6C-0000F8080861}\NoSlowLink and \NoGPOListChanges)

+ **Scripts policy processing** lets you apply the following three options to processing startup, logon, logoff, and shutdown scripts: Allow Processing Across a Slow Network Connection, Do Not Apply During Periodic Background Processing, and Process Even If the Group Policy Objects Have Not Changed. The effect of these options is identical to that described for preceding policies. (HKLM\Software\Policies\Microsoft\ Windows\Group Policy\{42B5FAAE-6536-11D2-AE5A-0000F87571E3}\NoSlowLink, \NoBackgroundPolicy, and \NoGPOListChanges)

+ **Security policy processing** lets you apply the same three options to Security Policy policies. (HKLM\Software\Policies\Microsoft\Windows\Group Policy\{827D319E-6EAC-11D2-A4EA-00C04F79F83A}\NoSlowLink, \NoBackgroundPolicy, and \NoGPOListChanges)

+ **IP Security policy processing** lets you apply the same three options to IP Security policies. (HKLM\Software\Policies\Microsoft\Windows\Group Policy\{E437BC1C-AA7D-11D2-A382-00C04F991E27}\NoSlowLink, \NoBackgroundPolicy, and \NoGPOListChanges)

✦ **EFS recovery policy processing** lets you apply the same three options to the Encrypted Data Recovery Agents policy. (HKLM\Software\Policies\Microsoft\ Windows\Group Policy\{B1BE8D72-6EAC-11D2-A4EA-00C04F79F83A}\ NoSlowLink, \NoBackgroundPolicy, \NoGPOListChanges)

✦ **Disk Quota policy processing** lets you apply the same three options to the Disk Quotas policy. (HKLM\Software\Policies\Microsoft\Windows\Group Policy\{3610EDA5-77EF-11D2-8DC5-00C04FA31A66}\NoSlowLink, \NoBackgroundPolicy, and \NoGPOListChanges)

NOTE: Taking into consideration that policies ordinarily are updated only when changed, the preceding five policies might qualify as "gratuitous granularity." However, you can take advantage of these and the other "policy processing" policies to prevent specific types of policies from being updated while users (especially developers and designers) are working at their computers.

Windows File Protection

Location: Computer Configuration\Administrative Templates\System\Windows File Protection

Windows File Protection (WFP) is intended to preserve Windows 2000's system file integrity in the event that users or rogue programs delete or overwrite essential DLLs. If a DLL is missing or replaced by an unsigned copy, the System File Checker tool, Sfc.exe, attempts to replace it with a copy stored in the \Winnt\System32\Dllcache folder. If a copy isn't available in Dllcache, Sfc attempts to obtain a copy from the Windows 2000 file distribution source (network share or CD-ROM). WFP protection uses the following four policies:

✦ **Set Windows File Protection scanning** offers the following three options for running Sfc.exe: Do Not Scan During Startup (the default), Scan During Startup (scans each time the user starts Windows 2000), and Scan Once (scan only during the next startup). If this policy isn't applied or you select the default, Sfc.exe runs only after an application or patch is installed. (HKLM\Software\Policies\Microsoft\Windows NT\Windows File Protection\SfcScan)

✦ **Hide the file scan progress window** prevents display of a dialog that provides status information when Sfc.exe runs. According to Microsoft, this dialog "might confuse novices." (HKLM\Software\Policies\Microsoft\Windows NT\Windows File Protection\SfcShowProgress)

✦ **Limit Windows File Protection cache size** lets you set the maximum amount of file space devoted to DLL caching. The default is 50 MB for Windows 2000 Professional and is unlimited for Windows 2000 Server. (HKLM\Software\Policies\Microsoft\ Windows NT\Windows File Protection\SfcQuota)

✦ **Specify Windows File Protection cache location** lets you change the location of the Dllcache folder to another volume or folder name. (HKLM\Software\Policies\ Microsoft\Windows NT\Windows File Protection\SFCDllCacheDir)

Network

Location: Computer Configuration\Administrative Templates\Network

The Network node has two subnodes: Offline Files and Network and Dial-up Connections. The Network and Dial-up Connections node has a *very important* policy.

Offline Files

Location: Computer Configuration\Administrative Templates\Network\Offline files

Offline Files has 17 policies that control whether users can utilize the Offline Files feature and its behavior, if it is enabled. Many of the following policies have obscure interactions:

✦ **Enabled** forces users to implement the Windows 2000 Offline Files feature. If enabled, this policy takes effect on the next reboot. If disabled, users can't use Offline Files, and no other Offline Files policies you enable take effect. (HKLM\Software\ Policies\Microsoft\Windows\NetCache\Enabled)

✦ **Disable user configuration of Offline Files** prevents users from changing the Offline Files behavior you specify with the following policies. If configured for both computers and users, the computer setting applies. (HKLM\Software\Policies\ Microsoft\Windows\NetCache\NoConfigCache)

✦ **Synchronize all offline files before logging off** causes a full synchronization with the server of all offline files when a user logs off. The default is a quick synchronization that ensures that files are intact, but not necessarily current, and allows the user to change the synchronization behavior. If configured for both computers and users, the computer setting applies. (HKLM\Software\Policies\Microsoft\Windows\NetCache\ SyncAtLogoff)

✦ **Default cache size** lets you alter the maximum percentage of total disk space that's allocated to locally cached offline files. The default is 10 percent. (HKLM\Software\ Policies\Microsoft\Windows\NetCache\DefCacheSize)

✦ **Action on server disconnect** offers the following two options when disconnected from the server storing offline files: Work Offline (use locally cached copies) and Never Go Offline (prevents use of cached copies). If configured for both computers and users, the computer setting applies. The descriptions of the choices on the Policy page for this policy are incorrect. (HKLM\Software\Policies\Microsoft\Windows\ NetCache\GoOfflineAction)

◆ **Non-default server disconnect actions** lets you specify what happens when a user is disconnected from servers you specify by name in a list. Each server has a value entry, 0 for Work Offline and 1 for Never Go Offline. This policy overrides values you set in the previous policy if you include the default server in the list. If configured for both computers and users, the computer setting applies. (HKLM\Software\Policies\ Microsoft\Windows\NetCache\CustomGoOfflineActions\CustomGoOfflineActions subkey)

◆ **Disable "Make Available Offline"** removes the View Files button from the Offline Files folder. It doesn't prevent users from working offline or using Explorer to view server files. If configured for both computers and users, the computer setting applies. (HKLM\Software\Policies\Microsoft\Windows\NetCache\NoMakeAvailableOffline)

◆ **Prevent use of Offline Files folder** disables the Offline Files folder. If configured for both computers and users, the computer setting applies. (HKLM\Software\ Policies\Microsoft\Windows\NetCache\NoCacheViewer)

◆ **Files not cached** lets you provide a comma-separated list of file types (extensions) that should not be cached locally. One example is file-shared databases (*.mdb for Jet files) to which multiple users connect. If configured for both computers and users, the computer setting applies. (HKLM\Software\Policies\Microsoft\Windows\ NetCache\ExcludeExtensions)

◆ **Administratively assigned offline files** lets you generate a list of UNC paths for files, folders, or both to which all users of the computer should have access. When adding items to the list, leave the value empty. If configured for both computers and users, the computer setting applies. (HKLM\Software\Policies\Microsoft\Windows\ NetCache\AssignedOfflineFolders\AssignedOfflineFolders subkey)

◆ **Disable reminder balloons** removes the balloons that appear above the Offline Files icon in the status bar when a network connection is lost or reconnected. Enabling this policy moots the settings of the following three policies. If configured for both computers and users, the computer setting applies. (HKLM\Software\Policies\Microsoft\Windows\NetCache\NoReminders)

✦ **Reminder balloon frequency** lets you change the update interval for reminder balloons. If configured for both computers and users, the computer setting applies. (HKLM\Software\Policies\Microsoft\Windows\NetCache\ReminderFreqMinutes)

✦ **Initial reminder balloon lifetime** lets you set the duration of the first reminder balloon for a network status change. If configured for both computers and users, the computer setting applies. (HKLM\Software\Policies\Microsoft\Windows\NetCache\InitialBalloonTimeoutSeconds)

✦ **Reminder balloon lifetime** lets you set the duration of successive reminder balloons. If configured for both computers and users, the computer setting applies. (HKLM\Software\Policies\Microsoft\Windows\NetCache\ReminderBalloonTimeoutSeconds)

NOTE: The preceding three reminder balloon policies are some of the more egregious examples of policy minutiae.

✦ **At logoff, delete local copy of user's offline files** deletes locally cached copies of online files *without synchronizing them*, even if you enable the Synchronize All Offline Files Before Logging Off policy. If you decide to enable this dangerous policy for security purposes, make sure to disable the Disable User Configuration of Offline Files policy so users can perform a full manual synchronization before logging off. (HKLM\Software\Policies\Microsoft\Windows\NetCache\PurgeAtLogoff)

✦ **Event logging level** lets you specify the events logged by Offline Files in the Application log. A value of 0 records offline cache corruption, 1 adds server disconnection, 2 adds client disconnection and reconnection, and 3 adds server reconnection events. If configured for both computers and users, the computer setting applies. (HKLM\Software\Policies\Microsoft\Windows\NetCache\EventLoggingLevel)

✦ **Subfolders always available offline** specifies that subfolders are always available offline when the parent folder is made available offline. If you don't enable this policy, users are asked whether they want to make subfolders available. Why users would not want to make subfolders always available is another unsolved policy mystery. (HKLM\Software\Policies\Microsoft\Windows\NetCache\AlwaysPinSubFolders)

Network & Dial-Up Connections

Location: Computer Configuration\Administrative Templates\Network\Network & Dial-up Connections

The following policy is the single most important policy in the entire collection:

✦ **Allow configuration of connection sharing** specifies that the local Administrator can enable, disable, and configure the Internet Connection Sharing feature of a dial-up connection. *Disable this policy at the domain level and never enable it at the OU level.*

NOTE: Internet Connection Sharing (ICS) is a dubious replacement for Windows 2000 Server's Network Address Translation (NAT) in a small-office/home-office (SOHO) configuration. No user within an organization that employs Group Policies should be given the ability to implement ICS.

Printers

Location: Computer Configuration\Administrative Templates\Printers

For most organizations, the default (Not Configured) state is satisfactory for Printers policies. The following 13 policies apply primarily to print servers, but some can be used with workstations that share printers:

✦ **Allow printers to be published** is the default when this policy isn't configured. Disabling this policy prevents printers managed by this computer from appearing in AD and disables the effect of most of the following policies. (HKLM\Software\Policies\Microsoft\Windows NT\Printers\PublishPrinters)

✦ **Automatically publish new printers in Active Directory** is the default when adding printers with the Add Printer Wizard. Disabling this policy prevents automatic publishing. (HKLM\Software\Policies\Microsoft\Windows NT\Printers\Wizard\Auto Publishing)

✦ **Allow pruning of published printers** is the default. DCs prune (delete) AD entries for printers managed by computers that can't be contacted on the network. When the computer reconnects, the DC republishes the printer in AD. (HKLM\Software\Policies\Microsoft\Windows NT\Printers\Immortal)

✦ **Printer browsing** is enabled by default, and shared printers appear in the Browse for Printer dialog of the local Add Printer Wizard. Disabling this policy hides the printer from the Wizard. (HKLM\Software\Policies\Microsoft\Windows NT\Printers\ServerThread)

◆ **Prune printers that are not automatically republished** has the following three options: Never (the default; don't prune under any circumstance), Only If Print Server Is Found (and the printer doesn't respond), and Whenever Printer Is Not Found. (HKLM\ Software\Policies\Microsoft\Windows NT\Printers\PruneDownlevel)

◆ **Directory pruning interval** lets you change the default interval (8 hours) between DC tests for printer connectivity. This policy applies only to DCs. (HKLM\Software\ Policies\Microsoft\Windows NT\Printers\PruningInterval)

◆ **Directory pruning retry** lets you alter the number of printer contact retries before the AD entry is pruned. The default is two retries. This policy applies only to DCs. (HKLM\Software\Policies\Microsoft\Windows NT\Printers\PruningRetries)

◆ **Directory pruning priority** lets you specify the DC's thread priority of printer pruning operations, ranging from Lowest to Highest. The default is Normal. This policy applies only to DCs. (HKLM\Software\Policies\Microsoft\Windows NT\ Printers\PruningPriority)

◆ **Check published state** lets you alter the interval at which computers verify that their printers are published in AD. The default is on startup; you can change the interval from 30 minutes to Never. (HKLM\Software\Policies\Microsoft\Windows NT\Printers\VerifyPublishedState)

◆ **Web-based printing** determines whether a server supports Internet printing, which lets users print over the Internet or an intranet. Allowing Internet printing is the default. This policy applies only to print servers. (HKLM\Software\Policies\Microsoft\ Windows NT\Printers\DisableWebPrinting)

◆ **Custom support URL in the Printers folder's left pane** lets you add a customized Web page link to the Printers folder of clients. The defaults are links to a Microsoft Web page and, in most cases, a link to the printer vendor's site. (HKLM\Software\ Policies\Microsoft\Windows NT\Printers\SupportLink, SupportLinkName)

◆ **Computer location** specifies the default location criteria used when searching for printers with the Location Tracking feature. Location Tracking lets users browse for printers by the location specification scheme you institute. You must enable the next policy for this policy to have effect. (HKLM\Software\Policies\Microsoft\Windows NT\ Printers\PhysicalLocation)

◆ **Pre-populate printer search location text** overrides the default IP address and subnet mask that estimates printer proximity to the user and enables the preceding policy to take effect. (HKLM\Software\Policies\Microsoft\Windows NT\Printers\ PhysicalLocationSupport)

User Configuration Policies

User Configuration policies apply to the user account and load when the user logs on to the computer. By default, User Configuration policy settings override Computer Configuration policies at each level of the policy application sequence (local, site, domain, OU, called LSDOU), unless the policy description states otherwise. Set the User Group Policy Loopback Processing Mode policy of the Computer Configuration\Administrative Templates\System\ Group Policy node to cause Computer Configuration policies to prevail.

Like the Computer Configuration node, the User Configuration node has three subnodes: Software Settings, Windows Settings, and Administrative Templates. With the exception of Software Settings, these subnodes differ significantly in content from the corresponding Computer Configuration subnodes. Figure A-10 illustrates the organization of the primary User Configuration subnodes. All User Configuration policies are set to Not Configured (or its equivalent) by Default Domain Policy or Default Domain Controllers Policy.

Software Settings

Location: User Configuration\Software Settings

Like its Computer Configuration counterpart, Software Settings has only a single subnode: Software Installation. For instructions on how to add Windows Installer and downlevel .zap packages for users, see the "Software Settings" section of Computer Configuration at the beginning of this chapter. Unlike with the computer-based version, you can assign *or* publish application packages for users in specific sites, domains, or OUs.

The Registry stores pointers to assigned packages as data for the policies value of the \HKEY_CURRENT_USER\Software\Microsoft\Windows\CurrentVersion\Group Policy\AppMgmt key.

Windows Settings

Location: User Configuration\Windows Settings

The Windows Settings node has five subnodes: Internet Explorer Maintenance, Scripts (Logon/Logoff), Security Settings, Remote Installation Services, and Folder Redirection. The Scripts (Logon/Logoff) node is identical to that of Computer Configuration\Windows Settings.

Internet Explorer Maintenance

Location: User Configuration\Windows Settings\Internet Explorer Maintenance

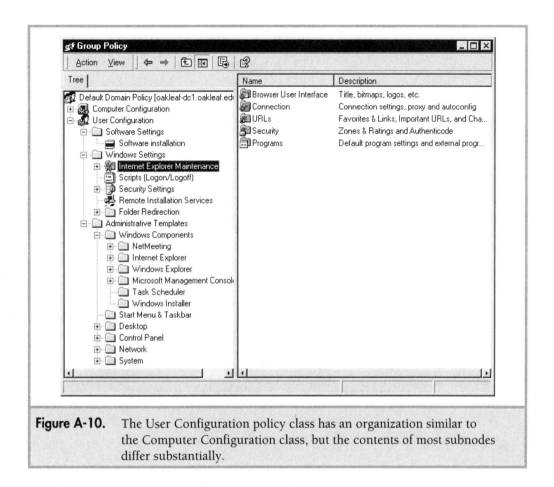

Figure A-10. The User Configuration policy class has an organization similar to the Computer Configuration class, but the contents of most subnodes differ substantially.

The Internet Explorer Maintenance node lets you customize the appearance and behavior of IE 5.0+ for users. This node has five subnodes: Browser User Interface, Connection, URLs, Security, and Programs. The UI for customizing user-specific IE properties differs dramatically from that for setting all other policies. Many additional policies for locking down IE are located under the User Configuration\Administrative Templates\Windows Components\Internet Explorer node. Microsoft devotes more policies to IE than to any other Windows 2000 "component."

Figure A-11 illustrates the typical design of dialogs for customizing IE features. Unlike other policy dialogs, IE dialogs have a Help button that opens the corresponding subtopic of the Internet Explorer Maintenance, Administering Microsoft Internet Explorer topic of the Group Policy online help file.

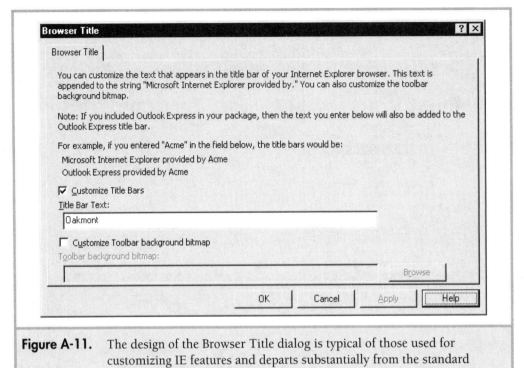

Figure A-11. The design of the Browser Title dialog is typical of those used for customizing IE features and departs substantially from the standard *PolicyName* Properties dialog for other policy categories.

Right-clicking the Internet Explorer Maintenance node offers the following three context menu choices:

✦ **Export Browser Settings** opens a dialog that lets you export your IE settings to .ins and .cab files for use with computers running Windows NT and 9x. You have the option to digitally sign the .cab file.

✦ **Preference Mode** adds a sixth Advanced subnode, which lets you specify Corporate Settings (from the \Winnt\Inf\Inetcorp.adm template) and Internet Settings (from \Winnt\Inf\Inetset.adm). Preference mode disables some browser policy settings.

✦ **Reset Browser Settings** erases any changes you've made to the IE settings and returns the settings for all IE policies to their default values.

TIP: If you're interested in using Preference mode's Advanced features, be sure to make your decision before changing standard browser policy settings. You must choose Reset Browser Settings before you can apply Preference mode.

Browser User Interface

Location: User Configuration\Windows Settings\Internet Explorer Maintenance\Browser User Interface

The Browser User Interface node offers the following four policies:

✦ **Browser Title** lets you append "provided by *TitleText*" to the "Microsoft Internet Explorer" title bar caption, as shown in Figure A-11. You also can substitute your own bitmap for IE's standard background bitmap behind the toolbar buttons. This policy isn't available in Preference mode.

✦ **Animated Bitmaps** lets you replace IE's upper-right corner bitmap with an animated bitmap you (laboriously) create. You must supply both small (22-by-22-pixel) and large (38-by-38-pixel) versions with four lead-in cells and any number of additional cells that loop while the user browses. This policy isn't available in Preference mode.

✦ **Custom Logo** lets you replace IE's "e" logo with your own small and large static bitmaps. This policy isn't available in Preference mode.

✦ **Browser Toolbar Buttons** gives you the dubious opportunity to add to or replace IE's toolbar buttons and text. You must provide 20-by-20-pixel button bitmaps for both the active and inactive states and write a script or executable file to perform the buttons' actions.

Connection

Location: User Configuration\Windows Settings\Internet Explorer Maintenance\Connection

The ability to lock down user connection-related IE settings for specific users can save a substantial amount of help desk assistance time. Consider implementing these policies, especially if you have proxy servers in use.

The Connection node offers the following four policies:

✦ **Connection Settings** lets you import the current IE connection settings for the machine on which you're authoring Group Policies. To establish the settings to be imported, select the Import the Current Connection Settings option and click Modify Settings to open Control Panel's Internet Options tool's Connection page. Specify the dial-up or LAN settings, or both, that you want to assign users and click OK.

✦ **Automatic Configuration** opens a dialog that lets you specify Automatic Configuration by specifying the URL of an auto-config .ins file (see the "Export Browser Settings" bulleted point on the previous page); an auto-proxy .js, .jvs, or .pac file; or both. You also can set the interval (in minutes) at which auto-config occurs. Settings you make for this policy override the Connection Settings policy.

✦ **Proxy Settings** opens a dialog in which you can type the IP address and port number of proxy servers that provide HTTP, HTTPS, FTP, Gopher, and Sockets services. Settings you make for this policy override those for the Connection Settings policy.

✦ **User Agent String** appends a custom entry to the end of the default IE browser identification string, Mozilla/4.0 (compatible; MSIE 5.0; Windows NT). You can use a customized identification string to verify that intranet users haven't substituted another copy of IE 5.0 for that managed by group policies. This policy isn't available in Preference mode.

URLs

Location: User Configuration\Windows Settings\Internet Explorer Maintenance\URLs

The URLs node lets you customize default URLs for IE's Favorites, Links, Home, Search, Support, and (believe it or not) Channels. The URLs node offers the following three policies, which add a (Preference mode) suffix if you have that feature turned on:

✦ **Favorites and Links** lets you add Favorites and Links entries to those included by Microsoft with IE and (better yet) lets you delete all favorite links before adding your own. You can add URLs and folders that contain URLs to the Favorites and Links dialog's list, or you can import them from a folder you specify.

✦ **Important URLs** opens a dialog in which you can set the home page, search bar, and Online Support URLs to those of your own choosing, rather than Microsoft's.

✦ **Channels** resurrects a widely deplored IE 4.0 feature, but does give you the ability to delete existing channels, if present. Don't mark the Turn on Desktop Channel Bar by Default check box unless you have an overwhelming urge (or a direct command) to implement Channels.

Security

Location: User Configuration\Windows Settings\Internet Explorer Maintenance\Security

The Security node lets you import security-related settings by importing them from the computer on which you author policies. The two Security policies, which add a (Preference mode) suffix if you have that feature turned on, are

✦ **Security Zones and Content Ratings** lets you import IE security settings from the Security and Content Advisor pages, respectively, of the Internet Options dialog.

✦ **Authenticode Settings** lets you remove the names of software publishers from your existing Trusted Publishers list. You can't add new items to the list.

Programs

Location: User Configuration\Windows Settings\Internet Explorer Maintenance\Programs
The Programs node contains the following policy:

✦ **Programs** (Preference mode) lets you specify on the Programs page of the Internet Options dialog the default programs for HTML editing (Notepad), e-mail (Outlook Express), newsgroups (Outlook Express), Internet calls (NetMeeting), Calendar (no default), and Contact List (Address Book).

Advanced

Location: User Configuration\Windows Settings\Internet Explorer Maintenance\Advanced
The Advanced node appears only if you have turned on Preference mode. Advanced has two nodes, Corporate Settings and Internet Settings, which rely on the two special .adm files mentioned in the "Preference Mode" bulleted item earlier in this "Internet Explorer Maintenance" section. The Advanced settings are for control freaks who insist on tuning virtually *every* IE option for users.

Corporate Settings   Opens a dialog with a tree view list containing the following four nodes:

✦ **Temporary Internet Files (User)** lets you specify whether users check for newer versions of stored pages Automatically (the default), Every Visit to the Page, Every Time You Start Internet Explorer, or Never. You also can specify the maximum amount of disk space devoted to storage of these files; the default is 20 MB per user (see Figure A-12).

✦ **Temporary Internet Files (Machine)** lets you set the maximum amount of disk space devoted by the computer to storage of these files for all users; the default is 20 MB.

✦ **Code Download** provides for additional URLs from which to download code specified in the CODEBASE tag of a page. The default string is CODEBASE;<http:// activex.microsoft.com/objects/ocget.dll>, which first attempts the URL specified in the tag and then checks the Microsoft ActiveX site. Use this policy to redirect users to download components from an intranet site. You can replace or add to the Microsoft link; separate URLs with semicolons.

✦ **Related Sites and Errors** lets you select from one of the following options: Show the Menu Item, but Do Not Turn on the Toolbar Button (default), Show the Menu Item, and Turn on the Toolbar Button, and Disable the Menu Item and Browser Toolbar Button.

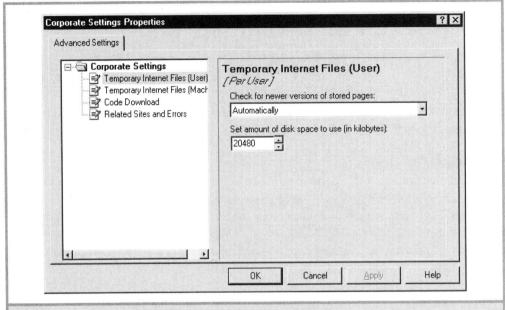

Figure A-12. The two Advanced subnodes, Corporate Settings and Internet Settings, open dialogs that have a tree view of additional customization settings for IE.

Internet Settings Opens a dialog with a tree view list containing the following five nodes:

✦ **AutoComplete** has the following six check boxes: Use Inline Autocomplete for Web Addresses, Use Inline Autocomplete in Windows Explorer (default), Use Autocomplete for Web Addresses (default), Use Autocomplete for Forms, Use Autocomplete for User Names and Passwords on Forms (default), and Prompt to Save Passwords (default).

✦ **Display Settings** lets you specify the default Text Size (Medium), Background Color (gray), Text Color (black), Link Color (blue), Visited Link Color (purple), and Hover Color (red) and whether to use Windows colors. You specify the colors with comma-separated RGB values.

✦ **Advanced Settings** has a scrollable list that enables the setting of 31 properties in the following categories: Connection (Enable Autodialing), Browsing , Multimedia, Security, Microsoft VM, Printing, Searching, and HTTP 1.1 Settings. The ability to disable Autodialing is the most useful of these options.

✦ **URL Encoding** lets you specify that the user always sends URLs in UTF-8 format (the default).

◆ **Component Updates** has text boxes in which you can alter the default URLs for IE updates (the Microsoft IE update site), the update check interval (30 days), and the source of the current IE High (128-bit) Encryption Pack (Microsoft). Set these policies if you want users to obtain their updates from an intranet.

Scripts (Logon and Logoff)

Location: User Configuration\Windows Settings\Scripts

Scripts (Logon and Logoff) has the following two policies:

◆ **Logon** lets you specify a startup script that runs when the user logs on to the network.

◆ **Logoff** runs the specified script when the user logs off.

Adding these scripts follows the same procedure as for Computer Configuration startup and shutdown scripts, except that logon and logoff scripts are stored in the *DomainName*\Sysvol*DomainName*\Policies*GUID*\User\Scripts\Logon and \Logoff shares, respectively, for replication between DCs.

Security Settings

Location: User Configuration\Windows Settings\Security Settings\Public Key Policies

The Security Settings node has a subnode, Public Key Policies, that contains the following policy:

◆ **Enterprise Trust** contains a Certificate Trust List (CTL) of Root Certificate Authorities (CAs). To add an entry, right-click the node and choose New | Certificate Trust List to start the Certificate Trust List Wizard.

As with the Enterprise Trust policy for computers, you must be running Certificate Services in your domain and have previously specified or created the appropriate certificates to take advantage of this policy.

Remote Installation Services

Location: User Configuration\Windows Settings\Remote Installation Services

The Remote Installation Services node also has a single policy:

◆ **Choice Options** for Remote Installation Services (RIS and RIPrep) are set by a dialog that opens when you double-click the Choice Options icon in the right pane. You can specify Allow, Don't Care, or Deny Permissions for Automatic Setup, Custom Setup, Restart Setup (in case of a failed installation) and support tools, such as the Administrative Tools (Adminpak.msi).

Folder Redirection

Location: User Configuration\Windows Settings\Folder Redirection

The Folder Redirection node has four subnodes: Application Data, Desktop, My Documents (which has a My Pictures subnode), and Start Menu. Folder Redirection, which stores user data and desktop configuration settings on a server, is one of the IntelliMirror features discussed in Chapter 4. The primary advantage of setting Folder Redirection policies is that you don't need to manually specify settings for each user.

To specify policies for these features, right-click the node and choose Properties to open the Target page of the *NodeName* Properties dialog. The Setting list offers the following three options:

✦ **No administrative policy specified** (the default) is the equivalent of Not Configured for the policy.

✦ **Basic - Redirect everyone's folder to the same location** lets you specify a single location for storing all users' redirected folders. Type in the Target Folder Location text box the path to the share in *ServerName**ShareName*\%username% format.

✦ **Advanced - Specify locations for various user groups** lets you specify individual servers and shares for storing redirected folders of specific user groups (see Figure A-13).

TIP: Don't let users with digital cameras redirect their My Pictures folders to a server. You're likely to end up with several gigabytes of photos of children, vacation trips, or worse. If you apply quotas to drives on which users store My Pictures, it's likely that quotas will become filled by photos, which ultimately prevents the user from updating the server-stored My Documents and Application Data folders. Fortunately, Microsoft didn't add redirectable My Music and My Videos folders to Windows 2000.

The Settings page of the *FolderName* dialog has the following options:

✦ **Grant the user exclusive rights to *FolderName*** (default) prevents anyone but the user and the local system from gaining access to the user's folder. Be sure to clear this check box if you want members of the Administrators group to have access to the folder.

✦ **Move the contents of *FolderName* to the new location** (default) moves the user's existing local *FolderName* to the designated server and share. If you don't mark this check box, you defeat the purpose of redirecting the folder.

✦ **Leave the folder in the new location when policy is removed** (default) lets the user continue to use Folder Redirection when the policy is revoked.

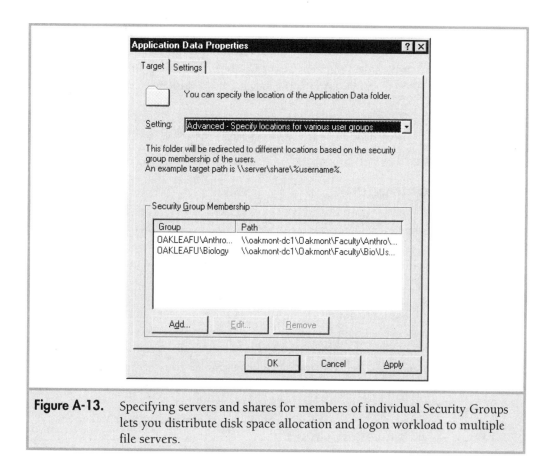

Figure A-13. Specifying servers and shares for members of individual Security Groups lets you distribute disk space allocation and logon workload to multiple file servers.

✦ **Redirect the folder back to the local user profile location when policy is removed** disables Folder Redirection when the policy is revoked.

Administrative Templates

Location: User Configuration\Administrative Templates

User-based Administrative Templates have a structure similar to those of Computer Configuration. Both classes of templates have Windows Components, System, and Network subnodes. The User Configuration Administrative templates add Start Menu & Taskbar and Desktop nodes for desktop configuration and lockdown.

Registry key names with value names appended are included with policy descriptions; key and value names were abstracted from the Users class of the appropriate template (.adm) file. All User Configuration Registry entries are in subkeys of the HKEY_CURRENT_USER (HKCU) hive. A typical entry is HKCU\Software\Microsoft\Windows\CurrentVersion\ Policies\Uninstall\NoAddRemovePrograms for the Disable Add/Remove Programs policy of User Configuration\Administrative Templates\Control Panel\Add/Remove Programs.

NOTE: Except as noted in particular policy descriptions, the effect of applying the policy is described.

Windows Components

Location: User Configuration\Administrative Templates\Windows Components

The Windows Components node has six subnodes: NetMeeting, Internet Explorer, Windows Explorer, Microsoft Management Console, Task Scheduler, and Windows Installer. The majority of the policies disable a particular feature or an element of the feature.

NetMeeting

Location: User Configuration\Administrative Templates\Windows Components\NetMeeting

Availability of low-cost, computer-mounted video cameras and video capture cards has increased corporate interest in using NetMeeting as a substitute for face-to-face conferences. If you're using or intend to use NetMeeting on your intranet or over the Internet, consider establishing at least some of these policies for Windows 2000 clients. The template for NetMeeting policies is Conf.adm.

The NetMeeting node has three subnodes (Application Sharing, Audio & Video, and Options Page) and the following 14 policies:

+ **Enable Automatic Configuration** configures NetMeeting to download settings from the URL listed in the Configuration URL text box during startup. (HKCU\Software\ Policies\Microsoft\Conferencing\Use AutoConfig and \ConfigFile)

+ **Disable Directory Services** prevents users from logging on to an Internet Locator Service (ILS) directory server when NetMeeting starts, so users can't view or place calls from a NetMeeting directory. (HKCU\Software\Policies\Microsoft\Conferencing\ NoDirectoryServices)

+ **Prevent adding Directory servers** prohibits users from adding ILS servers to the default list. (HKCU\Software\Policies\Microsoft\Conferencing\ NoAddingDirectoryServers)

+ **Prevent viewing Web directory** prohibits users from viewing directories as Web pages. (HKCU\Software\Policies\Microsoft\Conferencing\NoWebDirectory)

✦ **Set the intranet support Web page** lets you specify the URL displayed when users choose Help | Online Support. (HKCU\Software\Policies\Microsoft\Conferencing\ IntranetSupportURL)

✦ **Set Call Security options** lets you set security levels for outgoing and incoming NetMeeting calls. The choices are Disable or Required. (HKCU\Software\Policies\ Microsoft\Conferencing\CallSecurity)

✦ **Prevent changing Call placement method** prohibits users from changing the method of placing calls (directly or via a gatekeeper service). (HKCU\Software\Policies\ Microsoft\Conferencing\NoChangingCallMode)

✦ **Prevent automatic acceptance of Calls** prohibits users from turning on automatic acceptance of incoming calls, so other users can't connect when the user isn't present. (HKCU\Software\Policies\Microsoft\Conferencing\NoAutoAcceptCalls)

✦ **Prevent sending files** prohibits users from sending files to others in a conference. (HKCU\Software\Policies\Microsoft\Conferencing\NoSendingFiles)

✦ **Prevent receiving files** prohibits users from receiving files from other conference members. (HKCU\Software\Policies\Microsoft\Conferencing\NoReceivingFiles)

✦ **Limit the size of sent files** lets you set the maximum file size (in bytes) sent by conference members. (HKCU\Software\Policies\Microsoft\Conferencing\ MaxFileSendSize)

✦ **Disable Chat** prevents users from running NetMeeting's Chat feature. (HKCU\Software\Policies\Microsoft\Conferencing\NoChat)

✦ **Disable NetMeeting 2.x Whiteboard** eliminates the NetMeeting 2.x whiteboard compatibility feature. (HKCU\Software\Policies\Microsoft\Conferencing\ NoOldWhiteBoard)

✦ **Disable NetMeeting Whiteboard** disables NetMeeting's T.126 whiteboard feature. Enabling this and the preceding policy prevents use of the whiteboard feature entirely. (HKCU\Software\Policies\Microsoft\Conferencing\NoNewWhiteBoard)

Application Sharing   Contains the following seven policies:

✦ **Disable Application Sharing** prevents users from using this feature. (HKCU\Software\Policies\Microsoft\Conferencing\NoAppSharing)

✦ **Prevent Sharing** prohibits the user from sharing his or her applications or desktop, but doesn't prevent the user from viewing others' applications and desktops. (HKCU\Software\Policies\Microsoft\Conferencing\NoSharing)

✦ **Prevent Desktop Sharing** prohibits the user from sharing his or her desktop, but does not prevent application sharing. (HKCU\Software\Policies\Microsoft\Conferencing\ NoSharingDesktop)

✦ **Prevent Sharing Command Prompts** augments Disable Application Sharing by preventing others from using the command prompt to launch apps. (HKCU\Software\Policies\Microsoft\Conferencing\NoSharingDosWindows)

✦ **Prevent Sharing Explorer Windows** further augments Disable Application Sharing by preventing others from launching apps from the user's Explorer. (HKCU\Software\Policies\Microsoft\Conferencing\NoSharingExplorer)

✦ **Prevent Control** causes the user's shared applications to be read-only for other conference members. (HKCU\Software\Policies\Microsoft\Conferencing\NoAllowControl)

✦ **Prevent Application Sharing in True Color** reduces the bandwidth requirement for conferencing. (HKCU\Software\Policies\Microsoft\Conferencing\ NoTrueColorSharing)

Audio & Video   Offers the following six policies:

✦ **Limit the bandwidth of Audio and Video** lets you specify the maximum data rate of the conference in bps (not kbps as indicated by the dialog). The default and maximum are 621,700, and the minimum is 85,000 bps. (HKCU\Software\Policies\ Microsoft\Conferencing\MaximumBandwidth)

✦ **Disable Audio** prevents sending or receiving of sound, which severely limits the utility of NetMeeting conferences. (HKCU\Software\Policies\Microsoft\ Conferencing\No Audio)

✦ **Disable full duplex Audio** prevents hearing of sound while the user is transmitting audio. Enable this policy only if you need to support early sound cards that have problems with full-duplex audio. (HKCU\Software\Policies\Microsoft\Conferencing\ NoFullDuplex)

✦ **Prevent changing DirectSound Audio** disables the user's DirectSound setting. Don't apply this policy unless you must deal with old-timey audio adapters that don't have DirectSound drivers. (HKCU\Software\Policies\Microsoft\Conferencing\ NoChangeDirectSound)

✦ **Prevent sending Video** precludes users from transmitting talking heads or office panoramas. Users with video cameras on their desktop or laptop won't like this policy. (HKCU\Software\Policies\Microsoft\Conferencing\NoSendingVideo)

✦ **Prevent receiving Video** does exactly that, and no one will like this policy. (HKCU\Software\Policies\Microsoft\Conferencing\NoReceivingVideo)

Options Page   Contains the following five self-explanatory policies that hide or disable NetMeeting options users access from NetMeeting's Tool | Options menu choice:

✦ **Hide the General page.** (HKCU\Software\Policies\Microsoft\Conferencing\NoGeneralPage)

✦ **Disable the Advanced Calling button.** (HKCU\Software\Policies\Microsoft\Conferencing\NoAdvancedCalling)

✦ **Hide the Security page.** (HKCU\Software\Policies\Microsoft\Conferencing\NoSecurityPage)

✦ **Hide the Audio page.** (HKCU\Software\Policies\Microsoft\Conferencing\NoAudioPage)

✦ **Hide the Video page.** (HKCU\Software\Policies\Microsoft\Conferencing\NoVideoPage)

Internet Explorer

Location: User Configuration\Administrative Templates\Windows Components\Internet Explorer

Policies under the Internet Explorer node and its subnodes let you disable virtually every user-accessible option of IE. Group Policies extend the options of the IEAK to Soviet-style lockdown of IE running on Windows 2000 clients. Unlike with Internet Explorer Maintenance policies, you can't export these settings to an .ins or .cab file for use with downlevel clients. The template for Internet Explorer policies is Inetres.adm.

This node has six subnodes (Internet Control Panel, Offline Pages, Browser (M)enus, Toolbars, Persistence Behavior, and Administrator Approved Controls) and the following 30 policies:

✦ **Search: Disable Search Customization** disables the Customize button of the Search Assistant so users can't change search options. (HKCU\Software\Policies\Microsoft\ Internet Explorer\Infodelivery\Restrictions\ NoSearchCustomization)

✦ **Search: Disable Find Files via F3 within the browser** prevents use of F3 to search with Internet Explorer or Windows Explorer, which prevents users from searching the Internet or their fixed disks for specific files. (HKCU\Software\Policies\ Microsoft\Internet Explorer\Restrictions\NoFindFiles)

✦ **Disable external branding of Internet Explorer** ensures that third parties (such as ISPs) can't customize IE's and Outlook Express's logos and title bars. (HKCU\ Software\Policies\Microsoft\Internet Explorer\Restrictions\NoExternalBranding)

✦ **Disable importing and exporting of favorites** prevents users from exporting or importing favorite links with the Import/Export Wizard. (HKCU\Software\Policies\Microsoft\Internet Explorer\DisableImportExportFavorites)

✦ **Disable changing Advanced page settings** prevents users from altering settings on the Advanced page of the Internet Options dialog. (HKCU\Software\Policies\ Microsoft\Internet Explorer\Control Panel\Advanced)

✦ **Disable changing home page settings** prevents users from altering the Home page URL. (HKCU\Software\Policies\Microsoft\Internet Explorer\Control Panel\ HomePage)

✦ **Use Automatic Detection for dial-up connections** forces Automatic Detection from DHCP settings to configure dial-up settings for users. (HKCU\Software\Policies\ Microsoft\Windows\CurrentVersion\Internet Settings\DialupAutoDetect)

✦ **Disable caching of Auto-Proxy scripts** prevents storing these scripts locally, and causes IE to download the scripts from the server when launched. (HKCU\Software\Policies\Microsoft\Windows\CurrentVersion\Internet Settings\EnableAutoProxyResultCache)

✦ **Display error message on proxy script download failure** displays an error message if the client can't run specified proxy scripts. (HKCU\Software\Policies\Microsoft\ Windows\CurrentVersion\Internet Settings\DisplayScriptDownloadFailureUI)

 TIP: The following seven settings, which apply to properties set on the General page of the Internet Options dialog, are self-descriptive. An alternative to applying all of these policies is to apply the Disable the General page policy in the Internet Control Panel subnode so user's can't access the settings.

✦ **Disable changing Temporary Internet files settings** (HKCU\Software\Policies\Microsoft\Windows\CurrentVersion\Internet Settings\Cache)

◆ **Disable changing history settings**
(HKCU\Software\Policies\Microsoft\Windows\CurrentVersion\Internet Settings\History)

◆ **Disable changing color settings**
(HKCU\Software\Policies\Microsoft\Windows\CurrentVersion\Internet Settings\Colors)

◆ **Disable changing link color settings**
(HKCU\Software\Policies\Microsoft\Windows\CurrentVersion\Internet Settings\Links)

◆ **Disable changing font settings**
(HKCU\Software\Policies\Microsoft\Windows\CurrentVersion\Internet Settings\Fonts)

◆ **Disable changing language settings**
(HKCU\Software\Policies\Microsoft\Windows\CurrentVersion\Internet Settings\Languages)

◆ **Disable changing accessibility settings**
(HKCU\Software\Policies\Microsoft\Windows\CurrentVersion\Internet Settings\Accessibility)

TIP: The following four settings apply to properties set on the Connections page of the Internet Options dialog. Apply the Disable the Connections page policy if you don't want users to have access to any settings.

◆ **Disable Internet Connection wizard**
(HKCU\Software\Policies\Microsoft\Windows\CurrentVersion\Internet Settings\Conwiz Admin Lock)

◆ **Disable changing connection settings**
(HKCU\Software\Policies\Microsoft\Windows\CurrentVersion\Internet Settings\Connection Settings)

◆ **Disable changing proxy settings**
(HKCU\Software\Policies\Microsoft\Windows\CurrentVersion\Internet Settings\Proxy)

◆ **Disable changing Automatic Configuration settings**
(HKCU\Software\Policies\Microsoft\Windows\CurrentVersion\Internet Settings\Autoconfig)

TIP: The following five settings apply to the Content page of the Internet Options dialog. Apply the Disable the Content Page policy if you don't want users to have access to any settings.

✦ **Disable changing ratings settings**
(HKCU\Software\Policies\Microsoft\Windows\CurrentVersion\Internet Settings\Ratings)

✦ **Disable changing certificate settings**
(HKCU\Software\Policies\Microsoft\Windows\CurrentVersion\Internet Settings\Certificates)

✦ **Disable changing Profile Assistant settings**
(HKCU\Software\Policies\Microsoft\Windows\CurrentVersion\Internet Settings\Profiles)

✦ **Disable AutoComplete for forms**
(HKCU\Software\Policies\Microsoft\Windows\CurrentVersion\Internet Settings\FormSuggest)

✦ **Do not allow AutoComplete to save passwords**
(HKCU\Software\Policies\Microsoft\Windows\CurrentVersion\Internet Settings\FormSuggest Passwords)

TIP: The following four settings apply to the Programs page of the Internet Options dialog. Apply the Disable the Programs Page policy if you don't want users to have access to any settings.

✦ **Disable changing Messaging settings**
(HKCU\Software\Policies\Microsoft\Windows\CurrentVersion\Internet Settings\Messaging)

✦ **Disable changing Calendar and Contact settings**
(HKCU\Software\Policies\Microsoft\Windows\CurrentVersion\Internet Settings\CalendarContact)

✦ **Disable the Reset Web Settings feature**
(HKCU\Software\Policies\Microsoft\Windows\CurrentVersion\Internet Settings\ResetWebSettings)

✦ **Disable changing default browser check**
(HKCU\Software\Policies\Microsoft\Windows\CurrentVersion\Internet Settings\Check_If_Default)

◆ **Identity Manager: Prevent users from using Identities** prevents the user from adding, deleting, or changing identities with Outlook Express's Identity Manager. (HKCU\Software\Policies\Microsoft\Windows\CurrentVersion\Identities\Locked Down)

Internet Control Panel   Has the following six policies that remove (not just disable) the page from the Internet Options dialog:

◆ **Disable the General page** (HKCU\Software\Policies\Microsoft\Internet Explorer\Control Panel\GeneralTab)

◆ **Disable the Security page** (HKCU\Software\Policies\Microsoft\Internet Explorer\Control Panel\SecurityTab)

◆ **Disable the Content page** (HKCU\Software\Policies\Microsoft\Internet Explorer\Control Panel\ContentTab)

◆ **Disable the Connections page** (HKCU\Software\Policies\Microsoft\Internet Explorer\Control Panel\ConnectionsTab)

◆ **Disable the Programs page** (HKCU\Software\Policies\Microsoft\Internet Explorer\Control Panel\ProgramsTab)

◆ **Disable the Advanced page** (HKCU\Software\Policies\Microsoft\Internet Explorer\Control Panel\AdvancedTab)

Offline Pages   Has the following 11 policies that affect channels, offline pages, and subscriptions:

◆ **Disable adding channels** prevents users from adding channels to IE or channel-based content to their desktop. If you want to prevent user access to the infamous Channel Bar, enable the Disable Channel User Interface Completely policy. (HKCU\Software\ Policies\Microsoft\Internet Explorer\Infodelivery\Restrictions\NoAddingChannels)

◆ **Disable removing channels** prevents users from disabling channel synchronization in Internet Explorer. Enable this policy if, for some (presumably good) reason, you've set up channels for your users. (HKCU\Software\Policies\Microsoft\Internet Explorer\Infodelivery\Restrictions\NoRemovingChannels)

◆ **Disable adding schedules for offline pages** prevents users from specifying Web pages for offline viewing and adding new schedules for downloading offline content. (HKCU\Software\Policies\Microsoft\Internet Explorer\Infodelivery\Restrictions\ NoAddingSubscriptions)

✦ **Disable editing schedules for offline pages** prevents users from changing an existing schedule for offline viewing or displaying the schedule properties of offline pages. (HKCU\Software\Policies\Microsoft\Internet Explorer\Infodelivery\Restrictions\ NoEditingSubscriptions)

✦ **Disable removing schedules for offline pages** prevents users from clearing preconfigured settings for offline pages; they receive pages whether or not they want them. (HKCU\Software\Policies\Microsoft\Internet Explorer\Infodelivery\Restrictions\ NoRemovingSubscriptions)

✦ **Disable offline page hit logging** prevents channel providers from recording information about the use of offline pages by users. (HKCU\Software\Policies\ Microsoft\Internet Explorer\Infodelivery\Restrictions\NoChannelLogging)

✦ **Disable all scheduled offline pages** eliminates all scheduled offline page downloads (HKCU\Software\Policies\Microsoft\Internet Explorer\Infodelivery\ Restrictions\ NoScheduledUpdates)

✦ **Disable channel user interface completely** prevents users from displaying the Channel Bar and is the favorite IE policy of most admins. (HKCU\Software\Policies\ Microsoft\Internet Explorer\Infodelivery\Restrictions\NoChannelUI)

✦ **Disable downloading of site subscription content** is another admin favorite. (HKCU\Software\Policies\Microsoft\Internet Explorer\Infodelivery\Restrictions\ NoSubscriptionContent)

✦ **Disable editing and creating of schedule groups** disables the Add, Edit, and Remove buttons from the Schedule page. (HKCU\Software\Policies\Microsoft\Internet Explorer\Infodelivery\Restrictions\NoEditingScheduleGroups)

✦ **Subscription Limits** has four spin boxes for setting the maximum size and number of downloaded subscription content, the number of minutes between scheduled updates, the period during which scheduled updates are prevented (such as working hours), and the maximum crawl depth (0 to 3) when downloading linked pages. (HKCU\Software\Policies\Microsoft\Internet Explorer\Infodelivery\Restrictions\ MaxSubscriptionSize, \MaxSubscriptionCount, \MinUpdateInterval, \UpdateExcludeBegin, \UpdateExcludeEnd, and \MaxWebcrawlLevels)

Browser Menus   Has the following 16 self-explanatory policies that disable or hide menu choices and options:

✦ **File menu: Disable Save As menu option**
(HKCU\Software\Policies\Microsoft\Internet Explorer\Restrictions\NoBrowserSaveAs)

- **File menu: Disable New menu option**
  (HKCU\Software\Policies\Microsoft\Internet Explorer\Restrictions\NoFileNew)

- **File menu: Disable Open menu option**
  (HKCU\Software\Policies\Microsoft\Internet Explorer\Restrictions\NoFileOpen)

- **File menu: Disable Save As Web Page Complete**
  (HKCU\Software\Policies\Microsoft\Internet Explorer\InfoDelivery\Restrictions\
  NoBrowserSaveWebComplete)

- **File menu: Disable closing the browser and Explorer windows**
  (HKCU\Software\Policies\Microsoft\Internet Explorer\InfoDelivery\Restrictions\
  NoBrowserClose)

- **View menu: Disable Source menu option**
  (HKCU\Software\Policies\Microsoft\Internet Explorer\InfoDelivery\Restrictions\
  NoViewSource)

- **View menu: Disable Full Screen menu option**
  (HKCU\Software\Policies\Microsoft\Internet Explorer\InfoDelivery\Restrictions\
  NoTheaterMode)

- **Hide Favorites menu**
  (HKCU\Software\Policies\Microsoft\Internet Explorer\Restrictions\NoFavorites)

- **Tools menu: Disable Internet Options menu option**
  (HKCU\Software\Policies\Microsoft\Internet Explorer\InfoDelivery\Restrictions\
  NoBrowserOptions)

- **Help menu: Remove 'Tip of the Day' menu option**
  (HKCU\Software\Policies\Microsoft\Internet Explorer \Restrictions\
  NoHelpItemTipOfTheDay)

- **Help menu: Remove 'For Netscape Users' menu option**
  (HKCU\Software\Policies\Microsoft\Internet Explorer\ Restrictions\
  NoHelpItemNetscapeHelp)

- **Help menu: Remove 'Tour' menu option**
  (HKCU\Software\Policies\Microsoft\Internet Explorer\ Restrictions\
  NoHelpItemTutorial)

- **Help menu: Remove 'Send Feedback' menu option**
  (HKCU\Software\Policies\Microsoft\Internet Explorer\ Restrictions\
  NoHelpItemSendFeedback)

✦ **Disable Context menu** (HKCU\Software\Policies\Microsoft\Internet Explorer\Restrictions\NoBrowserContextMenu)

✦ **Disable Open in New Window menu option** (HKCU\Software\Policies\Microsoft\Internet Explorer\Restrictions\ NoOpenInNewWnd)

✦ **Disable Save this program to disk option** (HKCU\Software\Policies\Microsoft\Internet Explorer\Restrictions\ NoSelectDownloadDir)

Toolbars   Offers the following three policies to manage IE's toolbar button behavior:

✦ **Disable customizing browser toolbar buttons** removes the View | Toolbars | Customize menu choice. (HKCU\Software\Microsoft\Windows\CurrentVersion\ Policies\Explorer\NoToolbarCustomize)

✦ **Disable customizing browser toolbars** removes the View | Toolbars | *toolbar names* menu choices. (HKCU\Software\Microsoft\Windows\CurrentVersion\ Policies\Explorer\NoBandCustomize)

✦ **Configure Toolbar Buttons** displays a dialog with 20 check boxes that let you select which IE buttons (standard and nonstandard, such as Encoding) appear on the toolbar. (HKCU\Software\Microsoft\Windows\CurrentVersion\ Policies\Explorer\Btn_Forward ... \Btn_Encoding)

Persistence Behavior   Has five policies that let you specify the maximum amount of storage space that a Web site and page can consume as a result of implementing DHTML Persistence in a security zone:

✦ **File size limits for Local Machine zone** default to 1,024 kB per site and 128 kB per page. (HKCU\Software\Policies\Microsoft\Internet Explorer\Persistence\0\ DomainLimit and \DocumentLimit)

✦ **File size limits for Intranet zone** default to 10,240 kB per site and 512 kB per page. (HKCU\Software\Policies\Microsoft\Internet Explorer\Persistence\1\DomainLimit and \DocumentLimit)

✦ **File size limits for Trusted Sites zone** default to 1,024 kB per site and 128 kB per page. (HKCU\Software\Policies\Microsoft\Internet Explorer\Persistence\2\ DomainLimit and \DocumentLimit)

✦ **File size limits for Internet zone** default to 1,024 kB per site and 128 kB per page. (HKCU\Software\Policies\Microsoft\Internet Explorer\Persistence\3\DomainLimit and \DocumentLimit)

✦ **File size limits for Restricted Sites zone** default to 640 kB per site and 64 kB per page. (HKCU\Software\Policies\Microsoft\Internet Explorer\Persistence\4\DomainLimit and \DocumentLimit)

Administrator Approved Controls

Location: User Configuration\Administrative Templates\Windows Components\Internet Explorer\Administrator Approved Controls

Administrator Approved Controls policies let you specify whether members of a specific set of ActiveX controls are designated as Administrator Approved, which lets the controls run within security zones that require such approval. Mark the check box on the Policy page of the *ControlGroupName* Policy dialog for the particular control you want to approve. Controls aren't approved unless you enable the policy and mark the check box. Using check boxes to approve multiple controls in the same policy makes it easier for Microsoft to add new controls without adding new control groups. Registry values are based on the GUID of the control, not its name.

Following are the 12 policies for control groups:

✦ **Media Player** lets you specify approval of Active Movie Control and Windows Media Player. (HKCU\Software\Policies\Microsoft\Windows\CurrentVersion\Internet Settings\AllowedControls\{05589FA1-C356-11CE-BF01-00AA0055595A} and \{22D6F312-B0F6-11D0-94AB-0080C74C7E95})

✦ **Menu Controls** include the MCSi Menu, Popup Menu Object, and Ikonic Menu Control. (HKCU\Software\Policies\Microsoft\Windows\CurrentVersion\Internet Settings\AllowedControls\{275E2FE0-7486-11D0-89D6-00A0C90C9B67}, \{7823A620-9DD9-11CF-A662-00AA00C066D2}, and \{F5131C24-E56D-11CF-B78A-444553540000})

✦ **Microsoft Agent** has only a Microsoft Agent Control check box. (HKCU\Software\Policies\Microsoft\Windows\CurrentVersion\Internet Settings\AllowedControls\{D45FD31B-5C6E-11D1-9EC1-00C04FD7081F})

✦ **Microsoft Chat** has only a MSChat Control check box. (HKCU\Software\Policies\Microsoft\Windows\CurrentVersion\Internet Settings\AllowedControls\{D6526FE0-E651-11CF-99CB-00C04FD64497})

◆ **Microsoft Survey Control** has only a Microsoft Survey Control check box. (HKCU\Software\Policies\Microsoft\Windows\CurrentVersion\Internet Settings\AllowedControls\{BD1F006E-174F-11D2-95C0-00C04F9A8CFA})

◆ **Shockwave Flash** has only a Shockwave Flash check box. (HKCU\Software\Policies\Microsoft\Windows\CurrentVersion\Internet Settings\AllowedControls\{D27CDB6E-AE6D-11CF-96B8-444553540000})

◆ **NetShow File Transfer Control** has only a check box of the same name. (HKCU\Software\Policies\Microsoft\Windows\CurrentVersion\Internet Settings\AllowedControls\{26F24A93-1DA2-11D0-A334-00AA004A5FC5})

◆ **DHTML Edit Control** has a single check box. (HKCU\Software\Policies\Microsoft\Windows\CurrentVersion\Internet Settings\AllowedControls\{2D360201-FFF5-11D1-8D03-00A0C959BC0A})

◆ **Microsoft Scriptlet Component** also has a single check box. (HKCU\Software\Policies\Microsoft\Windows\CurrentVersion\Internet Settings\AllowedControls\{AE24FDAE-03C6-11D1-8B76-0080C744F389})

◆ **Carpoint** has a single check box. (HKCU\Software\Policies\Microsoft\Windows\CurrentVersion\Internet Settings\AllowedControls\{DED22F57-FEE2-11D0-953B-00C04FD9152D})

◆ **Investor** has MSN Investor Chart Control and MSN Investor Ticker check boxes. (HKCU\Software\Policies\Microsoft\Windows\CurrentVersion\Internet Settings\AllowedControls\{9276B91A-E780-11d2-8A8D-00C04FA31D93} and \{52ADE293-85E8-11D2-BB22-00104B0EA281})

◆ **MSNBC** has a single MSN News control. (HKCU\Software\Policies\Microsoft\Windows\CurrentVersion\Internet Settings\AllowedControls\{2FF18E10-DE11-11D1-8161-00A0C90DD90C})

Windows Explorer

Location: User Configuration\Administrative Templates\Windows Components\Windows Explorer

The Windows Explorer node has a single subnode (Common File Open Dialog) and the following 20 policies that control behavior of Explorer windows, including My Computer and My Network Places:

◆ **Enable Classic Shell** disables Active Desktop, Web view, and thumbnail views, which creates an Explorer UI similar to that of Windows NT 4.0. This policy overrides the Enable Active Desktop policy of the User Configuration\Administrative Templates\

Desktop node. (HKCU\Software\Microsoft\Windows\CurrentVersion\Policies\ Explorer\ClassicShell)

✦ **Remove the Folder Options menu item from the Tools menu** prevents users from opening the Folder Options dialog and setting Explorer properties. (HKCU\Software\ Microsoft\Windows\CurrentVersion\Policies\Explorer\NoFolderOptions)

✦ **Remove File menu from Windows Explorer** prevents users from performing file operations with Explorer. (HKCU\Software\Microsoft\Windows\CurrentVersion\Policies\Explorer\NoFileMenu)

✦ **Remove "Map Network Drive" and "Disconnect Network Drive"** removes these toolbar buttons and Tools menu choices. This prevents users from connecting logical drives to network shares or removing mapped drives. (HKCU\Software\Microsoft\ Windows\CurrentVersion\Policies\Explorer\NoNetConnectDisconnect)

✦ **Remove Search button from Windows Explorer** prevents users from opening the Search for Files and Folders frame. (HKCU\Software\Microsoft\Windows\ CurrentVersion\Policies\Explorer\NoShellSearchButton)

✦ **Disable Windows Explorer's default context menu** prevents shortcut menus from appearing when users right-click an item. (HKCU\Software\Microsoft\Windows\ CurrentVersion\Policies\Explorer\NoViewContextMenu)

✦ **Hides the Manage item on the Windows Explorer context menu** prevents users from seeing the Manage choice when right-clicking the My Computer desktop icon. (HKCU\Software\Microsoft\Windows\CurrentVersion\Policies\Explorer\ NoManageMyComputerVerb)

✦ **Only allow approved Shell extensions** restricts shell extension applications to those in the list under the HKLM\Software\Microsoft\Windows\CurrentVersion\Shell Extensions\Approved key. (HKCU\Software\Microsoft\Windows\CurrentVersion\ Policies\Explorer\EnforceShellExtensionSecurity)

✦ **Do not track Shell shortcuts during roaming** prevents Explorer from attempting to track missing shortcut targets when a roaming user profile is in use. (HKCU\Software\Microsoft\Windows\CurrentVersion\Policies\Explorer\ LinkResolveIgnoreLinkInfo)

✦ **Hide these specified drives in My Computer** lets you select individual or combinations of drive letters (A, B, C, and D) to hide from the user. The default is Restrict All Drives. (HKCU\Software\Microsoft\Windows\CurrentVersion\ Policies\Explorer\NoDrives)

♦ **Prevent access to drives from My Computer** has the identical effect of the preceding policy, but doesn't hide the icons for the drive. The user receives an error message when attempting any action on the restricted drives. (HKCU\Software\Microsoft\ Windows\CurrentVersion\Policies\Explorer\NoViewOnDrive)

♦ **Hide Hardware tab** removes the Hardware page from Control Panel's Mouse, Keyboard, and Sounds and Multimedia tools and from the Properties dialog of all local drives. (HKCU\Software\Microsoft\Windows\CurrentVersion\ Policies\Explorer\NoHardwareTab)

♦ **Disable UI to change menu animation setting** prevents users from enabling the option to animate window, menu, and list movement. (HKCU\Software\ Microsoft\Windows\CurrentVersion\Policies\Explorer\NoChangeAnimation)

TIP: Enabling this policy can substantially improve the UI responsiveness on Windows 2000 Professional clients that have marginal hardware, such as 64 MB RAM (or less) or slow video adapters.

♦ **Disable UI to change keyboard navigation indicator setting** causes accelerator key underlining to appear without pressing the ALT key. (HKCU\Software\Microsoft\ Windows\CurrentVersion\Policies\Explorer\NoChangeKeyboardNavigationIndicators)

♦ **Disable DFS tab** removes the Distributed File System page, which is present only in a Properties dialog for a DFS share. (HKCU\Software\Microsoft\Windows\CurrentVersion\ Policies\Explorer\NoDFSTab)

♦ **No "Computers Near Me" in My Network Places** hides this icon. (HKCU\Software\ Microsoft\Windows\CurrentVersion\Policies\Network\NoComputersNearMe)

♦ **No "Entire Network" in My Network Places** hides this icon and disables network browsing. Enabling this and the preceding policy renders My Network Places close to useless. (HKCU\Software\Microsoft\Windows\CurrentVersion\Policies\ Network\NoEntireNetwork)

♦ **Maximum number of recent documents** sets the number of items that appear in the Start | Documents menu. The default is 15 documents. (HKCU\Software\Microsoft\ Windows\CurrentVersion\Policies\Network\MaxRecentDocs)

♦ **Do not request alternate credentials** prevents users from seeing the Install Programs As Other User dialog and using Run As to install a program. (HKCU\Software\ Microsoft\Windows\CurrentVersion\Policies\Network\NoRunasInstallPrompt)

♦ **Request credentials for network installations** displays the Install Programs As Other User dialog when the user attempts network installation of an application. (HKCU\Software\Microsoft\Windows\CurrentVersion\Policies\Network\ PromptRunasInstallNetPath)

Common Open File Dialog   Has the following three policies that affect the Common Open File dialog, regardless of the program that employs it:

♦ **Hide the common dialog places bar** removes the Outlook-style shortcut bar. (HKCU\Software\Microsoft\Windows\CurrentVersion\Policies\Comdlg32\NoPlacesBar)

♦ **Hide the common dialog back button** removes the Back button from the toolbar. (HKCU\Software\Microsoft\Windows\CurrentVersion\Policies\Comdlg32\NoBackButton)

♦ **Hide dropdown list of recent files** removes the list of most recently used (MRU) files. (HKCU\Software\Microsoft\Windows\CurrentVersion\Policies\Comdlg32\ NoFileMru)

TIP: If you enable all three of the preceding policies, the Open File dialog's behavior emulates that of Windows NT 4.0.

Microsoft Management Console

Location: User Configuration\Administrative Templates\Windows Components\Microsoft Management Console

The Microsoft Management Console node has a single subnode (Restricted/Permitted snap-ins) and the following two policies, which apply to all permitted snap-ins:

♦ **Restrict the user from entering author mode** prevents users from opening MMC itself in Author mode, opening console (.msc) files in Author mode, and opening any .msc files that open in Author mode by default. This policy prevents users from opening an empty console or adding or removing snap-ins from a console. (HKCU\Software\Policies\Microsoft\MMC\RestrictAuthorMode)

♦ **Restrict users to the explicitly permitted list of snap-ins** prevents users from opening any snap-in except those you enable in the following sections. By default, users can open all snap-ins installed on the computer. (HKCU\Software\Policies\Microsoft\MMC\RestrictToPermittedSnapIns)

Restricted/Permitted Snap-ins   Is a laundry list of the 29 standard snap-ins included with Windows 2000 Professional and Server, plus those installed by the server Administrative

Tools (Adminpak.msi) for AD management. This node also has two subnodes: Extension Snap-ins and Group Policy.

Clicking a standard snap-in item opens the Policy page of a conventional *PolicyName* Properties dialog with the standard Not Configured, Enabled, and Disabled options. If you apply the Restrict User to the Explicitly Permitted List of Snap-ins policy, only those snap-ins to which you apply the Enabled policy are available to users. Otherwise, all snap-ins installed on the user's computer are available, except those you specifically designate as Disabled. The Explain page is identical for all policies in this subnode.

Registry entries for these policies appear in the HKCU\Software\Policies\Microsoft\ MMC*SnapInGUID* key as the Restrict_Run value (0 for Enabled, 1 for Disabled). A typical value entry is HKCU\Software\Policies\Microsoft\ MMC\{E355E538-1C2E-11D0-8C37-00C04FD8FE93}\Restrict_Run for the Active Directory Users and Computers snap-in. Table A-1 lists the names of the standard snap-ins and their GUIDs. In most cases, you can enter the first few characters of the GUID when searching the Registry for the key.

Restricted/Permitted Snap-In	Globally Unique Identifier (GUID)
Active Directory Users and Computers	{E355E538-1C2E-11D0-8C37-00C04FD8FE93}
Active Directory Domains and Trusts	{EBC53A38-A23F-11D0-B09B-00C04FD8DCA6}
Active Directory Sites and Services	{D967F824-9968-11D0-B936-00C04FD8D5B0}
Certificates	{53D6AB1D-2488-11D1-A28C-00C04FB94F17}
Component Services	{C9BC92DF-5B9A-11D1-8F00-00C04FC2C17B}
Computer Management	{58221C67-EA27-11CF-ADCF-00AA00A80033}
Device Manager	{90087284-d6d6-11d0-8353-00a0c90640bf}
Disk Management	{8EAD3A12-B2C1-11d0-83AA-00A0C92C9D5D}
Disk Defragmenter	{43668E21-2636-11D1-A1CE-0080C88593A5}
Distributed File System (Dfs)	{677A2D94-28D9-11D1-A95B-008048918FB1}
Event Viewer	{975797FC-4E2A-11D0-B702-00C04FD8DBF7}
FAX Service	{753EDB4D-2E1B-11D1-9064-00A0C90AB504}
Indexing Service	{95AD72F0-44CE-11D0-AE29-00AA004B9986}
Internet Authentication Service (IAS)	{8F8F8DC0-5713-11D1-9551-0060B0576642}
Internet Information Services (IIS)	{A841B6C2-7577-11D0-BB1F-00A0C922E79C}
IP Security (IPSec)	{DEA8AFA0-CC85-11d0-9CE2-0080C7221EBD}

Table A-1.   Standard MMC Snap-Ins and Their GUIDs in the Registry of the User's Computer

Restricted/Permitted Snap-In	Globally Unique Identifier (GUID)
Local Users and Groups	{5D6179C8-17EC-11D1-9AA9-00C04FD8FE93}
Performance Logs and Alerts	{7478EF61-8C46-11d1-8D99-00A0C913CAD4}
QoS Admission Control	{FD57D297-4FD9-11D1-854E-00C04FC31FD3}
Removable Storage Management	{3CB6973D-3E6F-11D0-95DB-00A024D77700}
Routing and Remote Access	{1AA7F839-C7F5-11D0-A376-00C04FC9DA04}
Security Configuration and Analysis	{011BE22D-E453-11D1-945A-00C04FB984F9}
Security Templates	{5ADF5BF6-E452-11D1-945A-00C04FB984F9}
Services	{58221C66-EA27-11CF-ADCF-00AA00A80033}
Shared Folders	{58221C65-EA27-11CF-ADCF-00AA00A80033}
System Information	{45AC8C63-23E2-11D1-A696-00C04FD58BC3}
Telephony	{E26D02A0-4C1F-11D1-9AA1-00C04FC3357A}
Terminal Services Configuration	{B91B6008-32D2-11D2-9888-00A0C925F917}
WMI Control	{5C659257-E236-11D2-8899-00104B2AFB46}

Table A-1.   Standard MMC Snap-Ins and Their GUIDs in the Registry of the User's Computer *(continued)*

Extension Snap-ins

A list of 26 second-level extension snap-ins are available for use by the standard MMC consoles. The process of setting policies for these snap-ins and their Registry entries is the same as for the standard snap-ins described in the preceding section. Table A-2 is a list of the extension snap-ins and their GUIDs.

Restricted/Permitted Extension Snap-In	Globally Unique Identifier (GUID)
AppleTalk Routing	{1AA7F83C-C7F5-11D0-A376-00C04FC9DA04}
Certification Authority	{3F276EB4-70EE-11D1-8A0F-00C04FB93753}
Connection Sharing (NAT)	{C2FE450B-D6C2-11D0-A37B-00C04FC9DA04}
DCOM Configuration	{9EC88934-C774-11D1-87F4-00C04FC2C17B}
Device Manager	{74246BFC-4C96-11D0-ABEF-0020AF6B0B7A}

Table A-2.   Extension MMC Snap-Ins and Their GUIDs in the Registry of the User's Computer

Restricted/Permitted Extension Snap-In	Globally Unique Identifier (GUID)
DHCP Relay Management	{C2FE4502-D6C2-11D0-A37B-00C04FC9DA04}
Event Viewer	{394C052E-B830-11D0-9A86-00C04FD8DBF7}
IGMP Routing	{2E19B602-48EB-11d2-83CA-00104BCA42CF}
IP Routing	{C2FE4508-D6C2-11D0-A37B-00C04FC9DA04}
IPX RIP Routing	{90810502-38F1-11D1-9345-00C04FC9DA04}
IPX Routing	{90810500-38F1-11D1-9345-00C04FC9DA04}
IPX SAP Routing	{90810504-38F1-11D1-9345-00C04FC9DA04}
Logical and Mapped Drives	{6E8E0081-19CD-11D1-AD91-00AA00B8E05A}
OSPF Routing	{C2FE4506-D6C2-11D0-A37B-00C04FC9DA04}
Public Key Policies	{34AB8E82-C27E-11D1-A6C0-00C04FB94F17}
RAS Dialin – User Node	{B52C1E50-1DD2-11D1-BC43-00C04FC31FD3}
Remote Access	{5880CD5C-8EC0-11d1-9570-0060B0576642}
Removable Storage	{243E20B0-48ED-11D2-97DA-00A024D77700}
RIP Routing	{C2FE4504-D6C2-11D0-A37B-00C04FC9DA04}
Routing	{DAB1A262-4FD7-11D1-842C-00C04FB6C218}
Send Console Message	{B1AFF7D0-0C49-11D1-BB12-00C04FC9A3A3}
Service Dependencies	{BD95BA60-2E26-AAD1-AD99-00AA00B8E05A}
SMTP Protocol	{03F1F940-A0F2-11D0-BB77-00AA00A1EAB7}
SNMP	{7AF60DD3-4979-11D1-8A6C-00C04FC33566}
System Properties	{0F3621F1-23C6-11D1-AD97-00AA00B88E5A}

Table A-2. Extension MMC Snap-Ins and Their GUIDs in the Registry of the User's Computer (*continued*)

Group Policy
The following affect the Group Policy snap-in only:

✦ **Group Policy snap-in** enables or disables use of this snap-in. (HKCU\Software\Policies\Microsoft\MMC\{8FC0B734-A0E1-11D1-A7D3-0000F87571E3}\Restrict_Run)

✦ **Group Policy Tab for Active Directory Tools** enables or disables the Group Policy page of the Properties dialog for objects opened in Active Directory Users and Computers, Domains and Trusts, and Sites and Services. (HKCU\Software\Policies\Microsoft\MMC\{D70A2BEA-A63E-11D1- A7D4-0000F87571E3}\Restrict_Run)

The Explain pages of the following policies incorrectly refer to these policies as enabling or disabling snap-ins. These 10 policies enable or disable the user's ability to open the following individual nodes or subnodes of Computer Configuration and User Configuration trees in the Group Policy Editor:

Restricted Node or Subnode	Globally Unique Identifier (GUID)
Administrative Templates (Computers)	{0F6B957D-509E-11D1-A7CC-0000F87571E3}
Administrative Templates (Users)	{0F6B957E-509E-11D1-A7CC-0000F87571E3}
Folder Redirection	{88E729D6-BDC1-11D1-BD2A-00C04FB9603F}
Internet Explorer Maintenance	{FC715823-C5FB-11D1-9EEF-00A0C90347FF}
Remote Installation Services	{3060E8CE-7020-11D2-842D-00C04FA372D4}
Scripts (Logon/Logoff)	{40B66650-4972-11D1-A7CA-0000F87571E3}
Scripts (Startup/Shutdown)	{40B6664F-4972-11D1-A7CA-0000F87571E3}
Security Settings	{803E14A0-B4FB-11D0-A0D0-00A0C90F574B}
Software Installation (Computers)	{942A8E4F-A261-11D1-A760-00C04FB9603F}
Software Installation (Users)	{BACF5C8A-A3C7-11D1-A760-00C04FB9603F}

Task Scheduler

Location: User Configuration\Administrative Templates\Windows Components\Task Scheduler

The Task Scheduler policies for users are the same as those for computers. The only difference is the location of the Registry key (HKCU instead of HKLM). Following are the seven Task Scheduler 5.0 policies:

◆ **Hide Property Pages** prevents all users from viewing or changing the properties of an existing scheduled task by disabling user access to the task's Properties dialog. If configured for both computers and users, the computer setting applies. (HKCU\Software\Policies\Microsoft\Windows\Task Scheduler5.0\Property Pages)

◆ **Prevent Task Run or End** prevents all users from starting or stopping scheduled tasks manually. If configured for both computers and users, the computer setting applies. (HKCU\Software\Policies\Microsoft\Windows\Task Scheduler5.0\Execution)

◆ **Disable Drag-and-Drop** prevents all users from using drag-and-drop or copy-and-paste methods to move or copy programs in the Scheduled Tasks folder. If configured for both computers and users, the computer setting applies. (HKCU\Software\Policies\Microsoft\Windows\Task Scheduler5.0\DragAndDrop)

◆ **Disable New Task Creation** prevents all users from adding new scheduled tasks. If configured for both computers and users, the computer setting applies. (HKCU\Software\Policies\Microsoft\Windows\Task Scheduler5.0\Task Creation)

♦ **Disable Task Deletion** prevents all users from removing scheduled tasks. If configured for both computers and users, the computer setting applies. (HKCU\Software\Policies\Microsoft\Windows\Task Scheduler5.0\Task Deletion)

♦ **Disable Advanced Menu** prevents all users from viewing or changing the properties of new tasks during their creation. This policy doesn't affect existing tasks (see the Hide Property Pages and Prohibit Browse policies). If configured for both computers and users, the computer setting applies. (HKCU\Software\Policies\Microsoft\ Windows\Task Scheduler5.0\Disable Advanced)

♦ **Prohibit Browse** restricts all users to Start menu items when creating new scheduled tasks and prevents them from changing existing tasks. If configured for both computers and users, the computer setting applies. (HKCU\Software\Policies\Microsoft\ Windows\Task Scheduler5.0\AllowBrowse)

Windows Installer

Location: User Configuration\Administrative Templates\Windows Components\ Windows Installer

There are far fewer user-based than computer-based Windows Installer policies. Following are the four Installer policies you can set for users:

♦ **Always install with elevated privileges** causes Windows Installer to use system permissions when installing any .msi pr .zap file. (HKCU\Software\Policies\ Microsoft\Windows\Installer\AlwaysInstallElevated)

♦ **Search order** opens a dialog that lets you type a string to specify the device search order for installation files: Network (n), CD Media (m), or URL (u). Combinations such as "nmu" (the default), "nu," and "um" are valid. (HKCU\Software\Policies\ Microsoft\Windows\Installer\Search Order)

♦ **Disable rollback** prevents saving of files required to reverse an interrupted or unsuccessful installation and revert to the computer's original configuration. If configured for both computers and users, the computer setting applies. Don't enable this policy for either computers or users. (HKCU\Software\Policies\Microsoft\ Windows\Installer\DisableRollback)

♦ **Disable media source for any install** prevents users from installing from removable media: CD-ROMs, DVDs, and diskettes. (HKCU\Software\Policies\Microsoft\ Windows\Installer\Disable Media)

Start Menu & Task Bar

Location: User Configuration\Administrative Templates\Start Menu & Taskbar

The 24 following policies let you preconfigure the user's Start menu and task bar and restrict the user's ability to change the configuration:

- ✦ **Remove user's folders from the Start Menu** hides the user-specific (upper) section of the Start menu. The primary purpose of this policy is to prevent redirected folders from appearing in the user-specific and main (bottom) sections of the Start menu. (HKCU\Software\Microsoft\Windows\CurrentVersion\Policies\Explorer\NoStartMenu SubFolders)

- ✦ **Disable and remove links to Windows Update** prevents users from connecting to the Windows Update Web site. (HKCU\Software\Microsoft\Windows\CurrentVersion\Policies\Explorer\NoWindowsUpdate)

- ✦ **Remove common program groups from Start Menu** removes items in the All Users profile from the Programs menu on the Start menu; the user sees only items in his or her profile. (HKCU\Software\Microsoft\Windows\CurrentVersion\Policies\Explorer\NoCommonGroup)

- ✦ **Remove Documents menu from Start Menu** hides the Documents menu choice. (HKCU\Software\Microsoft\Windows\CurrentVersion\Policies\Explorer\NoRecentDocsMenu)

- ✦ **Disable programs on Settings menu** prevents users from running Control Panel, Printers, and Network and Dial-up Connections from the Settings menu and from My Computer and Windows Explorer. (HKCU\Software\Microsoft\Windows\CurrentVersion\Policies\Explorer\NoSetFolder)

- ✦ **Remove Network and Dial-up Connections from Start Menu** prevents user access to Network and Dial-up Connections. (HKCU\Software\Microsoft\Windows\CurrentVersion\Policies\Explorer\NoNetworkConnection)

- ✦ **Remove Favorites menu from Start Menu** prevents users from adding a Favorites choice to the Start menu. (HKCU\Software\Microsoft\Windows\CurrentVersion\Policies\Explorer\NoFavoritesMenu)

- ✦ **Remove Search menu from Start Menu** disables the Search feature, including Search in Explorer. (HKCU\Software\Microsoft\Windows\CurrentVersion\Policies\Explorer\NoFind)

✦ **Remove Help menu from Start Menu** hides the Help menu choice. This policy doesn't affect behavior of other features' Help menus or buttons. (HKCU\Software\Microsoft\Windows\CurrentVersion\Policies\Explorer\NoSMHelp)

✦ **Remove Run menu from Start Menu** hides the Run choice from the Start menu and removes the New Task (Run) command from Task Manager. (HKCU\Software\Microsoft\Windows\CurrentVersion\Policies\Explorer\NoRun)

✦ **Add Logoff to the Start Menu** adds a Log Off *LogonID* choice to the Start menu. (HKCU\Software\Microsoft\Windows\CurrentVersion\Policies\Explorer\ ForceStartMenuLogOff)

✦ **Disable Logoff on the Start Menu** has the opposite effect of the preceding policy. (HKCU\Software\Microsoft\Windows\CurrentVersion\Policies\Explorer\ StartMenuLogOff)

✦ **Disable and remove the Shut Down command** prevents users from shutting down and restarting Windows 2000. The policy doesn't prevent users from using the power switch or pulling the power plug to shut down, (HKCU\Software\Microsoft\Windows\ CurrentVersion\Policies\Explorer\NoClose)

✦ **Disable drag-and-drop context menus on the Start Menu** prevents users from reordering or removing items from the Start menu and removes its context menus. (HKCU\Software\Microsoft\Windows\CurrentVersion\Policies\Explorer\ NoChangeStartMenu)

✦ **Disable changes to Taskbar and Start Menu Settings** removes the Taskbar & Start Menu choice from Settings on the Start menu and prevents users from opening the Taskbar Properties dialog. (HKCU\Software\Microsoft\Windows\CurrentVersion\ Policies\Explorer\NoSetTaskbar)

✦ **Disable context menu for taskbar** hides the pop-up menus for the taskbar and the items it contains. (HKCU\Software\Microsoft\Windows\CurrentVersion\Policies\ Explorer\NoTrayContextMenu)

✦ **Do not keep history of recently opened documents** disables most recently used (MRU) choices from the Documents menu. (HKCU\Software\Microsoft\Windows\ CurrentVersion\Policies\Explorer\NoRecentDocsHistory)

✦ **Clear history of recently opened documents on exit** removes MRU choices from the Documents menu when the user logs off. (HKCU\Software\Microsoft\Windows\ CurrentVersion\Policies\Explorer\ClearRecentDocsOnExit)

✦ **Disable personalized menus** causes all menu choices to appear, rather than only MRU choices. (HKCU\Software\Microsoft\Windows\CurrentVersion\Policies\ Explorer\Intellimenus)

TIP: Personalized menus, once called IntelliMenus, tend to confuse users who find menu choices suddenly "missing." You can save considerable help desk support time by applying the Disable Personalized Menus policy to all domain users.

◆ **Disable user tracking** prevents the system from saving the information required to enable personalized menus, effectively disabling that feature. (HKCU\Software\ Microsoft\Windows\CurrentVersion\Policies\Explorer\NoInstrumentation)

◆ **Add "Run in Separate Memory Space" check box to Run dialog box** lets users run 16-bit apps in a dedicated (not shared) Virtual DOS Machine (VDM). (HKCU\Software\Microsoft\Windows\CurrentVersion\Policies\Explorer\ MemCheckBoxInRunDlg)

◆ **Do not use the search-based method when resolving shell shortcuts** prevents the system from searching for the missing target executable of a shortcut. (HKCU\Software\Microsoft\Windows\CurrentVersion\Policies\Explorer\ NoResolveSearch)

◆ **Do not use the tracking-based method when resolving shell shortcuts** disables the file-tracking method (for NTFS only) of the search for a shortcut's missing target. (HKCU\Software\Microsoft\Windows\CurrentVersion\Policies\Explorer\ NoResolveTrack)

◆ **Gray unavailable Windows Installer programs Start Menu shortcuts** identifies partially installed assigned packages. When the user launches a partially installed program, Windows Installer runs to complete the installation process. Installing the GroupPol application from GroupPol.msi is an example of a two-step installation; after you click OK in the startup dialog, Installer runs before GroupPol's main window opens. (HKCU\Software\Microsoft\Windows\CurrentVersion\Policies\ Explorer\GreyMSIAds)

Desktop

Location: User Configuration\Administrative Templates\Desktop

The Desktop node has two subnodes (Active Desktop and Active Directory) and the following 10 policies that relate to desktop management:

◆ **Hide all icons on Desktop** removes all icons, shortcuts, and other default and user-defined items from the desktop, leaving the desktop empty. Enabling this policy initially shocks and then confounds users. (HKCU\Software\Microsoft\ Windows\CurrentVersion\Policies\Explorer\NoDesktop)

- **Remove My Documents icon from desktop** removes the My Documents icon not only from the desktop, but also from Explorer, programs that use the Explorer windows, and the common Open File dialog. (HKCU\Software\Microsoft\ Windows\CurrentVersion\Policies\NonEnum\{450D8FBA-AD25-11D0-98A8-0800361B1103})

- **Remove My Documents icon from Start Menu** does what it says. (HKCU\Software\Microsoft\Windows\CurrentVersion\Policies\Explorer\NoSMMyDocs)

- **Hide My Network Places icon on desktop** is equally self-descriptive. (HKCU\Software\Microsoft\Windows\CurrentVersion\Policies\Explorer\NoNetHood)

- **Hide Internet Explorer icon on desktop** also does what it says. (HKCU\Software\Microsoft\Windows\CurrentVersion\Policies\Explorer\NoInternetIcon)

- **Do not add shares from recently opened documents to the My Network Places folder** prevent icons for remotely shared folders from being added to My Network Places after a network document is opened. (HKCU\Software\Microsoft\ Windows\CurrentVersion\Policies\Explorer\NoRecentDocsNetHood)

- **Prohibit user from changing My Documents path** prevents users from typing a new path to My Documents in the Target textbox of its Properties dialog. (HKCU\Software\Microsoft\Windows\CurrentVersion\Policies\Explorer\ DisablePersonalDirChange)

- **Disable adding, dragging, dropping and closing the Taskbar's toolbars** prevents users from adding or removing toolbars from the desktop and dragging toolbars onto or off of docked toolbars. (HKCU\Software\Microsoft\Windows\CurrentVersion\ Policies\Explorer\NoCloseDragDropBands)

- **Disable adjusting desktop toolbars** prevents users from adjusting the length of desktop toolbars or repositioning items or toolbars on docked toolbars. (HKCU\Software\ Microsoft\Windows\CurrentVersion\Policies\Explorer\NoMovingBands)

- **Don't save settings at exit** prevents the system from saving changes, such as the positions of open windows and the size and position of the taskbar. This policy doesn't affect desktop shortcuts. (HKCU\Software\Microsoft\Windows\ CurrentVersion\Policies\Explorer\NoSaveSettings)

Active Desktop

Location: User Configuration\Administrative Templates\Desktop\Active Desktop

These policies don't apply if you enabled the Enable Classic Shell policy under the User Configuration\Administrative Templates\Windows Components\Windows Explorer node. If you insist on implementing Active Desktop, the following 11 policies apply:

+ **Enable Active Desktop** forces users into Active Desktop mode. (HKCU\Software\Microsoft\Windows\CurrentVersion\Policies\Explorer\ ForceActiveDesktopOn)

+ **Disable Active Desktop** does the opposite of the above and prevents users from enabling Active Desktop. (HKCU\Software\Microsoft\Windows\CurrentVersion\ Policies\Explorer\NoActiveDesktop)

NOTE: The following nine policies let you inactivate the Active Desktop by prohibiting or disabling normal Active Desktop user activities.

+ **Disable all items** removes Active Desktop content and prevents users from adding Active Desktop content, thereby defeating the purpose of this dubious feature. (HKCU\Software\Microsoft\Windows\CurrentVersion\Policies\ActiveDesktop\ NoComponents)

+ **Prohibit changes** prevents users from adding Active Desktop content. (HKCU\Software\Microsoft\Windows\CurrentVersion\Policies\Explorer\ NoActiveDesktopChanges)

+ **Prohibit adding items** prevents users from adding Web content. (HKCU\Software\ Microsoft\Windows\CurrentVersion\Policies\ActiveDesktop\ NoAddingComponents)

+ **Prohibit deleting items** prevents users from removing content. (HKCU\Software\Microsoft\Windows\CurrentVersion\Policies\ActiveDesktop\ NoDeletingComponents)

+ **Prohibit editing items** prevents users from changing the properties of Web content items. (HKCU\Software\Microsoft\Windows\CurrentVersion\Policies\ActiveDesktop\ NoEditingComponents)

+ **Prohibit closing items** causes items added to the Active Directory to remain open on the desktop at all times. (HKCU\Software\Microsoft\Windows\CurrentVersion\ Policies\ActiveDesktop\NoClosingComponents)

+ **Add/Delete items** lets you add space-separated lists of the URLs of items to add to or delete from the Active Desktop. (HKCU\Software\Microsoft\Windows\CurrentVersion\ Policies\ActiveDesktop\AdminComponents\Add and \Delete)

✦ **Active Desktop Wallpaper** lets you specify a local or UNC path to a graphics file that contains a wallpaper image. You also can specify whether the wallpaper is centered, stretched, or tiled. (HKCU\Software\Microsoft\Windows\CurrentVersion\ Policies\Explorer\Wallpaper and \WallpaperStyle)

✦ **Allow only bitmapped wallpaper** restricts wallpaper to the .bmp or .dib format. (HKCU\Software\Microsoft\Windows\CurrentVersion\Policies\ActiveDesktop\ NoHTMLWallpaper)

Active Directory

Location: User Configuration\Administrative Templates\Desktop\Active Directory

The following three policies have no relationship to the desktop, but the Law of Conservation of Features requires every feature to be somewhere:

✦ **Maximum size of Active Directory searches** lets you limit the maximum number of objects returned by an AD search. The default is 10,000 objects, and the maximum is 4 million. You can expect clients and servers to be tied up for a substantial period of time when filling a list with 4 million object names. A better setting is 2,000 objects, the default for the number of objects displayed by an Active Directory Users and Computers container. (HKCU\Software\Policies\Microsoft\Windows\Directory UI\ QueryLimit)

✦ **Enable filter in Find dialog box** adds a filter bar above the list filled by an AD search. The filter bar allows users to refine a search, if users understand how to apply filters. (HKCU\Software\Policies\Microsoft\Windows\Directory UI\EnableFilter)

✦ **Hide Active Directory folder** prevents the Active Directory icon from appearing in the My Network Places window. (HKCU\Software\Policies\Microsoft\Windows\ Directory UI\HideDirectoryFolder)

Control Panel

Location: User Configuration\Administrative Templates\Control Panel

Not surprisingly, the Control Panel node's policies restrict users ability to take full (or any) advantage of Control Panel tools. This node has four subnodes (Add/Remove Programs, Display, Printers, and Regional Options) and the following three policies:

✦ **Disable Control Panel** specifies that users can't run Control.exe, the Control Panel choice is removed from the Start menu, and the Control Panel folder is removed from Explorer. (HKCU\Software\Microsoft\Windows\CurrentVersion\Policies\Explorer\ NoControlPanel)

◆ **Hide specified control panel applets** lets you specify in the Show Contents list which Control Panel tools to hide from users. You must type the *ToolFile*.cpl file name in the Add Item dialog; you can't browse for the files. This policy overrides the following policy. (HKCU\Software\Microsoft\Windows\CurrentVersion\Policies\ Explorer\DisallowCpl)

◆ **Show only specified control panel applets** displays all Control Panel tools except those you disallow in the Show Contents list. (HKCU\Software\Microsoft\Windows\ CurrentVersion\Policies\Explorer\RestrictCpl)

Add/Remove Programs

Location: User Configuration\Administrative Templates\Control Panel\Add/Remove Programs
The following 10 policies apply the Add/Remove Programs tool:

◆ **Disable Add/Remove Programs** prevents users from installing and removing programs with this tool. (HKCU\Software\Microsoft\Windows\CurrentVersion\ Policies\Uninstall\NoAddRemovePrograms)

◆ **Hide Change or Remove Programs page** removes the Change or Remove Programs button from the Add/Remove Programs shortcut bar, which prevents users from uninstalling, repairing, adding, or removing features of installed programs with this tool. (HKCU\Software\Microsoft\Windows\CurrentVersion\Policies\Uninstall\ NoRemovePage)

◆ **Hide Add New Programs page** removes the Add New Programs button from the shortcut bar, which prevents users from installing programs published or assigned by a system administrator with the tool. (HKCU\Software\Microsoft\Windows\ CurrentVersion\Policies\Uninstall\NoAddPage)

◆ **Hide Add/Remove Windows Components page** removes the Add/Remove Windows Components button from the shortcut bar, which prevents users from reconfiguring installed services with the Windows Component Wizard. (HKCU\Software\Microsoft\ Windows\CurrentVersion\Policies\Uninstall\NoWindowsSetupPage)

◆ **Hide the "Add a program from CD-ROM or floppy disk" option** removes the Add a Program from CD-ROM or Floppy Disk section and its CD or Floppy button from the Add New Programs page, so users can't install programs from removable media. (HKCU\Software\Microsoft\Windows\CurrentVersion\Policies\Uninstall\NoAddFrom CDorFloppy)

◆ **Hide the "Add programs from Microsoft" option** removes the Add Programs from Microsoft section and its Windows Update button from the Add New Programs page to prevent users from connecting to the Windows Update URL from this tool. (HKCU\Software\Microsoft\Windows\CurrentVersion\Policies\Uninstall\ NoAddFromInternet)

✦ **Hide the "Add programs from your network" option** hides the list box and category list so users can't see what programs are available for installation over the network. (HKCU\Software\Microsoft\Windows\CurrentVersion\Policies\Uninstall\ NoAddFromNetwork)

✦ **Go directly to Components wizard** is supposed to run the Windows Components Wizard when users click the Add/Remove Windows Components button. If you disable this policy, users have access to the Set Up Services section of the Add/Remove Programs page. Tests of this policy indicate that the policy doesn't work and doesn't change its value setting in the Registry. (HKCU\Software\ Microsoft\Windows\CurrentVersion\Policies\Uninstall\NoServices)

✦ **Disable Support Information** removes links to the Support Info dialog, which might include troubleshooting text and hyperlinks to a vendor support URL. (HKCU\Software\ Microsoft\Windows\CurrentVersion\Policies\Uninstall\NoSupportInfo)

✦ **Specify default category for Add New Programs** lets you type a category name for added programs if the program doesn't have an assigned category name. (HKCU\Software\Microsoft\Windows\CurrentVersion\Policies\Uninstall\ DefaultCategory)

Display

Location: User Configuration\Administrative Templates\Control Panel\Display

The following 10 policies restrict user interaction with Control Panel's Display tool:

✦ **Disable Display in control panel** prevents the Display tool from running. (HKCU\Software\Microsoft\Windows\CurrentVersion\Policies\System\NoDisplayCpl)

✦ **Hide Background tab** removes the Background page, so users can't change the pattern or wallpaper on the desktop. (HKCU\Software\Microsoft\Windows\ CurrentVersion\Policies\System\NoDispBackgroundTab)

✦ **Disable Changing Wallpaper** This policy prevents users from adding or changing the background wallpaper of the desktop. (HKCU\Software\Microsoft\Windows\ CurrentVersion\Policies\ActiveDesktop\NoChangingWallpaper)

✦ **Hide Appearance tab** removes the Appearance page so users can't change the Windows color scheme. (HKCU\Software\Microsoft\Windows\CurrentVersion\ Policies\System\NoDispAppearancePage)

✦ **Hide Settings tab** removes the Settings page so users can't change the display settings, such as color depth, resolution, refresh rate, and other display properties. (HKCU\Software\Microsoft\Windows\CurrentVersion\Policies\System\ NoDispSettingsPage)

✦ **Hide Screen Saver tab** removes the Screen Save page to prevent users from changing the screen saver. (HKCU\Software\Microsoft\Windows\CurrentVersion\Policies\ System\NoDispScrSavPage)

✦ **No screen saver** disables all screen savers and prevents users from changing screen saver options. (HKCU\Software\Policies\Microsoft\Windows\Control Panel\Desktop\ ScreenSaveActive)

✦ **Screen saver executable name** lets you specify use of a particular screen saver by its local path and file name. You can't specify networked .scr files. (HKCU\Software\Policies\ Microsoft\Windows\Control Panel\Desktop\SCRNSAVE.EXE)

✦ **Password protect the screen saver** requires screen savers to be password protected. The default is optional password protection. (HKCU\Software\Policies\Microsoft\ Windows\Control Panel\Desktop\ScreenSaverIsSecure)

✦ **Screen Saver timeout** lets you specify computer idle time in seconds before activating the screen saver. The default is 15 minutes, and the nominal maximum is 24 hours. (HKCU\Software\Policies\Microsoft\Windows\Control Panel\Desktop\ ScreenSaveTimeOut)

Printers

Location: User Configuration\Administrative Templates\Control Panel\Printers

As expected, this node restricts use of Control Panel's Printers tool with the following five policies:

✦ **Disable deletion of printers** prevents users from using the tool to delete local and network printers. (HKCU\Software\Microsoft\Windows\CurrentVersion\Policies\ Explorer\NoDeletePrinter)

✦ **Disable addition of printers** prevents users from using the tool to add local and network printers, including adding printers by dragging a printer icon into the Printers folder. This policy doesn't prevent users from adding printers with the Add New Hardware Wizard. (HKCU\Software\Microsoft\Windows\CurrentVersion\ Policies\Explorer\NoAddPrinter)

✦ **Browse the network to find printers** lets users search the network for shared printers with the Add Printer Wizard. If this policy is disabled, users must type the full network path to the printer when using the Add Printer Wizard. (HKCU\Software\Policies\Microsoft\Windows NT\Printers\Wizard\Downlevel Browse)

✦ **Default Active Directory path when searching for printers** lets you specify the full LDAP path to the starting point of user's AD searches for network printers, instead of beginning at the domain root. The format of the entry is LDAP:\\[OU=*OUName*,][DC=*ChildDomainName*,]DC=*DomainName*,DC=*Ext*, and the maximum length is 255 characters. (HKCU\Software\Policies\Microsoft\ Windows NT\Printers\Wizard\Default Search Scope)

✦ **Browse a common web site to find printers** lets you add a URL to the Add Printer Wizard for a Web page with links to Internet-enabled printers. The usual format of the URL is http://www.*domain.ext*/printers, although http://*xxx.xxx.xxx.xxx*/printers, where *xxx.xxx.xxx.xxx* is the IP address of the Web server, also works. (HKCU\Software\Policies\Microsoft\Windows NT\Printers\Wizard\Printers Page URL)

Regional Options

Location: User Configuration\Administrative Templates\Control Panel\Regional Options

The Regional Options subnode has only the following policy:

✦ **Restrict selection of Windows 2000 menus and dialogs language** restricts users to a specified language selected from the dialog's or the default language, English. Users can't make their own language selection. (HKCU\Software\Policies\Microsoft\Control Panel\Desktop\MultiUILanguageID)

Network

Location: User Configuration\Administrative Templates\Network

The Network node has two subnodes: Offline Files and Network and Dial-up Connections.

Offline Files

Location: User Configuration\Administrative Templates\Network\Offline Files

The user-based Offline Files policies are a subset of the corresponding computer-based policies under the User Configuration\Administrative Templates\Network\Offline Files node. Registry entries are in the HKCU hive instead of HKLM. The following 12 Offline Files policies apply to users:

✦ **Disable user configuration of Offline Files** prevents users from changing the Offline Files behavior you specify with the following policies. If configured for both computers and users, the computer setting applies. (HKCU\Software\Policies\ Microsoft\Windows\NetCache\NoConfigCache)

✦ **Synchronize all offline files before logging off** causes a full synchronization with the server of all offline files when a user logs off. The default is a quick synchronization that ensures that files are intact, but not necessarily current, and allows the user to change the synchronization behavior. If configured for both computers and users, the computer setting applies. (HKCU\Software\Policies\Microsoft\Windows\ NetCache\SyncAtLogoff)

✦ **Action on server disconnect** offers the following two options when disconnected from the server that stores offline files: Work Offline (use locally cached copies) and Never Go Offline (prevents use of cached copies). If configured for both computers and users, the computer setting applies. The descriptions of the choices on the Policy page for this policy are incorrect.
(HKCU\Software\Policies\Microsoft\Windows\NetCache\GoOfflineAction)

✦ **Non-default server disconnect actions** lets you specify what happens when a user is disconnected from servers you specify by name in a list. Each server has a value entry: 0 for Work Offline and 1 for Never Go Offline. This policy overrides values you set in the previous policy if you include the default server in the list. If configured for both computers and users, the computer setting applies. (HKCU\Software\Policies\Microsoft\Windows\NetCache\CustomGoOfflineActions\ CustomGoOfflineActions subkey)

✦ **Disable "Make Available Offline"** removes the View Files button from the Offline Files folder. It doesn't prevent them from working offline or using Explorer to view server files. If configured for both computers and users, the computer setting applies. (HKCU\Software\Policies\Microsoft\Windows\NetCache\NoMakeAvailableOffline)

✦ **Prevent use of Offline Files folder** disables the Offline Files folder. If configured for both computers and users, the computer setting applies.
(HKCU\Software\Policies\Microsoft\Windows\NetCache\NoCacheViewer)

✦ **Administratively assigned offline files** lets you generate a list of UNC paths for files, folders, or both to which all users of the computer should have access. When adding items to the list, leave the value empty. If configured for both computers and users, the computer setting applies. (HKCU\Software\Policies\Microsoft\Windows\ NetCache\AssignedOfflineFolders\AssignedOfflineFolders subkey)

✦ **Disable reminder balloons** removes the balloons that appear above the Offline Files icon in the status bar when a network connection is lost or reconnected. Enabling this policy causes the system to disregard the following three policies. If configured for both computers and users, the computer setting applies. (HKCU\Software\Policies\Microsoft\Windows\NetCache\NoReminders)

✦ **Reminder balloon frequency** lets you change the update interval for reminder balloons. If configured for both computers and users, the computer setting applies. (HKCU\Software\Policies\Microsoft\Windows\NetCache\ReminderFreqMinutes)

✦ **Initial reminder balloon lifetime** lets you set the duration of the first reminder balloon for a network status change. If configured for both computers and users, the computer setting applies. (HKCU\Software\Policies\Microsoft\Windows\NetCache\ InitialBalloonTimeoutSeconds)

✦ **Reminder balloon lifetime** lets you set the duration of successive reminder balloons. If configured for both computers and users, the computer setting applies. (HKCU\Software\Policies\Microsoft\Windows\NetCache\ ReminderBalloonTimeoutSeconds)

✦ **Event logging level** lets you specify the events logged by Offline Files in the Application log. A value of 0 records offline cache corruption, 1 adds server disconnection, 2 adds client disconnection and reconnection, and 3 adds server reconnection events. If configured for both computers and users, the computer setting applies. (HKCU\Software\Policies\Microsoft\Windows\NetCache\ EventLoggingLevel)

Network and Dial-up Connections

Location: User Configuration\Administrative Templates\Network\Network and Dial-up Connections

Unlike with most other policies, which restrict or disable Windows 2000 features when enabled, enabling some Network and Dial-up Connections policies enforce Windows 2000's defaults. Enabling most of the policies extends to users rights that, by default, are reserved to administrators. To apply restrictions, you must disable the policy. The Network and Dial-up Connections node has the following 19 policies:

✦ **Enable deletion of RAS connections**, when set to Disabled, prevents users and administrators from deleting private (per-user) RAS connections. (HKCU\Software\Policies\Microsoft\Windows\Network Connections\ NC_DeleteConnection)

- **Enable deletion of RAS connections available to all users** allows users to delete shared (all-user) connections. Normally, only administrators can delete shared RAS connections. Disabling the preceding policy overrides this policy. (HKCU\Software\Policies\Microsoft\Windows\Network Connections\ NC_DeleteAllUserConnection)

- **Enable connecting and disconnecting a RAS connection**, when set to Disabled, prevents users from connecting and disconnecting dial-up connections using the connection icon. The user can, however, connect or disconnect using the connection's Status page. (HKCU\Software\Policies\Microsoft\Windows\Network Connections\NC_RasConnect)

- **Enable connecting and disconnecting a LAN connection**, when set to Disabled, prevents users from connecting and disconnecting network connections using the connection icon. The user can, however, connect or disconnect using the connection's Status page. (HKCU\Software\Policies\Microsoft\Windows\Network Connections\NC_LanConnect)

- **Enable access to properties of a LAN connection**, when set to Disabled, prevents users from viewing the *ConnectionName* Properties dialog for the network connection. (HKCU\Software\Policies\Microsoft\Windows\Network Connections\ NC_LanProperties)

- **Allow access to current user's RAS connection properties**, when set to Disabled, prevents users from viewing the *ConnectionName* Properties dialog for a private RAS connection. (HKCU\Software\Policies\Microsoft\Windows\Network Connections\ NC_RasMyProperties)

- **Enable access to properties of RAS connections available to all users**, when set to Disabled, prevents users from viewing the *ConnectionName* Properties dialog for a shared RAS connection. Disabling the preceding policy overrides this policy. (HKCU\Software\Policies\Microsoft\Windows\Network Connections\ NC_RasAllUserProperties)

- **Enable renaming of connections, if supported** lets users rename all connections, including their private dial-up connections. Disabling the policy restricts users to renaming only their private connections. (HKCU\Software\Policies\Microsoft\ Windows\Network Connections\NC_RenameConnection)

- **Enable renaming of RAS connections belonging to the current user**, when set to Disabled, prevents users from renaming their private RAS connections. (HKCU\Software\Policies\Microsoft\Windows\Network Connections\ NC_RenameMyRasConnection)

- **Enable adding or removing components of a RAS or LAN connection**, when set to Disabled, prevents users from adding and removing network components with the Install and Uninstall buttons in Network and Dial-up Connections or with the Windows Components Wizard. (HKCU\Software\Policies\Microsoft\Windows\ Network Connections\NC_AddRemoveComponents)

- **Allow connection components to be enabled or disabled**, when set to Disabled, prevents users from enabling or disabling components used by dial-up and local area connections for users. (HKCU\Software\Policies\Microsoft\Windows\Network Connections\NC_ChangeBindState)

- **Enable access to properties of components of a LAN connection**, when set to Disabled, prevents users from viewing the *ComponentName* Properties dialog for components of the network connection. (HKCU\Software\Policies\Microsoft\ Windows\Network Connections\NC_LanChangeProperties)

- **Enable access to properties of components of a RAS connection**, when set to Disabled, prevents users from viewing the *ComponentName* Properties dialog for components of the RAS connection. (HKCU\Software\Policies\Microsoft\Windows\ Network Connections\NC_RasChangeProperties)

- **Display and enable the Network Connection wizard**, when set to Disabled, prevents users from creating new network connections with the Network Connection Wizard. (HKCU\Software\Policies\Microsoft\Windows\Network Connections\ NC_NewConnectionWizard)

- **Enable status statistics for an active connection**, when set to Disabled, prevents users from viewing the Status page for an active connection. (HKCU\Software\Policies\Microsoft\Windows\Network Connections\NC_Statistics)

- **Enable the Dial-up Preferences item on the Advanced menu**, when set to Disabled, removes the Dial-up Preferences choice from the Advanced menu of Network and Dial-up Connections. This prevents users from creating or changing connections before logon and configuring AutoDialing and callback features. (HKCU\Software\Policies\Microsoft\Windows\Network Connections\ NC_DialupPrefs)

✦ **Enable the Advanced Settings item on the Advanced menu,** when set to Disabled, removes the Advanced Settings choice from the Advanced menu in Network and Dial-up Connections. This prevents users from viewing and changing bindings, the order in which connections occur, network providers, and print providers. (HKCU\Software\Policies\Microsoft\Windows\Network Connections\ NC_AdvancedSettings)

✦ **Allow configuration of connection sharing,** when set to Disabled, prevents users from configuring the Internet Connection Sharing feature of a dial-up connection. (HKCU\Software\Policies\Microsoft\Windows\Network Connections\ NC_ShowSharedAccessUI)

TIP: As recommended in the earlier "Computer Configuration Policies" section, always disable Internet Connection Sharing (ICS) for all computers in the domain. Disable the Allow Configuration of Connection Sharing policy under the Computer Configuration\Administrative Templates\Network\Network & Dial-up Connections node. Disabling this policy in User Configuration provides insurance against users accidentally or maliciously setting up ICS.

✦ **Allow TCP/IP advanced configuration,** when set to Disabled, prevents users from using Network and Dial-up Connections to configure TCP/IP, DNS, and WINS settings in the Advanced TCP/IP Settings Properties dialog. (HKCU\Software\Policies\ Microsoft\Windows\Network Connections\NC_AllowAdvancedTCPIPConfig)

System

Location: User Configuration\Administrative Templates\System

The user-based System node has many policies in common with the Computer Configuration\Administrative Templates\System node; common policies are identified by an asterisk (*) following the policy name. The System node has two subnodes (Logon/Logoff and Group Policy) and the following 10 policies:

✦ **Don't display welcome screen at logon*** hides the Getting Started with Windows 2000 dialog. (HKCU\Software\Microsoft\Windows\CurrentVersion\Policies\ Explorer\NoWelcomeScreen)

✦ **Century interpretation for Year 2000** lets you specify in a spin box the year that determines century rollback from 2000 to 1999 or vice-versa when dealing with two-digit year values. By default, the rollback year is 2029. In this case, 20 precedes two-digit year values less than 29, and 19 precedes values of 29 or greater.

(HKCU\Software\Policies\Microsoft\Control Panel\International\Calendars\
TwoDigitYearMax)

◆ **Code signing for device drivers** lets you select what occurs when a user attempts
to install device driver files that are not digitally signed. Choices are Ignore, Warn,
or Block. The default is Warn. (HKCU\Software\Policies\Microsoft\Windows NT\
Driver Signing)

◆ **Custom user interface** lets you specify an alternate executable file to replace
Windows Explorer as the shell for the user.
(HKCU\Software\Microsoft\Windows\CurrentVersion\Policies\System\Shell)

◆ **Disable the command prompt** prevents users from opening the Command window
and from running batch (.bat and .cmd) files, but doesn't prevent scripts that use
WSH from running.
(HKCU\Software\Policies\Microsoft\Windows\System\DisableCMD)

CAUTION: Don't enable this policy if the affected computers or users use startup, logon,
logoff, or shutdown scripts or run Terminal Services.

◆ **Disable registry editing tools** prevents users from running Regedit.exe and
Regedt32.exe to view and edit the Registry. (HKCU\Software\Microsoft\Windows\
CurrentVersion\Policies\System\DisableRegistryTools)

TIP: This is the most important user-based policy. Enable this policy for all ordinary users in
the domain. In almost all cases, only administrators, help desk personnel, and developers need
access to the Registry.

◆ **Run only allowed Windows applications** lets you create a List of Allowed Applications
by adding the name of allowed executable files, such as Excel.exe, Winword.exe, and
so on. This restriction applies only to applications launched by Explorer and doesn't
prevent users from running apps from the command prompt. (HKCU\Software\
Microsoft\Windows\CurrentVersion\Policies\Explorer\RestrictRun subkey)

NOTE: According to Microsoft Knowledge Base article Q263179, "'Run Only Allowed Applications' List in Organizational Group GPO Becomes Corrupted," adding long file names and creating a list that has 1,025 or more characters causes list corruption. Microsoft has a patch for the problem, but the fix isn't included in SP1.

✦ **Don't run specified Windows applications** is the opposite of the preceding policy. You add the names of embargoed executable files to the List of Disallowed Applications. This restriction applies only to applications launched by Explorer and doesn't prevent users from running disallowed apps from the command prompt. (HKCU\Software\Microsoft\Windows\CurrentVersion\Policies\Explorer\ DisallowRun subkey)

✦ **Disable Autoplay*** disables autostarting of CD-ROM setup programs and opening of CD Player or Windows Media Player when inserting an audio CD. You have the option of disabling CD-ROM drives or all drives. (HKCU\Software\Microsoft\Windows\ CurrentVersion\Policies\Explorer\NoDriveTypeAutoRun)

✦ **Download missing COM components*** enables the computer to search AD's Class Store for missing Component Object Model (COM and COM+) components required by an application. (HKCU\Software\Policies\Microsoft\Windows\App Management\ COMClassStore)

Logon/Logoff

Location: User Configuration\Administrative Templates\System\Logon/Logoff

The Logon/Logoff subnode shares some policies with those under the Computer Configuration\Administrative Templates\System\Logon/Logoff node. An asterisk (*) following the policy name identifies common policies. Following are the 14 Logon/Logoff policies:

✦ **Disable Task Manager** prevents users from running Taskman.exe. (HKCU\Software\Microsoft\Windows\CurrentVersion\Policies\System\DisableTaskMgr)

✦ **Disable Lock Computer** prevents users from locking the system by pressing CTRL+ALT+DEL and selecting Lock Computer. (HKCU\Software\Microsoft\Windows\ CurrentVersion\Policies\System\DisableLockWorkstation)

✦ **Disable Change Password** prevents users from changing passwords unless prompted to do so by the system. (HKCU\Software\Microsoft\Windows\CurrentVersion\ Policies\System\DisableChangePassword)

✦ **Disable Logoff** prevents users from logging off the network. (HKCU\Software\ Microsoft\Windows\CurrentVersion\Policies\Explorer\NoLogoff)

✦ **Run logon scripts synchronously*** causes logon script processing to complete before the user's desktop configuration appears. Long-running logon scripts delay the user's ability to start work. (HKCU\Software\Microsoft\Windows\CurrentVersion\ Policies\System\RunLogonScriptSync)

✦ **Run legacy logon scripts hidden** doesn't display the Command window when running Windows NT–type logon scripts. (HKCU\Software\Microsoft\Windows\ CurrentVersion\Policies\System\HideLegacyLogonScripts)

✦ **Run logon scripts visible** displays all logon scripts in the Command window. (HKCU\Software\Microsoft\Windows\CurrentVersion\Policies\System\HideLogonScripts)

✦ **Run logoff scripts visible** displays all logoff scripts in the Command window. (HKCU\Software\Microsoft\Windows\CurrentVersion\Policies\System\HideLogoffScripts)

✦ **Connect home directory to root of the share** causes the %HOMESHARE% and %HOMEPATH% environment variables to point to the network locations used by Windows NT 4.0. Disabling or not configuring this policy permits use of the full UNC path to folders under the shared folder. (HKCU\Software\Microsoft\Windows\ CurrentVersion\Policies\System\ConnectHomeDirToRoot)

✦ **Limit profile size** lets you specify the maximum size of a roaming user profile and the message that appears when a roaming user profile reaches the maximum size. You also can set the interval between reminders to the user. If enabled, the default maximum size is 30 MB; if disabled or not configured, the profile size is unlimited or is limited by server disk quotas. (HKCU\Software\Microsoft\Windows\CurrentVersion\ Policies\System\EnableProfileQuota)

✦ **Exclude directories in roaming profile** lets you exclude folders that normally are included in the user's profile by typing a semicolon-separated list of folders. The History, Local Settings, Temp, and Temporary Internet Files folders are excluded by default. Excluded folders aren't stored on the network server and don't follow users to other computers. (HKCU\Software\Policies\Microsoft\Windows\System\ ExcludeProfileDirs)

✦ **Run these programs at user logon*** lets administrators type a list of applications to run or documents to open when any user logs on. If configured for both computers and users, the computer setting applies. To add a program to run or document to open, choose the Enabled option, click the Show button to open the Show Contents dialog, click Add to open the Add Item dialog, type the well-formed path or UNC path to the file, and click OK to add the item to the Show Contents list. (HKCU\Software\Microsoft\Windows\CurrentVersion\Policies\Explorer\Run subkey)

✦ **Disable the run once list*** ignores a customized run-once list that executes one or more programs the next time the computer boots, but not thereafter. If configured for both computers and users, the computer setting applies. (HKCU\Software\Microsoft\Windows\CurrentVersion\Policies\Explorer\DisableLocalMachineRunOnce)

✦ **Disable legacy run list*** ignores the Windows NT 4.0 equivalent of the Run These Programs at User Logon policy's list. If configured for both computers and users, the computer setting applies. (HKCU\Software\Microsoft\Windows\CurrentVersion\Policies\Explorer\DisableLocalMachineRun)

Group Policy

Location: User Configuration\Administrative Templates\System\Group Policy

The last four of the following six policies of this subnode apply to administrators setting Group Policies:

✦ **Group Policy refresh interval for users** lets you set the frequency of Group Policy updates while the user is logged on. The default rate for updates is every 90 minutes, with a random offset of 0 to 30 minutes. You can set the maximum interval to 64,800 minutes (45 years) or 0 minutes; setting 0 results in a refresh interval of 7 seconds. The randomizing time interval can be set from 0 to 1,440 minutes (24 hours). (HKCU\Software\Policies\Microsoft\Windows\System\GroupPolicyRefreshTime and \GroupPolicyRefreshTimeOffset)

✦ **Group Policy slow link detection** lets you define a slow connection for purposes of applying and updating Group Policy for the user. The default defines less than 500 kbps as a slow connection. (HKCU\Software\Policies\Microsoft\Windows\System\GroupPolicyMinTransferRate)

✦ **Group Policy domain controller selection**, when enabled, lets you select which domain controller is used by the Group Policy Editor (GPE). The choices are Use the Primary Domain Controller, Inherit from the Active Directory Snap-ins, or Use Any Available Domain Controller. The DC performing the PDC Emulator FSMO role is the default. (HKCU\Software\Policies\Microsoft\Windows\Group Policy Editor\DCOption)

✦ **Create new Group Policy object links disabled by default** creates all new Group Policy object links in the disabled state, so they aren't applied to users until you enable them. The purpose of this policy is to let you configure multiple policies and then apply them to users after all policies are configured. (HKCU\Software\Policies\ Microsoft\Windows\Group Policy Editor\NewGPOLinksDisabled)

✦ **Enforce Show Policies Only** prevents administrators from viewing or using Group Policy preferences. Preferences are policies, such as Windows NT System Policies, that affect Registry entries other than those specified in Windows 2000 .adm files. (HKCU\Software\Policies\Microsoft\Windows\Group Policy Editor\ ShowPoliciesOnly)

✦ **Disable automatic update of ADM files** prevents Administrative Templates source (.adm) files from being updated automatically when you open the GPE. This policy is of interest only if you make custom modifications to .adm files. (HKCU\Software\ Policies\Microsoft\Windows\Group Policy Editor\DisableAutoADMUpdate)

Appendix B

Using the GroupPol Application to Create Active Directory Objects

M any of the examples in this book use GroupPol.exe (GroupPol), a compiled Visual Basic 6.0 application, to generate sample user and computer accounts in one or two Windows 2000 or Windows NT 4.0 domains. You can download the GroupPol Microsoft Installer file (GroupPol.msi, 4.4 MB) for Windows 2000 Server and a conventional Visual Basic Setup.exe installation program with setup files (GPSetup.zip, 12 MB) for Windows NT 4.0 SP4+ from the Admin911 Web site at http://www.admin911.com.

Understanding the Role of the GroupPol Application

Windows 2000 user and computer accounts created by GroupPol are contained within a hierarchical OU structure that's specifically designed for creation and testing of multiple Group Policy scenarios. The three first-level OUs are Faculty Members, Non-Faculty Staff, and Students when you specify a single domain. Each first-level OU has sub-OUs for academic department, staff function, and school year, respectively. GroupPol also creates sets of Security Groups that you can use to filter Group Policy Objects (GPOs) by user title, such as Professor or Teaching Assistant for faculty and Manager or Department Head for staff. Student groups are based on academic major subject. Chapter 3 and Chapter 4 describe GroupPol's OU and Security Group structure.

Most Windows 2000 Server–related books rely on domain examples with one or two sample OUs and a few Security Groups with a couple of users each. That's understandable, because manually adding a bunch of AD containers and populating them with members is downright tedious. If you don't have ready access to a large-scale Windows NT test network with multiple domains and hundreds or thousands of users that you can use to emulate in-place upgrades or domain restructure, GroupPol is a great time-saver. For instance, GroupPol running under Windows 2000 lets you automatically create a total of 93 new OUs and Security Groups in about 20 seconds; each OU has a shared folder, which is published in AD and contains a sample text file.

With moderate-speed hardware, you can add Windows 2000 user and optional computer accounts to the OUs at a rate of two or more per second. The GroupPol.mdb database contains records for 2,275 employee accounts and 25,344 student accounts. (Any resemblance between GroupPol's fictional user names and names of real persons, living or dead, is purely coincidental, by the way.) User accounts sport a complete set of common Active Directory attribute values—first and last names, title, address, telephone number, and so on—and optional home directory, local U: drive mapping to a home folder, user profile location, and logon script for downlevel (NetBIOS) clients. Each user automatically becomes a member of the Security Groups for his or her OU and rank in the organization's hierarchy. You can't run real-world tests on many AD features, such as LDAP filters, without a *lot* of users, an appropriate set of Security Groups, and many attribute values on which to base the filter.

NOTE: If you're interested in uncovering performance issues with the current version of Active Directory Users and Computers, try adding 10,000 or more student computer accounts to the Students, Computers OU. Because of performance problems with large numbers of objects in a container, Active Directory Users and Computers by default displays a maximum of 2,000 objects. To increase the maximum number of objects displayed, click the Set Filter Options button and type **10000** (or more) in the Maximum Number of Items Displayed per Folder text box.

GroupPol uses Active Directory Service Interfaces (ADSI) 2.5 to create and manipulate AD objects via the Lightweight Directory Access Protocol (LDAP). If you're an accomplished VBScript programmer and have a lot of spare time, you can write ADSI-based scripts to add OUs and Security Groups and then write more scripts to add user and computer accounts. For examples of VBScript code for cloning AD objects, check out the Clone*.vbs files of the Windows 2000 Support Tools. Gaining a firm grasp of ADSI syntax isn't easy, and you should count on five hours of debugging for each hour of script coding. Before taking the plunge into LDAP scripting, download the latest version of the ADSI SDK from http://www.microsoft.com/windows2000/library/howitworks/activedirectory/adsilinks.asp.

Running GroupPol under Windows NT 4.0 Server (SP4+) lets you create local and global groups and generate user and computer accounts in Windows NT domains. The Windows NT security group structure that GroupPol sets up lets you take advantage of Microsoft's Active Directory Migration Tool (ADMT) to copy or move user accounts to AD OUs based on group membership. If you have only a single test server, you can run an in-place Windows 2000 Server upgrade on a single Windows NT domain. You use security group membership to assign members to OUs you add to AD. Your Windows NT user accounts have all available property values populated, including options to specify home directories, user profiles, and logon scripts. Most of the property values migrate to AD attribute values during cloning or in-place upgrade operations.

If you have access to a production Windows NT domain structure, you can clone (copy) your existing security groups and user and computer accounts to Windows 2000's AD with ADMT. Cloning live Windows NT objects for a test domain requires you or the network admin to connect your test servers to the production network. A common response to such a proposal is: "When pigs fly" (or worse). To overcome this reluctance, run GroupPol to emulate a production Windows NT network on an isolated test PDC. Then use ADMT to demonstrate to doubters that cloning doesn't eat production NT objects, because ADMT simply clones Windows NT group and account objects to AD. Appendix C describes production-safe object cloning methods.

GroupPol removes all traces of the objects it adds, except the Member Servers OU, when you no longer need the program. The Remove All feature deletes only those objects added by GroupPol, including added shared folders and test files. The parent shared folders you add aren't removed.

Running GroupPol Under Windows 2000

You need at least one test machine running Windows 2000 Server that's configured (or configurable) as a DC to run GroupPol. You also can run GroupPol from a Windows 2000 Professional client that's a member of the test DC's domain. If you run GroupPol on a client, install the Administrative Tools (Adminpak.msi) so you run Active Directory Users and Computers from the client. Alternatively, install Terminal Services in Administrative mode and add the Terminal Services client to your workstation.

TIP: Running GroupPol on a domain client lets you log on to the DC with a user account created by GroupPol to test account properties. You also get a performance boost, because GroupPol isn't competing with AD for server resources when adding new users. Unless you change Domain Controller Security Policies, users aren't permitted to log on interactively to a DC.

GroupPol running under Windows 2000 consumes about 5 MB of disk space, usually in the *d*:\Program Files\GroupPol folder. You must have Administrators privileges for the machines on which you install GroupPol, and Enterprise or Domain Admins privileges to run GroupPol. Running GroupPol under Windows 2000 with two domains requires membership in the Enterprise Admins group.

CAUTION: GroupPol throws a fatal error when you attempt to add new user accounts to a Windows 2000 or NT domain whose security policy doesn't permit zero-length passwords. If the policy requires complex passwords, users get empty passwords, and adding user accounts slows dramatically.

Installing GroupPol on a Server or Workstation

Installing GroupPol creates a *d*:\Program Files\GroupPol folder to contain GroupPol.exe and its support files, plus Read1st.rtf and ReadGP.doc (user documentation). The installer also adds a GroupPol icon to your Start menu and an icon to the desktop.

Here's the drill for installing GroupPol on either a workstation or a server:

1. If you haven't run Dcpromo.exe on your test server to promote it to a DC, do so now. Unless you have a good reason to do otherwise, specify **oakmont.edu** as the domain name and **OAKMONTU** as the downlevel (NetBIOS) name. Install AD-integrated DNS during the AD upgrade and accept the remaining default values in the Active Directory Installation Wizard's dialog.

TIP: Using GroupPol's default domain names makes setup easier. If your test server already is a DC and you don't need to retain the existing test domain, run Dcpromo.exe to demote the server, change the server's name to oakmont-dc1, and then run the Wizard again to create a new initial root domain with Active Directory–integrated DNS. Re-creating the domain also ensures a clean AD installation.

2. If you intend to run GroupPol from a workstation that's not a member of the test domain, use the workstation's System Properties dialog to join the new test DC's domain. Log on as a member of the Domain or Enterprise Admins group of the test domain.

3. Download GroupPol.msi, a standard Microsoft Installer file (about 4.5 MB), from http://www.admin911.com to a temporary folder on the DC or workstation.

4. Double-click GroupPol.msi's icon to start the installation process, which closely resembles that for installing the Administrative Tools (Adminpak.msi). Figure B-1 shows the installer's opening dialog.

5. Accept the installation defaults by clicking Next. The next-to-last installation dialog displays the ReadMe file (Read1st.rtf), which includes the license agreement for use of the GroupPol program (see Figure B-2). Read the license agreement and any last-minute information about installation and use of the software. Click Next and Close to complete the installation.

Figure B-1.   The splash screen starts the GroupPol installation process.

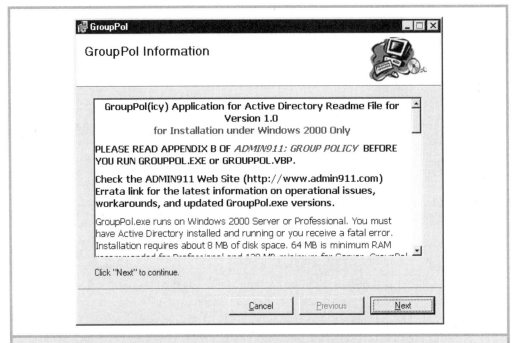

Figure B-2. Review late-breaking updates to Group Pol installation and brief operating instructions in the GroupPol Information dialog.

Running GroupPol for the First Time

GroupPol requires you to create one or two parent shared folders before you execute GroupPol.exe the first time. If you intend to use only a single domain, one shared folder on the DC, typically named and shared as Oakmont, holds the Faculty, Staff, and Students folders that GroupPol creates on startup. If you have a separate child domain for student accounts (typically students.oakmont.edu), create a Students folder and share on the child domain's DC. Initially, assign the Everyone group Full Control privileges on the folders and shares. If you've installed GroupPol on a Windows 2000 Professional client, verify access to the shares before proceeding.

TIP: If you intend to use logon scripts for Windows NT and 9x clients, the shares must reside on the PDC emulator DC of the domain. You use Group Policy to specify logon scripts for Windows 2000 clients.

After creating the shares, do the following to set up and run GroupPol for the first time:

1. On the DC, choose Programs | Administrative Tools | Domain Security Policy to open the snap-in. Navigate to Windows Settings\ Security Settings and click Account Policies.

2. If the Minimum Password Length policy's setting is greater than 0 characters, double-click the entry in the Policy pane to open the Security Policy Setting dialog and change the value in the spin box to 0.

3. If the Password Must Meet Complexity Requirements policy is set to Enabled, double-click the entry and select the Disabled option in the dialog.

4. If you made a change in step 2 or 3, at the command prompt run **secedit/ refreshpolicy machine_policy/enforce** to make the policy changes effective immediately. If you're running GroupPol from a workstation, run the same secedit command on the workstation.

5. Click the Admin911 GroupPol desktop shortcut or choose Start, Admin911 GroupPol to open the startup dialog.

6. Edit the employee and student domain names and UNC share names to correspond to your domain structure. The defaults are oakmont.edu and \\OAKMONT-DC1\Oakmont, respectively, for both domains (see Figure B-3).

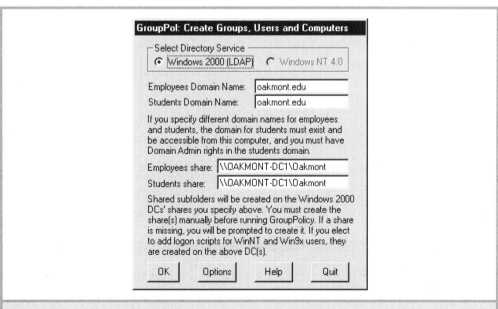

Figure B-3.   Specify domain names and UNC paths to required shared folders in the startup dialog.

7. Click the Options button to open the Options dialog (see Figure B-4). Mark the check boxes for the options you want. The default set of options is a good starting point for most of the examples in this book. If you add home directory paths for employees, which enables adding a user profile path, acknowledge the explanatory message. Adding logon scripts for Windows NT and 9x users requires at least Modify permissions for the DC's Netlogon share.

NOTE: Unlike domain and share names, option settings don't persist between GroupPol sessions. If you specify nondefault options, the next time you start GroupPol, be sure to reset the option values before clicking the OK button of the startup dialog.

8. Click OK to close the Options dialog and click OK in the startup dialog to open the main GroupPol form. If GroupPol can't connect to the shares, you receive a warning message, and the program exits. If the shares and your domain credentials are okay,

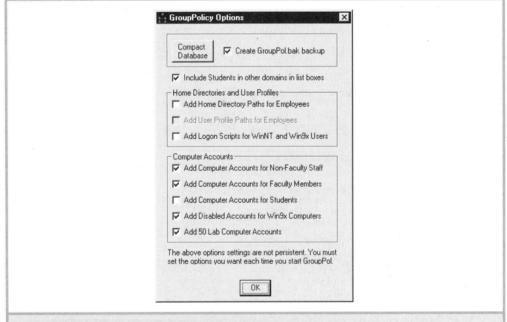

Figure B-4. Set options for user and computer accounts in the Options dialog. The default settings omit adding home employee directory paths and logon scripts and don't add accounts for student computers.

Windows Installer runs for a few seconds before the GroupPol form opens for the first time. Your current set of Security Groups and OUs appear in the upper-left Groups list box, and user accounts appear in the upper-right Users list box. Each list entry shows the full LDAP path to the AD object.

9. Click the Administrators item in the Groups list to display Security Group members and click the Administrator item in the Users list to show the user's Security Group and OU membership (see Figure B-5).

10. Click the Add OUs and Groups button to add the 93 GroupPol containers and, if specified in the Options dialog, 50 lab computers administered by the Computer Science department. Click the LDAP://OU=Lab Computers,DC=Oakmont,DC=edu OU entry to display the 50 serially numbered computer accounts in the lower-left list box.

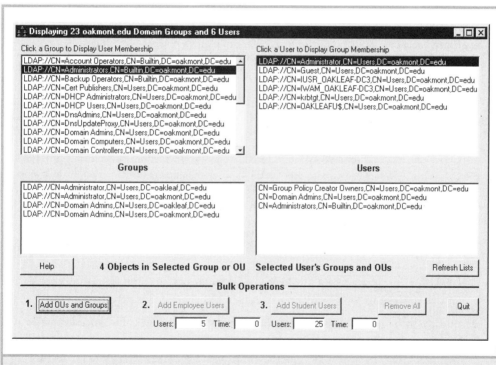

Figure B-5. Clicking a group or OU item in the Groups list displays the container's membership. Similarly, clicking a user item in the User list shows the Security Groups and OUs to which the user belongs.

11. Launch My Network Places, navigate to the shares you created, and verify presence of the Faculty, Staff, and Students folders and their subfolders. Each folder and subfolder is published in AD and contains a text file related to the folder name.

12. If you want to verify the ability of GroupPol to remove the AD objects it creates, click Remove All and then repeat step 6.

TIP: Use GroupPol to learn LDAP object naming syntax. GroupPol displays the full LDAP path of the Distinguished Name (DN) for every AD object it creates, as well as the default AD objects created by running Dcpromo. Applying LDAP filters to many object classes, such as Security Groups, requires you to specify the full LDAP path (without the LDAP:// prefix) of the container.

Adding Employee and Student User and Computer Accounts

As mentioned earlier, you can add up to 2,275 employee accounts, which consist of 1,648 faculty and 627 staff members, and 25,344 student accounts. The more user accounts you add, the longer it takes to fill the main form's list boxes on startup.

TIP: If you specify logon scripts for Windows NT and 9x clients, logon scripts are created in the Netlogon share when you click OK in the startup dialog; the logon script names are LogonWinNT.bat and LogonWin9x.bat, respectively. If you want to alter the contents of the logon scripts, do it before adding user accounts. Client computers are assigned the following operating system types by a pseudo-random pattern: Windows 2000 Professional, Windows NT 4.0 Workstation, Windows 95, Windows 95 OSR2, Windows 98, and Windows 98 SE.

To add user and computer accounts and verify account attributes in Active Directory Users and Computers, do this:

1. Click Add Employee Users to add five faculty and staff accounts and then click Add Student Users to add 25 student accounts to test user account creation.

2. In the Groups and OUs list box, scroll to and click the Political Science department OU to display objects in the OU.

3. Click the John Kinunen item to automatically search the Users list for his entry and display his group membership.

4. Double-click the selected item in the Users list to display user account attribute values in the Selected User's Account Attributes list (see Figure B-6). At this point, each user account has values for 25 attributes.

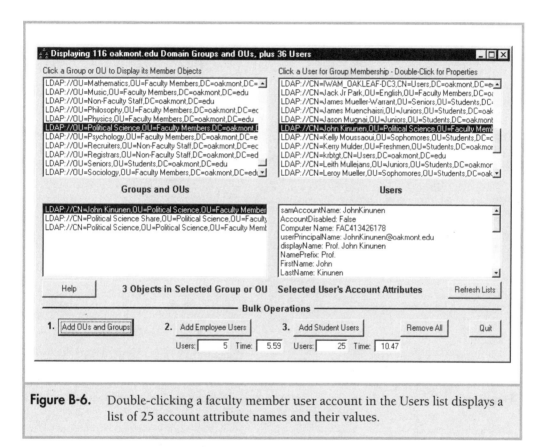

Figure B-6.   Double-clicking a faculty member user account in the Users list displays a list of 25 account attribute names and their values.

5. Launch Active Directory Users and Computers, expand the Faculty Members OU, click the Political Science node, and double-click the John Kinunen item to open the General page of the John Kinunen Properties dialog (see Figure B-7). GroupPol sets all attribute values on this page. John Kinunen is an Adjunct Professor, so he doesn't have an on-campus office.

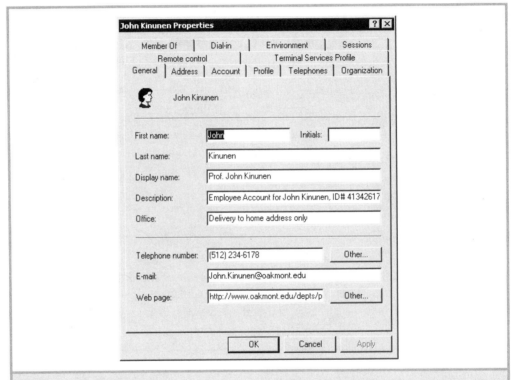

Figure B-7. The General page of the Properties dialog for a user account displays eight attribute values populated by GroupPol.

6. Click the Account tab to display logon attributes and account options (see Figure B-8). AD generates the Windows 2000 and downlevel logon IDs. The default password is "password" for Windows 2000 clients. If you don't disable the complex password requirement, you must log on with an empty password and change it to a complex password during the logon process.

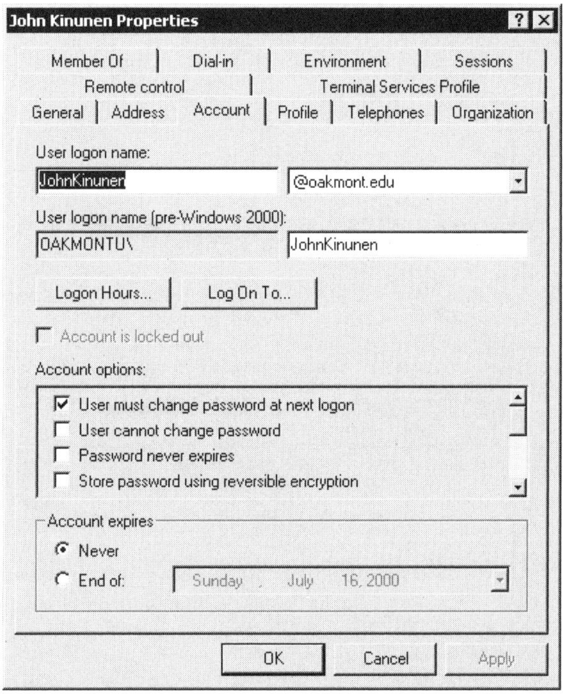

Figure B-8. The Account page displays logon information for the user. Depending on how the user logs on, a default password ("password") or empty password is required.

7. Click the Member Of tab to display the Security Group membership of the user (see Figure B-9). All users added by GroupPol are members of three groups: the default Domain Users group, a Global academic department group, and a Global group based on academic pecking order (Deans, Department Chairs, Professors, Lecturers, and Teaching Assistants). The Domain Local Faculty Members group contains the academic department groups. The title-based group is required for Group Policy filtering and for assigning permissions to shared folders.

8. Click the Organization tab to display the user's Title, Department, and Company attribute values added by GroupPol (see Figure B-10). GroupPol also can add Manager Name and Direct Reports attribute values for faculty users, but you must add all 2,275 employee accounts before you see the option to add these values.

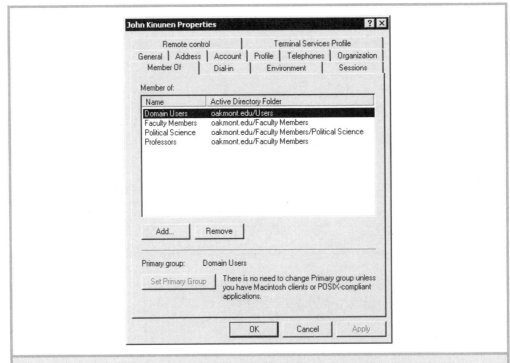

Figure B-9. GroupPol assigns employees to three Security Groups; a typical Faculty Member account is shown here. Staff accounts are assigned to the Non-Faculty Staff Domain Local group and the Global staff division and title groups.

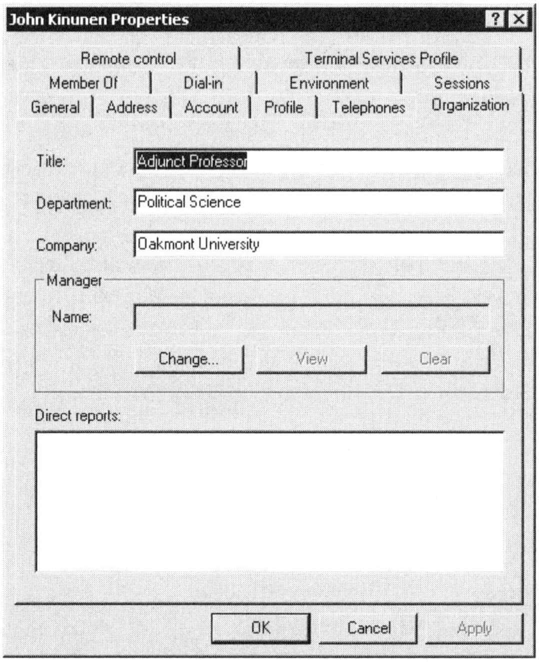

Figure B-10.   GroupPol adds organization-based attributes to all user accounts. Title is an important attribute value for sorting and searching. The Department value is independent of OU membership, but GroupPol sets this value to the name of the user's OU.

User accounts for members of the Non-Faculty Staff departments have similar attribute values. In Active Directory Users and Computers, expand the Non-Faculty Staff OU, click the Executive Staff OU, and then click a user account to display the *UserName* Properties dialog. Staff members don't have Web Page attribute values.

When you manually add new Windows 2000 or NT computers to your Windows 2000 network, the required computer accounts fall into the default Computers container and are members of the Domain Computers Security Group. To avoid ending up with thousands of computers in the Computer container, it's a better practice to add computer accounts to OUs. Creating OUs to hold different classes of computer accounts lets you apply Group Policies to each computer class. GroupPol adds computer accounts to the Computers sub-OU of Faculty Members, Non-Faculty Staff, and Students, if you specify the Add

Computer Accounts for Students option. GroupPol associates each computer account with a user account and adds a description that you can use to filter computer accounts by department (see Figure B-11). GroupPol populates Operating System attribute values (Name, Version, and Service Pack); these values are overwritten when the user's Windows 2000 or NT computer joins the network. GroupPol classifies Faculty Members computer accounts by two Security Groups: Network Computers and Remote Computers.

TIP: To see the User Principal Name (UPN) associated with the computer account, double-click a security group, click the Members tab, and click the Add button to open the Select Users, Contacts, or Computers dialog. Scroll to the employee computer accounts, which display the UPN in parentheses. This attribute value doesn't appear on the property pages for the computer account or elsewhere in Active Directory Users and Computers.

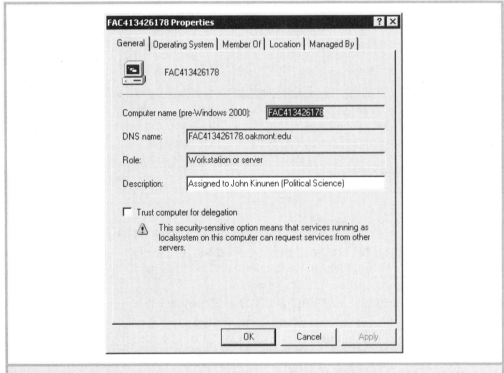

Figure B-11. If you accept the default Add Computer Accounts for Non-Faculty Staff and Faculty Members and Add Disabled Accounts for Win9x Computers options, every employee gets a computer account having DNS Name and Description attribute values.

After you add all 2,275 employee accounts, you have the option of adding to the computer account a Managed By attribute value, which points to a member of the Non-Faculty Staff, Information Technology, Helpdesk Technicians group.

NOTE: Microsoft recommends that membership of Security Groups be limited to "a few thousand users." The actual limit is 5,000 accounts. The reason for this limit becomes evident when you click the Members tab of the Domain Computers group in a large domain with a "few thousand" computer accounts; it can take a minute or longer to open the Members page. Apparently, Microsoft is counting on a client population with a relatively small percentage of Windows 2000 and NT users in the current incarnation of Active Directory Users and Computers.

Add as many more employee users as you want by typing the number of users to add in the text box below the Add Employee Users button and clicking the button. The process for adding student users is similar. When you add all employee users, a message box opens with the option to add Reports To and Direct Reports attribute values to faculty accounts. Adding these attribute values with GroupPol takes advantage of ADSI 2.5's LDAP- and SQL-based query syntax, but is a relatively slow process. You can add the previously mentioned Managed By attribute for employee computer accounts.

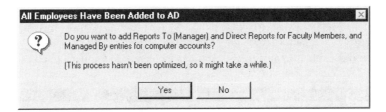

Running GroupPol Under Windows NT 4.0

A conventional Visual Basic 6.0 setup program installs GroupPol under Windows NT Workstation or Server 4.0 with SP 4+. GroupPol's default Windows NT 4.0 domain name is OAKMONT, which permits running the Windows NT and 2000 versions of GroupPol on the same network. When running GroupPol under Windows NT, you have the option of using LDAP to add AD objects to one or two existing Windows 2000 domains, or using the WinNT ADSI provider to add Windows NT objects to an existing Windows NT domain. You must be logged on to the domain with Administrator credentials to install GroupPol.

Before running Setup.exe for GroupPol under Windows NT, you must install the ADSI 2.5 components by running Ads_nt.exe, which also registers the components. Windows 2000 installs Microsoft Data Access Components (MDAC) 2.5 during the setup process, but MDAC isn't a standard element of Windows NT 4.0. Thus, GroupPol setup also adds MDAC 2.5 (build 2.50.4403.12) components to your system, if they aren't already present. The extra component overhead causes the Windows NT version of GroupPol to require about 10 MB of free disk space.

NOTE: If you have MDAC 2.5 or later installed on your Windows NT machine, the MDAC 2.5 components don't overwrite the currently installed MDAC version. For more information on MDAC 2.5, go to http://www.microsoft.com/data/. If you want to verify the version of MDAC on your test computer, download and expand Microsoft's Component Checker tool (cc.exe). The reason you can't run GroupPol under Windows 9x is because Microsoft doesn't provide an ADSI 2.5 installer for these operating systems.

Installing GroupPol on a Windows NT Machine

To obtain and set up GroupPol under Windows NT 4.0 Server or Workstation, do the following:

1. Download GPSetup.zip from the Admin911 Web site at http://www.admin911.com/grouppol.asp to a temporary folder.

2. Expand GPSetup.zip into the temporary folder. GPSetup.zip includes the following files: Setup.exe, Setup.lst, GroupPol.cab, Ads_nt.exe, and Read1st.txt

3. Double-click Ads_nt.exe to display the Active Directory Service Interfaces 2.5 message and click OK to open the End User License Agreement (EULA) dialog.

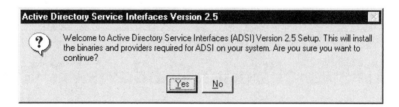

4. Click Yes to extract and install the ADSI 2.5 components and then acknowledge the message indicating that installation is complete.

CAUTION: If you don't run Ads_nt.exe before running Setup.exe, GroupPol crashes with a runtime error.

5. Double-click Setup.exe to begin the installation process. If you receive an out-of-date files message, click OK to install the files, click OK when requested to reboot the computer, and run Setup.exe again.

6. Click OK in the first Admin911:GroupPol for Windows NT Setup dialog.

7. If you're satisfied with the location of the GroupPol program files, click the large button. Otherwise, click Change Directory and choose another folder.

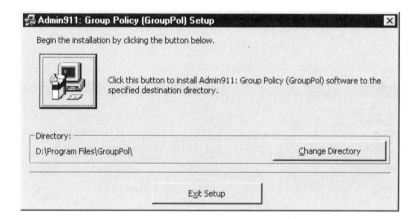

8. After Setup copies the files to the designated application folder, click OK to close the "completed successfully" message box.

Running GroupPol for the First Time under Windows NT

GroupPol requires you to create one or two parent shared folders before you execute GroupPol.exe for the first time. If you intend to use only a single domain, one shared folder on the server (typically named and shared as Oakmont) holds the Faculty, Staff, and Students folders that GroupPol creates on startup. If you have a separate domain for student accounts (typically STUDENTS), create a Students folder and share on a server in the STUDENTS domain. Initially, accept the default Everyone group's Full Control privileges on the folders and shares. If you've installed GroupPol on a Windows NT 4.0 Workstation client, log on as Administrator of the test domain and verify access to the shares before proceeding.

After creating the shares, do the following to run GroupPol.exe the first time:

1. Choose Programs | Group Policy to open the startup dialog, which defaults to the ADSI LDAP provider with server-specific binding to a Windows 2000 DC. (Running GroupPol under Windows 2000 uses serverless binding, which automatically connects to the first DC in a site.)

2. If you already have a Windows 2000 test domain accessible from your Windows NT server or workstation and have added the required shares, edit the domain names and UNC shares text boxes. You must enter Domain or Enterprise Admins logon credentials for the Windows 2000 domains to use server-specific binding (see Figure B-12). Otherwise, select the Windows NT option and skip to step 4.

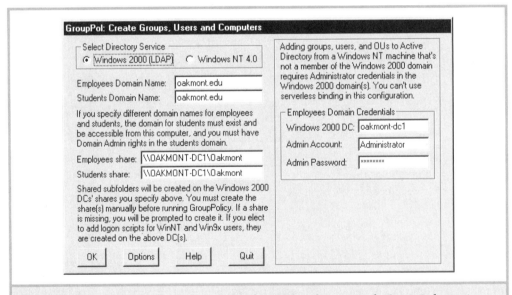

Figure B-12. Adding AD objects to a Windows 2000 domain with GroupPol running under Windows NT 4.0 requires server-specific binding and Domain Admins or better credentials for the destination domains.

3. Clicking OK with the LDAP option selected opens GroupPol's main form and displays AD objects in the specified domain. The full LDAP path to server-specific bound objects includes the name of the DC, as shown in Figure B-13. Click Quit and restart GroupPol if you want to create Windows NT objects.

CAUTION: Don't attempt to add user and computer accounts to a Windows 2000 domain that you created with GroupPol running on another machine. You receive a duplicate account warning and must exit the program.

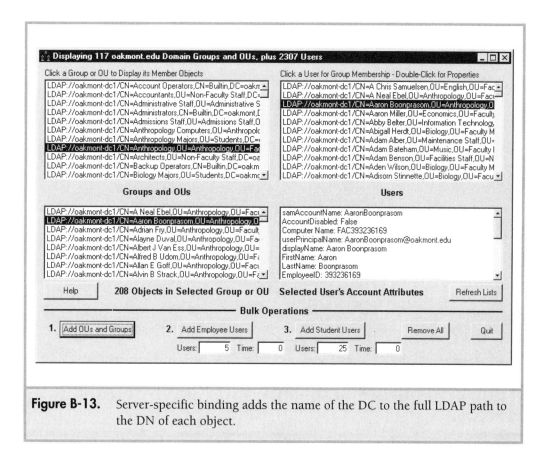

Figure B-13. Server-specific binding adds the name of the DC to the full LDAP path to the DN of each object.

4. Select the Windows NT option and accept or edit the default NetBIOS domain names and UNC share paths (see Figure B-14).

5. Click Options to display the Options dialog for user and computer accounts, which are identical to those for Windows 2000 (refer to Figure B-4). After setting the options you want, click OK to return to the startup dialog.

TIP: If you want to add logon scripts for Windows NT and 9x users, add the Administrators group to the Access Through Share Permissions dialog's list for the folder of the Netlogon share, *d*:\Winnt\Winnt32\Repl\Import\Scripts. Give the group Full Control permissions on the share. If Administrators don't have at least Change permissions on the share, you receive a message that you can't add logon script files for users.

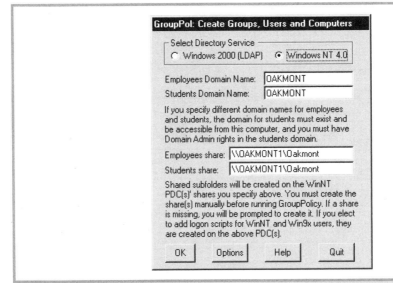

Figure B-14. GroupPol's Windows NT 4.0 option requires you to log on as Administrator in the Employees domain. If you specify a different Students domain, the startup dialog expands to let you add your Administrator credentials in the second domain.

6. Click OK to open GroupPol's main form with the domain's current Windows 2000 groups and users displayed. The WinNT ADSI provider substitutes WinNT://*DOMAINNAME* for LDAP://*DCName*.

7. Click Administrators in the Groups list to display user membership in the lower-left list box.

8. Click Administrator in the Users list to display group membership for the account (see Figure B-15). Displaying group membership with the WinNT ADSI provider is slower than for Windows 2000, because the code must iterate all user accounts to test group membership.

GroupPol with the WinNT provider lets you add or delete groups and users manually, a feature that isn't available when you use the LDAP provider.

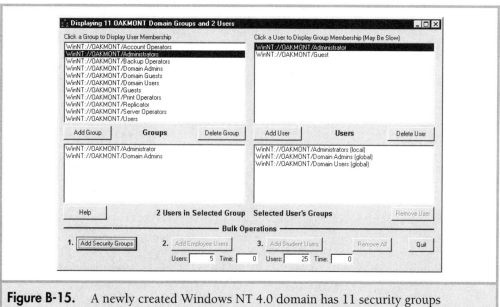

Figure B-15.   A newly created Windows NT 4.0 domain has 11 security groups and two users.

Adding Windows NT User and Computer Accounts

To add user and computer accounts and verify account attributes in User Manager and Server manager, do the following:

1. Click Add Employee Users to add five faculty and staff accounts and then click Add Student Users to add 25 student accounts to test user and computer account creation. Windows NT user accounts have "password" as the default password and don't require users to change their accounts during the first logon.

2. If you want to compare the performance of GroupPol running the WinNT and LDAP providers, add the same number of accounts as for your Windows 2000 domain (see Figure B-16).

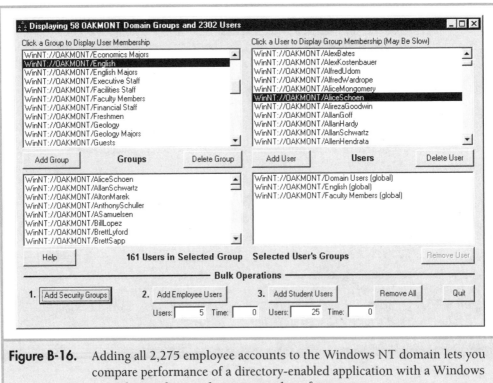

Figure B-16. Adding all 2,275 employee accounts to the Windows NT domain lets you compare performance of a directory-enabled application with a Windows 2000 domain having the same number of users.

NOTE: WinNT list boxes load about 15 times faster than LDAP when running GroupPol on a workstation in a 100BaseT network. The longer LDAP paths generate more network traffic, but more bytes on the wire don't explain the substantial difference in performance between Windows NT's SAM database and AD. Windows NT user and computer accounts are added at least twice as fast as Windows 2000 user and computer accounts.

3. Launch User Manager to display the Description property values for users and groups (see Figure B-17). When you clone or upgrade a Windows NT domain to Windows 2000, you can filter on User Description values to assign users to OUs and Security Groups.

4. If you specified home directories, profile paths, and logon scripts for Windows NT and 9x clients in the Options dialog, double-click an employee user account in User

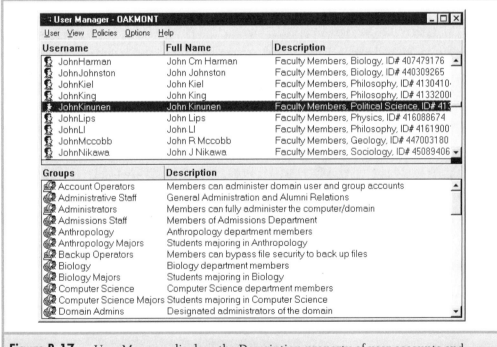

Figure B-17. User Manager displays the Description property of user accounts and security groups.

Manager and click Profile to open the User Environment Profile dialog. Figure B-18 illustrates User Profile Path, Logon Script Name, and Home Directory property values added by GroupPol. The %username% variable changes to the users logon ID and creates the home directory folder when you close the dialog. (Windows 2000 doesn't create the directory until the new user logs on.) The home folder path is intended for testing conversion to Windows 2000 only; it isn't valid on a Windows NT machine.

5. Open Server Manager to display the 50 lab computer accounts added during the Add Groups process, plus the employee computers corresponding to user accounts. Unlike with Windows 2000 computer accounts, the Description column is empty, and all accounts are disabled until the user logs on from the designated Windows NT or 2000 computer.

NOTE: You can't set the Description property value of a Windows NT Computer object with ADSI code. Descriptions you type in Server Manager's *ComputerName* Properties dialog don't propagate to Windows 2000 Computer objects during in-place upgrading or when cloning computer accounts with ADMT. You can set Division and Owner property values with ADSI code, but you can't read the values in the UI. Microsoft provides no explanation for these oddities.

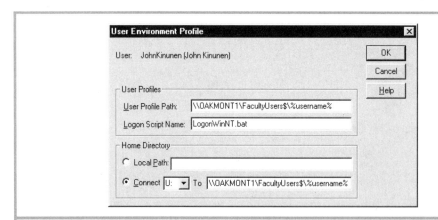

Figure B-18. Specifying home directory, profile path, and logon script options for employee users adds property values to the User Environment Profile.

Testing GroupPol User and Computer Accounts

After you've added a few user and computer accounts, it's a good practice to verify correct behavior of logons with the server and client operating systems in use before applying Group Policies. Because of the method GroupPol uses to assign operating system types to client computers, you must add 50 or more employee users to obtain one Faculty Member computer account for each of the supported operating systems. Table B-1 lists the logon ID and computer name for each supported client operating system.

Following are pointers for testing GroupPol user logons and precreated computer accounts:

✦ **Windows 2000 Professional computer accounts** To test behavior of Windows 2000 clients connecting to the network with precreated computer accounts in an OU, on the System Properties dialog's Network Identification page, demote the workstation to a member of a temporary workgroup. After rebooting, change the computer name to a valid Windows 2000 account, such as FAC455423293, and try to use the associated user account (RReynolds, password) to add the computer to the domain. If joining the domain fails, use your Domain Admins account to use the existing computer account.

✦ **Windows NT Workstation accounts** Windows NT domains place all workstation accounts in a single Computers container. You can join a computer running Windows NT Workstation to a Windows 2000 domain in a manner similar to that for Windows 2000 workstations.

Operating System	Logon ID	Computer Name
Windows 95	JackPark	FAC452365840
Windows 95 OSR2	GregoryRussell	FAC428394950
Windows 98	OwenDelapaz	FAC399857238
Windows 98 SE	NormanUllstad	FAC435498512
Windows NT Workstation 4.0	JohnKinunen	FAC413426178
Windows 2000 Professional	RReynolds	FAC455423293

Table B-1. Faculty Member Logon IDs and Computer Names for Each Supported 32-bit Client Operating System

NOTE: ADMT lets you specify an OU for computer accounts you clone from Windows NT 4.0 domains.

✦ **Passwords**   Use "password" to log on to the Windows 2000 or NT domain with a new user account. If logon fails with "password" because complex passwords are required, use an empty password, which you must change before completing the logon process.

✦ **User home directories**   If you specified the user home directory option, verify that the client's logical U: drive connects to the proper location. Windows 9x clients require logon scripts to set the U: drive share.

✦ **Logon scripts**   If you specified optional logon scripts for Windows NT and Windows 9x domains, verify that the logon scripts execute successfully. If they don't, check the contents of the LogonWinNT.bat or LogonWin9x.bat file in the \\ServerName\Netlogon share. Add a temporary PAUSE command at the end of the logon script if you want to debug the logon scripts with test clients.

✦ **User profile directories**   Test roaming user profiles with each type of 32-bit client you support. Roaming user profiles for Windows 2000 clients are one of the subjects of Chapter 4. Chapter 8 discusses server-stored user profiles for Windows NT and 9x clients.

Removing GroupPol from Your Machine

Click Remove All to remove all AD objects you created before removing the GroupPol program. Otherwise, you must manually delete the Faculty Members and Non-Faculty Staff OUs to clean up AD.

Use Control Panel's Add/Remove Programs tool to remove the Windows 2000 or Windows NT version of GroupPol. Click OK to acknowledge the warning that the GroupPol (Clear).mdb file isn't found. If you no longer intend to run GroupPol on the machine, you can safely delete the *d*:\Program Files\GroupPol folder that contains GroupPol.mdb.

NOTE: When you run GroupPol for the first time, GroupPol (Clear).mdb is renamed to GroupPol.mdb. This prevents installation of an updated version from overwriting user-specific, persistent data stored in the database.

Appendix C

Cloning Windows NT Domains with the Active Directory Migration Tool (ADMT)

The Holy Grail of Windows 2000 is Total Cost of Ownership (TCO). One of the benefits that Microsoft uses to justify the increased licensing cost of Windows 2000 Server and its clients is the system's ability to reduce the number of Windows NT domains, and thus the quantity of PDCs and BDCs, required to provide equal or better services to clients. Multimaster replication, flexible site topology, transitive trusts, and administrative delegation combine to make the process of restructuring (also called coalescing) Windows NT account and resource domains attractive for even mid-size networks.

Few things in life are simple, and regenerating a large-scale, geographically disperse Windows NT network isn't one of them. In-place upgrading of live PDCs to Windows 2000 DCs is a chancy proposition, at best. The fallback procedure (promoting an offline BDC to a PDC) in the event of a PDC upgrade failure doesn't appeal to most network admins. In-place PDC upgrades and mixed-mode domains don't accommodate domain restructure objectives; for example, each PDC retains its downlevel (NetBIOS) domain name. The alternative and more conservative approach is to create a new Windows 2000 network that runs in parallel with the existing Windows NT network. OUs, not domains, segregate user and computer accounts in the new network's domains. Classifying users and computers by OU enables you to delegate account management and selectively apply Group Policies to users and computers in each OU.

You also need a method that permits testing of incremental user and computer migration to the new Windows 2000 network. Incremental migration lets you evaluate scenarios with typical users and various combinations of client hardware and operating systems. The most common approach is to first migrate Windows 2000 clients to the new domain, which permits evaluating user reaction to an initial set of Group Policies. If users have issues with the configuration of their new Windows 2000 accounts, they need the ability to return to their old accounts in the Windows NT domain. After you correct the problems, users can retry their Windows 2000 accounts with revised Group Policies.

Restructuring Domains and Migrating Users the Hard Way

During the Windows 2000 beta test period, the missing link for widespread adoption of Windows 2000 Server was a GUI tool for domain restructuring, incremental user migration, or both. Domain restructuring involves creating a single forest having a minimum number of domain trees (preferably one). AD's ability to accommodate many more objects, especially user and computer accounts, than Windows NT's SAM database makes it feasible to progressively decommission PDCs and BDCs for resource domains that hold computer accounts, as well as deliver database, messaging, intranet, and other services to clients. During the migration process, users must retain access to resources in the Windows NT and 2000 domains.

MoveTree, NetDom, and Intraforest Migration

Installation of the Windows 2000 Support Tools provides MoveTree, a command-line tool for moving OUs and their user accounts between source and target (destination) domains in a single forest of domain trees. When you use MoveTree for domain restructuring, OUs moved to the target domain retain their links to existing Group Policy Objects (GPOs). The linked GPOs remain in the source domain, which causes a performance hit when users subject to the linked GPOs log on. You can't move Domain Local and Global Security Groups that contain members to the target domain, so you must re-create memberships in these groups after making the move. If MoveTree halts during the migration process, orphaned OUs and user accounts end up in the Lost And Found folder of Active Directory Users and Computers. MoveTree has several other serious limitations, and its arcane command-line syntax isn't easy to master.

NOTE: Microsoft uses "destination domain" in much of its documentation concerning domain migration. The ADMT wizards substitute "target" for "destination." For consistency with the wizard terminology, "target domain" (the Windows 2000 domain) is used throughout this appendix.

MoveTree doesn't move computer accounts; you must use the NetDom command-line Support Tool to handle this task. NetDom copies one computer account at a time, so you use batch files for moving a large number of computer accounts. NetDom offers the option to specify an OU for computer accounts copied to the target domain. Computer accounts remain in the source domain; if the source domain runs Windows 2000, the moved computer accounts are disabled. NetDom's syntax is somewhat simpler than MoveTree's, but "somewhat simpler" is damnation by faint praise.

ClonePrincipal and Interforest Migration

The Windows 2000 Support Tools include a series of sample Visual Basic scripts primarily for creating copies of (cloning) Windows NT local and global security groups, and user accounts in a native-mode Windows 2000 domain. Microsoft calls this process *interforest migration*. The scripts rely on the ClonePrincipal library (Clonepr.dll) to handle the interaction between the Windows NT SAM database and Windows 2000's AD. Accounts added to AD receive a new primary security identifier (SID), which ordinarily would prevent user accounts from accessing Windows NT resources for which users have permissions. ClonePrincipal generates a new Windows 2000 account attribute, sIDHistory, which contains a user's SIDs in the Windows NT domains to which he or she has access. Security groups also have a sIDHistory attribute. AD generates a GUID for each user account and security group you migrate.

The sIDHistory attribute, which is available only in Windows 2000 native-mode domains, makes incremental migration of user accounts practical. You can learn more about sIDHistory by reading the ClonePrincipal User Guide (Clonepr.doc) in \Program Files\Support Tools. The User Guide also includes a useful glossary of the terms involved in migrating accounts. You also can use ClonePrincipal to move groups and users between Windows 2000 domains in different forests. To take full advantage of the five sample Visual Basic scripts that use ClonePrincipal, you need experience running and, in some cases, debugging VBScript code. Another limitation is that ClonePrincipal scripts aren't capable of migrating computer accounts.

Easing Restructure and Migration with ADMT

The operational limitations and missing ease-of-use features of MoveTree, NetDom, and ClonePrincipal made development of a graphical tool for domain restructure and account migration mandatory. In June 1999, Microsoft licensed Mission Critical Software's (http://www.missioncritical.com) Domain Migrator technology for Windows NT, and the two firms set about developing a Microsoft Management Console snap-in, the Active Directory Migration Tool, to simplify domain restructuring and account migration. During the Windows 2000 beta period, ADMT was available only to members of the Rapid Deployment Program, Joint Development Program participants, and a few other technical beta testers. Microsoft released version 1.0 of ADMT in March 2000, so ADMT isn't on the Windows 2000 Server distribution CD-ROM, nor is it on the Service Pack 1 CD-ROM. You must download ADMT as Admt.exe (2.3 MB) from http://www.microsoft.com/windows2000/downloads/deployment/admt/default.asp. Admt.exe is a wrapper around the installer file.

NOTE: Chapters 9 and 10 of Microsoft's *Domain Migration Cookbook* offer detailed instructions for migrating Windows NT groups and user and computer accounts with ADMT. The *Cookbook* example, however, has only two user accounts and one global and two local groups. You can download the *Cookbook* from http://www.microsoft.com/windows2000/library/planning/activedirectory/cookbook.asp.

ADMT Requirements

The basic requirements for cloning Windows NT groups and accounts or performing interforest and intraforest migrations with ADMT are the same as those for running ClonePrincipal scripts. Following are brief descriptions of these prerequisites:

◆ ADMT must run on a computer running Windows 2000 Professional or Server that's a member of the Windows 2000 target domain. Microsoft recommends that you run ADMT on a DC, preferably the PDC emulator. Unless you've changed it, the PDC emulator is the first DC you installed on the network.

✦ The target domain must run in native mode. Running in native mode orphans any Windows NT BDCs in your target domain (they don't receive AD updates) and prevents you from adding new Windows NT BDCs with Netdom.exe. The PDC emulator, like a Windows NT PDC, is a single point of failure for downlevel client account changes. If the PDC emulator is dead, you can't add new Windows NT or 9x users or Windows NT computers, and downlevel users can't change their passwords. You can't revert to mixed mode from native mode.

✦ A pair of *uplevel* nontransitive trusts must exist between the Windows NT source and the target domains. An uplevel trust is one created in Active Directory Domains and Trusts and confirmed in Windows NT's User Manager. All sIDHistory operations fail with *downlevel* trusts; downlevel trusts are maintained with other Windows NT domains when you upgrade a Windows NT PDC to a Windows 2000 DC. If you upgraded the target domain from a PDC, you must delete and re-create the trusts with the source domain PDC. The next section describes how to create the uplevel trusts. Microsoft Knowledge Base article Q256250, "ClonePrincipal and ADMT Require Uplevel Trust to Migrate Objects Between Windows 2000 Domains," has more information about issues with downlevel trusts.

✦ If you're performing a domain restructure with a Windows 2000 DC as the source domain controller, the source domain can run in mixed or native mode.

✦ You must enable success/failure auditing of User and Group Management (Windows NT) or Audit Account Management (Windows 2000) in the source domain, and Audit Account Management in the target domain.

✦ You must log on to the DC with an account having at least Domain Admins rights in the target domain and membership in the Administrators group of the source domain. The Domain Admins group of the source domain must be a member of the Administrators group of the target domain, and vice versa.

✦ Administrative shares (ADMIN$, C$, D$, and so on) must exist on the target domain DC and on computers running Windows 2000 or NT whose accounts you intend to migrate to Windows 2000. Windows NT and 2000 create the required Administrative shares during installation, but there's always a remote chance that these shares could be missing. The Domain Admins group of the target domain must be a member of the migrated client's Administrators group for successful migration of computer accounts.

✦ Modifications to the source domain's Registry (addition to HKEY_LOCAL_MACHINE\ System\CurrentControlSet\Control\LSA of a TcpipClientSupport key with a value of 0x1) and addition of a *SourceDomainName*$$$ local security group also are required. When you first run ADMT against the source PDC, the program handles these two chores for you. If you have problems cloning Windows NT objects, you should verify that both modifications have succeeded on the PDC. Knowledge Base article Q260871, "How to Set Up ADMT for Windows NT 4.0 to Windows 2000 Migration," has more detailed information on these alterations.

TIP: If you're starting with a new DC to serve as the initial root DC of your network, verify that all network services, such as DNS, DHCP, and WINS (if necessary), are operating correctly. Make sure that AD-integrated Dynamic DNS is operational by checking for the presence of the four server locator (SRV) record folders (_msdcs, _sites, _tcp, and _udp) under the forward lookup zone node for your DC's domain.

Domain Restructure Test Scenarios with ADMT

If you're setting up a Windows 2000 test network to emulate an existing Windows NT installation, install and synchronize a BDC with the Windows NT PDC for a production account domain, remove the BDC from the production network, and promote the BDC to a PDC in the test network. Then you can use ADMT in one or both of the following ways:

✦ Use the PDC as the source domain for a newly created (pristine) DC of a native-mode target domain that uses the DNS and NetBIOS names you plan to use in production. Migrate the directory objects to the appropriate OUs in the target domain. Repeat the BDC installation for each additional account and resource domain you plan to coalesce into your single Windows 2000 domain.

✦ Upgrade the PDC to a Windows 2000 DC for a new child domain or domain tree in an existing native-mode domain. Use ADMT to move all AD objects contained in the added domain into OUs of the existing domain.

In either of the preceding two scenarios, you decommission the PDC after the migration or after you coalesce the upgraded Windows NT domain into the existing Windows 2000 domain.

CAUTION: Never reconnect to the production network an isolated test PDC that you've upgraded in place to Windows 2000. You receive a "duplicate name on the network" message if you do, and you might temporarily disable the production PDC having the same NetBIOS name.

Configuring the Domains and Installing ADMT

The most common use of ADMT is to clone production directory objects from existing Windows NT 4.0 domains. The following procedure, which assumes a newly created target DC and a Windows NT account domain PDC on the network, works equally well for test or production domains and supports incremental client migration:

1. If you haven't already done so, download Admt.exe from http://www.microsoft.com/windows2000/downloads/deployment/admt/default.asp to a temporary folder.

2. Launch Active Directory Domains and Trusts, right-click the node for your target domain, and choose Properties to open the DomainName Properties dialog. If your target domain isn't running in native mode (see Figure C-1), click the Change Mode button and click Yes when you receive the message that converting to native mode is not reversible. The Change Mode button disappears, and the Domain Operating Mode text box displays Native Mode (No pre–Windows 2000 Domain Controllers).

NOTE: The figures in this chapter use the default domain names of the GroupPol application: oakmont.edu and OAKMONTU for the target domains, and OAKMONT for the source domain. Substitute the names of your Windows 2000 test and Windows NT production domains for the names shown in the figures.

3. Click the Trusts tab and click the upper Add button to open the Add Trusted Domain dialog. Type the name of the source domain, a password for the trust, and a confirmation of the password in the three text boxes (see Figure C-2). Click OK to close the dialog and then acknowledge the message that advises that the trust can't be confirmed.

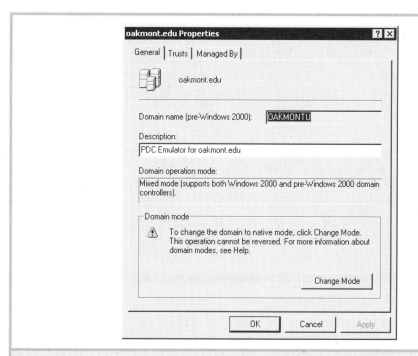

Figure C-1. Presence of the Change Mode button indicates that your Windows 2000 target domain isn't running in native mode, which ADMT requires.

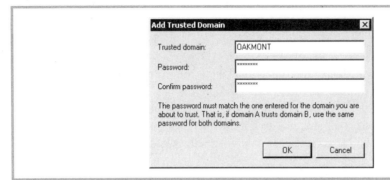

Figure C-2. Add a nontransitive trust to the source domain in the Trusts page's Add Trusted Domain dialog; then add a similar trust from the source domain in the Add Trusting domain.

4. Click the lower Add button to open the Add Trusting Domain dialog and type the same information as in the previous step. Click OK, click No when asked if you want to verify the trust, and acknowledge the message that advises that the trust can't be confirmed. Repeat this step for each resource domain to which the users you migrate need access.

NOTE: If you plan to add local groups that have members whose accounts reside in other domains, you must repeat steps 3 through 6 to create reciprocal trusts with each domain in which those member accounts are defined. Reciprocal Administrators group membership also is required in each additional domain.

5. On the Windows NT PDC, launch User Manager and choose Options | Trusts to open the Trust Relationships dialog. Click the upper Add button to open the Add Trusted Domain dialog and type the downlevel (NetBIOS) name of the target domain and the password you typed in step 4 (see Figure C-3). Click OK to close the dialog and click OK again to acknowledge the message that the trust relationship was established successfully.

6. Repeat step 5 for the Trusting Domain. In this case, you must type and confirm the password you used in step 3. Click OK three times to return to User Manager.

7. Double-click the Administrators group in User Manager to open the Local Group Properties dialog, click Add to open the Add Users and Groups dialog, and select the target domain in the List Names From list.

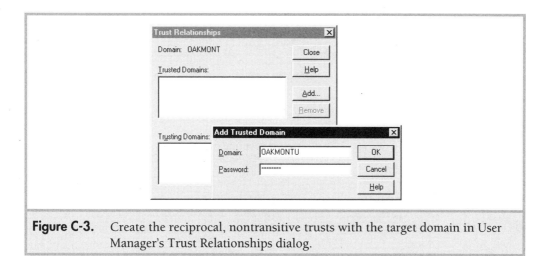

Figure C-3.   Create the reciprocal, nontransitive trusts with the target domain in User Manager's Trust Relationships dialog.

8. Double-click the Domain Admins group and Administrator account to add them to the Add Names list (see Figure C-4) and click OK twice to close the dialogs and add the group and account to the source domain's Administrators group.

9. In User Manager, choose Policies | Audit to open the Audit Policy dialog. Select the Audit These Events option and mark the Success and Failure check boxes for User and Group Management auditing (see Figure C-5). Close User Manager.

10. Synchronize the system time of the source PDC with that of the target DC. Keeping system time in sync makes analysis of event logs on the two servers easier.

11. On the Windows 2000 DC, choose Programs | Administrative Tools | Domain Controller Security Policy to open the eponymous snap-in and then expand the Security Settings and Local Policies nodes.

12. Click Audit Policy and double-click the Audit Account Management icon to open the Security Policy Setting dialog. Mark the Define These Policy Settings check box and then mark the Success and Failure check boxes (see Figure C-6). Click OK to close the dialog and exit the snap-in.

13. Launch Active Directory Users and Computers, click the Builtin container node, and double-click the Administrators item to open the General page of the Administrators Properties dialog.

14. Click the Members tab and click Add to open the Select Users or Groups dialog. Select the source domain in the Look In list and double-click the Administrator and Domain Users items in the list to add the names to the text box (see Figure C-7). Click OK twice to return to Active Directory Users and Computers.

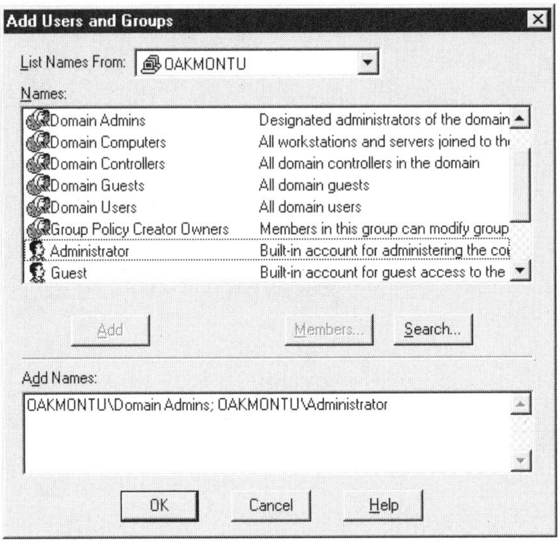

Figure C-4. Add the target domain's Domain Admins group and, optionally, add the Administrator account to the source domain's Administrators group.

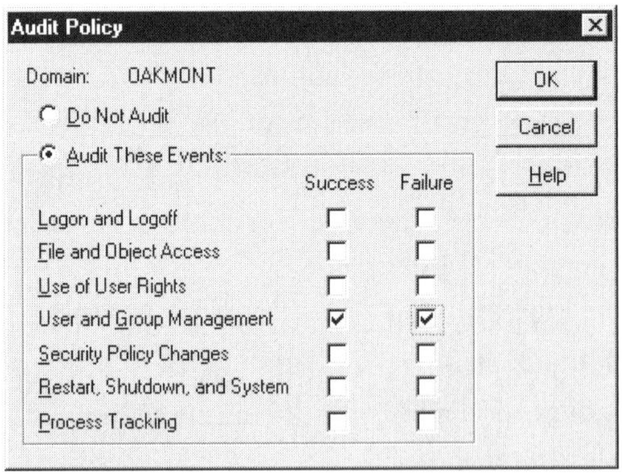

Figure C-5. ADMT requires auditing of changes to the source domain's user and group accounts.

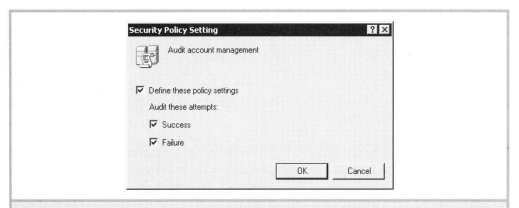

Figure C-6. Enable auditing of the target domain's account management operations in the Domain Controller Security Policy snap-in.

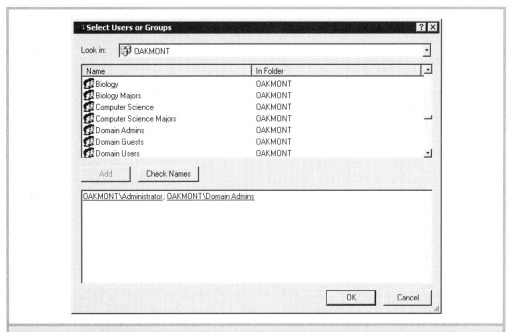

Figure C-7. ADMT also requires the source domain's Domain Admins group and, optionally, Administrator account to be members of the target domain's Administrators group.

15. Double-click Admt.exe to unwrap Admt.msi and start the Active Directory Migration Tool Setup Wizard. Click Next to bypass the Welcome dialog.

16. In the License Agreement dialog, select the I Accept the License Agreement option and click Next.

17. Accept or change the default installation folder and click Next twice to install ADMT. Click Finish when installation completes.

TIP: Complete every step in the preceding list, preferably in the given order. If you miss a step, count on receiving error messages when you attempt to run one of the ADMT wizards for the first time.

Using the ADMT Wizards

Choose Programs | Administrative Tools | Active Directory Migration Tool to open the ADMT snap-in, which displays only the Active Directory Migration Tool node and a Reports subnode. ADMT is a wizard-based console; all but report viewing operations run from context-menu choices of the console's root node. Figure C-8 illustrates the menu choices available when running ADMT for the first time.

Following are brief descriptions, in the order of the function of the ADMT wizards:

✦ The Reporting Wizard specifies the names and location of HTML reports generated for the actions of several wizards. You view the reports by clicking the Reports subnode and then clicking the name of the report you want in the Name pane.

✦ The Trust Migration Wizard analyzes trusts in the source domain and compares them to the trusts you've created in the target domain. You must create any missing trusts in the target domain manually.

✦ The Group Mapping and Merging Wizard lets you change the name of a group in the target domain. By default, migrated groups retain their source domain names. You also can use this Wizard to combine the membership of more than one source group into a single target group. If your source domain groups and their membership are reasonably well organized, you don't need to use this Wizard.

✦ The Group Migration Wizard lets you copy global security groups from the source (Windows NT) domain to OUs you add to the target domain. Optionally, you can add the group's user accounts when you copy a group. Adding groups and users together simplifies the migration process. You also can copy local groups (other than existing groups that are included in AD's Builtin container). For initial test migration of conventional user accounts, you can omit the local accounts.

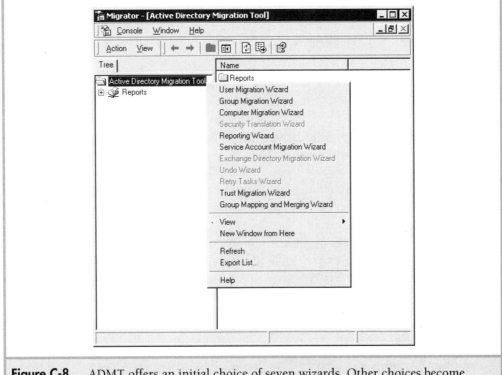

Figure C-8.   ADMT offers an initial choice of seven wizards. Other choices become available after you migrate Windows NT directory objects.

✦ The User Migration Wizard adds user accounts to existing OUs independently of their group membership. Membership in all groups is updated as you add the users. Adding user accounts after migrating groups is the better approach if your users are members of several groups.

✦ The Service Account Migration Wizard adds user accounts that run services on multiple domain controllers. Microsoft Exchange Server and SQL Server often use service accounts. Unless you want to migrate servers running such services, you can skip this step.

✦ The Computer Migration Wizard migrates computer accounts into the Computers container or OUs you specify. To delegate management or apply different Group Policies to subsets of computers, you must place the computer accounts in corresponding OUs. If you use an OU structure based on organizational structure, you can create sub-OUs to further classify computer accounts by operating system or other attribute values.

✦ ADMT enables the Exchange Directory Migration Wizard only if the Exchange Server administrative tools are installed on the target DC. Running your first migration enables the Undo Wizard, and migrating computer accounts enables the Retry Tasks Wizard.

Adding OUs for Groups and User Accounts

Before you use any Migration Wizard, create the OU structure to contain your source groups and user accounts. The only means of dividing Windows NT user accounts into subsets for migration is group membership. You must decide which of the available user groups creates the OU structure you want and migrate those groups and users after migrating other groups. If you don't have an appropriate security group structure for classifying users by organization function (or another classification method you use), consider adding the required global groups and populating them with members before performing the initial migration.

The example migration uses the security group structure generated for the sample OAKMONT domain by the GroupPol application running under Windows NT, as described in the "Running GroupPol Under Windows NT 4.0" section of Appendix B. Each employee user is a member of the Faculty Members or Non-Faculty Staff group and also is a member of a global department-based group, such as Anthropology or Admissions Staff. Department-based OU membership is the most practical approach for delegating responsibility for management of the OU. Title-based groups are better suited to filtering Group Policy Objects. Read Chapter 2 and Chapter 3 for detailed information on designing OU and security group structures.

Students are members of the Students OU and sub-OUs based on school year (Freshmen, Sophomores, and so on), as well as their major academic subject. Students who pass a sufficient number of courses move between school years, so these groups are the better choice. Academic-major group membership is better suited to assigning permissions for accessing major-related shares.

Running the Reporting Wizard

To specify the location and types of reports you want to view, do the following:

1. Launch the Reporting Wizard and click Next to bypass the Welcome dialog.

2. In the Domain Selection dialog, select the source and target domains in the two drop-down lists (see Figure C-9) and click Next.

3. In the Folder Selection dialog, accept or change the location for the report files and click Next.

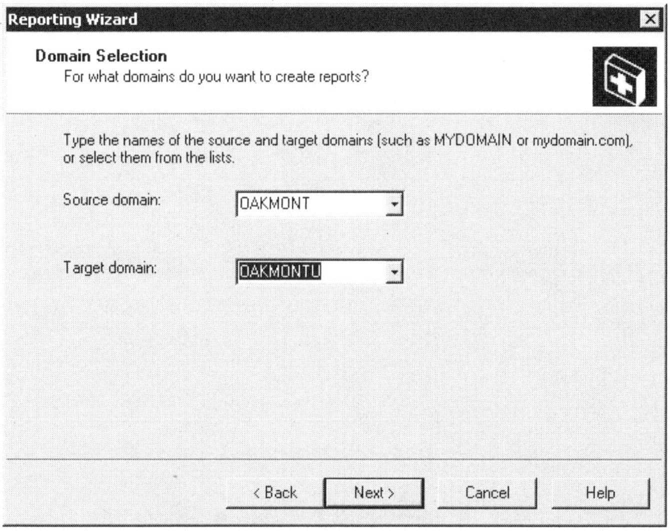

Figure C-9.   The Domain Selection dialog is the same for most ADMT wizards. The lists contain the NetBIOS names of all accessible domains and workgroups, regardless of whether you're created trusts to them.

4. In the Report Selection dialog, multiselect the reports you want to review (see Figure C-10). Migrated User Accounts, Migrated Computer Accounts, and Expired Accounts are the most common choices. Click Next.

5. Selecting Expired Accounts opens the Migration Progress dialog that tests computer password age. Click View Log to view in Notepad a list of computers with expired passwords, if any. Close Notepad and click Close to terminate the Wizard and return to the ADMT snap-in, which has added nodes for each type of report you specified in step 4.

6. Click each of the Reports subnodes to display the HTML table header for the report.

If you have no computers with expired passwords, none of the reports have data rows at this point.

Performing a Test Group and User Migration

It's easy to remove migrated groups and user accounts if you add them to OUs; you simply delete the OU, which removes all traces of the objects it contains. ADMT's Undo Wizard also makes it easy to remove most objects you migrate. Thus, there's no risk of irreparable

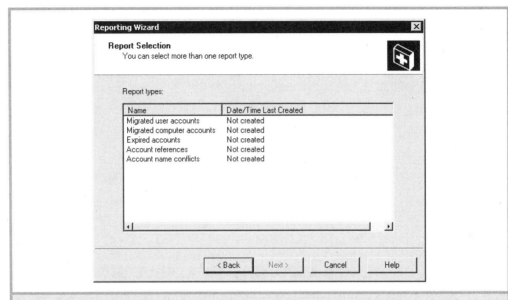

Figure C-10. Specify the reports you want to view before or after migration in the Reporting Wizard's Report Selection dialog.

damage to the target domain. The following examples use a small subset of the OUs created by running the GroupPol application under Windows 2000 (see Figure C-11). All the sample OUs are empty prior to performing the migration.

Copying Secondary Groups

Secondary groups are security groups on which you don't want to base user account migration. After creating the required OUs to serve as containers for the objects you plan to migrate, do the following:

1. Choose Group Migration Wizard in the context menu to launch the Group Account Migration Wizard and then click Next to bypass the Welcome Dialog.

2. In the Test or Make Changes dialog, select the Migrate Now option and click Next.

3. In the Domain Selection dialog, the source and target domains you set in the preceding section are the defaults for successive wizards. The DNS name, rather than the NetBIOS name, appears in the Target Domain list. Click Next.

4. In the Group Selection dialog, click Add to open Active Directory's Select Groups dialog. Multiselect the groups that you don't use to add user accounts to an OU and then click Add to add the selected groups to the text box. Select only those groups

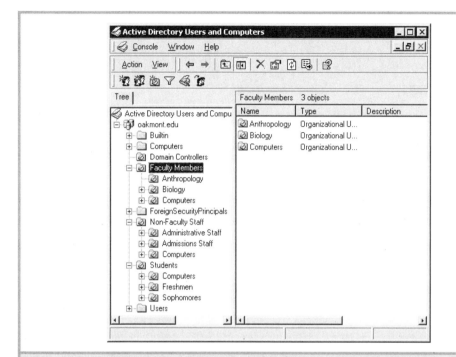

Figure C-11. The OU hierarchy for the test migration contains only a small subset of the OUs added by the GroupPol application when running under Windows 2000.

that are to be included in a single OU (see Figure C-12). For this example, the Students OU stores all academic major groups. Click OK to return to the Wizard's Select Groups dialog, review your selection, and click Next.

5. In the Organizational Unit Selection dialog, click Browse to open the Browse for Container dialog, select the OU to contain the groups, and click OK. The full LDAP path for server-specific binding appears in the Target OU text box (see Figure C-13). Click Next.

NOTE: The full LDAP path for server-specific binding adds the LDAP://*DCName*/ prefix to the distinguished name (DN) of the destination AD object in the target domain.

6. In the Group Options dialog, mark the Update User Rights and Migrate Group SIDs to Target Domain check boxes (see Figure C-14). Make sure that the Copy Group Members check box is clear, because you don't migrate users to the OU for the groups you selected in step 4. Click Next.

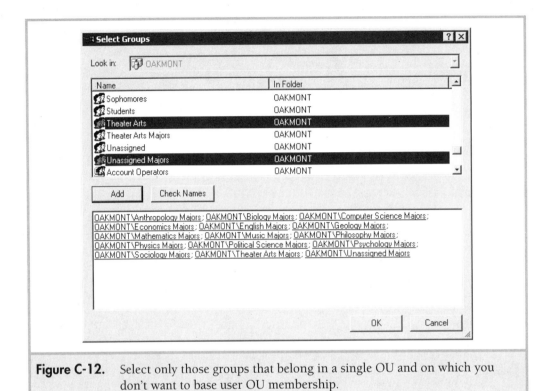

Figure C-12. Select only those groups that belong in a single OU and on which you don't want to base user OU membership.

7. When the first of three mislabeled error messages appears, click Yes to create the special *DOMAINNAME*$$$ local group on the source PDC.

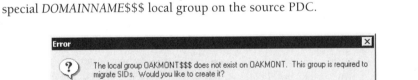

8. In the second error message, click Yes to add the TcpipClientSupport key to the source PDC's registry.

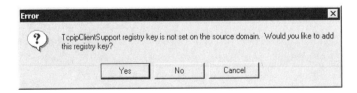

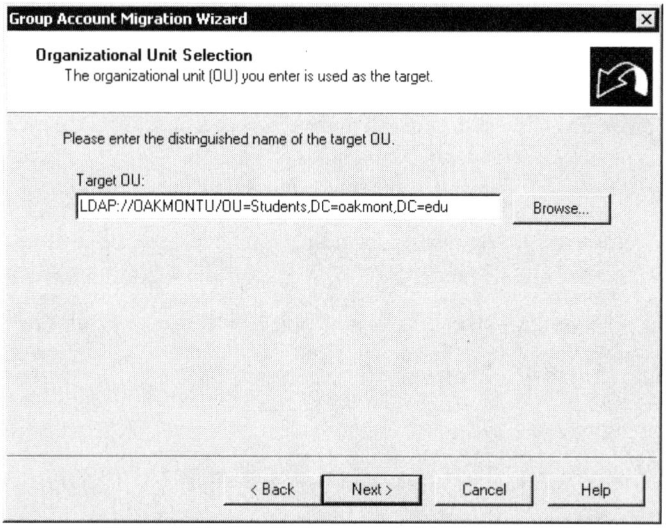

Figure C-13. ADMT uses LDAP syntax to specify target domain objects. Server-specific binding adds the name of the DC to the path.

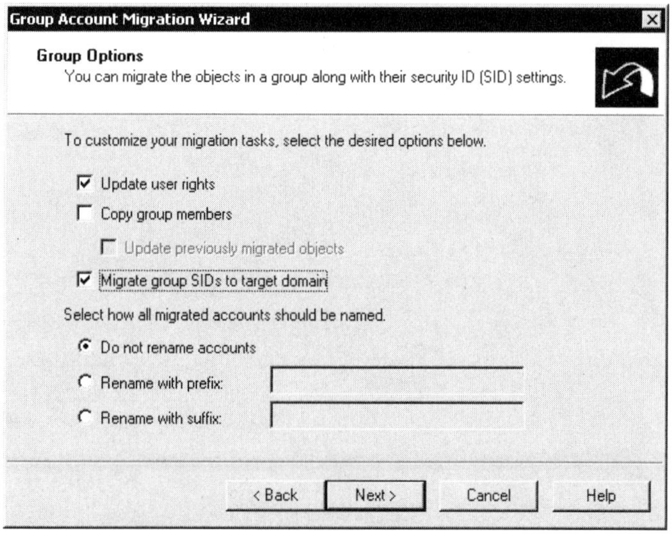

Figure C-14. Don't mark the Copy Group Members check box for groups on which you don't want to base user OU membership.

9. In the third error message, click Yes to reboot the source PDC remotely.

> **NOTE:** The three message boxes represent only potential errors; they let you automatically perform the preceding three operations. If the first two operations succeed, you don't see these messages again until you change source domains. If either fails, you can't proceed with migration and must add any missing elements manually to the source PDC.

10. In the User Account dialog, type your administrative user name and password and accept the source domain name in the three text boxes. Click Next.

11. In the Naming Conflicts dialog, accept the default Ignore Conflicting Accounts and Don't Migrate option (see Figure C-15). The target OU is empty, so naming conflicts aren't a factor. Click Next, review your choices, and then click Finish to start the group copying operation.

12. The Migration Progress dialog displays the number of groups copied and errors, if any (see Figure C-16).

13. When the copying process is complete, click the View Log button to open the Migration.log file in Notepad (see Figure C-17). Near the end of the log, entries indicate that user accounts couldn't be added to the groups because you haven't added user accounts yet. Close Notepad.

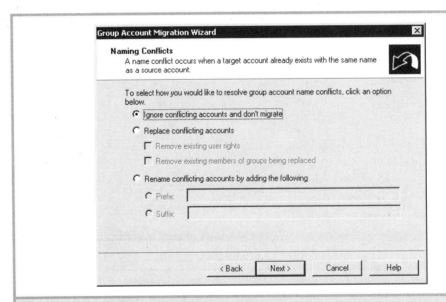

Figure C-15. Don't worry about naming conflicts when copying accounts to OUs without member objects.

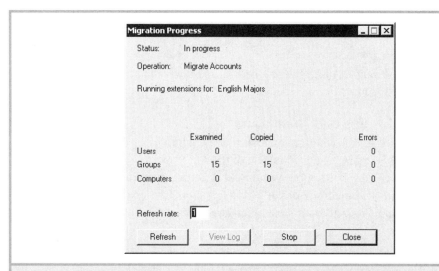

Figure C-16.   Each wizard that copies objects displays a progress dialog with a description of the current operation, the number of objects copied, and the errors, if any.

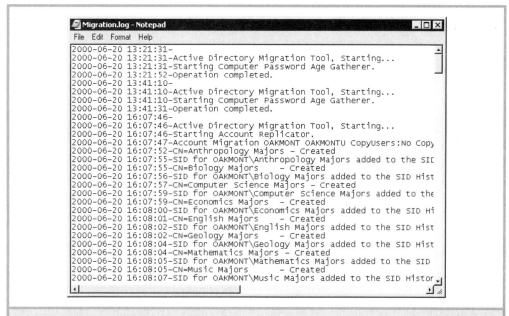

Figure C-17.   The Migration.log file includes entries for each operation processed by the Wizard.

14. Click Close to get rid of the Migration Progress dialog and return to the ADMT snap-in. Confirm in Active Directory Users and Computers addition of the groups to the target OU.

15. Repeat steps 1 through 14 for each security group on which you don't want to base user OU membership.

Copying Primary Groups and Their Users

Primary groups have the user account membership on which to base addition of users to a predetermined OU. This example adds members of the Anthropology group to the Faculty Members, Anthropology OU. The sample Windows NT source domain has 250 employee and 250 student accounts, which provides at least a few users in every security group.

To add a group and its user accounts to a precreated OU, run this abbreviated (no "click Next") drill:

1. Launch the Group Migration Wizard, select the Migrate Now option, and accept the default source and target domains.

2. In the Group Selection dialog, specify the single security group with the user account membership to copy to the OU (Anthropology for this example).

3. In the Organizational Unit Selection dialog, browse to the OU for the group and user accounts (Faculty Members).

4. In the Group Options dialog, mark the Update User Rights, Copy Group Members, Update Previously Migrated Objects (security groups), and Migrate Group SIDs to Target Domain check boxes (see Figure C-18).

5. Complete the entries in the User Account dialog and accept the Ignore Conflicting Accounts and Don't Migrate options.

6. In the Group Member Options dialog, accept the default Set Password to User Name and Leave Both Accounts Active options (see Figure C-19). If you specify the Generate Complex Passwords option, the Wizard creates a password list so you can advise users of their new passwords. You must generate complex passwords if you've set the Passwords Must Meet Complexity Requirements policy under the Security Settings | Account Policies | Password Policies node of the Domain Security Policies snap-in. Don't mark the Translate Roaming User Profiles check box when performing an initial test migration.

CAUTION: You can do repairable damage to your source domain if you're not careful when making selections in the Group Member Options dialog during a production migration. Choosing the Disable Source Accounts option when copying user accounts from a production domain will make users *very unhappy* and require you to reenable all disabled accounts with User Manager.

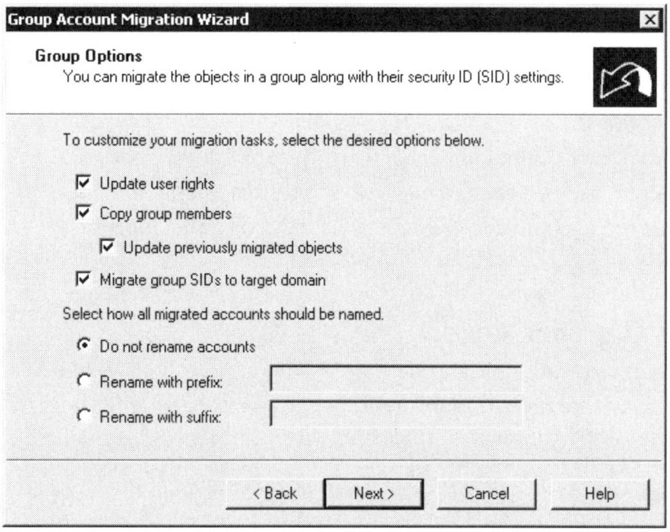

Figure C-18.   Copy the user accounts along with the security group to the OU for users.

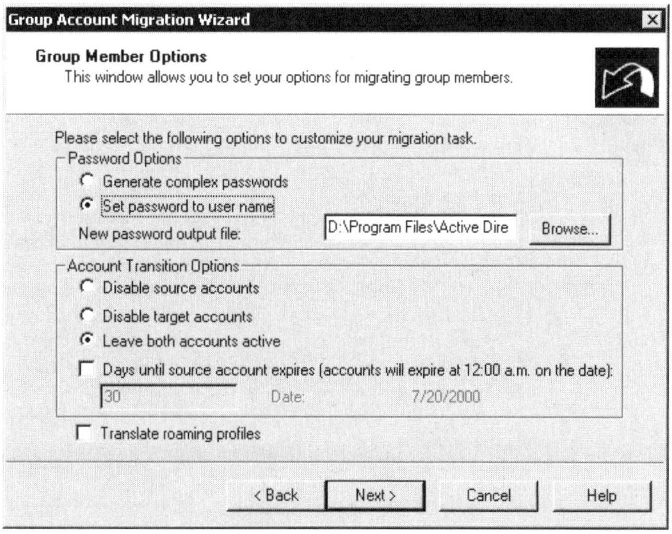

Figure C-19.   For a test migration, the Group Member Options dialog's defaults are satisfactory.

7. Finish the group and user account migration, open the Migrate.log file, and scroll to the bottom to review the Wizard's actions.

8. Launch or refresh Active Directory Users and Computers, open the target OU, and verify that the group and user accounts are in the correct container (see Figure C-20).

9. Double-click one of the Global Security Groups added by ADMT, Anthropology for this example, to open the *GroupName* Properties dialog and click the Members tab to verify that the users in the OU have been added to the appropriate Security Group (see Figure C-21).

Updating the Migration Report

ADMT doesn't automatically update the reports you've selected after you run a migration operation. To update the reports, run the Reporting Wizard again, select the reports to update in the Report Selection dialog, and complete the Wizard sequence. Click the node

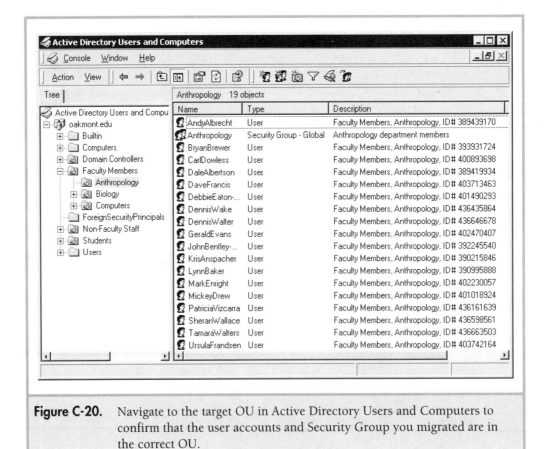

Figure C-20. Navigate to the target OU in Active Directory Users and Computers to confirm that the user accounts and Security Group you migrated are in the correct OU.

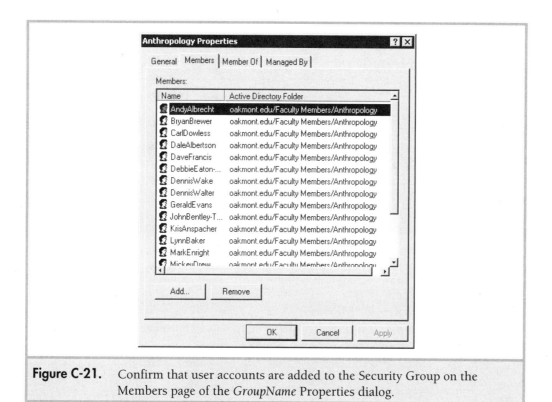

Figure C-21.   Confirm that user accounts are added to the Security Group on the Members page of the *GroupName* Properties dialog.

for the report you want to view and scroll to the end of the report to check the latest entries. Figure C-22 illustrates the first few rows for multiple-group migration in the Migrated User and Group Accounts report. The rows generated by adding group and user accounts are at the bottom.

Using the Undo Wizard

The Undo Last Migration Wizard lets you reverse the changes made to the target domain by your action. In other words, ADMT has a single undo level. ADMT uses a Jet (Access) database, Protar.mdb, that holds a record for each migration operation you perform. The Reporting Wizard uses Protar.mdb data to generate HTML migration report tables, and the Undo Wizard uses data in Protar.mdb to reverse the last action. If you have Access 97 or later, you can open Protar.mdb and view the ActionHistory, MigratedObjects, and other ADMT tables. The MigratedObjects table lists every directory object copied to the target domain. In a production migration with a large number of users, Protar.mdb (and Migration.log) can become quite large.

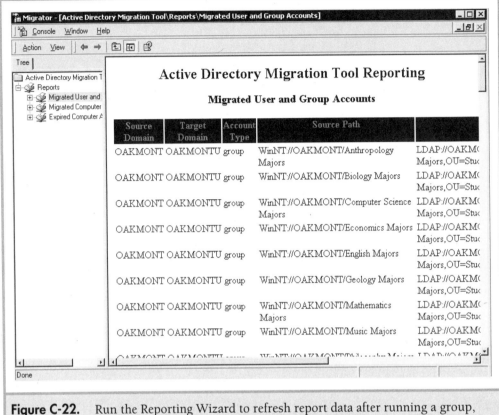

Active Directory Migration Tool Reporting

Migrated User and Group Accounts

Source Domain	Target Domain	Account Type	Source Path	
OAKMONT	OAKMONTU	group	WinNT://OAKMONT/Anthropology Majors	LDAP://OAKM(Majors,OU=Stu<
OAKMONT	OAKMONTU	group	WinNT://OAKMONT/Biology Majors	LDAP://OAKM(Majors,OU=Stu<
OAKMONT	OAKMONTU	group	WinNT://OAKMONT/Computer Science Majors	LDAP://OAKM(Majors,OU=Stu<
OAKMONT	OAKMONTU	group	WinNT://OAKMONT/Economics Majors	LDAP://OAKM(Majors,OU=Stu<
OAKMONT	OAKMONTU	group	WinNT://OAKMONT/English Majors	LDAP://OAKM(Majors,OU=Stu<
OAKMONT	OAKMONTU	group	WinNT://OAKMONT/Geology Majors	LDAP://OAKM(Majors,OU=Stu<
OAKMONT	OAKMONTU	group	WinNT://OAKMONT/Mathematics Majors	LDAP://OAKM(Majors,OU=Stu<
OAKMONT	OAKMONTU	group	WinNT://OAKMONT/Music Majors	LDAP://OAKM(Majors,OU=Stu<

Figure C-22. Run the Reporting Wizard to refresh report data after running a group, user, or computer account migration operation.

CAUTION: If you use Access 2000 or later to view Protar.mdb, choose the Open Database option, *not* the Convert Database option, when first opening the database. If you convert the database to a later Jet version, ADMT can't open it, and you must remove and reinstall ADMT to recover.

To reverse (unmigrate) the last ADMT operation you performed, do the following:

1. Launch the Undo Wizard and click Next to bypass the Welcome dialog.

2. Review your last migration action in the Last Migration dialog (see Figure C-23) and click Next.

3. The Completing the Undo Last Migration dialog confirms the unmigrate operation. Click Finish to open the Migration Progress dialog.

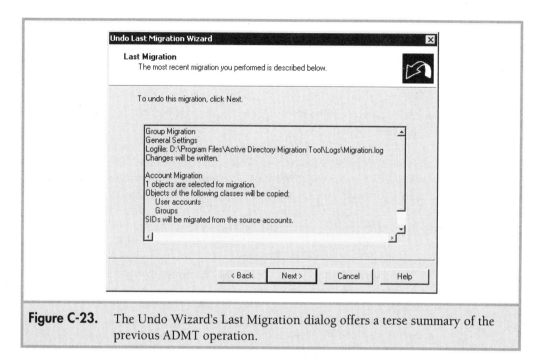

Figure C-23.   The Undo Wizard's Last Migration dialog offers a terse summary of the previous ADMT operation.

4. When the undo process completes, verify in Active Directory Users and Computers that the previously migrated objects have departed.

Migrating Computer Accounts

It's possible for Windows NT and 2000 clients to retain their computer accounts in the source Windows NT domain and log on with accounts in the target Windows 2000 domain. In this scenario, Windows 2000 Professional clients don't receive Computer-based Group Policies during the boot process. Thus, it's advantageous, at least for Windows 2000 clients, to change the computer's domain to the source domain. To do so requires copying computer accounts from the source domain and then changing the computer's domain affiliation on the Network Identification page of the client's System Properties dialog. Changing the computer's domain requires a reboot.

NOTE: Users with computer accounts that are authenticated by a Windows NT PDC or BDC and user accounts authenticated by a Windows 2000 DC receive User Configuration but not Computer Configuration Group Policies.

Migrating computer accounts with ADMT is a two-stage process. In the first stage, the Computer Migration Wizard copies the computer accounts from the source to the target domain's container. In the second stage, ADMT dispatches an agent, which runs as a service on the client, to automatically change the domain affiliation of client computers to the target domain. The agent requires that your administrative account for the *target domain* be a member of each client computer's local Administrators group; you can accomplish this by adding the target domain's Domain Admins group to the Administrators group. All client computers selected for migration must be live on the network for the agent to succeed. If some clients are down when you dispatch the agent, you can use the Retry Tasks Wizard after the previously missing clients reconnect to the network.

NOTE: The User and Group Migration Wizards with default options don't affect the source domain or its clients. Alternating user logons between the source and target domains simply requires users to log off and log back on to the other domain with the same user ID and, depending on user preference, the same or a different password. The Computer Migration Wizard, however, automatically alters (or attempts to alter) the domain affiliation of computer accounts. Users who must return their computer account into its original domain need to know how to use the Network Identification page of the System Properties dialog. They also need patience, because it usually takes at least a couple of minutes to rejoin the original domain, and a reboot is necessary.

To run a trial migration of computer accounts, do the following:

1. Launch the Computer Migration Wizard, bypass the Welcome dialog, and specify the source and target domains, if necessary.

2. In the Computer Selection dialog, click Add and multiselect the computer accounts to move in the Select Computers dialog (see Figure C-24).

3. In the Organizational Unit Selection dialog, browse to and select the Computers container.

TIP: Migrate computer accounts to the default Computers container and then manually move the accounts to OUs you add to classify computer accounts. Moving computer accounts to OUs lets you delegate computer account management and apply computer-based Group Policy at the OU level.

4. In the Translate Objects dialog, mark all the check boxes (see Figure C-25). Security translation adds (or replaces) the Access Control Entries (ACEs) in the Access Control Lists (ACLs) of security descriptors for network resources to which the client computer has access. Security translation is necessary because the client has a new Security ID (SID) in the target domain.

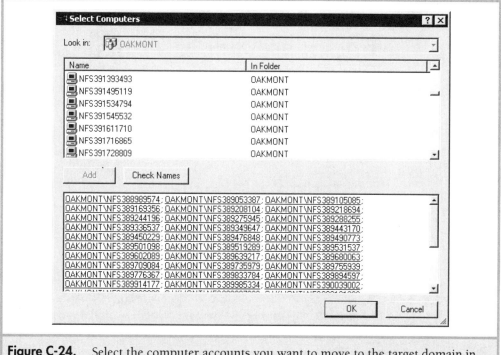

Figure C-24.   Select the computer accounts you want to move to the target domain in the Select Computers dialog.

5. In the Security Translation Options dialog, select the Add option (see Figure C-26). Adding the ACEs for the new client SID leaves intact the original ACEs in the source domain. This translation option permits client computers to return to their prior domains in the event of a problem in the target domain.

6. Complete the User Account dialog's administrative account entries, accept or change the default five-minute client reboot delay setting in the Computer Options dialog, and accept the default Do Not Rename Computers option. Accept in the Naming Conflicts dialog the default Ignore Conflicting Accounts and Don't Migrate option.

7. Click Finish in the Completing the Computer Migration Wizard dialog to open the Migration progress dialog and start copying computer accounts. The Wizard creates each account and then sets the password for secure channel communication with the DC.

8. When copying is complete, click the Close button to begin dispatching agents to the computers you selected. After the agents are dispatched, you receive a report on the ability of the agent to perform its duties on each selected client on the Server List

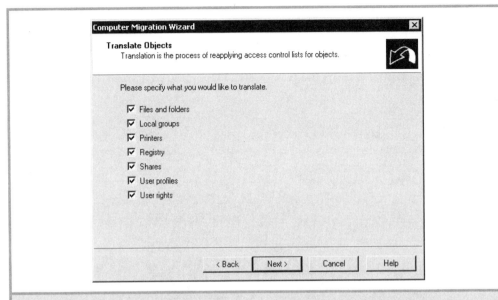

Figure C-25. Selecting all objects for security translation ensures that the client has access to network objects when joining the target domain.

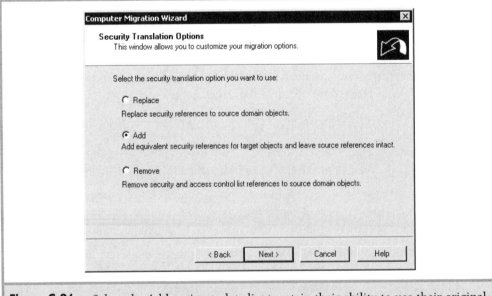

Figure C-26. Select the Add option to let clients retain their ability to use their original ACEs in the source domain.

page of the ADMT Monitor dialog (see Figure C-27). If the clients can't be contacted, you receive "The RPC Server Is Unavailable" messages. After the agent runs on an active computer, you receive a "Completed" message.

TIP: If the agent fails with an "Access Denied" message, the most likely cause is your failure to add the target domain's Domain Admins group to the local Administrators group of the client. Check the Dispatch.log file to see if the reason for the failure is listed. Another possibility is that remote Registry access has been turned off on the client. Remote Registry access is enabled by default on Windows 2000 and NT clients. Use Regedt32.exe and attempt to connect to the remote computer's Registry. You ordinarily can disregard "Completed with Errors" messages; the errors refer to objects you selected in the Translate Objects dialog that aren't present on the client.

A "System Shutdown" message appears on each client after the agent completes its assigned duties. The message indicates the time in HH:MM:SS format before automatic reboot occurs. User's can't forestall the reboot.

Active Directory Migration Tool Agent Monitor

Summary   Server List   Monitoring Settings

Computer	Last Checked	Status	Message
NFS388989574	2000-06-21 15:07:54	Running	
NFS389053387	2000-06-21 15:06:53	Install Failed	The RPC serv
NFS389105085	2000-06-21 15:06:53	Install Failed	The RPC serv
NFS389169356	2000-06-21 15:06:53	Install Failed	The RPC serv
NFS389208104	2000-06-21 15:06:53	Install Failed	The RPC serv
NFS389218694	2000-06-21 15:06:53	Install Failed	The RPC serv
NFS389244196	2000-06-21 15:06:53	Install Failed	The RPC serv
NFS389275945	2000-06-21 15:06:54	Install Failed	The RPC serv
NFS389288255	2000-06-21 15:06:53	Install Failed	The RPC serv
NFS389336537	2000-06-21 15:06:53	Install Failed	The RPC serv
NFS389349647	2000-06-21 15:06:53	Install Failed	The RPC serv
NFS389443170	2000-06-21 15:06:54	Install Failed	The RPC serv
NFS389450229	2000-06-21 15:06:53	Install Failed	The RPC serv
NFS389476848	2000-06-21 15:06:54	Install Failed	The RPC serv
NFS389499772	2000-06-21 15:06:54	Install Failed	The RPC serv

Agent Detail   View Dispatch Log

Close   Cancel   Apply   Help

Figure C-27.   In this computer account migration, only the first client (NFS388989574) was active when the Wizard dispatched the agent.

After running the agent on clients, it's a good practice to check the success of the agent's operation by verifying on the Network Identification page of the System Properties dialog that the new domain affiliation has taken effect.

Restructuring Windows 2000 Domains

In addition to migrating Windows NT objects to Windows 2000, you also can use ADMT to restructure domains, as mentioned near the beginning of this appendix. Restructuring a domain requires that the target domain run in native mode, but the source domain can run in mixed or native mode and be in the same forest as the target (intraforest migration) or in another forest (interforest migration). You can migrate any AD object except DCs from the source to the target domain. The primary application for restructuring Windows 2000 domains is coalescing Windows NT resource domains that you in-place upgrade to Windows 2000.

Another use for ADMT is cloning a production Windows 2000 domain and its AD objects to a test domain. A cloned test domain that's not connected to the production network or is in a different forest of domain trees lets you set up and test clients with different Group Policies before placing the policies in production.

 CAUTION: Don't run the Computer Migration Wizard when cloning a production domain in test mode. Although you can prevent agents from running on production clients by omitting the target domain's account membership in the Administrators group of the clients, there's always the possibility that the agent will succeed. In that case, someone must reconnect the clients to their original domain.

The process for restructuring or cloning Windows 2000 domains is almost identical to that for migrating objects from Windows NT. The only basic change in the foregoing procedures for group, user, and computer accounts is substituting the production Windows 2000 domain for the Windows NT domain in the Wizards' Select Domains dialogs.

Index